The Mythology of Crime and Criminal Justice

Third Edition

The Mythology of Crime and Criminal Justice

Third Edition

Victor E. Kappeler
Eastern Kentucky University

Mark Blumberg
Central Missouri State University

Gary W. Potter
Eastern Kentucky University

WAVELAND

PRESS, INC.

Prospect Heights, Illinois

For information about this book, write or call:
Waveland Press, Inc.
P.O. Box 400
Prospect Heights, Illinois 60070
(847) 634-0081
www.waveland.com

Chapter Opener Photo Credits
Chapter 1, © Robert Maass/CORBIS; Chapter 3, Jan Weissman; Chapter 4, © David Vondrak/CORBIS; Chapter 5, © Charles O'Rear/CORBIS; Chapter 6, © Robert Maass/CORBIS; Chapter 7, © Roger Ressmeyer/CORBIS; Chapter 8, © UPI/CORBIS-Bettman; Chapter 9, *Los Angeles Times* photo by Juanito Holandez; Chapter 12, © Joseph Sohm, ChromoSohm Inc./CORBIS; Chapter 13, © Owen Franken/CORBIS; Chapter 14, *Chicago Tribune* photo by Bob Fila; Chapter 15, © AFP/CORBIS.

About the Authors

Victor E. Kappeler is Associate Professor of Police Studies at Eastern Kentucky University in Richmond, Kentucky. He received undergraduate degrees in Police Administration and Juvenile Corrections as well as a master's degree in Criminal Justice from Eastern Kentucky University. His doctoral degree in Criminal Justice is from Sam Houston State University in Huntsville, Texas. Dr. Kappeler has written articles on issues related to police deviance, law, and civil liability published in *Justice Quarterly*, the *American Journal of Criminal Law*, the *American Journal of Police*, the *Journal of Police Science and Administration*, the *American Journal of Criminal Justice*, *Criminal Law Bulletin*, the *Journal of Criminal Justice*, and *Police Chief*, among others. He is the author of *Critical Issues in Police Civil Liability* and editor of *Police and Society: Touchstone Readings*. He is co-author of *Policing in America*, *Forces of Deviance: Understanding the Dark Side of Policing*, and co-editor of *Constructing Crime: Perspectives on Making News and Social Problems*. Dr. Kappeler served as editor of *Justice Quarterly* and was the founding editor of *Police Liability Review* and *Police Forum*.

Mark Blumberg is Professor of Criminal Justice at Central Missouri State University in Warrensburg, Missouri. He received his undergraduate and master's degrees in Sociology from the University of Kansas, Lawrence. He received an additional master's and doctoral degree in Criminal Justice from the State University of New York, Albany. Dr. Blumberg has written extensively on both police use of deadly force and on the impact of AIDS on various criminal justice issues. Dr. Blumberg has authored numerous book chapters and journal articles. His work has appeared in *Crime and Delinquency*, *Criminal Law Bulletin*, *Justice Professional*, the *Prison Journal*, *Journal of Criminal Justice*, and the *American Journal of Police*, as well as in other publications. He is the author of an edited book entitled *AIDS: The Impact on the Criminal Justice System*.

Gary W. Potter is Professor of Police Studies at Eastern Kentucky University in Richmond, Kentucky. He received his doctorate in Community Systems Planning and Development from Pennsylvania State University. Dr. Potter is the author of *Criminal Organizations: Vice, Racketeering, and Politics in an American City* and *The Porn Merchants*. He has co-authored *Drugs in Society*, *Organized Crime*, *The City and the Syndicate*, and co-edited *Constructing Crime: Perspectives on Making News and Social Problems*. He has written articles on issues related to organized crime published in the *American Journal of Police*, *Corruption and Reform*, the *American Journal of Criminal Justice*, *Deviant Behavior*, *Criminal Justice History*, *Police Forum*, *Criminal Justice Policy Review*, *Policy Studies Review*, and the *Journal of Criminal Justice*, among others.

Acknowledgments

Our book made its way into print through the vision of many people who directly contributed to the work or who contributed to the authors' development. Not the least of these people are Carol and Neil Rowe of Waveland Press, Inc. They either took a risk or just became tired of reading traditional criminal justice textbooks. We openly acknowledge their vision and contribution to our work and to the field of criminal justice. We also note the special contribution of Dr. Philip Jenkins for allowing us to include his excellent chapter on serial murder.

One of the demands of "scholarly" writing is to credit the source of information and ideas. We have attempted to meet this demand but have found it a difficult task since ideas are often the product of past conversations, education, and misplaced readings that tend to fold into one another. We gratefully acknowledge the contributions of the following persons to our development: Dorothy Bracey, Dennis Longmire, Frank Williams, Victor G. Strecher, Peter B. Kraska, Larry K. Gaines, Stephen Mastrofski, William Chambliss, Donald Wallace, James J. Fyfe, Lawrence W. Sherman, Douglas Heckathorn, Robert Antonio, Roger C. Barnes, Geoffrey Alpert, and the late Donald J. Newman. Writing this book was a collaborative effort—three authors plus the contributions acknowledged above, aided by all the influences whose origins cannot be clearly delineated.

Preface

In some respects, *The Mythology of Crime and Criminal Justice* may seem an improbable book. In a humorous vein, it is somewhat unlikely that graduates from the Pennsylvania State University, State University of New York, and Sam Houston State University would collaborate on anything more than professional conferences or occasional forays for field research purposes. It is said that these institutions of higher education approach issues of crime and justice from very divergent perspectives and produce very different scholars of justice. Perhaps this too is a myth of criminal justice. Admittedly, we do have very diverse backgrounds and interests; thus, perhaps it was unusual that we would collectively produce a book that addresses "myths" in criminal justice given the broad range of possible topics. That is, however, one of the wonders of academia and one of the strengths of the social sciences. Divergent people, ideas, and approaches to understanding contribute to an environment where varying perspectives, interests, and backgrounds can blend to create unique works.

On a more serious note, the most unlikely part of this collaboration is that a publisher would agree to expend the resources and energies required to produce and market this work. It is not that each author has not published books in the past or made scholarly contributions to the literature (or so we would like to think). Rather, this book does not fit neatly into any specific academic category. The book is not pure sociology, criminology, or criminal justice. It is certainly not a work that would fall under any single recognized ideological or theoretical framework. It is neither a radical nor a traditional approach to criminology, conflict, or functionalist sociology. It is also not a traditional systems or empirical approach to criminal justice.

What we have tried to create is a work that focuses on very popular issues of criminal justice—issues that have captured the attention of the public as well as the scholarly community. Our hope is that the work challenges many popular notions of crime, criminals, and crime control. Unlike many other texts available, this book offers students of crime and justice an alternative to traditional criminal justice texts. Each chapter of this book questions our most basic assumptions of crime and justice and traces the development of a crime problem from its creation to society's integration of a myth into popular thinking and eventually social policy.

At the risk of characterizing the work as everything to everybody, we feel that it has broad application. The issues selected challenge habitual perspectives. Although the book was written for the undergraduate student, it could also stimulate discussion in the graduate classroom. It can be used as an alternative to standard introductory treatments of criminal justice or as a supplement to criminology or issues-orientated classes. Even though we feel the work has broad application, it was not intended to be the last word in myths of crime or justice. Rather, we hope that the text will serve as a very good starting point for understanding the realities of criminal justice and as an alternative to reinforcing crime myths in the classroom.

Victor E. Kappeler
Eastern Kentucky University

Mark Blumberg
Central Missouri State University

Gary W. Potter
Eastern Kentucky University

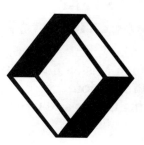

Contents

3 THE MYTH AND FEAR
OF CHILD ABDUCTION   49

4 MYTH AND MURDER
THE SERIAL KILLER PANIC   65

5 OF STALKERS AND MURDER
SPREADING MYTH TO COMMON CRIME   85

6 BLUE SMOKE AND MIRRORS
THE "WAR" ON ORGANIZED CRIME   99

The Social Construction of Crime Myths

People study social problems for a variety of reasons. The most obvious is to find solutions to society's concerns. Sometimes the solution must be sought not only in the content of the issue itself but in why a particular problem becomes more prominent than another. Many scholars in many disciplines look at the origins, diffusion, and consequences of social issues that capture the public's attention. Two very different perspectives can be used to explain the existence of a social problem. One perspective is taken by people who have been characterized as "claims-makers," "moral entrepreneurs," "political activists," "social pathologists," and "issue energizers." These individuals have vested interests in the problem they bring to the public's attention. They usually advocate formal social policy to address the new problem, which they feel is real, unique in its characteristics, and grave in its consequences.

The other perspective is taken by people who study the construction of social problems. These people view social problems as constructed from collective definitions rather than from individual views and perceptions. From this perspective, social problems are composite constructions based on accumulated perceptions and presentations of information; they can never actually exist in the collective, socially distorted form. People who see social problems in these terms often attribute the conception and definition of the problems to the mass media (Fishman, 1998), urban legend (Best & Horiuchi, 1985), group hysteria (Medalia & Larsen, 1958), ideology (Ryan, 1976), political power (Quinney, 1970), or some other often latent social force that directs public attention and shapes the nature and characteristics of emerging social problems. We will use this viewpoint to examine several myths of crime and justice.

We have chosen the term "myth" to describe some of the collective definitions society applies to certain crime problems and their solutions. The word myth seems most appropriate to the social definition of many different kinds of criminal behavior brought to the public's attention. One common meaning of myth is a traditional story of unknown authorship, with a historical basis, serving to explain some event. The events of myth are based on exaggeration or heightening of "ordinary" events in life. Other uses of the term carry the connotation of nonscientific, spoken, or written fiction used as if it were a true account of some event.

The phrase "crime myth" does not stray too far from these accepted definitions. Crime myths are usually created in nonscientific forums through the telling of crime-related fictions or sensational stories. These crime fictions often take on new meanings as they are told and retold—and at some point evolve into truth for many people.

The fiction in crime myth comes not only from fabrication of events but from the transformation and distortion of events into social and political problems. Many of our contemporary issues of crime and justice are the product of some real event or social concern. Whether or not these events are based on "truth" is largely irrelevant because they "gain their persuasiveness and motivating power from their larger-than-life quality" (Bromley et al., 1979, p. 44). As crime-related issues are debated and redebated, shaped and reshaped in public forums, they become distorted. Once transformed and repeatedly played out in public arenas, the mythical social problems are incorporated into the public consciousness. Crime myths are so powerful and can become so compounded that they shape our thoughts about and reactions to almost any issue related to criminal justice.

This book focuses on the processes by which criminal events and issues of criminal justice become distorted and are given unprecedented social consideration. Single authors of short, crime-related fictions are given scant attention. Instead, we attempt to illustrate the range of social processes by which popular thought concerning a crime issue transforms the original concern into a crime problem taking on the characteristics of myth. This distortion of the reality of crime and criminal justice issues into myths emerges from a "collective," sometimes "unconscious" enterprise (Mannheim, 1936). Our inquiry concentrates on current issues in crime and justice that have reached or are near their mythic potential and the costs of myth production to society.

◈

THE FUNCTION OF CRIME MYTHS

The study of myths in crime is not a novel or merely academic undertaking. Crime myths are real in the minds of their believers and have definite social consequences. Crime myths have numerous effects on our perceptions; we may not even be conscious that they are at work. Myths tend to organize our views of crime, criminals, and the proper operation of the criminal justice system. They provide us with a conceptual framework from which to identify certain social issues as crime-related, to develop our personal opinions on issues of justice, and to apply ready-made solutions to social problems.

The organization of views through crime myths contributes to the cataloging of social actors into artificial distinctions between law-abiding citizens, criminals, crime fighters, and victims. Casting certain segments of society into the category of "criminal" offers others a reassuring self-conception.

> For many people, it is comforting to conceive of themselves as law abiding citizens . . . No doubt there are a few paragons of virtue, but not many. Most people manifest common human frailties. For example, evidence suggests that over 90% of all Americans have committed some crime for which they could be incarcerated. (Bohm, 1986, pp. 200–201)

Yet, when we think of criminals we do not think of ourselves, our families, or our friends—we think of people very different from ourselves.

Myths support and maintain prevailing views of crime, criminals, and the criminal justice system, strengthening the tendency to rely on established conceptions of crime and justice. Myths reinforce the current designation of conduct as criminal, support existing practices of crime control, and provide the background assumptions for future designation of conduct as criminal. Once a crime myth has been generated and accepted by the public, it provides the necessary pre-understandings to generate other myths of crime and justice. In a sense, society becomes intellectually blinded by the mythology of crime and justice. The established conceptual framework may not enable us to define issues accurately, to explore new solutions, or to find alternatives to existing socially constructed labels and crime control practices.

Myths tend to provide the necessary information for the construction of a "social reality of crime" (Quinney, 1970). Crime myths become a convenient mortar to fill gaps in knowledge and to provide answers to questions social science either cannot answer or has failed to address. Where science, empirical evidence, and education have failed to provide answers to the public's crime concerns, mythology has stepped in to fill the knowledge void.

> One of the major contradictions that confronts American society is that one of the wealthiest and most technologically advanced countries in the world contains widespread poverty, unemployment and crime. Historically, a myth that has been perpetrated to resolve this contradiction is that crime is an individual problem . . . Conceived this way there is no social or structural solution to the problem of crime. (Bohm, 1986, p. 203)

Crime myth not only explains a social contradiction, it tells us where in society the crime problem resides; where we should look to find solutions; and what solutions are acceptable. Because of the manner in which the myth is framed, acceptable solutions are usually those that do not disrupt existing social arrangements regardless of the extent to which they contribute to understanding or control. Collectively, myths create our social reality of crime and justice.

Finally, crime myths provide an outlet for emotionalism and channel emotion into action. Myth "imperatively guides action and establishes patterns of behavior" (Fitzpatrick, 1992, p. 20). Myths not only allow for interpretation of general social emotions and sentiment but direct those emotions to designated targets. When we cast criminals into roles as social deviants and evildoers preying on innocent victims, we invite and feel justified in advocating draconian punishment. Crime myths condone social action based on emotionalism while providing justification for established views of behavior, social practice, and institutional responses to crime.

◊

CRIMINAL MYTHMAKERS

The social construction of myths of crime and criminal justice seems to follow a series of recurrent patterns. These patterns allow a disproportionate amount of social attention to be focused on a few isolated criminal events or issues. This attention is promoted by concentrated, but often brief, mass media coverage of a chosen problem. Intense social concern with an issue is achieved by a variety of means. The mass media, government, law enforcement officials, and the interests of reform groups all play a major role in focusing the public's attention on select social problems. There is, if you will, a myth-producing enterprise in our society. The largest and most powerful mythmakers in this enterprise are the mass media.

Modern mass communication has virtually replaced traditional vehicles of communicating myth. Mass communication is a formalized and institutionalized system of conveying messages. It consists of sending messages by way of technology to large groups of people. The traditional process of communication and myth distribution, once based solely on word of mouth and later extended by the written word, has been replaced by rapid, electronic-based communication. This modern mass communication system has enabled unprecedented numbers of myths to spread with frightening speed. More than fifty years ago, Edwin H. Sutherland (1950) noted that "Fear is produced more readily in the modern community than it was earlier in our history because of increased publicity" (p. 143). Technology has enhanced our ability to generate, refine, distribute, and reinforce myths. What were once stories restricted in dissemination to small interactive social groups are now instantly projected to millions of people internationally by the mass media.

The process works in reverse as well. The modern media maintain their ability to localize their national and international messages by presenting hometown examples of crime myths. It is not uncommon for local news stations to develop their lead story based on a theme set by the major television broadcasters (Potter & Kappeler, 1998). A government press release on drunk driving reported in the national news is likely to be followed by an interview of a hometown victim of drunk driving on the local news. A national news story on the "good life" that prisoners have—complete with phone, television, and Internet privileges—can spawn a local news reporter's investigation of a local jail. This practice creates the illusion that the national theme is of local consequence and affects us all.

The increased ability to project myths and the tendency to localize them have been accompanied by a shrinking number of people who control the means and mediums of myth production. Fewer than 15 corporations control most of the newspaper circulation in the United States, and Time, Inc. controls about 40% of all magazine sales. The Walt Disney Corporation includes ABC and ESPN. Viacom is the parent company of Paramount Pictures, MTV, Nickelodeon, Nick at Nite, Comedy Central, Showtime, The Movie Channel, All News Channel, UPN, Blockbuster, and CBS. Pearson Publishing includes Prentice-Hall, Allyn and Bacon, Longman, and Addison-Wesley. This restricted number of mythmakers has given the modern media, reform groups, and government almost a monopoly on the myth industry. Today, the media and government select our crime problems for us and focus our attention on social issues. The roles of individuals and small social groups no longer predominate in the dissemination of modern crime mythology.

◇

MEDIA AS MYTHMAKER

The media choose and present crime problems for public consumption. The selection of crime problems is often limited to the most bizarre or gruesome act a journalist or investigator can uncover. Incident and problem selection are driven by the competitive nature of modern media. By promoting unique and fascinating issues for public exhibition, the media insure the marketability and success (measured by number of viewers and advertising dollars) of a given media production. Once an incident has been selected, it is then presented as evidence of a representative, common crime problem.

In the print media the practice of using sensational stories to attract readers and to increase profit became known as "yellow" journalism. Television news followed the economic lure of sensationalism. Local stations learned "late in the 1960s, that news could make money—lots of money. By the end of the 1970s, news was frequently producing 60% of a station's profits . . . and a heavily entertainment-oriented form of programming began to evolve" (Hallin, 1990, p. 2). News as entertainment used public fascination with sensational crime to attract viewers; "if it bleeds it leads" became the mantra. Crime has become a media product that sells perhaps better than any other media commodity. Like any for-profit organization, the media merely respond to the dynamics of the economy by marketing their crime products "to attract a large viewing audience which, in turn, sells advertising" (Bohm, 1986, p. 205).

Prompted by the nature of the media industry, television and newspaper reporters focus on "hot topics" of entertainment value. In the early stages of myth development, a media frenzy develops that allows for expanded coverage of isolated and unique events. Typically, the appearance of an uncritical newspaper or magazine article exploring a unique social problem starts the chain of events. The journalist has uncovered a "new" social evil. Other journalists, who can't afford to be left out, jump on the bandwagon. The multiple accounts may eventually blossom into highly publicized quasi-documentaries or even movies that graphically portray the problem. Social problems reach their media-driven myth potential when sensationalism reaches its height and when they are reported by tabloid-television investigators. Isolated incidents thus become social issues and eventually, through politicalization, crime problems.

Media frenzies often start in single newsrooms and quickly spread across information mediums, giving the false impression of order and magnitude to criminal events. As Mark Fishman (1998) points out in his discussion of "crime waves":

> Journalists do not create themes merely to show an audience the appearance of order . . . In particular, editors selecting and organizing the day's stories need themes. Every day, news editors face a glut of "raw materials" . . . out of which they must fashion relatively few stories . . . The chances that any event or incident will be reported increase once it has been associated with a current theme in the news. (pp. 58–59)

Once a theme has been set by the lone newsroom, selection of newsworthy stories is based on that theme. Other events that may or may not be related to the existing news theme are then culled from an abundance of material and are fashioned to fit within the crime theme of the day. Themes then spread across communication mediums giving the impression of a crime epidemic.

The media reach enormous audiences instantly. Unfortunately, the ability to disseminate information quickly comes at a cost. In an editorial, Mortimer Zuckerman (1994) warned that public events require context, an understanding of the past, and explanations of complexities. "Television, in particular, is so focused on pictures and so limited by time that in the normal run of reporting it cannot begin to provide the context that gives meaning and perspective" (p. 64). Incidents of violence are collected and then condensed into 120 seconds of compelling footage. In Zuckerman's words "graphic images of pain and outrage [are] beamed into our homes," increasing pressure for immediate commitment to a plan—any plan—to stop the wanton violence. The editorial quotes Walter Lippmann on the process: "the public will arrive in the middle of the third act and will leave before the last curtain, having stayed just long enough perhaps to decide who is the hero and who the villain."

While the media play an important role in the identification and construction of crime myth, they are not the sole participants in the enterprise. Journalistic freedom of topic selection is often guided by events and influences external to the media. While the media may be guilty of not reporting an incident in the proper perspective, the media are not solely to blame for sensational reporting. Unfortunately, repugnant crimes do occur. Some events that are blown out of proportion still warrant public attention. Each myth considered in this book contains legitimate cause for public concern. Yet, social policy should not be developed based on distortion, sensationalism, or a few newsworthy events. We will return to the media's role in constructing crime myths later.

◇

GOVERNMENT AS MYTHMAKER

There are other methods beyond the naturally occurring bizarre and unusual crimes captured by the media that begin the myth construction process. These sometimes contrived or directed government events help alert the media to a new "hot topic." In some cases, the directed information helps refocus a media frenzy. The government has a vested interest in maintaining the existing social definition of crime and extending this definition to groups and behaviors that are perceived to be a threat to the existing social order.

Similarly, the government has an interest in seeing that the existing criminal justice system's response to crime is not significantly altered in purpose or function. While some "system tinkering" is permissible, major change in the system's response to crime is never implemented because the status quo serves the interests of government, crime control agencies, and social elites. We build more prisons, mete out longer prison terms, reinstate the death penalty, and move more offenders through the criminal justice system at faster speeds, but all these changes are intellectually bonded by a myth-based philosophy of punishment and crime control that reflects the interests of government and the criminal justice system.

The government secures its interest in identifying crime and criminals and maintaining the established criminal justice system by promoting crime myths. Since the government can control, direct, and mold messages, it is one of the most powerful mythmakers in the crime production enterprise.

> The public is far more likely to accept the pronouncements of a federal department than a voluntary private organization. There is the element of propaganda development. Due to its public nature, a federal department is more skilled in dealing with the public and in preparing propaganda for public consumption. (Dickson, 1968, p. 147)

The government can suppress information for national security reasons; it can punish "obscenity"; it can reward the media for presenting official versions of crime myths; and it can "bring a wide range of pressures to bear on its critics" (Dickson, 1968, p. 147). Shaping the content of messages and rewarding the media for myth presentation are frequently done under the guise of public service announcements, controlled press briefings, and the release of research reports.

The government functions as a controller and director of the mass media; it is also a form of media. The government controls extensive print publication resources, commissions and funds research, operates radio stations, and exposes the television-viewing audience to government-sponsored messages. With great regularity governmental agencies like the Federal Bureau of Investigation (FBI), the Bureau of Justice Statistics (BJS), and the National Institute of Justice (NIJ) distribute press releases about crime statistics to the media. One must remember that these press releases are written by the same people who fund the research and decide what statistics should be collected and shared with the public. While much of the research that these agencies release provides basic and needed information, it is often oversimplified and sometimes designed to elicit social concern—at a minimum, it is filtered through a political process. We discuss some of this research in greater detail in the next chapter, but for the moment consider the "Uniform Crime Reports" published by the FBI. These reports are released annually and often employ techniques of presentation that distort our image of crime.

One of the most misleading techniques is the FBI's crime clock that presents the number of crimes committed in either minutes or seconds. Presenting data in this fashion implies a crime epidemic. In a nation with about 271 million citizens and a day with only 24 hours, crime (and virtually any social behavior) will seem to occur with alarming regularity and speed in this type of visual representation. In 1997, the FBI's crime clock showed a murder every 29 minutes, a rape every 5 minutes, a robbery every minute, and an assault every 31 seconds (UCR, 1998). Presenting almost any social phenomenon in this form results in the appearance of alarming statistics. By way of comparison, there is a fatal car accident involving alcohol every 2 seconds, and 2 traffic accidents every second. Similar constructions can be created for behaviors ranging from hospital admissions to eating at fast-food restaurants.

In addition to providing the media and public with distorted statistics on crime, the government also disseminates a highly selective ideology of crime and justice. The media need constant sources of information to feed their demand for news products. Convenient sources like police officials and political leaders respond eagerly to media inquiries. Favorite sources for journalists' inquiries are often those who are readily available or those who reliably provide quotable statements.

In this pipeline to the media, governmental officials, criminal justice practitioners, and politicians have a distinct advantage over researchers and scholars. Welch, Fenwick, and Roberts (1998) examined the sources major newspapers used to craft their feature crime stories. These researchers found a striking ideological difference between governmental and academic sources. Generally, governmental spokespersons were more likely to advance a crime control ideology, whereas academics were more likely to discuss crime causation. Likewise, politicians and criminal justice practitioners were more likely to construct crime in terms of deterrence and the personal pathology of criminals, whereas academics were more likely to discuss the social factors that contribute to crime. Additionally, governmental spokespersons were more likely to advocate stringent crime control efforts packaged in slogans like "three strikes and you're out" and "get-tough-on-crime," while their academic counterparts subscribed to crime control measures like education, the provision of social services, and reducing economic disparity and racism. "Reporters' dependence on authorities makes them—and by extension media consumers—particularly vulnerable to deliberate attempts to mislead by governments and agencies" (Hynds, 1990, p. 6).

All of these capabilities contribute to the role of government as myth generator. The government directs media attention to specific crime issues and incidents; the "war on drugs" is an excellent illustration. While drug scares in the United States can be traced back over two hundred years, the government's role has been most evident in the last forty years (Reinarmann, 1996). The highest offices in government have been used as stages for constructing the public's conception of crime. In the 1970s, President Nixon was careful to call drug abuse "public enemy number one" and characterized it as "the worst threat the country ever faced." Hinting at a solution, he employed the war metaphor, equating drug abuse to "foreign troops on our shores" (see Dumont, 1973, p. 534). Nixon's call for a war on drugs was sounded against a backdrop of drug hysteria that began at least forty years earlier when the Bureau of Narcotics attempted to expand its organizational power.

The Bureau of Narcotics' 1937 campaign against marijuana under the leadership of Harry Anslinger is a classic example of the media's dissemination of government-sponsored crime myths. The Bureau of Narcotics, wanting to expand its bureaucratic domain by adding marijuana to the list of controlled substances it was responsible for monitoring, put together a series of mythological and outrageous stories about atrocities committed by people allegedly under the influence of marijuana. These stories included the murder of a Florida family and their pet dog by a wayward son who had taken one toke of marijuana. Newspapers printed this story and others like it.

Thus, the myth of the "dope fiend" was born out of the minds of law enforcement officials. The media involvement with the Bureau of Narcotics disinformation campaign continued with editorial calls for the suppression of the dangerous drug. In fact, such hysteria resulted that the Bureau's own legal counsel recommended discontinuation of the propaganda campaign. During the height of the media frenzy and while the Marijuana Tax Act of 1937 was being debated in Washington, news stories covering the testimony of leading medical experts about the relative safety of the drug and objections by the scientific community to the criminalization of marijuana were lost in the coverage of the government-created crime wave (see Dickson, 1968; Galliher & Walker, 1977).

In the 1980s President Reagan rekindled the drug hysteria and further solidified the war solution in the minds of many citizens by abandoning the treatment orientation of the Carter administration.

> Almost immediately after his election, Reagan outlined a seven-step plan to eradicate drugs from society. This included a diversion of $708.8 million from education, treatment, and research programs to law enforcement programs. An additional $127.5 million were appropriated for increasing prison space, and to increase the personnel of the Drug Enforcement Administration. (Kraska, 1990, p. 117)

Municipal law enforcement agencies revitalized their narcotics units, created drug task forces, and organized multi-jurisdictional strike teams with the influx of federal funds generated by the government's renewed drug propaganda and the attendant public hysteria. Law enforcement was revitalized to wage yet another war on drugs.

In 1990 President Bush's administration arranged for the Drug Enforcement Administration (DEA) to conduct a high-profile drug arrest. Public focus on the "drug war" had waned due to concern over other social problems; the administration needed an event to refocus public and political attention. Following a DEA drug bust just outside the White House, the president made a national television address concerning the drug issue. It was later learned that the DEA had to go to considerable means to persuade the drug dealer to meet the agents at the desired location—just outside the White House. Following the arrest, President Bush went on national television holding a baggie of white powder and instructing the nation that drugs had encroached to the steps of the White House. Public attention had been successfully redirected to the drug issue.

President Clinton used the myth-generating power of the government to shift attention in another direction; he actively contributed to an unprecedented level of fear of violent crime in the United States. He warned citizens about the rise of violent crime and its dreadful effect on children by appearing in public-service announcements with his arms around children, answering questions in town meetings, and making speeches across the nation. Similarly, Attorney General Janet Reno emphasized the growing problem of child abuse and exploitation. Yet with presidential approval, Reno ordered the Federal Bureau of Investigation (FBI) to storm the Branch Davidians' home in Waco, Texas. The raid resulted in the death of at least seventy-nine people—many of whom were children.

Ironically, the siege at Waco triggered the rage that resulted in the bombing of the Alfred P. Murrah Federal Building in Oklahoma City—two years to the date after the FBI raid. Stories about "Terror in the Heartland" filled the airwaves in 1995. Fears of such massive, random violence prompted calls for fewer restrictions on government surveillance. The Clinton administration furthered simplistic solutions to complex crime problems, advocating the deployment of thousands of additional police officers, broadening the powers of the police to conduct warrantless searches of housing projects, adopting a "three strikes and you're out" correctional policy, and expanding the use of the death penalty. By the end of the 1990s, the Clinton administration had effectively shifted public attention away from the drug war and focused social concern on violent, predatory urban crime.

The media and the government, whether independently or in concert, focus public attention on unique social problems. These two powerful entities establish the seriousness of the problem and inform the public of viable solutions. In the process, they sow the seeds of crime myths. As we will discuss later, these preliminary events comprise all the necessary ingredients for creating crime myths.

◈

MERGING MYTHMAKERS

During the latter part of the 1980s, a new form of television programming began to emerge. Following the format of information-commercials (programs appearing as fact-based presentations of information but designed to sell products), television crime programs began to blend entertainment and government-sponsored messages. These shows used government officials, well-known relatives of crime victims, and law enforcement officers to inform the public about crime. This type of television programming, broadcast from local stations across the nation under various names like *Crime Solvers*, *Secret Witness*, and *Crime Line*, increased in number from forty-eight shows in 1980 to at least five hundred in 1984. The programs encourage viewers to report crime and criminals in exchange for monetary rewards. They were predecessors of the government's national media campaign, *Take a Bite Out of Crime*, which mustered citizen participation in support of crime prevention, citizen self-protection, and neighborhood cooperation (Tunnell, 1992).

The growth of this new form of crime-news entertainment did more than just advocate crime prevention and citizen cooperation and support these efforts with monetary rewards. Using government officials as spokespersons gave viewers the impression of official credibility. Television shows like *Unsolved Mysteries*, *Rescue 911*, *48 Hours*, *America's Most Wanted*, *Cops*, and *Top Cops* reenacted crimes accompanied by narratives from law enforcement officials. As the name *Unsolved Mysteries* suggests, often the facts of the particular crime had yet to be uncovered. Still, these and other programs filled fact voids by reconstructions born out of the minds of law enforcement officials.

In 1989, *Unsolved Mysteries* added a new segment to the show called *FBI Alert*. The segment was hosted by FBI director William Sessions and spent its time describing American fugitives. *America's Most Wanted* was hosted by John Walsh, the father of Adam Walsh who was abducted and murdered. *Bad Girls* and *Gangs, Cops, and Drugs*, both broadcast by the National Broadcasting Company (NBC), featured drug czar William Bennett. These shows and the numerous versions that have appeared since then contribute to an unprecedented level of fear of crime in U.S. society (Cavender & Bond-Maupin, 1998) and use the authority and credibility of government officials to legitimize their activities.

As mentioned earlier, TV creates its own graphic images of reality. Producers massage the message, which is further affected by hot lights and microphones. Members of the Police Executive Research Forum commented on the merits of reality programs like *Cops*. They noted that the presence of television encourages more aggressive behavior from police officers. "They don't doctor the tapes but they only depict a portion of policing . . ." (Goode, 1994, p. 53). Viewers who rely on such information may end up with a distorted view of the world as more dangerous than it really is.

Do the selective presentations of atypical, serious, and violent crime on these shows really have any effect on the viewing public? The following incident serves as an illustration of one destructive consequence of merging mythmakers. One evening Rudell Combs and several other employees of a tool manufacturing company watched *America's Most Wanted*. On this particular evening, the show was featuring fugitive Don Moore, a former teacher from Los Angeles who was wanted by the police for twenty-one counts of fondling, masturbation, oral copulation, and sexual intercourse with several fifth-grade students. While watching the program Combs and his fellow employees became convinced that one of their coworkers, Richard Maxwell, was the fugitive. The following day they called *America's Most Wanted* and explained that Maxwell's age, appearance, and a missing fingertip matched the description of Don Moore. Compounding their suspicion, Maxwell failed to show up at work the day after the episode aired.

Staff from *America's Most Wanted* contacted a detective from the Los Angeles Police Department, and he faxed the *America's Most Wanted* information sheet to local police officers. The bulletin contained a photograph, a fingerprint classification, and specific identifiers which described Moore as a male Caucasian, 5'11", 175 pounds, with gray hair, green eyes, a fair complexion, a gray mustache, a goatee, and missing the tip of his left index finger. Local police officers went to the manufacturing company and summoned Maxwell. During the course of their interview with Maxwell they learned that he was a male Caucasian 6'5", 270 pounds, with gray hair, green eyes, a gray mustache and missing the tip of his left middle finger. Over his protests, Maxwell was arrested and taken to the local police department for fingerprinting. The fingerprints established conclusively that Maxwell was not Moore. He was returned to work—to the company of coworkers who had willingly suspended any personal knowledge of him in favor of a televised characterization, reported their suspicions to a television program, and watched those suspicions momentarily "confirmed" by his handcuffing and arrest.

His recourse for this embarrassing, reputation-destroying incident was to sue the city whose police officers had compounded the process initiated by the "reality" programming. A court reviewing the case made the following observations concerning the reliability of the television description of Moore and the acceptability of the police officers' actions:

> Presumably, a T.V. show such as *America's Most Wanted*, undoubtedly viewed by millions, would broadcast descriptions that have a high degree of reliability. Otherwise, one risks people fingering neighbors—co-workers—who loosely fit the description of one or another fugitive . . . Maxwell is a full six inches taller than Moore and weighs almost one hundred pounds more. While weight is a mutable characteristic, the size of the difference here should have given the police officers pause. In the same vein, Maxwell was missing the tip of his left middle finger, not his left index finger. Certainly a missing fingertip in an industrial plant cannot be so unusual that the officers would not have scrutinized more closely which particular fingertip was damaged. Furthermore, . . . neither the officers' affidavits nor their report indicate that any of them asked Maxwell about his work record or work history. And curiously, it appears that none of the officers asked him for an alibi, or even whether he would consent to finger-printing . . . No other factors in this instance can be construed as circumstances warranting an arrest . . . the officers had no grounds for suspecting Maxwell was engaging in any of the conduct Moore was charged with. (*Maxwell v. City of Indianapolis*, 1993, pp. 432–433)

America's Most Wanted was aware of Maxwell's anguish and the findings of the court. However, it seemingly did not find it necessary to implement safeguards against future occurrences. In 1994 it celebrated its 300th criminal capture. On the same program, it publicly apologized for inadvertently placing an innocent citizen's photograph on television accompanied by a story of criminal acts the citizen had *not* committed. Whether a televised apology is sufficient to recover one's reputation is debatable. Moreover, the incidents of mistaken identity have had lethal consequences as well as damage to reputations.

A violent shootout in Los Angeles, California resulted in the death of two sheriff's deputies and Homero-Isadoro Ibarra. Ibarra's children identified Cesar Mazariego-Molina, an undocumented worker from El Salvador, as the killer. The case was featured on *America's Most Wanted*. Two days later New York State police killed Molina with a shotgun blast to the back of the head. The owner of an orchard in Plattekill, New York, had recognized one of his workers as Molina. Within minutes of the arrival of police and FBI agents, he was shot dead. A subsequent search of the orchard, Molina's person, and his possessions uncovered no weapons.

Molina's family alleged that he was the victim of vigilante justice promoted by the intentional release of false information by the television show. *America's Most Wanted* had broadcast photos of Molina, interviews with angry deputies, and a detective's remarks that Molina "has no value for human life. Killing, to him, is like a hobby" (Gordon, 1992, p. 1). Host John Walsh characterized Molina as a murderer, rapist, and member of an El Salvadorian death squad. Family members denied that Molina was ever convicted of a crime or that he ever was a member of a death squad. They also insisted that he never carried weapons and that at the time of the alleged shooting he was not even in California. Spokespeople for *America's Most Wanted* said that they report what the police tell them, although Los Angeles County Sheriff's Department spokespersons said they could not verify any of the charges *America's Most Wanted* aired concerning Molina's background.

Days after Molina's death John Walsh was back on the air remarking that "the L.A. County Sheriff's Department asked for your help in finding the accused killer of one of their own. Deputies feared he might head for the border, but you answered the call. Three thousand miles away, and 48 hours later, the manhunt was over" (Gordon, 1992, p. 1). The killing of Molina was dubbed *America's Most Wanted's* 197th successful capture.

Media depictions of crime and justice in the United States have consequences that reach beyond the individual miscarriage of justice described above. They represent a new form of knowledge construction where crime and the response to it is a hybrid product of governmental ideology and media distortion. Even more disconcerting, official actions in some cases are not based on the collection of facts concerning the crime but rather on conjecture enhanced or fabricated by media presentations.

◊

CREATING CRIME MYTHS

Public attention and media focus alone cannot create a crime myth. Generally, public concerns are related in some measure to social or economic conditions. Erich Goode and Nachman Ben-Yehuda (1994) point out that "Fear and concern do, for the most part, grow out of very real conditions of social life. But no, they need not be commensurate with the concrete threat posed specifically by that which is feared" (p. 49). In order for a myth to develop to the point where it becomes more than a social concern for a majority of citizens, it must be properly packaged and marketed.

A requirement for myth production often repeated throughout this work is that the crime problem must be reported to occur in "epidemic" proportions. A quantum leap must occur from uncovering an incident to depicting it as pervasive. Only by exaggerating the magnitude of the problem can public attention be sustained for prolonged periods, fear be instilled, calls for institutional control be made, and public support be mustered to institute formal sanctions—all the ingredients required for a myth to reach its full potential.

Exaggeration of the magnitude of a problem and the manufacturing of a crime myth are accomplished by several means. First, the media can suddenly focus on crimes that they had previously ignored (Fishman, 1998). The organization of these presentations can create the image of a crime problem when they are taken out of their geographical, temporal, or social contexts. Crime myths are also created when the media fail to pursue stories beyond their initial reporting. Crimes reported as constituting a pattern may later be found to be unrelated or even conceptually distinct. There is, however, no requirement that the media or government correct their mistakes or recall their myths. Joel Best and Gerald Horiuchi's (1985) study of Halloween sadists' attacks against children found that the media greatly exaggerated their occurrence.

> There simply was no basis for *Newsweek's* (1975) claim that "several children had died." The newspapers attributed only two deaths to Halloween sadists, and neither case fit the image of a maniacal killer randomly attacking children. In 1970, five-year-old Kevin Toston died after eating heroin supposedly hidden in his Halloween candy. While this story received considerable publicity, newspapers gave less coverage to the follow-up report that Kevin had found the heroin in his uncle's home, not in his treats . . . In 1974, eight-year-old Timothy O'Bryan died after eating Halloween candy contaminated with cyanide. Investigators concluded that his father had contaminated the treat . . . Thus, both boys' deaths were caused by family members, rather than by anonymous sadists. (p. 490)

The fear generated from exaggerating Halloween sadism not only affected the general public but also organizations and individuals who are expected to have valid information regarding the reality of crime. In 1982 the International Association of Chiefs of Police (IACP) and the confectionery industry sponsored a "Halloween Candy Hotline." The hotline was devised to give police departments technical assistance with suspected candy tampering cases. According to a news item by the IACP, the hotline received sixty-eight calls in 1990, but the article failed to note if any of these calls resulted from actual tamperings ("Halloween," 1991). By 1994, a journalist's interview with IACP's Charles Higginbotham revealed that "He's one of the few who ever dials the number anymore; he calls each year to make sure it's working" (Dunn, 1994, p. 25). Although the Halloween hotline does serve as an example of a possible positive effect of exaggerating crime, it raises questions as to whether the nation's leading police executives are able to discern between actual crime problems and media-generated myths of crime.

How often do the media distort or exaggerate the crime problem in our society? Harry Marsh (1991, pp. 67–68) reviewed the research devoted to the study of the content of newspapers. His examination of the literature found the following patterns:

- The vast majority of newspaper crime coverage pertains to violent or sensational crimes.

- The high percentages of violent crimes reported in newspapers are not representative of the percentages reflected in official crime data.

- Overemphasis of violent crimes and failure to address personal risk and prevention techniques often lead to exaggerated fears of victimization in certain segments of society. Newspaper coverage tends to support police views and values about crime and criminals.

Robert Bohm's (1986) review of the research perhaps best captured the essence of the type of crime information consumed by the public:

> Crime-related television programs have been estimated to account for about one-third of all television entertainment shows. Information that the public receives from these shows is anything but accurate. Studies have indicated that: (1) the least committed crimes, such as murder and assault, appear more frequently than those crimes committed more often, such as burglary and larceny; (2) violent crimes are portrayed as caused by greed or attempts to avoid detection rather than by passion accompanying arguments as is more typical; (3) the necessary use of violence in police work is exaggerated; (4) the use of illegal police tactics is seemingly sanctioned; (5) police officers are unfettered by procedural law; and (6) the police nearly always capture the "bad guys," usually in violent confrontations. (citations omitted, p. 205)

To what extent does the public rely on the media to make judgments about crime, and what effects do these distortions have on the public's view of crime? "Ninety-six percent of the respondents [in a National Crime Survey] reported relying on the news media to learn about crime and criminals, and 49% of those surveyed believed the media gave the right amount of attention to stories about crime" (Tunnell, 1992, p. 295). Kenneth Tunnell goes on to report that, "At that time, more than 50% of the news stories were of violent crime, whereas only 6% of the actual crimes involved some form of violence. Not surprising, 88% of those surveyed overestimated the number of crimes they believed involved violence" [citations omitted]. Melissa Barlow, David Barlow, and Theodore Chiricos (1995a; 1995b) also studied crime news and found that the media escalate the threat of violent crime and play down property crimes. Clearly, the media's distortion of crime and justice has an impact on the public's conception of crime.

Misuse of statistics promotes crime myths. The misuse of statistical information can range from limiting public access to information to deliberate attempts to mislead the public by presenting false information or using deceptive formats to present information. Vested interests can manipulate "facts" when they have control of information, choose the mode of presentation, and control access to channels of dissemination (see Orcutt & Turner, 1993). As we shall see in later chapters, debates on "missing children" are particularly susceptible to misuse and control of information, as are discussions of rising crime rates. Statistics presented for public consumption are often clouded by broad definitions of crime that tend to group distinct behaviors, offenders, and victims into single categories giving the impression of an epidemic. In a study of the social reaction to sex crimes, Sutherland (1950) wrote, "Fear is seldom or never related to statistical trends in sex crimes. . . . Ordinarily, from two to four spectacular sex crimes in a few weeks are sufficient to evoke the phrase 'sex crime wave'" (p. 144).

Statistics and information often mislead the public when they are stripped from their original context and inferences are made between research studies. Causal links are often inferred or claimed between the crime myth under construction and some other more pervasive social concern. For example, in recent years the use of drugs has been linked to: other crimes, high school dropouts, decreased employee productivity, the rise of youth gangs, the corruption of the police, the spread of AIDS, the emergence of "crack babies," and a multitude of other social maladies. The incidence of drug use in society may or may not have been perceived as a major social threat without media coverage and claims-maker activities; when coupled with other social problems, the perception of an epidemic is insured. In later chapters we will explore the myth-built links between drug use and other social problems.

◊

CHARACTERIZATIONS OF CRIME MYTHS

In order for the momentum of a crime myth to be prolonged and public support for institutionalized controls to be generated, myths must be accompanied by certain characterizations. Momentum is achieved if the crime problem has traits that either instill fear or threaten the vast majority of society in some appreciable way. Not unlike Greek mythology, modern crime myths must follow certain themes for success. There must be "virtuous" heroes, "innocent" victims, and "evil" villains who pose a clear and certain threat to the audience. Only then can a crime myth reach its potential. Characterizations common among myths in crime and criminal justice include: (1) the identification and targeting of a distinct deviant population; (2) the presence of an "innocent" or "helpless" victim population; (3) the emergence of brave and virtuous heroes; and (4) the existence of a substantial threat to established norms, values, or traditional lifestyles.

Crime myths are often built around unpopular groups in society. This targeting helps to insure sustained support for a myth. Unpopular groups are particularly vulnerable as possible targets of mythical fears. Groups most vulnerable to myth targeting are those who are easily distinguishable from the dominant social group. Distinctions are often as crude as race, color, or national origin but need not be limited to visual appearance. Differences in religious beliefs, political views, or even sexual preferences are attractive targets for mythmakers. Hate groups, pro-slavery advocates, supporters of prohibition, and advocates of the death penalty have all portrayed their adversaries as posing grave threats to society. The we/they distinction has been used to develop crime control policy, enact criminal laws, and even bring nations to war.

The importance of this characterization of "difference" cannot be overstated. Scholars have observed the targeting of groups labeled as different. In his insightful book, *Blaming the Victim*, William Ryan (1976) states:

> This is a critical and essential step in the process, for difference is in itself hampering and maladaptive. The Different Ones are seen as less competent, less skilled, less knowing—in short less human. The ancient Greeks deduced from a single characteristic, a different language, that the barbarians—that is, the "babblers" who spoke a strange tongue—were wild, uncivilized, dangerous, rapacious, uneducated, lawless, and, indeed scarcely more than animals. [Such characterization] not infrequently justifies mistreatment, enslavement, or even extermination of the Different Ones. (p. 10)

Fear of minorities, foreigners, and differences in cultural or religious values has led to the creation of some shocking myths of organized crime. The birth of the Mafia myth in the United States is based on the created fear of cultural differences. The murder of New Orleans police chief David Hennessey in 1890 provides an excellent example. New Orleans was one of the cities that experienced a large influx of Italian immigrants during the end of the nineteenth century. Chief Hennessey was gunned down on a New Orleans street one night. As he was dying, the chief was said to have uttered "dagos, dagos." Officers later rounded up a large number of petty criminals of Italian descent and presented them before a grand jury that indicted them for the chief's murder. Since evidence of their involvement was lacking, the jury acquitted them of the charges. Acquittal did not deter the citizens of New Orleans who marched to the jail, seized the defendants (and others who were not even on trial) and killed eleven of them. This lynching and subsequent trials and acquittals of "different ones" is said to be the genesis of the American Mafia myth (Smith, 1975).

The difference requirement of the myth construction process is built into issues surrounding crime and justice. There is a convenient supply of unpopular people—those whom society labels criminal. Criminals are probably the most unpopular minority in any society, although they are difficult to identify visually aside from their undesirable conduct.

Another requirement for myth development is that "helpless" or "innocent" victims (people like ourselves) must be depicted as suffering the brunt of the newly found social evil. The more innocents perceived as being affected by the myth, the greater the likelihood of public attention and support for the creation of crime myths targeting unpopular groups. Women, children, law enforcement officers killed in the line of duty, or unwitting business people who become the victims of "organized" crime are often used as the virtuous victims who suffer at the hands of the unpopular deviant. Sutherland (1950) observed, "The hysteria produced by child murders is due in part to the fact that the ordinary citizen cannot understand a sex attack on a child. The ordinary citizen . . . concludes that sexual attack on an infant or girl of six years must be the act of a fiend or maniac. Fear is the greater because the behavior is so incomprehensible" (p. 144).

Casting victims as innocents authorizes the implementation of stiff criminal sanctions against the deviants—accompanied by feelings of moral superiority and the satisfaction of retribution. It is common for the media to dwell on the virtues of the innocent victim to the exclusion of the offender (see Drechsel, Netteburg & Aborisade, 1980; Karmen, 1978). After all, what parents do not feel their child is either a "good student," a "likable person," or "a good boy or girl." This is not to say that innocents do not become the targets of violent crime, but rather to illustrate that media coverage of crime stories often focuses extensively on the innocent person victimized by the evil stranger. The irony here is that "good" and "evil," "deviants" and "conformists" are creatures of the same culture, inventions of the same imagination (Messner & Rosenfeld, 1997, p. 2; citing Erikson). As we shall see in later chapters on child abduction and abuse, strangers are not the greatest threat to our nation's children. In the construction of crime mythology, there are no "ordinary" victims or criminals.

The subjects of myths are characterized as constituting a major threat to middle-class values, norms, or lifestyles. Myths of crime and justice when blended with threats to religious beliefs, economic systems, sexual attitudes or orientation, the traditional family, or political preference become a volatile mix. The characterizations of the deviant subjects of crime myths fuel emotionalism. The fear generated by this mixture of the unpopular offender, the innocent victim, and the perceived threat to traditional lifestyles can produce a formal and even violent social response. The argument is simple; a growing menace is plaguing society. Not only is the conduct characteristic of a deviant group, it is affecting innocents and endangering tradition.

The idea that "normal" life might break down adds to the value of a crime myth and provides for its continued existence long after media attraction has vanished. These characterizations insure that major social institutions become involved in the reform process, since the conduct is perceived as both a physical threat and a substantial threat to existing social arrangements and institutions. Crime myths in this guise are similar to moral panics; they clarify the moral boundaries of society and demonstrate that there are limits to how much diversity will be tolerated. Erich Goode and Nachman Ben-Yehuda (1994) assert that moral panics are "characterized by the feeling . . . that evildoers pose a threat to the society and to the moral order as a consequence of their behavior and, therefore, 'something should be done' about them and their behavior" (p. 31). The "something" usually means strengthening social controls, according to Goode and Ben-Yehuda

(1994): "more laws, longer sentences, more police, more arrests, and more prison cells. If society has become morally lax, a revival of traditional values may be necessary; if innocent people are victimized by crime, a crackdown on offenders will do the trick . . ." (p. 31).

The hysteria over child abduction in the 1980s led some parents to return to traditional parenting roles instead of child care. Such a focus reinforces traditional values and allows blame to be placed on parents rather than on the absence of positive alternatives to traditional child-rearing practices. "If only she had not worked outside the home," instead of "if only the government supported and monitored alternative child-care industries." The child-care issue was so entrenched in the public mind that it became part of the 1992 presidential campaign with President Bush coming under fire for vetoing the parental leave bill and President Clinton signing the bill as one of his first official acts. Ironically, the children we were so concerned with protecting in the 1980s have now become teenagers, and, if media messages and political commentary are to be believed, they have become the new criminal class. At the turn of the century the airwaves are full of images of "killer kids" and "juvenile superpredators."

Mythmaking and the characterization of crime problems as major threats to traditional values and society serve important political functions for law enforcement. Consider organized crime and vice. Leaders in the law enforcement community testifying before Congress and state legislators can present the issue in one of two ways. They can present a relatively safe myth, suggesting that organized crime is a foreign conspiracy (Italians, Colombians, Jamaicans, etc.) that has invaded the United States and threatens the peace and security of a homogeneous and righteous society. Organized crime corrupts otherwise incorruptible politicians and police; it makes people gamble away their life savings; it introduces drugs into the schools; it uses prostitutes to seduce family men. Even worse, organized crime is an intricate, highly structured foreign conspiracy that can only be eliminated with more money, more justice personnel, and more enforcement power. The myth is safe and convenient. It points to the different ones as the source of a problem, so we do not have to change our life-style or take responsibility for the problem. Finally, it explains why law enforcement has yet to win the war against organized crime in the United States.

The alternative would be to expose the myth. Organized crime is an integral part of U.S. society. It could not exist if the citizenry did not wish to have ready access to drugs, pornography, prostitution, gambling, no-questions-asked loans, or stolen goods. Many of the "crimes" of organized crime would not be important or profitable if the business community did not collaborate in money laundering, the illegal disposal of toxic wastes, and the fencing of stolen goods. Organized crime would find itself quite harried if an array of politicians, law enforcers, and others were not willing to "grease the skids" of organized crime. Uncovering the myth of crime and vice, however, carries no bureaucratic rewards for law enforcement or government; it would offend people and end law enforcement and political careers. A rational bureaucrat or politician will find characterizing crime in terms of those who are different and threats to traditional values more useful than fact.

◇

Techniques of Myth Characterization

Mythmakers do not simply uncover crime and transmit information; they structure reality by selecting and characterizing events—thereby cultivating images of crime (Gerbner, 1972; Lang & Lang, 1969; Schoenfeld et al., 1979). The characterization of criminal events is largely a process of bias and distortion. This distortion is often an unintended consequence of the process by which information is collected, processed, and prepared for dissemination by mass media, government, and interest groups. Research on the media, the news particularly, concludes that misrepresentation and distortion are not uncommon practices (Bohm, 1986; Marsh, 1991).

The collection of crime events for public presentation is often shaped by reporters' perceptions. Journalistic accounts are rarely the product of actual observation. When they are, they are often conducted by reporters largely untrained in field research. More often than not, reporting of crime is based on secondhand information a reporter gleans from witnesses or public officials. The process of listening to and interviewing witnesses and crime victims invites bias. Frequently, the wrong questions are asked, essential questions are omitted, and sensationalism becomes the reporter's focus. After all, journalists are in competition when creating a product for audience consumption. The untrained observer or journalist who is driven by the competitive nature of the modern mass media may selectively observe or interview with the end product in mind. Outcome and conclusion may already have been drawn before the investigator begins collecting information.

Following a journalist's selection of a topic and initial investigation of a potential media story, the reporter's observations must make a transformation to communicable material. It must be written for dissemination or presentation. In this process of moving from observation to presentation, several problems arise. First, there is the possibility of selective memory or even the injection of personal preference by the reporter. Forgotten statements or observations may later be recalled by the journalist in the process of constructing a crime story. As information is recalled, initially insignificant observations may take on new meaning as the story unfolds. Second, after initial drafts of the presentation are constructed, they must be edited. In this editorial process a story can change considerably. Reports are often edited by a series of people who are guided by numerous constraints. Editorial constraints often include the time available to present a story, the page space available, and the marketability of the final product. The audience and editorial ideology also influence decisions. This process requires persons often unassociated with the initial crime to make judgments about what should be said or what should be shown. Editorial decisions are not always made in conjunction with the advice of the original observer.

The selection of which stories eventually appear in the news is based on the ordering of stories into media themes, as mentioned earlier. Mark Fishman (1998) notes that:

> The selection of news on the basis of themes is one ideological production of crime news. . . . This procedure requires that an incident be stripped of the actual context of its occurrence so that it may be relocated in a new, symbolic context: the news theme. Because newsworthiness is based on themes, the attention devoted to an event may exceed its importance, relevance, or timeliness were these qualities determined with reference to some theory of society. . . . Thus, something becomes a "serious type of crime" on the basis of what is going on inside newsrooms, not outside them. (p. 60)

Finally, after the presentation of a story there is the possibility of selective observation and retention on the part of the audience. Many will only remember the bizarre or hideous part of a communication to the exclusion of other information. While media focus on crime myth is often short-lived, the visceral images created may linger with the audience long after the media have moved on to a different topic.

There are, however, other techniques used in the manipulation of information and the construction of crime myths. There is a rich history of research and literature on the use of propaganda by the media and government. Propaganda is a technique for influencing social action based on intentional distortions and manipulation of communications (remember the discussion about marijuana earlier). While not all media and government presentation, or even a majority of it, is a conscious attempt at propaganda, many crime myths are the product of propaganda techniques.

> One important point to remember is that objective reporting is a myth. Every reporter brings to the story his/her own biases and worldview. Each reporter has to make choices in writing the story: what to include, what to leave out, what sources to use. A few well-placed adjectives, a few uses of "alleged" or "so-called" can cast a definite ideological twist. (Hynds, 1990, p. 5)

These techniques tend to shape the presentation of a crime, create images for the uncritical audience, and promote social reaction. Some of the most common techniques employed by the media, government officials, and interest groups for characterizing crime myths include:

- *Creating criminal stereotypes.* This practice amounts to presenting crime as a unidimensional and nonchanging event. Certain phrases such as "crime against the elderly," "child abduction," "street crime," "organized crime," and "school crime" group wide varieties of behavior into single categories that have been previously characterized by the media. The use of stereotyped phrases links broad and popular conceptions of crime to diverse criminal behavior. For example, "organized crime" often creates the image of large "well-structured" groups of foreign-born individuals who engage solely in criminal enterprise.

- **Presentation of opinion as fact.** This practice involves injecting personal opinion into media presentations without factual basis. Phrases that present opinions as fact might include: "the police are doing all they can to prevent this crime," "the community is in a state of panic," "crime threatens our families," or "schools are unsafe."

- **Masking opinions through sources.** This activity involves collecting opinions of others that closely match the proponent's viewpoint on a given issue. A reporter may select people to interview on the basis of how well their opinions fit the theme of the story or the direction in which the reporter intends to take the story. Opinions that do not fit the predetermined theme of an article or presentation are either not solicited or simply omitted.

- **Value-loaded terminology.** Biased language is used to characterize and label crime, criminals, or victims. A serial murderer may "stalk" the victim; a group of individuals may be referred to as a "crime family"; or a group of youths may become a "gang" that "preys" on "unsuspecting" victims.

- **Selective presentation of fact.** Presenting certain facts to the exclusion of others strengthens a biased argument. To emphasize the issue of child abduction, a proponent could cite that thousands of children are missing each year without presenting the fact that the vast majority of missing children are runaways. Alternatively, a proponent of community policing may cite the fact that crime is declining without pointing out that crime began to decline long before the introduction of community policing.

- **Information management.** The editorial process by which a particular news story is shaped and selected for presentation to the exclusion of other stories is one way to manage information. Presenting stories about sensational crimes like serial murder, stalkers, crack babies, and child abduction to the exclusion of stories on corporate crime, securities fraud, and other more common crimes are examples of such management.

- **Undocumented sources of authority.** Vague references including statements like "many police officials feel" or "many people are saying" without specific reference to who is saying what and what constitutes "many" is a misleading reference to authority.

- **Stripping fact from its context.** A variation of the characteristic above is using facts or statements of authorities appropriate in one context

and transferring them to another to support a particular position or
injecting facts that are unrelated to the issue. A media presentation
on drug abuse that focuses on statistics about the high school drop-
out rate without addressing whether or not there is an empirical link
between the two is stripping fact from its original context.

- *Selective interviewing.* A final method of portraying a position as more
  solid than the facts indicate is interviewing one or two authorities on
  a topic and presenting their remarks as the generalized expert opinion on a given topic. For example, interviewing one or two criminologists and giving the audience the impression that those views are
  reflective of the criminological community.

In the chapters that follow, we will address specific myths of crime and
criminal justice. Each myth or series of myths presented in this text differ in
the fashion in which they rely on these practices and other characterizations
to create a crime myth.

◇

ANALYZING CRIME MYTHS

There are no traditional or standard crime myths. Myths have at their origin
unique events that may or may not be noticed by particular mythmakers in
society. A criminal event or series of events cannot become a myth unless a
sufficient number of people contribute to its transformation. The story that is
conceived but never told does not become an issue or a crime myth. Crime
myths are unique in that they are a product of the social, political, and economic atmosphere of a time. That is to say, the audience must be ready or be
made ready to accept a crime myth. A criminal event that has the potential
for becoming a crime myth at one given moment may not be a viable myth at
another point in time. Myths are constructed within a given context, and that
context includes existing myths of crime and justice.

Mythmakers are varied, and their roles are dynamic. Sometimes the
government is the mythmaker, and the media respond to the official myth.
Other times the government responds to the myths created by the media or
special interest groups. These varied mythmakers and shifting roles all make
crime myths unique. Crime myths also differ in their purposes and consequences. Some myths result in the criminalization of behavior while others
die quietly without social or political response. Some myths serve the interests of powerful groups in society or serve a needed social function, while others serve no useful social purpose.

The uniqueness of the origins, detection, construction, and consequence of crime myths does not lend itself well to traditional criminological
analysis. There are no master keys or magic statistical bullets to understand-

ing and solving all crime myths. There is no blanket sociological theory that explains the development and purpose of all crime myths. Each crime myth requires individualized treatment and analysis. Such a situation is an invitation for criticism. It is, however, also a strength. Wedding oneself to a particular theory, perspective, or method of knowing is like relying on a single sense to describe a garden of flowers. This work is grounded in a variety of perspectives and supports its numerous contentions with varying means of understanding. We shall leave it to the reader to judge whether we have described a rose or merely wandered into the bramble bush.

Crime Waves, Crime Fears and the Social Reality of Crime

What circumstances predict variations in citizen concern about safety in a modern industrial society? Franklin Zimring and Gorden Hawkins (1997) suggest that there are at least three major influences: (1) the amount and seriousness of violent crime, (2) the level of fear-arousing social conditions in the immediate physical environment, and (3) the amount and perceived seriousness of fear-arousing cues in the mass media and personal social universe (p. 13). In this chapter we contrast the statistics about crime and crime rates with the influences contributing to public perception and fears.

For almost a decade, polls have found that people in the United States are more worried about crime than about any other issue. Recent polls confirm the public's deeply held fear of crime. A Gallup (1998) poll found that 14% of Americans frequently worried about the possibility that they would be murdered. An even greater number expressed frequent worry that their homes would be burglarized (31%); they would be sexually assaulted (28%); they would be mugged on the streets (19%); or they would be attacked while driving their cars (18%). The General Social Survey (1994), which is an attempt to track public opinion by the government, found that 41.4% of Americans were afraid to walk in areas close to their homes after dark. Overall, Americans felt seriously threatened by crime and were certain that the threat was growing year after year. In the 1998 Gallup survey, 47% of the respondents said they felt

more threatened by crime than they did five years ago, and an additional 11%
said there had been no improvement in the crime problem in the last five years.

Data from the National Crime Victimization Survey seemingly confirm
public fears.

> In 1996 U.S. residents age 12 or older experienced nearly 37 million crim-
> inal victimizations. . . . Of these victimizations, 27.3 million involved prop-
> erty crimes against households, 9.1 million involved the violent crimes of
> rape, robbery, and assault, and 0.3 million involved personal thefts such
> as purse snatching.
>   Translated into the number of violent and property crimes per 1,000
> persons or households, crime rates for 1996 show 42 violent victimiza-
> tions per 1,000 persons and 266 property crimes per 1,000 households.
> (Bureau of Justice Statistics, 1997a)

These are shocking numbers that suggest drastic measures are called for
to deal with this national crisis. After all, if these reports are correct, we are
somewhere between three and six times more likely to be attacked by a violent
criminal than in the past, and about one in three Americans is in dire danger of
criminal victimization each and every year.

The crime trends as presented by Department of Justice officials are
frightening, but our perceptions of the individual who will probably inflict this
harm and the harm that will be inflicted are even worse. Jeffrey Reiman (1998)
suggests this image of the typical crime:

> Think of a crime, any crime. Picture the first "crime" that comes into your
> mind. What do you see? The odds are you are not imagining a mining
> company executive sitting at his desk, calculating the costs of proper safe-
> ty precautions and deciding not to invest in them. Probably what you see
> with your mind's eye is one person physically attacking another or rob-
> bing something from another via the threat of physical attack. Look more
> closely. What does the attacker look like? It's a safe bet he (and it is a *he*,
> of course) is not wearing a suit and tie. In fact, my hunch is that you—like
> me, like almost anyone else in America—picture a young, tough, lower-
> class male when the thought of crime first pops into your head. (p. 61)

And who exactly is the typical criminal?

> . . . the one whose portrait President Reagan described as "that of a stark,
> staring face, a face that belongs to a frightening reality of our time—the
> face of a human predator, the face of the habitual criminal. Nothing in
> nature is more cruel and more dangerous." . . . He is, first of all, a *he*. Out
> of 2,239,934 persons arrested for FBI Index crimes in 1995, 1,705,681, or
> 76%, were males. Of persons arrested for violent crimes, 80% were men.
> Second, he is a *youth*. Almost half (49.3%) of arrests for FBI index crimes
> were people aged 22 and under; 49.9% of men arrested were aged 22 and
> under. Third, he is predominantly *urban* . . . Fourth, he is disproportion-
> ately *black*—blacks are arrested for Index crimes at a rate two-and-a-half
> times that of their percentage in the national population, they make up
> 31.1% of Index crime arrests. Finally, he is *poor*; among state prisoners in

1991, 33% were unemployed . . . prior to being arrested—a rate four times that of males in the general population. Among state prisoners who had incomes prior to being arrested, 19% earned less than $3,000 a year . . . and half earned less that $10,000 a year. (Reiman, 1998, pp. 54–55)

Not only is crime rampant, dangerous and threatening to explode in America, but it is the worst kind of crime. It is the kind of crime portrayed by George Bush's infamous "Willie Horton" commercials during the 1988 presidential campaign. The Bush campaign took a single case where a convicted violent offender participating in Massachusetts' highly successful prison furlough program committed a violent crime while on furlough. The ad had a devastating effect on then Governor Michael Dukakis' campaign. It also played to the worst fears and prejudices about crime. Willie Horton was an African-American male whose predations were directed at white females. The Bush campaign played to the prevailing fear: violent crime committed by a sociopathic stranger with a weapon after being released by a "soft" criminal justice system.

These images explain why 81% of the public favors life imprisonment for anyone convicted of three serious crimes, and 65% of the public favors the imposition of a 10 P.M. curfew for citizens under the age of 18 (Lacayo, 1994, p. 53). Similarly according to the General Social Survey (1994), 84% of the population feels that the courts don't deal harshly enough with criminals, and 74.5% support the death penalty for those convicted of murder. Given those attitudes, is it surprising that politicians clamor for more police, more prisons, more severe sentences, and an ever-increasing panoply of crimes? Is it any wonder that the mood of the U.S. public is becoming increasingly ugly toward violent predators?

Sober reflection about this wave of crime allegedly gripping the United States and threatening the innocent yields a very different picture than the one promoted by the politicians, the media, and law enforcement officials. Facts have been curiously missing from the debate about crime in the United States, and the facts, once discovered, are startling:

- There is no crime wave in the United States. Criminal victimization has been steadily declining for the past two and a half decades. The U.S. crime wave is a myth.
- Of those crimes that do occur, the overwhelming majority are the result of minor incidents involving neither serious economic loss nor extensive injury. Most crimes are not the serious, violent, dangerous crimes that compose the public stereotype of the United States as a predatory jungle.
- Most of the violent crimes that do threaten our well-being are not committed by psychopathic, predatory strangers lurking in urban shadows but by relatives, intimate friends and acquaintances, those we trust the most.
- Most crimes, even violent crimes, do not involve the use of a weapon, nor do they involve serious injury.

- Most crimes, particularly violent crimes, are intraracial, thereby contradicting the subtle and not so subtle appeals to racism by crime warriors.
- While government bureaucracies, police officials and politicians inflame our passions with racist images of "street crime" using dubious statistics, questionable analyses and unreliable data, they also go to great lengths to obfuscate, confuse, and cover up more serious criminal threats to the nation's well-being. Every effort is made to hide the prevalence and harm of corporate crime and to direct attention away from the real problem of violence in the United States—attacks on women and children by relatives, intimates, and acquaintances within the framework of the politically hallowed "traditional family."

The socially constructed image of crime, created by the state and the media, that emphasizes street crimes committed by the poor, the young, and minority group members is substantially false. The socially constructed image of crime hides the real problems and subjects millions of Americans to serious threats of death and injury from the ones they love most and have been taught to respect.

◇

How Much Crime Is There?

Asking how much crime there is in the United States is a very tricky question. Crime statistics must be treated with great caution and not an inconsiderable amount of skepticism. When numbers are bandied about, purporting to reflect the danger of crime in society, two primary questions must be asked about their validity. First, are they measuring what they purport to measure? Second, where do these numbers come from? Do they emanate from a source that has something to gain from the way crime is presented to the public?

The Official Crime Rate

The most commonly recognized measures of crime in the United States are the FBI's *Uniform Crime Reports*. These reports are issued annually and are compilations of "crimes known to the police." The first problem with the UCR is that "crimes known to the police" is a relatively ambiguous category. For the most part they are composed of complaints from citizens indicating that a crime has occurred. Note that this does not mean that a crime has actually occurred. Unlike media depictions of crime and policing, only a very small percentage of arrests are made by the police while a crime is in progress. The FBI does not insist that a suspect be arrested, or, for that matter, that the crime even be investigated and "founded" (Chambliss, 1988, p. 29). The only requirement is that someone, somewhere, for some reason, believed that a crime may have been committed and reported it to the police.

Second, the UCR, while severely underestimating the total amount of crime because of its reliance on victim and witness reporting (only about 3–4%

of crimes are actually "discovered" by the police), seriously overdramatizes the seriousness of crime by exaggerating its classifications of serious crimes. The crime categories and definitions used by the FBI are designed in such a way as to maximize both the severity of the crime and the number of crimes that are reported by local police departments. In fact, police departments have a consistent record of overrating the seriousness of offenses they are reporting. Equally confusing is the fact that no two police agencies classify crime in exactly the same way, leading to highly unreliable counts (Sherman, 1998). For example, as Chambliss (1988) points out:

> The crime categories used in the *UCR* are often ambiguous. For example, burglary requires the use of force for breaking and entering in many states, but the FBI tells local police departments to report the crime as burglary simply if there is unlawful entry. Merging these two types of offenses makes statistics on "burglary" ambiguous. More important is the way police departments are instructed to fill out the forms. In every instance, the instructions are designed to show the highest incidence of crime possible. The *Uniform Crime Reporting Handbook* states: "If a number of persons are involved in a dispute or disturbance and police investigation cannot establish aggressors from the victims, count the number of persons assaulted as the number of offenses."
>
> In reporting homicides, the instructions to the police are equally misleading from the point of view of gathering scientifically valid information. The instructions tell police departments that they should report a death as a homicide regardless of whether other objective evidence indicates otherwise: ". . . the findings of coroner, court, jury or prosecutor do not unfound [change the report of] offenses or attempts which your [police] investigations establish to be legitimate." (pp. 29–30)

This exaggeration of serious violent crime gives the false impression that street crime is more dangerous and common than it actually is; it also minimizes the danger to women and children emanating from crimes that occur in the traditional family setting. This occurs in two ways. First, crimes by relatives, friends, and acquaintances are often classified as less serious than crimes between or among strangers. Instead of the Index crime of aggravated assault, many of these crimes are classified as misdemeanor assault, thereby downgrading them out of the UCR Index crimes. Second, crimes among intimates are far less likely to be reported because of victim fear, embarrassment, and the personal and private nature of the crime (Allison & Wrightsman, 1993; Eigenberg, 1990).

Third, in addition to exaggerating violent street crime and obfuscating the nature of violent crimes against women and children by intimates, the UCR ignores crimes by corporations and businesses. No data at all is presented on white-collar crime, which is arguably far more damaging both economically and in terms of personal injury (see chapter 7) than street crime. This serious omission once again contributes to the misimpression that people are in greatest danger from the "typical" criminal described above and hides the serious crime the state and politicians do not want to reveal (Simpson et al., 1995).

Fourth, social scientists have demonstrated with regularity that statistics from the police reporting of crime are subject to political manipulation. For example, former President Richard Nixon instituted a crime control experiment in Washington, D.C. to demonstrate the effectiveness of his crime control proposals for the nation. The Nixon administration wanted the crime rate to go down in order to claim success. The crime rate did indeed go down—not because of any diminution in crime, but because of a bureaucratic device related to the reporting of crime. The District of Columbia police simply began listing the value of stolen property at less than $50, thereby removing a vast number of crimes from the felony category and thus "reducing" the crime rate (Seidman & Couzens, 1974, p. 469).

Selke and Pepinsky (1984) studied crime reporting practices over a thirty-year period in Indianapolis. They found that local police officials could make the crime rate rise or fall, depending upon political exigencies. Other studies have also demonstrated the ease with which crime rates can be manipulated (Mcleary, Nienstedt & Erven, 1982).

Recently, serious questions have been raised about whether crime data reported to the FBI for inclusion in the UCR are routinely falsified by the reporting departments. During the 1980s the FBI had to drop reports from the states of Florida and Kentucky because of unreliability and sloppy reporting (Sherman, 1998). In fact, in the last several years police departments in Philadelphia, New York, Atlanta, and Boca Raton, Florida have all been caught falsely reporting crime statistics. The city of Philadelphia had to withdraw its crime reports for 1996, 1997, and 1998 because they were downgrading some crimes, underreporting other crimes, and because of "general sloppiness" in their data collection. Philadelphia police officials systematically devalued rape, assault, and robbery offenses reclassifying them as "hospital cases," "threats," and "investigations of persons." About 10% of Philadelphia's Index crimes were tampered with (Cox, 1998). In Boca Raton, the police department systematically downgraded property crimes (reminiscent of the fraudulent reporting in the District of Columbia), resulting in an 11% reduction in reported felonies in 1997 (Butterfield, 1998).

Fifth, UCR crime data are highly sensitive to things that have nothing at all to do with crime. For example, improved police record keeping or computerization can make the crime rate skyrocket. During the 1970s and 1980s many police departments computerized their record keeping and filing systems. The result was a higher rate of reported crime that did not necessarily reflect any real increase in crime overall. For example, in 1973 citizens reported 861,000 aggravated assaults in the National Crime Victimization Survey, but the police recorded only 421,000 (UCR). In 1988, citizens reported 940,000 aggravated assaults in the victimization survey and the police recorded 910,000 (UCR) (Reiss & Roth, 1993, p. 414). Victimization surveys showed a very small increase in aggravated assault, almost all of which could be explained by an increase in population, but police statistics show massive increases. Expansion of 911 emergency phone systems greatly increase the reporting of crime to police. Changes in victim reporting practices unrelated to the actual number of crimes committed make the UCR crime rates rise or fall. For example, increased awareness of rape and educational campaigns by rape crisis centers and women's groups have contributed to a significant increase in the reporting of that crime. An increase in reporting may give the impression of a substantial increase in the incidence of rape (Jensen & Karpos, 1993).

Sixth, police department practices give a misleading impression of crime and criminals when reported in UCR statistics. If the police concentrate personnel and funds on policing criminal activity in minority neighborhoods, the amount of crime reported for those neighborhoods will be higher than for neighborhoods not as intensely policed (Jackson & Carroll, 1981; Liska & Chamlin, 1984). As we shall see in a later chapter, the deployment of police personnel in the war on drugs has seriously aggravated this problem and has contributed substantially to an incorrect idea that young, urban, poor, male blacks constitute the bulk of the crime problem in the United States.

Finally, as mentioned in chapter 1, UCR data are presented in ways that are far from scientific. The FBI creates "crime clocks" and other visual gimmicks designed to exaggerate the incidence of crime and the threat it poses to the public. By taking a large number (the total number of index crimes) as the numerator and a small number (the number of seconds in a minute, minutes in an hour, and hours in a day) as the denominator a melodramatic and misleading ratio of crimes to minutes or hours can be created. These presentations of UCR data are designed to exaggerate the amount of crime in society and to leave the impression that violent victimization is imminent. As Chambliss (1988) comments:

> This makes good newspaper copy and serves to give the law enforcement agencies considerable political clout, which is translated into ever-increasing budgets, pay raises, and more technologically sophisticated "crime-fighting" equipment. It does not, however, provide policy makers or social scientists with reliable data. (p. 31)

Uniform Crime Reports crime rates tell us virtually nothing about crime. "Crimes known to the police" is an ambiguous category, subject to political manipulation and easily adjusted to the bureaucratic requirements of law enforcement agencies. They may tell us a little about police department practices and policies, but they tell us nothing useful about crime. Nonetheless, it is on the basis of "crime rates" that both criminal justice officialdom and the media inform us about the ever-increasing threat from crime and criminals.

Having said all of this, it may be startling to note that in its release of 1998 crime figures on May 16, 1999, the FBI reported that for the seventh straight year serious crime *decreased*. In fact, serious crime was down 7% from 1997 and overall crime was down 17% since 1991 (FBI, 1999). Even more surprising is the fact that reported crime rates today are lower than they have been in decades. In 1998 murder was at its lowest rate since 1967; the robbery rate is the lowest it has been in 29 years; and all other forms of crime show a downward spiral (UCR, 1999). Despite public perception that crime continues to increase, a crime measure that is designed to produce the highest possible estimates of serious, violent crime shows a steep decline for at least six years.

Even more startling is the fact that any decline in "crimes reported to the police" is remarkable for two reasons having nothing to with the incidence of crime. First, there are many more police on the streets today than in the past. The number of police officers has increased about 20% in the last two decades, meaning that we have about 750,000 police on the streets today. If the number of police officers increased 20%, we would expect the crime rate to increase about the same amount. More police, patrolling a greater area with greater frequency, should be reporting a greater amount of crime. Instead we find a prolonged decline. Second, citizen reporting of crime is up markedly in the past three decades. With the exception of rape, every single category of crime shows an increase in incidence of reporting. This means that the decrease in reported crime rates is even greater than it appears at first glance because more people are reporting much more crime.

Table 2.1
Crime Reported to the Police

Crime Reported	1973	1998	Change
Rape	49%	31.6%	−17.4
Robbery	52%	62.0%	+10.0
Aggravated Assault	52%	57.6%	+5.6
Simple Assault	38%	40.3%	+2.3
Household Burglary	47%	49.4%	+2.4
Motor Vehicle Theft	68%	79.7%	+11.7

Source: BJS (1999). *Criminal Victimization 1998*. Washington, D.C.: Bureau of Justice Statistics, p. 10.

As we shall see, this reported decline in the crime rate is not a result of greater care in the culling of data or a sudden change in the direction of the political manipulation of crime rate statistics. It is in fact a *vast understatement of just how much decline in the amount of crime there really has been.*

Victimization Rates

A better source of crime data is the National Crime Victimization Survey (NCVS). Since the survey's inception in 1972, the Department of Justice annually conducts a survey of 110,000 U.S. residents, age 12 or older, from 55,000 randomly selected households across the country, asking respondents if they or any member of their households have been a victim of crime in the past year. The victimization surveys are clearly superior to UCR data in that they measure both reported and unreported crime, and they are unaffected by technological changes in police record keeping, levels of reporting by victims to the police, and the other factors which call into question the validity of UCR data (BJS, 1993, pp. 2–4). The NCVS data come from questionnaires carefully designed for validity and reliability by social scientists; they are administered to a very large, demographically representative sample of the U.S. population. While no survey is perfect, the NCVS represents the best available source of data on crime victimization in the United States. How the data are reported is subject to political manipulation, but the data themselves are scientifically valid.

The National Crime Victimization Survey data speak volumes about crime in the United States. Most importantly, survey results show that crime has been *decreasing* for the past 25 years and that the decrease has been precipitous. From 1993 to 1998 personal crimes (rape, robbery, assault, and personal larceny) *decreased 27.4%*, and household crimes (burglary, household larceny, and motor vehicle theft) *decreased 31.8%*. The victimization rate for rape was down 50%; for robbery 33.3%, for aggravated assault 37.5%, and for burglary 33.8%. Simple assault was down 20.1% and motor vehicle theft decreased 43.2%. *The fact is that violent crime in the United States is down 26.7% and property crime is down 31.8%* (BJS, 1999). It appears that a massive decrease in the incidence of crime has somehow sparked a massive increase in concern about crime. As Samuel Walker (1998) succinctly puts it: "This is one of the longest and most significant declines in the crime rate in American history. Much of the public hysteria about crime is misplaced" (p. 5).

Table 2.2
Victimization Rates Per 1,000 Households

Crime	Victimizaton Rates			Victimization Rates		
	1973	1991	Change	1993	1998	Change
Rape	1.0	0.8	−11.6	1.0	0.5	−50.0
Robbery	6.7	5.6	−17.2	6.0	4.0	−33.3
Aggravated Assault	10.1	7.8	−22.2	12.0	7.5	−37.5
Simple Assault	14.8	17.0	+15.1	29.4	23.5	−20.1
Household Burglary	91.7	53.1	−42.1	58.2	38.5	−33.8
Motor Vehicle Theft	19.1	21.8	+14.3	19.0	10.8	−43.2

Source: Bastian, L. D. (1992). *Criminal Victimization 1991*. Washington, D.C.: Bureau of Justice Statistics, p. 4; BJS (1999). *Criminal Victimization 1998*. Washington, D.C.: Bureau of Justice Statistics, p. 9.

Let us be very clear about this. The only reliable, scientific data we have on crime in the United States tells us that crime is decreasing. Furthermore, those decreases are not small or marginal; they are consistent decreases that have resulted in a diminution in the amount of crime. The irony of this prolonged and significant decrease in crime juxtaposed against public hysteria about crime should not escape us.

In 1992 the NCVS was redesigned (Bastian, 1995). Categories of crime were changed. For example, rape was aggregated with sexual assault to create a new crime classification: aggravated and simple assault were combined with "attempted assault with a weapon" and "attempted assault without a weapon," thereby creating a new category of crime. This redesign may simply have been part of the annual methodological review of the NCVS that attempts to increase the reliability and validity of the study. Certainly the reformulation of questions on rape and sexual assault were in response to serious problems with the survey. Prior to 1992 the manner in which the NCVS attempted to solicit information about rape (asking questions about assault, but never directly mentioning rape) resulted in a severe underestimation (Eigenberg, 1990).

It is possible, however, that some of the redesign may have had other motivations. The NCVS recorded a decline in serious crime between 1973 and 1991, contrary to politicians' proclamations and public impressions. The data do not justify: immense new expenditures on law enforcement and prisons; the expansion of the criminal law; the extension of the death penalty to a plethora of new offenses; the incarceration of an additional one million Americans; and a "crime crisis" mentality in policy making. The reclassification of criminal acts in the redesigned survey makes it inevitable that the victimization rates and frequencies will be higher than in the surveys of the previous twenty years. Perhaps some of the survey's redesign was a bit of methodological legerdemain intended to give the appearance that the incidence of victimizations was increasing. Perhaps the intent was simpler. By changing the survey and the classification of crimes in that survey, the Justice Department has made it extremely difficult to continue a longitudinal comparison of data into the future. It is therefore not possible to determine if the clear trends of declining victimization have continued through 1992–1999. The Department of Justice has, intentionally or otherwise, made continuing analysis of a trend that negates the government's official position on crime impossible.

While the data from 1992 forward are no longer directly comparable with the earlier data, they still indicate a continuing decrease in serious crime. The 1998 NCVS property and violent crime rates were the lowest recorded since 1973 when the NCVS began reporting data (after rates were adjusted to take into account the 1992 redesign). In 1998 violent crime rates were 27% lower and property crimes were 32% lower than they were in the first redesigned survey of 1993. Between 1993 and 1998 no crime showed a victimization increase; in fact, all categories of crime had a decline ranging from 6 to 50% (BJS, 1999). Criminal victimizations have declined for 25 years. The justification for crime-war hysteria is clearly absent in both old and new victimization surveys.

◊
THE REALITY OF CRIME

The decrease in crime over the past quarter century is only a part of the story. *Approximately 96% of the U.S. population was not the victim of any kind of personal crime.* In addition, the bulk of crime reported by the NCVS that does occur is not the heinous, violent predatory crime that we imagine.

For 1998, the victimization rate for crimes of violence according to NCVS was 36.6 per thousand households. This suggests that roughly 4% of the population aged 12 and older was the victim of a violent crime. These crimes of violence include rape, robbery, and aggravated and simple assault. However, when the victimization rates for rape, robbery, and aggravated assault are combined, we arrive at a figure of about 15 victimizations per 1,000 households. This means that less than 1.5% of U.S. households were victims (or feared the threat of being victims) of serious violent crime—a fact diametrically at odds with public perceptions and official pronouncements.

Recall that the 1998 Gallup poll discussed earlier found that 14% of U.S. citizens worried about being murdered. Murder is the least frequent violent victimization, with about 7 murder victims for every 100,000 people in the population. So while 14% of the population is worried about being a murder victim,

Table 2.3
Victimization Rates for Personal and Property Crimes, 1998

Crime	Victimizations per 1,000 persons age 12 or older or per 1,000 househoulds
Personal Crimes	37.9
Crimes of Violence	36.6
Rape/Sexual Assault	1.5
Robbery	4.0
Assault	31.1
Aggravated	7.5
Simple	23.5
Property Crimes	217.4
Household Burglary	38.5
Motor Vehicle Theft	10.8
Theft	168.1

Source: BJS (1999). *Criminal Victimization 1998*. Washington, D.C.: Bureau of Justice Statistics, p. 9.

only .007% are actually murdered. In the same Gallup poll 19% of the population worried about being "mugged." Yet, the NCVS data show that only 3.5% of all households will actually be victims of a completed robbery. The poll found that 280 of every 1,000 people worried about rape or sexual assault, yet the NCVS tells us that only about 1 of every 1,000 people will be victims of such crimes. In essence this means that Americans overestimate the danger of homicide by a factor of 2000 to 1 and overestimate the threat of robbery by a factor of 5 to 1.

Turning to crimes of theft we find a similar situation. The NCVS tell us that in 1997 the victimization rate for crimes of theft was 189.9 per 1,000 households, or roughly 9.5% of the population over age 12. But considerable ambiguity exists over these victimizations. For example, the rate of completed thefts of $250 or more was only 38 per 1,000 households or about 1.8% of the U.S. population, meaning that 80% of thefts involved only very minor losses. In the 1998 Gallup poll 31% of the U.S. population worried frequently about their homes being burglarized, yet NCVS data for 1997 tells us that 1.8% of the population will be the victim of a completed burglary. Once again Americans overestimate the threat of burglary by a factor of 17 to 1.

Strangers and Crime

There are strong indicators that the "typical criminal" is less of a threat than the popular stereotype would have us believe. For example, according to the 1998 NCVS data 54% of all violent crime victimizations were by "nonstrangers" compared to 44% by the feared stranger predator (in 1% of the cases the relationship was unknown). About three-quarters of all rapes of females were perpetrated by someone known to the victim, not by a stranger lurking in an alley or hiding behind bushes. NCVS data for 1998 indicated that 74% of all rapes and sexual assaults were committed by "nonstrangers"; 25% were committed by strangers. In the case of homicides the numbers are even more striking. Contrary to the assertions of politicians, three times as many murder victims (45%) are killed by relatives, friends, or acquaintances. The popular image of a homicide as being related to youth gangs, drug trafficking, and burglary accounts for less than 15% of all homicides.

There are excellent reasons to believe that these are severe underestimates of the actual amount of violent victimizations by friends, relatives, and acquaintances. Scott Decker (1993) reviewed all 792 homicides occurring in St. Louis between 1985 and 1989. He found that 58% of these murders were committed by friends or acquaintances; 12% by perpetrators involved in romantic relationships with the victims; and 8% by other relatives. Only 18% were by strangers. Simply put, people were four times as likely to be killed by someone close to them as by a stranger. Another research project sponsored by the government reviewed murder cases in the 75 largest counties in the United States in 1988 and found that 16% involved family members, 64% friends and acquaintances, and only 20% strangers (Dawson & Langan, 1994). Clearly, it is not the lurking stranger we should fear; those closest to us pose the greatest danger.

The issue of stranger homicides is vital to understanding the unfounded public hysteria over crime and the role of the state in creating that fear. In 1994, despite the fact that the murder rate had been relatively stable for two decades, the FBI suggested that the public should be concerned with the nature of murder, not the number of murders. In fact, the *Uniform Crime Reports* argued, "something has changed in the constitution of murder to bring about the unparalleled level of concern and fear confronting the nation" (FBI, 1994, Section V). The FBI claimed that murder was more threatening because it was becoming more random. Random killing is the most frightening type of crime because it entails innocent victims killed by strangers for no apparent reason.

The media immediately seized the theme. Page one of *USA Today* proclaimed, "Random Killings Hit a High" with the subtitle "All have 'realistic chance' of being victim, says FBI" (Davis & Meddis, 1994). The claim is simply untrue. Nor is there a discernible trend that would make such a claim true in the future. According to the FBI's own data, in 1976 13.8% of murders were committed by strangers; in 1980 13.3%; in 1985, 14.5%; in 1990, 14.0% and in 1993, 14.0% (Donziger, 1996, p. 77). Where do these numbers show a dramatic increase in random murder by strangers? Based on 1996 numbers, the chance of a U.S. citizen 12 years old or older being murdered is about 14,286 to 1. Creating a climate of fear is irresponsible at best. Random, stranger murder is an officially produced myth.

The most heinous and most feared crimes involve attacks on children, particularly the rape and murder of children. Legislators have been quick to pass laws similar to "Megan's Law" in New Jersey, which requires notification

Table 2.4
Victim and Offender Relationships, 1998

	Violent crime rate per 1,000		
	Stranger	**Nonstranger**	**Unknown**
*All victimization	44	54	1
Rape/Sexual Assault	25	74	2
Robbery	57	41	2
Aggravated Assault	48	50	2
Simple Assault	42	57	1

*The absence of murder increases the rate of stranger crimes; totals may not equal 100 because of rounding.
Source: BJS (1999). *Victimization 1998*. Washington, D.C.: Bureau of Justice Statistics, p. 7.

to the community of the presence of a "sex offender" and seeks to protect children against stranger-pedophiles, rapists, and murderers. Once again the emphasis on crimes by strangers is fundamentally misleading. As with the crimes of homicide and rape, the data clearly show that "nonstrangers" pose the greatest threat. In a study of state prisoners incarcerated for violent crimes against children under the age of 18, it was determined that 88% of the offenders had a prior relationship with their victims (Greenfield, 1996). In fact, in about one-third of the cases of rape and sexual assault against children the victim was the child or step-child of the assailant. When the child-victim was very young (12 or younger), family relationships accounted for 70% of incarcerated child rapists, compared to 6% of incarcerated child-rapists to whom the victim was a stranger (Langan & Harlow, 1994). In addition, in cases where the victim-offender relationship was known, 57% of child murders were committed by family, friends, and acquaintances; 33% of child murderers were family members; and only 10% were strangers (Greenfield, 1996).

Weapons, Injury, and Crime

Our images of crime are often filled with weapons wielded by violent strangers. However, the data indicate that such crimes are the exception, not the rule. Only one out of four violent crimes involves the use of a weapon (BJS, 1997a). Most violent victimizations do not involve weapons. In fact they typically do not involve injuries; when they do, the injuries are minor. Only about 8% of violent crime victims in the United States went to a hospital emergency room, and most of them were released the same day. About 1% of violent crime victims required a hospital stay of one day or more (BJS, 1994c, Tables 86 and 88). In addition, only 9% of all victims of violent crimes lost any time at all from work and only 10% incurred medical expenses as a result of the crime (BJS, 1993, pp. 15, 17). Unlike the picture of crime presented by the media, politicians, and the police, the truth is that even in violent crimes, very few people are injured and even fewer are seriously injured.

Race and Crime

Both crime reporting by the media and anti-crime railing by politicians and law-enforcement executives have played on a deeply ingrained racism in U.S. culture. The Willie Horton ad was designed to raise the image of a very specific type of criminal—a violent, black offender, the type of offender most feared by white, middle-class America. Similarly, tabloid media coverage of shootings of white tourists by young black men at rest stops, gang attacks on innocent passerbys in our cities, or acts of vigilantism by people like Bernard Goetz against minority youth prey on the same racist fears. The fact is, however, that interracial crime is very rare. Interracial crime images are blatant and insidious appeals. Only 15% of violent crimes involve white victims and black perpetrators, while 69% involve white victims and white perpetrators. Seventy-five percent of white crime victims are victimized by whites, and 85%

of black crime victims are victimized by blacks. In 80% of all violent crimes, the victims and offenders are of the same race (Zawitz et al., 1993, pp. 3, 23). The issue of interracial violent crime is totally unsubstantiated by the facts.

Kids and Crime

The government and the media have also gone to great lengths to create a totally unwarranted fear of crime by juveniles. Reports of violence by alleged juvenile "superpredators" and alleged increases in drug use by juveniles have fueled fears of crime committed by this segment of the population. Chapter 9 discusses this myth in detail. Here we highlight a few of the facts about juvenile crime and juvenile violence. The fact is that only 6 out of every 100 juvenile arrests involves a crime of violence, less than half the adult ratio. Rape and murder account for less than one-half of one percent of juvenile arrests (Donziger, 1996, pp. 132–133). Eighty-eight percent of murderers known to the police are over the age of 18 (UCR, 1999). Eighty-four percent of the 3,139 counties in the United States had no youth homicides in 1994. Despite the publicity given to school shootings, research indicates that 96% of the country's students experienced no violent crime in either 1995 or 1996 (NCIA Web site, 1999).

Claims have been made that teenage drug use is escalating and is at an all time high. This is also patently false. Teenage drug use declined throughout the 1980s. In the early 1990s teenage use of marijuana, alcohol, and tobacco increased slightly, indicating a change in social trends extending well beyond illegal drugs. The fact remains that the current rate of monthly marijuana use among teenagers stands at 8.2%, down from 16.7% in 1979. In addition, much was made of a claim that heroin use among teenagers had more than doubled between 1994 and 1995, rising from an estimated 0.3% to 0.7%. While technically true, this is in reality a false claim because the actual number of teen heroin users in the government's study rose from 14 to 32, much too small an increase considering the size of the sample to have any statistical significance (NCIA Web site, 1999).

◊

CRIME IMAGES

How can we explain the persistent, mounting public concern about crime? With serious crime declining over a long period of time, why do fear of crime and feelings of public punitiveness follow precisely the opposite pattern? At least three factors appear to be responsible for the lack of congruence between the facts and public perception: the media and its reporting of crime; alarms raised by the law enforcement establishment; and the politicalization of crime.

The Media

The media grossly distort our view of crime and its dangers through both news and entertainment programming. Tabloid television shows such as *Hard Copy*,

Inside Edition and *A Current Affair* regale us regularly with reports of serial murder, rest stop killings of tourists, and patricide among the privileged. After all, few viewers would stay tuned to watch a segment on the theft of a bicycle or a day in the life of a pickpocket. But viewers will tune in for sensational murders like the Menendez killings in California, or for lurid details about the serial murders of Ted Bundy, or for a segment on the murder of a tourist at a Florida highway rest stop. Despite the fact that such crimes are relatively rare events, they are emphasized and highlighted by these programs. The mundane, relatively unimportant crimes that make up 75–80% of all crimes committed do not attract viewers.

The same type of exaggeration of the violent and weird can be seen in news programming. The local evening news usually leads with a story about a murder committed in the course of a robbery, or even a robbery without a murder, as long as violence was threatened. The hundreds or thousands of mundane crimes that occur daily in every city are scarcely mentioned. Entertainment shows such as *NYPD Blue, The Practice,* and *Law and Order* feature crimes of violence and depredation. After all, few people want to see the prosecutors on *Law and Order* vigorously pursue a case of "personal larceny without contact" or Andy Sipowicz and his *NYPD Blue* colleagues rough up suspects over a troublesome case of misplaced luggage at Grand Central Station.

The news media make violent crime seem normal and commonplace. Crime coverage during the evening news programs of the three national networks nearly tripled from 571 stories in 1991 to 1,632 stories in 1993, despite the fact that crime rates and victimization rates fell sharply during the same period (Lichter & Lichter, 1994). The Center for Media and Public Affairs found that crime has been the most prominently featured topic on the evening news since 1993, with 7,448 stories, or about 1 in 7 evening news stories. The greatest increase was in the coverage of murder; it has increased by over 700% since 1993. During 1990–1992 homicide coverage averaged 99 stories per year. That number jumped to 714 in 1993 during a period when the homicide rate was falling drastically. Since 1993 one out of every twenty evening news stories has been about murder (CMPA, 1997). In addition to overreporting homicides, the media also distort the phenomenon. In a study of 9,422 homicides in Los Angeles County occurring between 1990 and 1994, researchers found that only specific types of homicides were selected by the media. The 13% covered by the *Los Angeles Times* had very specific characteristics. First, news coverage focused on homicides with victims who were either elderly or children; female; and highly educated. Contrast this with the 85% of homicides in Los Angeles County where the victims were young, minority males. Homicides selected for coverage tended to be stranger homicides that occurred in neighborhoods where the average household income was more than $25,000. As we learned earlier, nonstranger homicides are by far the most common. In addition homicide most frequently occurs in low-income neighborhoods (Beil, 1998).

Not satisfied by the excessive coverage of crime by both news and entertainment programming, the television industry invented a programming hybrid, a genetic cross between entertainment and the news, called "Reality TV." There are many national programs in this genre: *America's Most Wanted, Top Cops, American Detective, Unsolved Mysteries, Rescue 911*, and *Real Stories of the Highway Patrol* (Seagal, 1993, p. 51).

Research has demonstrated that the mass media are the primary and most consistent sources of information on crime, criminals, crime control policies, and the criminal justice system for most Americans (Barak, 1994; Ericson, Graber, 1980; Warr, 1995). Crime is good business for the media industry; it attracts readers and viewers. More readers and viewers mean greater newspaper and magazine circulation and larger television audiences—consequently larger advertising fees (Barkan, 1997). The evening news and reality crime shows know that salacious and exciting crime-related topics like police "hot pursuits"; violent crimes, particularly strange and particularly brutal crimes with innocent and unsuspecting victims; jury trials; and crime alleged to be committed by social deviants like pedophiles, prostitutes, satanists and cannibals attract the most viewers (Lichter & Lichter, 1983).

The media seek the most sensational and unusual crimes that fit news themes with moralistic messages. Over the years the media have created crime scares by formulating news themes around issues of "white slavery" in the prostitution industry; sexual psychopaths terrorizing major cities; Communists infiltrating vital industries and relaying national security data to the Soviet Union; satanists engaged in mass murder, child sacrifice and ritualistic child abuse; serial killers roaming the country; and many others.

> Consider how readily today's media link particular cases to larger social problems. We *problematize* events, turning particular criminal acts into examples of types of crime. . . . In addition to generalizing from particular cases, claims about crime waves imply changing levels—increases in criminality. We talk about crime waves as though there are fashions in crime: people didn't used to commit this crime . . . but now they do. (Best, 1999, pp. 35–36)

With such heavy exposure to crime themes in entertainment media and through news programming it would appear to be common sense that more media exposure should be directly related to a greater fear of crime (Barkan, 1997). Evidence exists that the media's impact on fear of crime and on the persistence of crime as a major national issue is both real and tangible. Researchers surveyed the residents of Phoenix in both 1979 and 1980 to study public attitudes toward crime (Baker et al., 1983; Livingston, 1996). Both surveys found roughly the same levels of crime victimization, but the 1980 survey showed a clear and marked increase in the percentage of residents who thought crime was increasing. Since actual crime incidents could not explain this increase in concern, the researchers turned to the media for clues. They found that during 1980 the local newspapers had intensified their coverage of two crime categories: homicides and robberies. The intensified coverage coincided with a change in police department leadership and increased dissemination of information about violent crime by the police department. In essence, a bureaucratic change in police procedures facilitated media access to data emphasizing violent crime. The subsequent increase in media coverage sparked an increase in citizen fear, despite the fact that the reality of crime had not changed. Other studies point to similar media influences. For example, Linda Heath's (1984) research demonstrated that newspaper stories focusing on random violent crimes had the effect of increasing public fear of crime. Liska and Baccaglini (1990) found that newspaper stories about local homicides increased fear of crime. This effect was especially strong for stories appearing in the first fifteen pages of the newspaper.

George Gerbner (1994), a leading media researcher at the Annenberg School of Communications at the University of Pennsylvania, has synthesized these media impacts into a theory of "the mean world syndrome." Gerbner argues that the research demonstrates that heavy viewers of television violence, whether in entertainment or news media, increasingly develop the feeling that they are living in a state of siege. Gerbner's research shows that heavy television viewers: (1) seriously overestimate the probability that they will be victims of violence; (2) believe their own neighborhoods to be unsafe; (3) rank fear of crime as one of their most compelling personal problems; (4) assume crime rates are going up regardless of whether they really are; (5) support punitive anti-crime measures; and (6) are more likely to buy guns and anti-crime safety devices. Other research demonstrates that "heavy viewers . . . exhibit an exaggerated fear of victimization and a perception that people cannot be trusted." (Carlson, 1995, p. 190).

In addition to increasing public fears, media crime coverage impacts other public perceptions and views of crime. Heavy coverage directs much public discourse on the crime issue. For example, the media regularly and falsely direct attention to crimes allegedly committed by young, poor, urban males, who are often members of minority groups (Reiman, 1998). Media coverage directs people's attention to specific crimes and helps to shape those crimes as social problems (i.e., drug use, gangs). Media coverage limits discourse on crime control options to present policies, suggesting that the only options are more police, more laws, more prisons, and longer sentences (Surette, 1998).

The Crime-Industrial Complex

Very much like the media, the criminal justice establishment also has a pecuniary interest in portraying crime as a serious and growing threat. Public spending on the criminal justice system is about $100 billion a year, up from $12 billion in 1972. In 1996, 2,343 state prosecutor's offices employed over 71,000 attorneys, investigators, and support staff, a 25% increase from 1992. There are about 420,000 employees working in state and federal correctional institutions and another 228,000 working in local jails (BJS, 1998b). At the state and local level in the United States there are about 15,000 police agencies, with 757,000 employees and annual budgets in excess of $28 billion. Add to these the approximately 60 federal agencies with budgets in excess of $12 billion and you will find quite a large interest group for crime control issues. This interest group is even more impressive in size when the 13,000–15,000 courts in the United States are added and the $37 billion spent in the past two decades on prison construction is considered (Smolowe, 1994a, p. 56). Overall there is about $100 billion of tax money spent annually on the criminal justice system in the United States (Donziger, 1996, p. 85).

It is in the interests of police administrators, prison officials, judges, and prosecutors to keep crime in the forefront of public debate. Enormous sums of money, millions of jobs, and bureaucratic survival depend on increasing concerns about crime. It is not surprising then, that official statistics consistently have been presented in ways to increase public fear and to downplay any decrease in criminal activity.

But it is not just money and jobs that are at stake for the criminal justice system in presenting crime as a major threat. Policy decisions and jurisdictional issues also come into play. For example, the "war on drugs" has resulted in the expansion of the jurisdiction and police powers of many federal law enforcement agencies, with the FBI, the keeper of crime statistics, as the primary beneficiary. Attempts to remove due process protections and to expand the scope of the legal code depend on an active public interest in crime matters.

In addition to a massive number of public employees in the criminal justice system, there is also a large and growing private crime-control industry. About $65 billion a year is spent on private security. Private industry produces a variety of "protective" devices at a substantial profit, everything from home security systems to the color-coordinated "Club" designed to prevent auto theft. In addition, many major defense contractors have begun marketing their wares for the crime-control industry. For example, recent "defense"-related products being sold to police departments include night vision goggles tested for use in "Desert Storm"; a listening device that attaches to lightposts, identifies the sound of a gunshot, and transmits the location to the precinct station; and, most remarkably, a wristwatch that is used to monitor vital signs of troops in battle. Other defense industry products may be less remarkable but no less profitable. Bulletproof vests, improved computer technology, equipment that forces cars to stop, and foam that freezes a suspect in place are all now readily available at a price (Donziger, 1996, p. 86).

The private prison industry is booming. The private corrections industry plays on fear of crime the way the defense industry played on fear of communist expansion during the cold war years. The old coalition of politicians, defense department bureaucrats, and corporations (the military-industrial complex) that drove U.S. foreign policy for some forty years has been replaced by a coalition of politicians, criminal justice bureaucrats, and corporations in a crime-industrial complex (Paulette, 1994, p. A1). Twenty-one corporations operate in the private prison industry. They manage 88 prisons and supervise about 50,000 inmates, realizing annual revenues of about $250 million a year. The private prison industry has experienced a 2,000% growth since 1984 and is growing four times as fast as state correctional systems (Thomas, 1995, p. vii).

Both public agencies and private corporations have a vested interest in fear of crime. In addition, as Nils Christie (1994) has pointed out in his book *Crime Control as Industry*, they all have a vested interest in a "war on crime." In order for public or private organizations to grow and profit, they require sufficient quantities of raw materials. In the criminal justice field, those raw materials are prisoners, and those profiting from crime and its control will do whatever is necessary in a capitalist society to assure that steady supply.

The Politicalization of Crime

Finally, both the media and the criminal justice system find ready allies among officeholders and office-seekers who must court the public. Crime is a relatively easy issue. No one is for it; being against it is a safe political issue. Exaggerating and distorting the amount and shape of the crime threat is standard fare for politicians.

But it is not just exaggeration and distortion that emanate from the politicalization of crime. Politicians create false fear, false portraits of the "typical criminal" and the "typical crime," and false views of how crime is handled by the criminal justice system. Examples of political disregard of the truth are legion; the case below highlights the extent to which the public is misled.

In the 1998 election for the 6th congressional seat in Kentucky, the Republican candidate, Ernest Fletcher, ran a dangerously deceptive crime ad. It featured a young, blonde woman named Jessica who said:

> It was the worst day of my life. My attacker was convicted and got six months in jail. Ernesto Scorscone [the Democratic candidate] was his lawyer.
>
> He must have thought six months was too harsh. Because twice Scorscone appealed just to get the case thrown out or the sentence reduced. Now Scorscone's telling us he's tough on crime.
>
> But he's not being honest with you. Everyone deserves a defense. But to me, Scorscone is more concerned with criminals' rights than victims' rights.

While "Jessica" is speaking the words "Raped," "Shot Twice," and "Left for Dead" appear on the screen.

This ad referred to a 1977 case, making the issue two decades old, a fact not reported by Fletcher. "Jessica" was walking alone at night and was abducted and taken to the campus of a local high school, where was she raped and shot in the neck and chest.

The ad drew several blatantly untruthful conclusions. First, it implied that Scorscone sought out this wanton stranger-predator as a client in order to shield him from justice. In fact, Scorscone was working in the public defender's office; he was *appointed* by a judge to represent the defendant. Second, the ad implied that Scorscone was responsible for a seemingly light sentence. Under Kentucky law at the time, the maximum sentence that could be given to a juvenile was detainment in a juvenile facility until he turned 21. The defendant was 17 years old at the time of the crime. The sentence was that he be held until he was 21, with a minimum sentence of six months. That was the most severe sentence allowed by the law. The third falsehood is the most troubling. The ad suggested that two appeals represented extraordinary efforts by Scorscone to help the rapist avoid punishment. In fact, the appeals addressed issues of innocence. The youth had taken a lie-detector test administered by the police and was found to be truthful in denying the attack. The police and prosecutors had mishandled the evidence used to provide corroboration for the victim's story. It turned out that prosecutors were unable to identify the source of the blood sample being used as evidence against the youth. They were unable to tell if the sample came from the rapist's semen, the victim's cervical fluid, or the victim's blood, an issue directly related to the accused's guilt (Baniak, 1998; Potter, 1998).

In addition to the factual errors in the ad, its implications about crime, victimization, and the criminal justice system were also very disturbing. The ad distorted the nature of crime by lying about the probability of victimization by a stranger in a rape case. It exploited rape victims by fundamentally misrepresenting the actual nature of rape, the probable source of rape, and normal circumstances surrounding rape. And it suggested that even in cases where severe evidentiary problems exist, accused criminals don't deserve quality representation—an assertion contrary to basic constitutional protections. Despite the fact that the ad was vigorously contested by attorneys, rape crisis center representatives and women's groups, Fletcher won a narrow victory in the election.

Both Democrats and conservative Republicans compete today to see who can spend the most money and appear the most punitive in putting together crime-control legislation. Adding police officers, building prisons, removing constitutional protections for individual rights, buying more hardware and expanding technology, and continually expanding the scope and reach of criminal law are the centerpieces of these policies. Explaining that crime is less of a threat today than it was in 1973 would not justify expanding the criminal justice system. Appeals to fear about drive-by shootings, carjackings, and violent predators will get new cops hired, new prisons built and more money spent on criminal justice.

◈

CONCLUSION

Whether a creation of the media, politicians, private corporations, criminal justice system bureaucrats, or a combination of all four the popular image of crime is a myth. The crime wave does not exist. Crime is decreasing and decreasing drastically. The typical criminal does not exist. Crime is committed, for the most part, in social settings by unarmed people who are relatives, friends, and acquaintances of the victims. The typical crime is also a myth. Most crime is minor in nature and content. And very little crime results in serious injury. We have been duped or have duped ourselves. We will return repeatedly to the same questions: how do myths become ingrained in the fabric of our social psyche, and whose interests do exaggerations and divisive images serve?

The Myth and Fear of Child Abduction

To be unaware of the issue of missing children in America is to be totally isolated from newspapers, television, mail, or other forms of communication. Beginning in the early 1980s, barely a week went by when the public was not exposed to photographs, stories, and debates on the issue of missing and abducted children. Virtually every form of media was used to circulate the faces and stories of missing children. From milk cartons to flyers in utility bills to television documentaries, Americans were made aware of the child abduction "epidemic." "Toy stores and fast-food restaurants distributed abduction-prevention tips for both parents and children. Parents could have their children fingerprinted or videotaped to make identification easier; some dentists even proposed attaching identification disks to children's teeth" (Best, 1987, p. 102).

Public concern with child abduction became so profound that in 1983 then President Ronald Reagan proclaimed May 25th National Missing Children's Day. A study in *Clinical Pediatrics* showed that parents were more frequently worried about abduction than about anything else, even car accidents (Stickler et al., 1991, p. 527). In 1997 a survey by the Princeton Survey Research Associates Poll found that child kidnapping, sexual abuse, and becoming the victim of a violent crime were among parents' highest concerns (Kantrowitz, 1997).

In 1995, the Family Protection Network took out full-page advertisements in major newspapers and magazines across the country. "If your child were missing, you'd think about it every minute." The copy described how the service would put a photograph of the child and other information into a database reaching numerous sources including the police, media and private investigators to help avert "the terrifying problem of child abduction." At the end of the advertisement, the $250 annual fee was mentioned, followed by "But think what you might get in return." The general manager denied that his company was preying on paranoia. "This is a prudent way for parents to prepare for their child's safety. No one has the dedicated massive resources we do, the private investigators, the technology, the commitment" (Zorn, 1995b, p. 1).

The National Center for Missing and Exploited Children (NCMEC) is the national clearinghouse and resource center funded by the Office of Juvenile Justice and Delinquency Prevention (OJJDP). It maintains a Web site (www.missingkids.com) and a toll-free number (1-800-THE-LOST). On the Web site, visitors can "click here" to report a sighting, use the CyberTipline to report child sexual exploitation, and take an interactive safety quiz (parent or child version). The Web site also has links to thirteen charter Web site sponsorships including Wal-Mart, Compaq, Continental Airlines, Sun Microsystems, and Polaroid. Thirty-nine sponsors are listed including Canon, which placed advertisements in national news magazines with 36 photos of missing children and the following copy:

> Every day, more than 2,200 children disappear. A staggering statistic. But there is good cause for hope. Working closely with law enforcement agencies across the country, the National Center for Missing and Exploited Children (NCMEC) has achieved substantial success in finding children. Canon is proud to join the effort by donating state-of-the-art equipment to help disseminate photos and information about missing children faster. We urge you to look at these children and see if you recognize any of them. Then take current photos of your own children just in case of an emergency. Because photos are the best way to help find missing children. For more information about this program, visit our Web site at www.picturethemhome.com.

At the bottom of the ad were small pictures of Canon products and this sentence in smaller italic type: "A recent poll among law enforcement found that pictures are the most important tool in the search for missing children. Canon is donating CanoScan™ scanners, Bubble Jet™ printers and PowerShot™ digital cameras to help get the photos out quickly."

The image of missing and exploited children commands public attention and causes emotional response in even the most callous individuals. One cannot be exposed to the stories and images of these victims and not feel some emotion. Shedding the issue of emotionalism, however, produces serious questions concerning the true magnitude of the missing children problem and the necessity of drastic social changes aimed at its prevention. Several factors have culminated in the creation of an unprecedented level of fear and concern about the possibility of child abduction in the United States. Combining the concepts of missing children and exploited children precipitates increased emotionalism and concern. The thought of a child being abducted conjures up images of strangers hiding under cover of darkness, lurking to whisk away someone's child, intending to commit some unspeakable crime.

◇
SENSATIONAL IMAGES

Indisputably, there are hideous acts committed against children. In 1981 the country's attention was riveted on missing children after the abduction and subsequent murder of Adam Walsh from a shopping mall in Hollywood, Florida. The image of his brutal murder was seared into the nation's consciousness. Incidents such as these receive great media attention and remain embedded in the public's mind for extended periods of time. The media focus extensively on sensational cases like the abductions and murders of Polly Klaas, Megan Kanka and Adam Walsh or the serial murders of children in Atlanta and Texas. The horror of such examples becomes the key ingredient in the public's perception of the child abduction problem. As one group of researchers remarked, the popular stereotype of kidnapping "draws its imagery from nationally notorious and tragic cases of abduction" (Finkelhor, Hotaling & Sedlak, 1992, p. 226).

Politics, Media and Advocacy
Politicians respond to the grieving parents and fearful citizens by passing legislation memorializing the dead children. In the eighteen-month period from 1997 to mid-1998, more than 50 laws were passed by state legislatures with names like Jenna's Law (New York), Amber's Law (Texas), and Stephanie's Law (Kansas). University of Chicago law professor Stephen Schulhofer commented, "policy issues are reduced to poster children and you have an up-and-down emotional vote as if you're choosing between the killer and a particular child" (cited in Glassner, 1999, p. 63).

The suffering of parents whose children die in such horrible circumstances lends urgency to advocacy groups such as the Adam Walsh Center and Vanished Children's Alliance. Spokespersons are popular sources when another incident occurs. In 1995 John Walsh was quoted as saying the United States was "littered with mutilated, decapitated, raped, strangled children" (cited in Glassner, 1999, p. 62). The murder of six-year-old JonBenet Ramsey in Boulder, Colorado on December 25, 1996 prompted massive media coverage. Walsh appeared on the program hosted by Geraldo Rivera. The mayor of Boulder had tried to reassure the residents that there was no need to panic. Walsh repeated his theme that *everyone* is at risk *anywhere* in the country.

On a subsequent program about child abductions, Rivera commented:

> This isn't a commentary, this is reality: they will come for your kid over the Internet; they will come in a truck; they will come in a pickup in the dark of night; they will come in the Hollywood Mall in Florida. There are sickos out there. You have to keep your children this close to you—this close to you [gesturing to signal close proximity]." (cited in Glassner, 1999, p. 64)

Linking Missing Children with Sexual Exploitation

In addition to drawing on the imagery of notorious cases, the media and politicians link child abduction with sexual exploitation. In 1981 when the issue of missing children was first taking shape, Senator Hawkins remarked that "once they [missing children] are on the street they are fair game for child molestation, prostitution, and other exploitation" (cited in Best, 1987, p. 105). Little has changed in the 1990s. In November of 1992 and again in May of 1993, the television show *America's Most Wanted* aired specials devoted to child abduction. To promote the first show, the producers ran advertisements in *TV Guide* stating that "over one million children are reported missing every year." The 1992 special spent considerable time forging the imagery of child abduction with talk of "serial child molesters" and "child predators," vowing to get "the people who hunt our children."

Government agencies also promote the linkage between missing children and sex offenders. In 1997 the OJJDP released "A Report to the Nation: Missing and Exploited Children." A press release for the report made the following observation:

> The report's findings reflect accomplishments across the nation in making child protection a priority. Yet law enforcement and local communities must continue this progress so that no child is ever exploited or victimized.
>
> All 50 states now have laws requiring the registration of convicted sex offenders upon their release from custody. In 1994, when the report was last issued, only 39 states had similar legislation. Most states also have missing children's clearinghouses that provide timely information on missing children's cases to law enforcement agencies. (p. 1)

Exploitation Has Many Faces

Media imagery aside, children can be missing without being the victims of sexual exploitation or abuse. Conversely, exploitation and abuse can occur in the child's own home; unfortunately, these acts are not limited to strangers. The media did eventually provide accurate information about a horrifying incident in 1994. Susan Smith initially reported that her two young sons were kidnapped in a carjacking. The nation watched in shock as it was later revealed that Susan Smith had released the parking brake on her car and let it roll into a lake with her sons strapped in their car seats (Gibbs, 1994).

> However bone-chilling the idea of stranger-danger, more children are murdered by parents than kidnapped by strangers. Susan Smith is more the norm than Richard Allen Davis [convicted for the murder of Polly Klaas]. Yet every magazine has had its cover stories on stranger-danger; every television show its scare segments; every school its lessons. In every home, parents wrestle with their terrors and with how to warn their children away from the unfamiliar. (Goodman, 1995, p. 11)

Countless other cases do not receive national attention. Consider a few incidents of "missing" and abused children that were given only passing mention by the media:

- Tanisha Nobles of Dayton, Ohio, who reported her son, Erick age two, missing from a shopping mall, was charged with murder after she admitted to police that she had drowned her child because he "got on her nerves" (*USA Today,* 1/14/93, p. 6A).
- A three-state investigation by the FBI and police has failed to turn up any sign of Katelyn Rivera-Helton, a 21-month-old child police say was taken from a babysitter's care by her father. Robert Rivera, 33, is being held without bail on kidnapping and assault charges. The baby disappeared August 10 (*USA Today,* 9/20/99, p. 14A).
- William Couch was sentenced to 18 years in prison for manslaughter in the 1998 scalding death of his 6-month-old son. Authorities said that Couch, 30, immersed his son in the bathtub while they were home alone. The scalding was an accident, but the case became criminal when Couch failed to seek help for the infant, prosecutors said (*USA Today,* 9/20/99, p. 14A).
- Reenee Lloyd and Bertha Toombs, the aunt and grandmother of five-year-old Marquisha Candler, were charged with murder after police uncovered the child's remains in a California desert. The two women had made public pleas for help in locating the missing child (*USA Today,* 9/30/92, p. 10A).

Distorted Definitions

The issue of child abduction is further complicated by the lack of a clear criterion for defining the term "missing children." While this may seem to be a trivial point, an analysis of the issue illustrates that the ambiguity of the definition "missing" distorts the public's perception of the "reality" and "extent" of the missing children problem. Joel Best (1987) insightfully captured the context in which the definition of missing children was constructed when he contended that reforms advocating new laws to address the missing children problem "preferred an inclusive definition of missing children" (p. 105). Under their definition a child would have included people as old as twenty and people missing for a few hours, and the events surrounding the child's disappearance would include most misadventures which might befall children" (Best, 1987, p. 105).

Eventually because of the political pressure generated by individuals, reform groups, and the media, Congress took action to address the problem of missing children in America. The Missing Children's Assistance Act (MCAA) of 1983 defined "missing child" as:

1. any missing person thirteen years of age or younger, or;

2. any missing person under the age of eighteen if the circumstances surrounding such person's disappearance indicate that such person is likely to have been abducted (Sec. 272).

The Missing Children's Assistance Act passed in 1984 created the NCMEC and defined "missing" in the following language:

1. "missing child" means any individual less than eighteen years of age whose whereabouts are unknown to such individual's legal custodian if—

   (A) the circumstances surrounding such individual's disappearance indicate that such individual may possibly have been removed by another from the control of such individual's legal custodian without such custodian's consent; or

   (B) the circumstances of the case strongly indicate that such individual is likely to be abused or sexually exploited... (Sec. 5772).

The text of the new law clearly linked sexual exploitation and child abduction. Persons encompassed by these definitions may be missing for a variety of reasons unrelated to stranger abductions or exploitation. Children can be abducted by a parent who does not have legal custody, an act commonly termed "child stealing." They may be missing because they ran away from home; they could be lost and injured as a result of an accident; they may be suffering from some form of illness such as amnesia; or in some cases they may have committed suicide. Clearly, not all children counted as missing are lost as a result of some stranger's criminality. Broad definitions of missing children distort the reality of the problem and lead to imprecise reporting of statistics. The failure to formulate clear typologies of missing children combined with law enforcement's merging of the two categories—exploited and missing—contribute to the public's misperception of the extent and context of the potential danger of a child being abducted by strangers.

◈
CREATING REALITY THROUGH MISLEADING STATISTICS

Beginning in 1983, the public was deluged with statistics on missing children published by sources varying from newspaper articles and private organizations to governmental reports. These reports generally indicated that anywhere between 1.5 and 2.5 million children were missing from their homes each year (*Congressional Record–Senate*, 1983; Dee Scofield Awareness Program, 1983a; Regnery, 1986; Treanor, 1986). Of those reported missing, it was predicted that as many as fifty thousand children would never be heard from again (Schoenberger & Thomas, 1985; Thornton, 1983). It was also estimated that as many as 5,000 of these missing children would be found dead (*Congressional Record–Senate*, 1983).

The Reality behind the Statistics

These were the statistics distributed by various sources for public consumption. A more critical examination of these statistics finds that nearly 1 million of the reportedly 1.5 million missing children were runaways (Regnery, 1986). Within some jurisdictions between 66 and 98% of those children listed as missing were in reality runaways and were not abducted at all (Treanor, 1986). Police departments receive many more reports of missing runaways than other types of cases of missing children. As many as 15% of missing children may be parental abductions (Schoenberger & Thomas, 1985). In fact one author has maintained that about 1 out of 22 divorces ends in child theft (Agopian, 1981). Others estimate that between 25,000 and 100,000 incidents of missing children are parental abductions *(Congressional Record–Senate,* 1983; Foreman, 1980).

In a Michigan study (Schoenberger & Thomas, 1985), the researchers found that 76% of the 428 entries examined in Michigan's lost children files should have been removed because the persons entered as missing had been located. These 325 children had been found but were not removed from the active files. The vast majority of children listed as missing in law enforcement records are found within twenty-four hours. Similarly, the Massachusetts State Police Missing Persons Unit estimated that 40% of their computer listings on missing persons were in reality solved cases that had not been removed from the data base (*Crime Control Digest,* 1985). The presence of inaccurate data in many law enforcement record systems has contributed to dramatically overestimating the number of children missing.

Bill Treanor (1986), Director of the American Youth Center, presented even more conservative figures:

> Up to 98% of so-called missing children are in fact runaway teenagers. . .
> Of the remaining 2% to 3%, virtually all are wrongfully abducted by a parent. That leaves fewer than two hundred to three hundred children abducted by strangers annually. The merchants of fear would have you believe that five thousand unidentifiable bodies of children are buried each year. In truth, it's less than two hundred dead from all causes, such as drowning, fire and exposure, not just murder. (p. 131)

To compound the problem, statistics are presented regarding the number of children murdered each year. It is maintained that approximately 2,500 children are murdered yearly including homicides committed by ". . . psychopathic serial murderers, pedophiles, child prostitution exploiters and child abusers" (Regnery, 1986, p. 42). However, of these 2,500 children murdered, the number reported missing prior to their victimization was not determined. Additionally, it is not reported how many of these victims were killed by their parents or other family members.

Researchers determined that out of 63 million children living in the United States, two to three hundred cases of missing children per year met the imagery of the stereotypic kidnapping (Finkelhor, Hotaling & Sedlak, 1992). The odds of a child being abducted by a stranger are about 1 in 250,200. In fact, the missing children on the milk cartons have most likely been taken by a non-custodial parent. These distinctions are easily blurred in the public's eyes. Statistics, often without qualification, are distributed to the public from official governmental sources.

Partners in Fear

Vague and misleading numbers magnify the missing children problem. The *Juvenile Justice Journal* (1998), a government publication, wrote that "Since May 25, 1979 many more children have disappeared from their homes" (p. 1). In his on-line message, the president of NCMEC explained that the FBI's National Crime Information Center (NCIC) reports include three categories for missing children. He reported that most missing children are entered in the "Juvenile" (J) file and that the 749,090 entries in 1998 were down 6.5% from 1997, but he went on to describe the two other categories.

> The "endangered" missing is defined as "missing and in the company of another person under circumstances indicating that his or her physical safety is in danger." In 1998 the number of endangered missing juveniles increased 5% from 1997.
>
> Finally, the "involuntary" missing juveniles, defined by the FBI as "missing under circumstances indicating that the disappearance was not voluntary (*i.e.*, abduction or kidnapping)." In 1998 there were 33,038 such cases, down 2.5% from 1997.
>
> We cannot rest when, on average, 2,200 children are reported missing every day. (Allen, 1999)

Despite reporting percentage decreases, the actual numbers cited were alarming—and misleading.

Businesses participate in awareness programs about child abduction. In 1999, Wal-Mart began running a series of advertisements in local newspapers for the "Picture Them Home" program. The program posts pictures of missing children on store bulletin boards, asks patrons to review the pictures, and encourages parents to keep updated pictures of their children on file—just in case. Their claims are presented in fear-invoking language. Consider this joint venture of Wal-Mart (1999) and the NCMEC.

> Child abduction is more than a reality. It's a tragedy common to parents, grandparents, brothers and sisters. Well over 100,000 children are abducted in this country each year. But the more people who are aware of this widespread catastrophe, the less of a problem it becomes.
>
> That's why in June 1996, Wal-Mart teamed up with The National Center for Missing and Exploited Children (NCMEC) to form The Missing Children's Network. NCMEC is a non-profit organization and the most widely recognized finder of missing children.
>
> Wal-Mart's Missing Children's Network consists of a bulletin board posted in every Wal-Mart store and Sam's Club nationwide. Each bulletin board contains several photos of missing children, along with relevant personal information, updated monthly. Listed with the photos and infor-

mation is the all-important toll-free hotline to the NCMEC (1-800-THE-LOST) so that the public can provide leads.

The visibility of these bulletin boards permeates big cities and small towns in every corner of the country, and provides tremendous exposure to the millions of people who shop each week in our stores. As of December 1996, in the short time since the Missing Children's Network was formed, 13 children had been recovered as a direct result of the bulletin boards. (p. 1)

Growing public awareness and concern over the missing children issue have been promoted through the use of inconsistent and inaccurate statistics regarding numbers and the ultimate fate of missing children in the United States. Such statistics and the effect they have on the public and its perception of the extent of the missing children problem have both obvious and unintended consequences.

◇

LATENT FUNCTIONS OF PREVENTION

The obvious goal of increased awareness of the problem of child abduction is prevention. Public preoccupation with child safety is evident in the proliferation of children's literature addressing safety and the prevention of abduction since the mid-1980s. With increasing frequency, books and other forms of media appeared illustrating the dangers of social contact with persons who were not members of the family or extended family unit. These texts informed children of the danger of speaking or having contact with strangers. For example, Stan and Jan Berenstain wrote *The Berenstain Bears Learn about Strangers* in 1985 (Jenkins, 1998, p. 140). Mark Klaas produced a videotape titled "Missing: What to Do If Your Child Disappears" (Kuczka, 1999). In February 1999, radio stations began airing "Among the Missing," a song written by Peter McCann and performed by Kathy Mattea and Michael McDonald. The CD jacket (in six versions), in-store promotions, and music video feature missing children registered in NCMEC's database (NCMEC, 1999).

There are at least three negative, latent consequences of books that discuss stranger danger. First, literature links feelings of danger with social contacts outside the family unit. This perception can result in increased social isolation and alienation of children from the community. As both parents and children begin to equate social contact outside the family with danger and impending harm, community interaction may decrease. The fear of child abduction, while limiting social interaction, may reduce the family's dependence on third parties for child care. Parents may begin to rely less and less on day-care facilities, in-house sitters, and other third-party child care sources. As parents take greater responsibility for the care of their children, the contact within the family unit may increase and greater dependence may be placed on the interactions of family members. The family unit may gain greater solidarity as social interaction with the community decreases, but the cost may be increased fear and stunted social development.

Second, these texts trigger anxieties about kidnapping, while targeting unlikely perpetrators. *On the Safe Side* (Statman, 1995) contains strategies to teach children to scare off potential molesters and abductors as well as surveillance methods for parents to use to check up on the conduct of baby-sitters and day care providers (Glassner, 1999, p. 65). Law enforcement has also contributed to the fear of child abduction. The following advice was published in a popular policing magazine.

> Never leave the child unattended; use a secret code word that persons must use before the child should go with them; encourage children to have a friend with them when they are going to be in vulnerable situations; instruct children in the use of the telephone; and instruct children in what to do if they believe they are being followed or are being confronted by someone they do not know well. (Wills, 1996, pp. 39–42)

Yet, the literature and research on both sexual abuse of children and child abduction indicates that children are more often victimized by acquaintances rather than strangers. Consider these statistics:

- A study of three states found that 96% of female rape victims under the age of twelve knew their attackers (BJS, 1994b, p. 2).
- A study of murder found that 63% of the children murdered under the age of twelve were killed by family members. In 57% of these cases, children were murdered by a parent (BJS, 1994d, p. 5).

As children are taught to run from unfamiliar persons, they are also being taught to run into the arms of those most often engaged in child abuse. These media promote the notion that if properly educated, children can distinguish between those individuals who are "safe" and those persons to avoid, a distinction even criminologists are reluctant to make. The fear invoked by the spread of prevention literature and the indoctrination of children with safety tips like avoiding strangers may be a zero sum game. Such prevention measures only replace the unfounded fear of child abduction with a new and equally unfounded fear of strangers.

These approaches to prevention may confuse children and promote paranoia and insecurity. "We must also begin to acknowledge the risks of protectiveness. Risks that come to a diverse society when kids grow up suspicious of others. Without even knowing it and with the best of intentions, we can stunt our children with our deep longing to keep them safe" (Goodman, 1995, p. 11). The fear generated by shortsighted prevention measures was so profound that a Roper Poll found that the number one concern of children was fear of being kidnapped (cited in Fass, 1997, p. 262). Where would a child abused by a family member turn given such mixed messages—to a stranger?

Third, the proliferation of literature on child safety stresses that it is the duty of the parents to educate their children. This responsibility in itself is not damaging and may very well contribute to prevention. However, placing blame on parents for failing to educate their children allows the responsibility for child safety to be shifted from social control agencies such as the police and society as a whole to individual family members. In effect, what these texts suggest is that if parents fail to educate their children and if children fail to heed their warnings, they will be abused or abducted and the responsibility rests on them alone—rather than on the offender or society as a whole. We in effect begin to "blame the victim" and shift focus from the offender and crime control agencies to the child and the nonvigilant parent.

The link between literature and the behavior of adolescents has been well illustrated by the works of David McClelland (1961). He found that the economic performance of a culture varied with the degrees of achievement portrayed in literature. Parallels were drawn between the declines and increases in achievement, and the decline and increase of literature depicting economic success. This research shows that literature has an effect on behavior. Whether it is motivation to excel economically or motivation to withdraw socially, the effect is profound. By depicting strangers as persons to fear and avoid due to the possibility of abduction and exploitation, we circumvent serious consideration of the extent to which relatives, friends, and family members are involved in child abuse and abduction. We also divert attention away from the fact that most missing children are runaways.

Another unintended consequence of awareness heightened by fear is that the sensational drowns out the most prevalent, potentially answerable, problems. Historian Paula Fass comments that kidnap stories haunt middle-class families far more than the dangers of neglect, abuse, and disadvantage that are much more common in children's lives (Bok, 1998, p. 63). Groups such as the National Safe Kids Campaign find that their objectives of educating parents about the actual leading causes of death and disability can't compete with the aggressive campaigns of missing children's advocacy groups. The media are not drawn to stories about preventable accidents. If parents and elected officials paid more attention to simple safety measures in homes and public places, lives could be saved and emergency room visits avoided (Glassner, 1999, p. 65). But such prevention campaigns do not sell newspapers, magazines, and advertising spots.

Concern for child safety and fear of child abduction have not been limited to children's literature. The fear of child abduction is beginning to motivate legal reform designed to criminalize a vast scope of behavior involving children. Society is turning to solutions to a problem that has been defined based on fear and inaccurate information.

◇

LEGAL REFORM: CREATING CRIME AND CRIMINALS

The emotional furor over the issue of child abduction has created an atmosphere conducive to the creation of a new crime and a new class of criminals. In California, prior to 1976, if a parent took his or her child in violation of a custody order, it was not considered a criminal offense. Since October 1, 1977, legislation in California has been enacted making it a criminal offense for parents to take custody of their own children in violation of a court custody order (Agopian, 1980; 1981).

The state of New York has enacted similar legislation, making parental child abduction a felony offense. In February of 1985, the National Governors' Association called for all states to adopt legislation making child snatching a felony offense, regardless of whether the violator was a parent or stranger to the child. By 1983, forty-eight states had adopted the Uniform Child Custody Jurisdiction Act and forty-two states had classified child snatching as a felony (Silverman, 1983). The legal response to this behavior has also been addressed at the federal level.

Prior to 1983, the United States Department of Justice restricted the issuance of warrants for the arrest of parents who took illegal custody of their children and subsequently crossed state lines. Since December 23, 1982, federal and local law enforcement officials can seek federal arrest warrants for child snatching even if there is no evidence to suggest the child is in physical danger *(United States Attorneys Bulletin,* 1983). In the Sixth Report to Congress on the implementation of the Parental Kidnapping Prevention Act of 1980, the Department of Justice indicated that during 1982, thirty-two "fugitive parents" were arrested by the Federal Bureau of Investigation (FBI). These arrests took place prior to removal of the warrant restrictions imposed by the Department of Justice. During the first nine months of 1983, after the removal of restrictions, the number of parents arrested by the FBI doubled to sixty-four (U.S. Department of Justice, 1983). With these reforms at both the state and federal levels, we have created the crime of child stealing and the criminal classifications of "fugitive parents" and "custody criminals."

While in some circles this easing of restrictions on the FBI and the criminalization of custody violations may be viewed as a positive step in solving the problem of child abduction by parents, there are certainly negative effects associated with the increased arrests of fugitive parents. An undetermined number of these children are physically and emotionally better off with the parent who committed the illegal act. This point was illustrated in the case of a Long Island girl who was abducted by her mother after the father was awarded custody. After lengthy consideration of the case, New York Justice Alexander Vitale ordered that the mother should retain custody of the child, having decided that this was in the best interest of the child's welfare. The best interests of the child are not always paramount in the court's decision-making process; jurisdictional concerns are often given equal importance in deciding custody cases after an abduction has occurred *(In re Nehra v. Ular,* 1977).

The second problem arises out of labeling as criminal the parent who removes his or her child from an abusive atmosphere. While not all parents who abduct their children do so with such noble intentions, these parents often have little recourse. They must decide either to comply with the law and allow their children to endure further abuse or to violate the law in the best interest of the child. Legal avenues are often closed to parents. Fees associated with custody battles often restrict a parent's ability to obtain legal redress in these matters. Regardless of the individual's ability to access the courts, child abduction is often seen as the last alternative to maintaining a full-time parental relationship (Agopian, 1980).

While some degree of formal social control may be required to prevent parental abductions, better screening and investigation by the courts before awarding custody could reduce the incidents of well-meaning child abduction. We can only speculate as to the motivations of a parent who would abduct a child or children from an apparently stable family, but the abducting party must (at a minimum) feel that an inadequate custody arrangement was made in the judicial process. More equitable custody arrangements may be one way of reducing child abduction by parents.

A more pragmatic consideration is the utility of fugitive warrants. A fugitive warrant does not allow the FBI to take a child into custody or even to return the child to the parent with legal custody. These children are often kept in foster homes or other community shelters while courts review the custody arrangements. In some cases these environments may be more damaging than staying with the abducting parent. Arrests on fugitive warrants do not reflect the number of children who are actually returned to their legal guardians as a result of arrest. Furthermore, the warrant does not allow agents to effect arrests of persons other than those named on the warrant, who may have materially participated in the abduction or currently have physical custody of the child.

The emotional atmosphere created by increased publicity of the dangers of child abduction has been used as a political tool to advocate stiffer punishments for offenders. In the cases of true stranger abductions, this may be a desirable prevention measure. It is, however, questionable whether stiffer sanctions would prevent hideous crimes against children. The desire to control and sanction stranger abduction often becomes politicized with calls for stiffer penalties for all offenders who commit crimes against children.

Calling for legislative "reform," Congressman Henry J. Hyde advocated mandatory life sentences for persons who kidnap a child and the death penalty for child abduction that results in death. The congressman stated, "I do not feel it is too harsh to say that one who kidnaps or murders a child has forfeited his right to freedom forever" ("Kidnapping," 1985, p. 4). A call for the death penalty for child snatchers has not been limited to the political arena. Private organizations devoted to the location of missing children have also called for legislative "reform." Dee Scofield Awareness Program (1983b), a private organization located in Tampa, Florida, recommends that child abduction be elevated to a federal offense punishable by either death or life imprisonment. The most disturbing point here is that the proposed reform failed to make a clear distinction between parental custody violations and stranger abductions.

◊

CONCLUSION

The manner in which a problem is defined is related to the type of social control systems available to address that problem. The problem of missing children in the United States is no exception. It becomes clear from the analysis of the missing children problem that the issue has been defined as epidemic in proportion and criminal in nature. Given this definition and perception of the issue, the current course of action—the criminalization of this behavior—is clearly a logical consequence.

Incorporating runaways into missing children statistics produces the perception of an epidemic. The inclusion of stranger abduction in the composite figures permits the problem to be defined as criminal. Linking sexual abuse and exploitation provokes emotionalism. Criminalizing all abductions permits no distinctions as to the perpetrator, further increasing the numbers and criminality.

As a society, we have defined the problem as an abnormal behavior on the part of a select group of individuals we have chosen to call criminal. We have chosen social control agencies and criminal sanctions as the solutions for this epidemic. In an attempt to prevent this behavior, we have subsequently created a new classification of crime and criminals without distinguishing the motives and reasoning behind this behavior. In short, we have defined missing children in the United States as a legal problem with legal solutions. As long as this definition and solution dominate the missing children problem, a solution is not forthcoming. The legal "solution" is merely a reaction to an undesirable behavior. However, if we define the scope of the problem more accurately and develop a clear understanding of the various types of incidents that collectively compose the problem, an alternative solution may yet emerge.

In order to begin to address the problem of missing children, we must first understand the problem in a social rather than a legal context. Only then can we begin to take preventive rather than reactive measures. The nature of family relationships must be explored in order to begin to understand why 1.5 million children flee their homes each year. We must also begin to realize that our legal system, both criminal and civil, is not a panacea for all social problems. One of the most preposterous illustrations of using the legal system to address a social problem took place in Will County, Illinois in 1995. Associate Judge Ludwig Kahar sentenced two sisters aged twelve and eight to spend the night in a foster home for refusing to visit their father in North Carolina, as mandated by a court-ordered visitation schedule. The following week, he sentenced the older girl to the county juvenile detention center. "Visit your father or go to jail" seems counterproductive to promoting familial relationships.

The fact that thousands of children each year are abducted by their parents raises serious questions about our legal system's ability to define family relations equitably through divorce and child custody orders. The adversarial trial system, often alluded to in the criminal process, is omnipresent in civil courts as well. The adversarial process fosters custody battles. These events create conflict, setting the stage for continued discord between the winners (those awarded custody) and the losers (those denied custody). Unless a more equitable process is developed—one void of the conflicts resulting from the current system—child stealing will remain an outcome. If we cannot adequately understand the behavior of runaway children and the reaction of parents who are denied the custody of their children, or develop workable solutions to custody arrangements, how can we hope to understand or prevent child abductions by strangers?

The true effects of increased awareness and fear may not become evident for some time. The preliminary indications are that we will continue to attempt to handle the issue of child abduction through increased legislation and stiffer penalties for offenders. However, it is evident that advocacy campaigns, while well intended, will have negative effects socially. It would appear prudent to consider the social effects of prescribing criminalization and prevention in mass dosages. Critical research that accurately reflects the scope of the problem of missing children in the United States is desperately needed. We should not implement prevention programs without first giving critical thought to both the manifest and latent social functions of these policies.

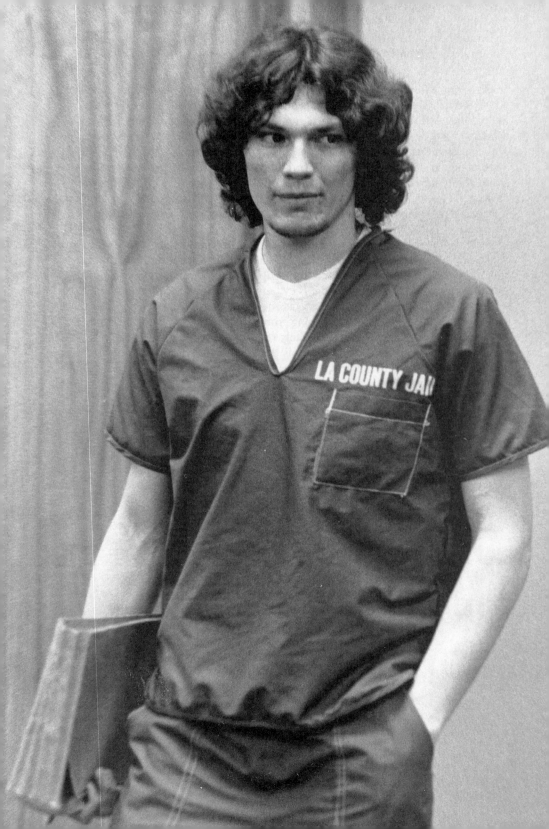

Myth and Murder
The Serial Killer Panic
Philip Jenkins[*]

If we relied solely on the evidence of the mass media, we might well believe that every few years a particular form of immoral or criminal behavior becomes so dangerous as to threaten the foundations of society. Some of these media scares or moral panics have been analyzed by social scientists, including the "dope-fiend" in his or her many guises (most recently, the crack enthusiast); the "sex-fiend" of the 1940s; and the white slavers of the Progressive Era (Becker, 1963; Duster, 1970; Tappan, 1955).

These panics are important in their own right for what they reveal about social concerns and prejudices—often based on xenophobia and anti-immigrant prejudice (Gusfield, 1981). Also, bureaucratic factors sometimes play a part when an agency promotes a panic in order to enhance its own power and prestige. An example often quoted in support of this theory is the view that Harry Anslinger and the Federal Bureau of Narcotics promoted a marijuana scare in the mid-1930s for just these ends. . . .

Describing such issues as panics does not imply that they are without some real foundation. There were and are rapists and pimps, and drugs can cause immense damage to individuals and communities. However, such a

* Pages 65–73 were excerpted from "Myth and Murder: The Serial Killer Panic of 1983–85." *Criminal Justice Research Bulletin,* 3(11): 1–7, 1988. The additional material was adapted from *Using Murder: The Social Construction of Serial Homicide,* Aldine de Gruyter, 1994 with the permission of the publisher.

"scare" period immensely inflates the perceived scale and prevalence of the original problem. . . . Severe legislation is proposed which in turn fuels . . . the original issue and compounds the process.

The 1980s were a particularly fruitful period for such media panics over crack, child sexual abuse, juvenile satanism, sex and violence in rock lyrics, and (in a rather different category) AIDS (Jenkins & Katkin, 1987). Each of these concerns had its particular stages of origin and growth and deserves study. Here, the focus will be on the source of another modern panic-serial murder. This is a topic at least as old as Jack the Ripper and his contemporaries.[1] However, between 1983 and 1985, serial murder suddenly attained a major place in media attention [and has retained that position] because of a number of specific incidents that we will examine.

It will be argued that the serial murder panic illustrates the way in which the media discover and publicize certain forms of criminality, but it also suggests certain important directions in contemporary views of the origins and causation of crime and deviancy.

◊

CREATING A MYTH

Between late 1983 and mid-1985, serial murder was the topic of numerous stories in magazines and newspapers, as well as television programs. Most of these stressed the same group of themes, which can be conveniently summarized from a front-page *New York Times* article of January 1984 (Lindsey, 1984). The key concepts were that serial murder was an "epidemic" in contemporary America; that there were a great many such offenders active at any given time . . . ; and that the new wave was qualitatively different from earlier occurrences, with more savage torture and mutilation of victims. Serial killers accounted for perhaps 20% of American murder victims, or some 4,000 a year, according to the accounts. It was also strongly implied that this appalling "disease" was largely a distinctive American problem.

According to Lindsey (1984), "the officials [quoted] assert that history offers nothing to compare with the spate of such murders that has occurred in the United States since the beginning of the 1970s" (p. 1). He quotes Robert O. Heck of the Justice Department for the view "that as many as 4,000 Americans a year, at least half of them under the age of eighteen, are murdered this way. He said he believes at least thirty-five such killers are now roaming the country." Many of their victims were to be found among the thousands of bodies that turned up each year unidentified and unexplained. As for the explanation of the new phenomenon, Lindsey quoted favorably the view that exposure to sexually explicit and sado-masochistic material tended to arouse the violent instincts of individuals already prone to extreme acts by an abusive upbringing.

The essentials of Lindsey's story were repeated extensively during 1984 and 1985, especially the estimate of 4,000 serial victims each year (Berger, 1984; Kagan, 1984). This was cited in a *Life* article, which placed particular emphasis on serial murder as an almost uniquely American problem, and in many leading newspapers and magazines (Darrach & Norris, 1984). In *Newsweek,* it was stated that "Law-enforcement experts say as many as two-thirds of the estimated 5,000 unsolved homicides in the nation each year may be committed by serial murderers" (Random Killers, 1984). . . .

The "unsolved" category from the Uniform Crime Reports would be frequently quoted in this context. Sometimes, a story about the importance of serial murder would cite the number of "unsolved" killings (roughly 5,400) and then go on to estimate how many of these might be serial victims—anywhere from one-tenth to two-thirds, as here. Some stories, however, would simply state the number of "unsolved" homicides without comment. This left the reader with the impression that this *was* the serial victim category.

The visual media strongly reinforced the concept of a new and appalling menace, with each story—almost without fail—beginning with the estimate of 4,000 victims a year. Each of the major news magazines of the *60 Minutes* format had at least one story of this type, while an *HBO America Undercover* episode was a documentary focusing on three well-known serial killers of the last decade: Ted Bundy, Edmund Kemper, and Henry Lee Lucas. Interviews with all three were featured, as were harrowing (and controversial) reconstructions, using actors.

◈

THE LUCAS CASE

Lucas was the most frequent vehicle for a news story on this topic, which customarily referred to FBI sources for background on the scale of the murder wave. Lucas was a convicted murderer and arsonist, who began confessing numerous murders in the fall of 1983. By the end of the year, his alleged "kill" had exceeded three hundred, and he did much to shape the stereotype of the multiple murderer.

Lucas gave plausibility to the estimate of thousands of victims each year. His case also placed emphasis on the serial killer as a wanderer, a drifter who traveled between many states and regions. The roaming killer was much cited in 1983–85, especially when media attention was focused on the nationwide murder spree of Christopher Wilder in the spring of 1984 (eleven victims in six states). This suggested the need for new federal or interstate agencies to combat the menace, for which local agencies were clearly inadequate. Finally, Lucas and his partner Otis Toole claimed responsibility for the murder of a number of child victims including Adam Walsh, a notorious case that gave rise to national concern about missing children. This helped ensure publicity and linked the murder issue with other contemporary panics in which unsubstantiated figures were being severely misused ...

During 1985, the Lucas case effectively collapsed under investigation from a number of journalists. The estimate of three hundred murders had fallen to about ten, spread over several states. The basis of at least part of the panic had disappeared. It should be noted incidentally that the credence given to Lucas had never been universally shared, and *The New York Times* had published a very critical article as early as November 1983 (Joyce, 1983). However, the case continued to be a media event well into the following year.

To return to the substance of the issue: how accurate were the claims made by writers on serial murder in these years? The Lucas affair does not discredit the existence of a real phenomenon, and the media were drawing very heavily on the opinions of major official agencies, above all in the Justice Department. The figure of 4,000 seems to have been orthodox opinion, but none of these reports recognized how far such a view departed from established views on the nature of murder. That in itself certainly would not disprove the idea, but it is a statistic with remarkable consequences. Each year (it appears), one American murder in five is committed by a serial killer like Ted Bundy or John Wayne Gacy—perhaps 40,000 victims between 1976 and 1986. If this is correct, then clearly our views of violent crime need to be radically reformed. So would our policies and funding priorities in law enforcement. This was also an important argument for a growing federal role in law enforcement, as only national coordination could prevent the depredations of a Wilder or a Lucas.

◊

THE REALITY OF SERIAL MURDER

There are a number of questions about this "murder wave" that must be handled separately. That this type of crime had become much more common is not in dispute. However, its numerical impact on the murder statistics may be challenged. Finally, how may this sudden concern about serial murder be explained, especially when reports of notorious multiple murder cases were no more frequent in 1983 than five or ten years previously?

In studying the reality of serial murder, there are a number of important problems. There is a sizeable literature on multiple murder, but it has important gaps and discontinuities. We have a distinguished psychiatric literature on the causation of this type of offense, and there is a superb and accessible synthesis of theories and typologies (see Abrahamsen, 1973, 1960, 1945; Lunde, 1976; Nettler, 1982; Toch, 1969). We have many case studies of killers, some of the "True Crime" type, but many rising above it to real insight; but the real lack is in systematic or "epidemiological" studies of the phenomenon. Without such a broad survey, changes in the frequency or distribution of serial murder are not possible. Only in 1985 did a really scholarly work of this nature appear (Fox & Levin, 1985), and even it made no attempt to compare the frequency of serial murder reports in the period studied (1974–79) with earlier periods (for the growing academic interest in the topic, see Egger, 1986, 1984; Hickey, 1986; Leyton, 1986; Vetter & Rieber, 1986).

The present study is based on media publications about serial killers, including a search of *The New York Times* since 1960. Only serial murder cases are noted, rather than mass murders, and killing for profit or political motive has been excluded—a decision that would by no means be accepted by all students of the topic. This exclusion is sometimes difficult, as in the case of Joseph Paul Franklin, reported in 1984 as a suspect in fifteen murders in eight states between 1977 and 1980. This would appear to be a "serial" case, but there is strong evidence that Franklin acted out of his political beliefs as a white supremacist who used violence against biracial couples. He was thus excluded from the present study, as were black racists Mark Essex and the "Zebra" gang. (For works consulted, see note 2. Other books used include Abrahamsen, 1985; Caute & Odell, 1979; Godwin, 1978; Keyes, 1986; Klausner, 1981; Lunde, 1976; Nettler, 1982; Olson, 1983; Wilson, 1972; Wilson & Seaman, 1983).

There are obvious problems in using news media as sources for determining the frequency or scale of serial murder. The nature and quality of reporting is likely to change over the years, while newspapers concentrate on what is likely to interest a local readership. From its prominence in the media, one might well think that the "Son of Sam" case of 1976–77 was uniquely serious or remarkable. In fact, the affair received so much attention chiefly because it occurred in the New York area, and thus near the headquarters of so many news organizations. This geographical bias might lead to the underrepresentation of offenses occurring in areas of the country that would be considered remote by the important news media, and our knowledge of serial murder would be slanted.

On the other hand, it is possible to defend the view that a media search is likely to produce a reasonably accurate list, at least of extreme serial offenders who killed (say) ten or more victims. Throughout the century, there has been intense media attention on any such case, suggesting that public interest is steady, if not precisely constant from decade to decade. In the 1920s and 1930s, massive publicity was devoted to the cases of American serial killers like Albert Fish, Earle Nelson, Joe Ball, Carl Panzram, and Gordon Stewart Northcott. In fact, coverage was more intense than for any comparable modern case because of the greater rarity of the offense in that era. It is not claimed that the present study can be truly comprehensive, but it is also unlikely that many cases have been omitted. The combination of newspaper records and secondary accounts is likely to yield a sizeable majority of the serial murder cases that actually occurred.

Assessing the scale of the problem and calculating a figure for the victims of serial murder are also real problems. In part, this is because serial offenders remain such a tiny proportion of the population that statistical comparisons are of little use. We are often dependent on the offenders themselves for estimates of their "kill" (the number of victims). False confessions sometimes appear to be part of the psychological make-up of such criminals.

Law enforcement agencies themselves play a vital part in shaping our perceptions here, and this may work in different cases either to swell or to diminish the alleged total of victims. In the late 1960s, for example, the still-anonymous "Zodiac" killed several people in northern California. Recently a journalist published a well-argued case for believing that the "Zodiac" attacks have continued into the present decade, with the consequence of almost fifty deaths (Graysmith, 1987). If this view is correct, the case would be a classic example of "linkage blindness"—the failure of law enforcement to perceive connections between incidents. On the other hand, bureaucratic self-interest might have the opposite effect, as there is so much pressure to avoid having uncleared cases—especially such glaring and publicized crimes. Law enforcement agencies wish to clear as many murders as possible as "solved," even if this means rather tenuous attributions of the crimes to currently notorious figures.

We are rarely in as reliable a position to estimate the number of victims as in the John Wayne Gacy case, where almost thirty bodies were found in his crawl space. However, even similar evidence can be disputed. In 1985, extensive remains were found at the California home of Leonard Lake, but the conclusions of the forensic investigation were variously interpreted. Lake appeared to be connected with the murders of somewhere between six and thirty people—hardly precise figures. . . .

Despite these problems of assessing scale, there is strong evidence for a dramatic increase in the prevalence of serial murder in the United States from the end of the 1960s. This can be seen if we compare cases between 1950 and 1970 with those since 1971. Between 1950 and 1970, there were only two cases in the United States where a serial murderer was definitely associated with over ten victims (these were Charlie Starkweather in 1958 and the "Boston Strangler" case of 1962–64). There were other celebrated serial cases, but these tended to involve at most eight or nine victims. . . . This is in sharp contrast with the years between 1971 and 1987. There have been at least nine cases where offenders were generally credited with over twenty victims in this period (see note 2). . . . There were also twenty-eight cases where people are believed to have killed between ten and twenty victims in the same period. We therefore have a total of thirty-seven cases, involving thirty-nine individuals (in at least two cases, the crimes were committed by pairs of killers).

The Justice Department appears to have somewhat underestimated the number of active serial killers. A 1983 study claimed that since 1973, there had been at least 30 individuals who had killed six or more victims serially. The present author would put the figure at well over 40 for that same decade. However, while understating the number of killers, the same study appears to have grossly exaggerated the number of their victims. A subsequent Justice

Department estimate gives a figure of 35 serial murderers active at any one time. Let us assume that this is correct. It is rare for such an offender to kill more than six victims in any particular year, which suggests that the real annual total for serial victims is unlikely to exceed 300 and may well be under 200. Even that may be far too many. In the present study, 71 cases were found where six or more people were killed serially between 1971 and 1987. Certainly, cases have escaped attention, but these 71 cases account for only 950–1000 victims in all—or about 50 to 60 each year.

There are occasional cases where a killer engages in a rampage—Paul Knowles in 1974, Christopher Wilder in 1984—but these usually attract major law enforcement attention and are soon stopped. In other words, someone who kills more than ten or so people in a single year is unlikely to continue his career for more than that one year.

Even if our estimate for the number of active killers is too small, as it may be, then serial murder might account for at most three or four hundred victims each year. This is a terrible figure, but it is far short of the much-quoted "four thousand." In other words, even during a wave of serial murder like the seventeen years between 1971 and 1987, this type of crime accounts for perhaps 2 or 3% of American homicides, rather than the 20% suggested in 1984. Multiple murder remains an extreme fringe of American crime. . . .

Multiple murderers—those credited with at least ten victims—generally do not "roam." Fox and Levin correctly note that such killers tend to act fairly close to home, often in or around one city, and this view can be confirmed from the cases listed here. Ted Bundy killed in four states, but this was unusual. Of the 39 killers in our sample, only ten killed in more than one state. Two (Wilder and Knowles) went on short-lived "murder sprees," and three were active in neighboring states. The stereotype of "roaming killer" applies best to the case of William Christensen, who was accused in 1985 of 15 murders in the northeastern United States and in Canada. A much more common pattern is the killer who finds and kills most of his victims in one city, or even a small area of that city—from East London in the 1880s to the Sunset Strip in the 1970s. . . .

◇
EXPLAINING A PANIC

Serial murder thus must be placed into context. It may have been a growing menace, and steps to curb it should have been vigorously encouraged. However, the official view of the problem was badly flawed. The reasons for misinterpretation were complex and include an element of pure accident. Lucas's confessions tended to cause both media and law enforcement agencies to lose proportion in examining the topic. But the way in which a "murder epidemic" was created is an illuminating example of the relationship between media and official agencies. Also required is an explanation of why Lucas's statements met with the credulity they did.

One consistent theme in the media coverage of 1983–85 was the misuse of UCR murder data, by both experts and lay people alike. Put simply, the argument suggests that motiveless murders had risen dramatically. The UCR stated that in 1966, there were eleven thousand murders in the United States. Of those, 644 (5.9%) involved no apparent motive. In 1982, there were twenty-three thousand murders, but the number of "motiveless" killings was now 4,118 (17.8%), the figure quoted by Lindsey. By 1984, this "motiveless" category had risen to 22%. It was suggested that the increase represented "serial" activity and that serial killers were claiming thousands of lives every year in the United States alone. The figure for recorded murders (some twenty thousand a year) could have actually understated the total, as many victims are not proven to have been murdered until many years later. The total of four thousand serial victims annually therefore seemed plausible. Other sources simply took the "unsolved" figure from UCR statistics. In 1983, 28% of murders fell into this category.

Both categories—unsolved and motiveless—require serious qualification, based on an understanding of how UCR data are compiled by individual police departments. When a murder occurs, the police will file a UCR report, with the deadline being the first five days of the month after the crime is reported. They also submit a supplementary homicide report, addressing topics like characteristics of the victim and offender; weapon; relationship of victim to offender; circumstances surrounding death; and so on. "Offenders" can be single, multiple, or unknown. At this early stage, the police might well know neither the offender, a motive, nor the exact circumstances of the death. All these would thus be recorded as unknown.

Weeks or months later, the situation might well change, and the correct procedure would be for the department to submit a new report to amend the first. Here, though, there is enormous room for cutting corners. The death has been reported, and whether a further correction is submitted depends on many factors. A conscientious officer in a professional department with an efficient record system would very probably notify the reporting center that the murder was no longer "unsolved" or "motiveless," especially in an area where murder was a rare crime. Other officers in other departments might well feel that they have more important things to do than to submit a revised version of a form they have already completed. This would in fact represent a third form on a single case.

The chance of follow-up information being supplied will depend on a number of factors: the frequency of murder in the community; the importance given to record keeping by a particular chief or supervisor; the organizational structure of the department (for instance, whether records and data are the responsibility of a full-time unit or of an individual); and the professional standards of the department. The vast majority of departments are likely to record the simple fact of a murder being committed. Only some will provide the results of subsequent investigations—although these are crucial to developing any kind of national statistical profile of U.S. homicide.

Murders depicted in the UCR as having a suspect and motive are likely to be those where there is a very clear-cut situation with the offender immediately identified. Any delay, and it is likely to fall into the limbo of "motiveless" crimes. If a suspect is not found within the same month as the murder, then the case is likely to be entered as "no suspect" and to remain so despite subsequent events. In this case, it is even likely that the later in the month a particular murder takes place, the more likely it is to be described as "motiveless" or lacking a suspect.

Even when no suspect is ever found, it does not necessarily mean that a serial killer is to blame. . . . The remarkable fact about the UCR is the number of murders with an immediate motive and suspect. As to the sharp rise in the number of murders lacking this information, a variety of explanations is possible. These include an increase in homicides arising from narcotics trafficking and gang activities and perhaps deaths resulting from an increase in violent robberies. Although some of the murders indeed indicated serial activity, this was far less than was reported. . . .

To equate either "motiveless" or "unsolved" crimes with the number of serial victims is wholly to misunderstand the nature and composition of that much-criticized set of data. It is remarkable that some (by no means all) of the Justice Department sources so frequently quoted tended to continue this confusion, with the results we have witnessed.

As the Justice Department was the source of so much of the information and interpretation about serial murder during 1983–85, it is necessary to ask exactly what was the nature of their interest in the topic. In order to understand the context, it should be recalled that the 1983 work on serial murder became a justification for a new center for the study of violent crime at the FBI Academy in Quantico, Virginia, with a new Violent Criminal Apprehension Program (VICAP). In the previous two years, attempts to expand FBI databanks had met serious challenges, both from civil libertarians and from local law enforcement agencies. Similar opposition might well have been expected to the new federal interest in violent criminals.

In practice, the serial killer panic helped to justify the new proposals, and the creation of a National Center for the Analysis of Violent Crime (NCAVC) was announced by President Reagan in June 1984, with an explicit focus on "repeat killers" (Michaud, 1986). Early NCAVC publicity emphasized how frequently serial crimes "transcend jurisdictional boundaries," while serial murderers were characteristically "highly transient criminals" (NCAVC, 1986). However, it was mentioned that in the future, the new databank would expand its attention—to "rape, child molestation, arson and bombing" (NCAVC, 1986). Serial murder thus provided a wedge for an expansion of the federal role in law enforcement intelligence.

It would be the worst sort of conspiracy theory to claim that the Justice Department created or promoted the post-Lucas murder panic. This is especially true when some FBI officials placed the estimated number of serial victims at several hundred rather than several thousand, contradicting what was quickly becoming orthodoxy. But it was in the interests of the agencies and spokespersons concerned to emphasize certain themes that did in fact emerge strongly in media coverage: the sudden and extreme danger posed by a murder wave—and above all, the national and interstate character of the "new" serial killers. Henry Lee Lucas—at least as he portrayed himself—was tailor-made for such a campaign.

Apart from the bureaucratic interests involved, the new emphasis on serial murder also suggested a shift in popular attitudes toward crime and criminals. The serial killer represented an extreme image of the newer and more conservative stereotype of the offender. The central element in the new concepts can perhaps be described as a quest for evil, a need to understand crime in terms of objective evil. Relativist ethics and environmental theories of causation were both discounted.

In the 1960s, environmental theories were widely held among the educated, though by no means universally. An understanding of the sociology of crime and justice did much to condition the attitudes of the Warren and early Burger Supreme Courts on issues such as capital punishment or defendants' rights. Environmental determinism undermined concepts of absolute responsibility, while rehabilitation was seen as an appropriate response for deviancy. "Evil" fitted poorly with such an intellectual climate.

By the late 1970s, ideas had changed considerably, although it is always a temptation to regard the writings of a few experts as indicating universal trends. Broadly, though, scholars of criminality tended to place more emphasis on the offender as a rational, responsible creature who could be deterred by the certainty and scale of punishment (Wilson & Herrnstein, 1985). Retribution was therefore more suitable than rehabilitation, which was seen as a failed goal. In the new political agenda, criminals were less victims of society than ruthless predators upon it. Solutions to crime were to be found in the justice system, rather than in social or family policy. In the more conservative tone of the 1980s, there was a series of cases where offenders appeared to be not only predators but creatures of extreme, pathological evil. Apart from the serial killers, there was concern about the mass sexual abuse of children, and even suggestions that some such offenses might be connected to devil-worship (Eberle & Eberle, 1986). A book entitled *The Ultimate Evil* suggested that a satanic cult was responsible for numerous serial murders, including those of the Manson family and "Son of Sam" (Terry, 1987).

If ever a moral panic was personified in one individual, then the concerns of the Reagan era were focused in the case of Richard Ramirez. In September 1985, he was arrested as a suspect in 68 offenses, including 14 murders attributed to the "Night Stalker" over the previous year. The allegations were those of a classic serial-murder case, while Ramirez himself seemed to be an archetypal "external enemy"—a drifter accused of brutal sexual violence against women. In court, he made apparently satanic references—a horned hand, and a cry of "Hail Satan!" The attention paid to this case—and the Green River case in Seattle—did much to prevent any public doubt that might have arisen as the Lucas case fell apart in the following month or two.

Public fears of the horrors of such atrocious crimes erased public opposition to the expansion of FBI powers. Federal officials stood to gain substantially by establishing serial murder as a growing menace. The Behavioral Sciences Unit (BSU) had been established in the early 1970s at the FBI National Academy. It needed validation for its efforts in profiling criminals (including interviews with convicted mass and serial killers) through extensive crime scene analysis. The profiles are not limited to how the crime was committed; behavioral analysis looks at possible interactions leading to the crime and at what the offender might do after the crime. The behavioral scientists at BSU use this process to construct detailed portraits of the offender—a process which has been labeled "mind-hunting" by some (Jenkins, 1994, p. 70). The FBI experts were extremely skillful in investing the word "serial" with much more significance than a simple definition of "repeated." Serial was linked in the public mind with sinister, irrational, compulsive, extremely violent, and inhuman acts committed by people who crossed state borders to spread their domain of horror (Jenkins, 1994, p. 213).

Extending jurisdiction by promoting their expertise was a common ploy by the FBI. Founded in 1908, it had little impact before the 1930s. At that time, the public was fearful of a perceived increase in kidnapping. The media presented the crime as the work of ruthless, itinerant predators snatching innocent children from the safety of their homes; the official response to the public anxiety created was to declare kidnapping a federal crime. Marijuana, organized crime, and bank robbers were the next areas annexed by the FBI which, in each case, suggested the problem threatened the public on a vast scale and was interjurisdictional in nature, thus requiring federal action. The FBI was portrayed as the appropriate agency because of its superior professionalism and forensic skills. It had enormous resources at its disposal to help support its claims; it had an inside track with Congress; and it cultivated relationships with journalists and other people in the media to help present compatible views of emerging problems (Jenkins, 1994, p. 214).

Serial murder further enhanced the FBI's image as an authoritative source. BSU agents not only offered a systematic overview, but they had actual contact with people who had committed unspeakable crimes. The news media had found a rich vein to mine—sensational stories anchored by the authority of federal law enforcement officials. BSU agent Robert Ressler described how his interaction with a *Chicago Tribune* reporter led to a flattering article in 1980. Immediately thereafter, a number of articles appeared in various publications, including *The New York Times*, *Psychology Today*, and *People*. He was also asked to appear on a number of radio and television programs (Jenkins, 1994, p. 216).

Media depictions reinforced the image of BSU experts as both knowledgeable and heroic and established a closed loop of information. The media reported the Justice Department's statistics without question; the intensity of the coverage helped support the claims of an increasing menace. High public visibility increased the profitability of media reporting of the topic. Any news story or fictional account of serial murder was legitimized by interviews with BSU; those very interviews added to the prestige of the Unit and insured that future stories would also rely on these unquestioned authorities (Jenkins, 1994, p. 217). In addition to interviews with agents, the FBI had the authority to grant or deny interviews with imprisoned killers. Anyone with access to the BSU had the potential for newsworthy stories. Particularly in 1983 and 1984, the FBI skillfully shared the information it was acquiring with accommodating journalists, academics, and filmmakers.

> There was somewhat of a media feeding frenzy, if not a panic, over this issue in the mid-1980s and we at the FBI and other people involved in urging the formation of VICAP did add to the general impression that there was a big problem and that something need be done about it. We didn't exactly go out seeking publicity, but when a reporter called, and we had a choice whether or not to cooperate on a story about violent crime, we gave the reporter good copy. In feeding the frenzy, we were using an old tactic in Washington, playing up the problem as a way of getting Congress and the higher-ups in the executive branch to pay attention to it. (Ressler & Schachtman 1992, p. 203, as quoted in Jenkins, 1994)

Serial murder offers an excellent illustration of the complex relationship between law enforcement, the media, and the public. Once public fears had been sufficiently aroused to view the threat as epidemic, the theme of serial killers was established. Innovative variations on that theme could then arise from any of the three segments and find support and acceptance from the other two (Jenkins, 1994, p. 223). The FBI formulated an image that was publicized and adapted to fictional accounts. This image directs public perceptions, and the media publish stories that address the established stereotype. Media images, in turn, affect the behavior of law enforcement officials. Even offenders are affected by the labeling process. Convicted killers often profess to match the prevailing stereotype. Ted Bundy discussed the terrible influence pornography had on him. Henry Lee Lucas claimed far more murders than he had actually committed. While there are numerous explanations for such admissions, their existence further complicates the feedback relationship between officials, the media, and the public (Jenkins, 1994, p. 225).

The FBI was successful in defining serial murder in terms of interjurisdictional cooperation, intelligence gathering, and overcoming linkage blindness. The crime was thus clearly established as a federal law enforcement problem, not a mental health issue or a social dysfunction. Fictional and media depictions had a major impact on the perception of the offenders—an image which dovetailed with that advanced by law enforcement. The serial killer in the 1980s was viewed as a ruthless, inhuman monster who could be stopped only by heroic "mind-hunters" (Jenkins, 1994, p. 16). Thus, the popular view of the extent of serial murder, the nature of the offender, and the only solution all matched the law enforcement image.

While the Justice Department played a significant role in shaping the image of serial murder, the statistics and portrayal they projected would have been irrelevant if the public was unconcerned and ignored the information. The Justice Department found an audience ready and willing to hear and to accept what they had to say. The statistics received instant credibility, with politicians calling for congressional hearings and the public responding. The media would not have maintained their interest in the topic if the public had not been receptive. The justice model was projected at an opportune time. As mentioned earlier, therapeutic models of crime had been rejected for justice-oriented approaches that emphasized the need to control predatory violence.

Problem construction is a cumulative process; new topics are usually based on predecessors, and the context of the times determines both the constraints and opportunities for new themes. Earlier memories and preconceptions shape current expectations and attitudes.

> Claims-makers must compete for attention. Social problems drop from view when they no longer seem fresh or interesting. New waves of claims-making may depend on the claims-makers' ability to redefine an issue, to focus on a new form of an old threat or to find other wrinkles. (Best 1989, p. 140, as quoted in Jenkins, 1994, p. 222)

The serial murder panic followed concerns raised earlier about missing children, child abuse, and the increase in homosexuality and its linkage with a killer disease.

Questionable statistics were readily accepted as credible because they served the purposes of a number of interest groups. Groups with far different agendas could find reasons to elevate the topic of serial murder. African-American groups could use the crime to illustrate a theme of systematic racial exploitation; feminists could find in serial killing another example of violence against women; children's rights activists linked missing and exploited children with the crime; and religious advocates could find evidence of satanic or ritual murder (Jenkins, 1994, p. 212). John Walsh, whose son Adam was kidnapped and murdered, testified before Senate judiciary hearings in 1982 that the issue of missing children was largely a problem of repeat killers. He alluded to Bundy, Gacy, and others and discussed how widespread the problem was and that linkage blindness made it possible for children to disappear without a trace, until they were located in a mass grave (Jenkins, 1994, p. 59). Conservatives could link sexually motivated multiple homicide with the decline of society's morals, easy access to pornography, media violence, and weakening of family values which allows killers easy access to "disposable" victims (Jenkins, 1994, p. 124).

Many of these interests coalesced around the concern for children. This became the unifying theme, which helps explain how a minor issue—statistically speaking—could achieve such prominence. The linkage of serial murder with the plight of children opened previously closed avenues. In the 1970s, the prevailing moral climate emphasized freedom of consenting adults to determine their private moral conduct. Groups who disapproved of homosexuality or pornography found little support in their attempts to label the behavior immoral. Shifting the focus to children provided a wedge. Children could not give legal consent, therefore the disapproved behavior was neither victimless nor consensual. Undertones of stigmatizing homosexuality could be masked by concerns about children. Serial murder was used to draw attention to the pedophile tendencies of serial killers and to associate homosexuals with violence (Jenkins, 1994, p. 18). Unapproved behavior serves as the basis from which to extrapolate other concerns and, in the process, to denounce a category of people and their lifestyle. Such stereotyping is possible only by exaggerating the prevalence of the offense and the composition of the offender population (Jenkins, 1994, p. 187).

Once a theme captures public attention, myths take hold that are difficult to dislodge. Perhaps inevitably, the accounts of the collapse of many of Lucas's claims in late 1985 received nothing like the national attention of his initial boasts. Probably the American public will long recall the transparent myth that "serial killers account for one-fifth of all murder victims in the United States." The myth is important because it confirms a traditional notion of an overwhelming threat by lethal predators and because it distracts attention away from the reality of most homicide—as an act committed between relatives or acquaintances, often in a domestic setting. Crime is thus transformed from the problem of individuals and groups in a particular environment to a war fought by semi-human monsters against society. The FBI's painstaking efforts to create the impression that only chesslike moves by supremely trained, high technology experts—also well-versed in psychology—could possibly catch diabolically clever criminals outlive documented contradictions.

Most serial killers are caught by police officers performing routine duties. Despite VICAP's existence, the typical case is usually discovered by chance. Joel Rifkin was stopped by Long Island police in 1993 for driving without a license plate. The decomposing remains of one of his victims were found in the car. In California, one suspect was captured when stopped for driving erratically, and police discovered a body in the passenger seat. Another offender made an illegal U-turn, was found to be violating parole, and was eventually linked with nineteen unsolved murders. Complaints from neighbors about noise and smell led to the arrests of both Jeffrey Dahmer and John Wayne Gacy (Jenkins, 1994, p. 109). Media stories rarely emphasize such facts. In fact, a BSU agent in his autobiography remarked, "The media have come around to lionizing behavioral science people as supersleuths who put all other police to shame and solve cases where others have failed" (Ressler & Schachtman 1992, p. 241, as quoted in Jenkins, 1994, p. 73). The myth of gladiatorial conflict between worthy heroes and reprehensible villains has much greater appeal to the public than the realities of happenstance.

Similarly, the overwhelming emphasis on sex killers like Ted Bundy leads the media to focus on crimes that most resemble the mythical stereo-type. Reinforcing the image of all serial killers as Jack-the-Ripper types can distract attention from other possibilities where opportunities are plentiful and avenues to mask the crimes are available, such as people in the medical or nursing-home professions or women killing children and blaming Sudden Infant Death Syndrome. It seems somehow more comprehensible to attach blame for unthinkable crimes to a conspiracy of organized evil, ritualistic kill-ings, or the work of a sexual sadist. The savagery of such crimes is apparently more "rational" if attached to the accepted stereotype.

Serial killers provide the most graphic illustration of dangerous outsid-ers. Their behavior is often marked by actions—including cannibalism and mutilation—abhorrent to civilized people. Serial murderers are portrayed in the same terms as those used by Cesare Lombroso in the 1870s in developing his theory of criminality:

> the problem of the nature of the criminal—an atavistic being who repro-duces in his person the ferocious instincts of primitive humanity . . . the irresponsible craving of evil for its own sake, the desire not only to extin-guish life in the victim, but to mutilate the corpse, tear its flesh and drink its blood. (Jenkins, 1994, p. 114)

The echoes of this characterization resonate today in calls for stringent laws against sexual predators:

> Chronic sexual predators have crossed an osmotic membrane. They can't step back to the other side—our side. And they don't want to. If we don't kill them or release them, we have but one choice. Call them monsters and isolate them. . . . I've spoken to many predators over the years. They always exhibit amazement that we do not hunt them. And that when we capture them, we eventually let them go. Our attitude is a deliberate in-terference with Darwinism—an endangerment of our species. (Andrew Vachss, 1993, as quoted in Jenkins, 1994, p. 118)

Once identified, the mere mention of serial killers' names is a rallying call for public revulsion. Names acquire mythic significance and evoke pow-erful images of horror—John Wayne Gacy's crawl space, Jeffrey Dahmer's apartment, Joel Rifkin's pickup truck (Jenkins, 1994, p. 222). Names serve as powerful rhetorical tools for weaving threads of the myth through other themes, as did John Walsh in his testimony before Congress.

Serial murder played a significant role in the debates over capital pun-ishment. In states where the death penalty was restored, serial killers were often the first to be executed. The public could dismiss previous views that the death penalty was reactionary and racist when it was applied to monsters for whom rehabilitation was futile (Jenkins, 1994, p. 131).

After the height of the serial murder panic in 1983–1985, the topic receded somewhat. In August 1990, five mutilation murders were reported on the University of Florida campus. Although these murders were not techni-cally "serial," the fact that the victims were students at another campus in the same state as Bundy's last murders created a media stir. Reports speculated on a number of current and unsolved cases around the country (Jenkins, 1994, p. 75). The boundaries between fiction and reality were blurred in 1991, pushing the subject of serial murder to new heights. Thomas Harris' 1988 novel, *The Silence of the Lambs,* was released as a motion picture (including location shots at Quantico, Virginia) in February 1991. Hannibal Lecter and Buffalo Bill resurrected all the images of incarnate evil established in the previous decade, while Clarice Starling and Jack Crawford embodied the fearless heroes using all their resources to save society. In July 1991, the real-life atrocities of Jeffrey Dahmer magnified the issue. Dahmer's case provided ample evidence for a number of claims.

> [T]hese crimes were hate-motivated. By focusing on Dahmer's alleged homosexuality, [the media] has overlooked the fact that many of his victims were homosexual. Regardless of Dahmer's actual sexual identity, it is clear that he hates homosexuals enough to want to kill them. It is also apparent Dahmer's murders were racially motivated. (as quoted in Jenkins, 1994, p. 180)

His trial was carried on *Court TV* and more than four hundred and fifty journalists covered it. Several other cases came to light in the months that followed. Television and the media continued to revisit the topic. Joel Rifkin's crimes and name were even the subtopic of a *Seinfeld* episode in 1994.

> Interest in the topic remains high: dozens of nonfiction books approach the topic from various angles, ranging from popular accounts to academic studies from disciplines as diverse as history, criminology, anthropology, psychiatry, and women's studies; and the diabolical serial murderer, striking at random, is a standard pop-culture icon in novels and movies. (Best, 1999, p. 5)

The interaction of bureaucratic agencies, the media, and the public create countless permutations of vested interests. The inherent newsworthiness of such crimes intersects with a growth of sensational television and radio programming. Nor does there appear to be any diminution of interest. With VICAP searching for links between unsolved murders, any increase found may be used as proof of a surging serial murder rate—rather than an indication of improvement in investigative technology. Points of similarity between geographically separated cases are bound to be noted, and there will be speculation about links. Unless care is taken, dozens or even hundreds of murders will be blamed on unknown hypothetical killers.

The "panic" is likely to be self-sustaining. There were warning signs to this effect from the British experience with that country's equivalent of VICAP, the Home Office Large Major Enquiry System (HOLMES). Use of the system initially produced claims of the existence of hypothetical serial child-murderers, by the linkage of what appear to have been very dissimilar cases. One arrest led to a rapid and embarrassing realization that at least one string of cases was in fact unrelated (Ballantyne, 1987). Demographic changes may result in the perception that the elderly are "new" victims. A future discovery may stir dormant fears of racial or cult conspiracies (Jenkins, 1994, p. 223).

In any given year, serial murder will account for approximately one out of every ten thousand deaths in the United States; 99.99% of Americans will die from causes other than multiple homicide (Jenkins, 1994). Despite the minimal threat statistically, the public remains fascinated with the topic and continues to frame it as a major problem. The harm that results from the crime when it occurs cannot be disputed. The reprehensible nature of the crime erases the necessity of establishing harm (as compared to victimless crime, for example). However, that very fact often encourages the use of serial crime as a weapon against other behaviors by linking the two (Jenkins, 1994). If the linkage is not questioned, policy and resources may target more than the indisputable wrong.

CONCLUSION

This chapter is emphatically not an attempt to trivialize or wish away the problem of serial murder. It is, however, intended as an illustration of the reasons why we should demand the highest standards of accuracy in the portrait of crime that is presented to the public both by law enforcement professionals and by academic researchers in this area—one that is quite literally a matter of life and death. Most clearly, there is the question of resources and the political priorities given to different areas. For example, it might be that a focus on serial murder might have an impact on this type of homicide, here estimated as accounting for perhaps two or three percent of homicides annually. It might also be that the homicide rate could be reduced still more dramatically by devoting the same resources to other activities. To put the problem in proportion: the total number of victims of serial murder across the United States in a particular year is considerably less than the annual total of homicide victims in Detroit alone. Should resources and activity be directed to a perceived national problem, or might they be better employed in a highly focused way in major metropolitan areas?

The problem of serial murder raises many of the perennial issues of criminal justice: public perceptions of the threat of crime as opposed to the very different reality; the tendency of agencies to direct resources to issues in the public view; and the role of the media in forming public perceptions of the crime problem. Social scientists often find cause to bemoan the myths portrayed by the media, especially in the area of crime and justice. The tendency is to blame sensationalist editors and journalists, but the relationship between the media, government, and the public is much more complex than that. There was sensationalism and also manipulation of the media by official agencies, but the media "panic" also resulted from a more subtle and general shift in public attitudes. The credulity apparent from reactions to the Lucas case is indicative of what has been described here as a "quest of evil," and this attitude forms the context of both public and official responses to a variety of legal and social issues in contemporary America. Understanding this attitude is an essential prerequisite to approaching the political debate over crime, law and order.

Notes

[1] In this article, I have taken what now appears to be the standard United States definition of serial murder, as several killings committed over a period of time. It should be noted that there are problems with this. Opinions differ on how frequently a person must kill to be counted in this category (four and six victims have been suggested). Also, the "period of time" remains undefined. If someone kills repeatedly over some hours, this is a mass murder. If days elapse, then it might be seen as a "serial" offense, though the exact dividing line is not clear. Finally, there is the problem of an individual committing one murder, and then another mass killing at a later date. Does he become a serial killer?

These points may appear pedantic, but they are important in developing a taxonomy of multiple murderers. It might be suggested that a mass murderer like Richard Speck was no different behaviorally or psychologically from a serial lust-murderer. It merely happened that he found himself with the opportunity to carry out so many of his fantasies at one place and time. Generally, though, there are substantial differences between mass killers like James Huberty and Patrick Sherrill and their serial counterparts, so the distinction is a useful one.

[2] Killers alleged to have claimed twenty or more victims are:

Name	Source
Ted Bundy	(Michaud & Aynesworth, 1983; Rule, 1980)
Dean Corll/Elmer Henley	(Olsen, 1974)
Juan Corona*	(Kidder, 1974)
Bruce Davis	
John Wayne Gacy	(Cahill, 1986; Sullivan & Maiken, 1983)
Donald Harvey	
Patrick Kearney*	(Godwin, 1978)
Gerald Stano	
"Green River Killer"	
Wayne Williams	(Detlinger & Prugh, 1983)

Those associated with between ten and twenty killings are:

Kenneth Bianchi/Angelo Buono*	(O'Brien, 1985; Schwartz, 1982)
William Bonin*	
William Christensen	
David J. Carpenter*	
Douglas D. Clark*	
Carroll Cole	
Robert Diaz*	
Larry Eyler	
Gerald Gallago	
Robert Hansen	
Frederick Hodge	
Calvin Jackson	(Godwin, 1978)
Edmund Kemper*	(Cheney, 1976; Lunde, 1967)
Paul Knowles	(Fawkes, 1978)
Randy Kraft*	
Leonard Lake*	
Bobby Joe Long*	
Henry Lee Lucas	
Bobby Joe Maxwell*	
Sherman McCrary	
Herbert Mullin*	(Lunde & Morgan, 1974)
Marcus Nisby*	
Richard Ramirez*	
Daniel Lee Siebert	
Coral Watts	
Christopher Wilder	
Randall Woodfield	(Stack, 1984)
"South Side Slayer"*	

(Asterisks denote individuals chiefly active in California)

Of Stalkers and Murder
Spreading Myth to Common Crime

Were the panics over child abduction and serial murder merely fads that caught public and government attention for a fleeting moment? Did the panics of the 1980s have an appreciable impact on our perceptions of crime and justice? Is it easier to spread myths and offer simplistic solutions to crime problems today than it was in the past? Events of the 1990s suggest that panics indeed have lasting effects and that previously constructed myths drive our current thoughts about crime. Crime myth is spreading beyond bizarre and unique criminal events into our views of more common crime. Before we consider these events, let's briefly recount some of the necessary techniques used to conjure up mythical crime.

Myths are exaggerations of reality; they form because of an inordinate amount of attention paid to sensational events or because of a sudden government or media fascination with a "newly" discovered behavior. These events or behaviors are presented in social forums that foster fear, accentuate danger, and focus almost exclusively on innocent victims and evil villains. Typically, before adequate definitions of criminal behavior are developed and before clear typologies emerge, dissimilar behaviors are fused to give the appearance of an epidemic. Targeted behaviors are characterized as increasing in frequency and severity. No one is immune from being preyed upon by the perpetrators of our most recent panic. Media depiction of these mythical crimes is accompanied by the language of fear. Strangers "hide" in the dark to steal away our children; serial murderers "prowl and prey"; and crime is "rampant" on urban streets. "Stalk" is another potent word, as in the case of California serial killer Richard Ramirez, the Night Stalker (Jenkins, 1994, p. 117).

◇

CONSTRUCTING THE MYTH OF STALKING

The panics of the 1980s served as perfect backdrops for the spread of myth into common forms of crime in the 1990s. "Problem construction is a cumulative or incremental process, in which each issue is to some extent built upon its predecessors, in the context of a steadily developing fund of socially available knowledge" (Jenkins, 1994, p. 220). Rising urban crime, child abduction, and serial murder panics provided the "intellectual environment" for the spread of crime myths into other behaviors. The stage had been set, the lines had been well rehearsed, and the public was ready to be incited when the murder of actress Rebecca Schaeffer made the news. Ms. Schaeffer, a star in the television series *My Sister Sam*, was killed by Robert Bardo—a "stalker." The young actress was gunned down at her California apartment. In a very short time, California citizens were informed of the Schaeffer murder as well as the murders of four other women by "stalkers" (Dawsey & Malnic, 1989). Other celebrities, including David Letterman and Madonna, later reported to the nation that they had been the victims of stalkers or that they were persistently harassed by obsessive fans (see Table 5.1).

Between 1989 and 1993, stalking became a major media issue (Jenkins, 1994). Articles on stalking appeared in a variety of national and local magazines like *U.S. News and World Report, People Weekly, Los Angeles Magazine*, and *Time* (see, Holmes, 1993). Popular media sources invoked the rhetoric of fear with phrases such as "the murderous obsession" and "the terror of stalking" (Beck, 1992; "Fatal," 1989; Puente, 1992). While the news media were capitalizing on the sensationalism associated with celebrity stalkings, the entertainment industry was cashing in at the box office. Movies like *Fatal Attraction, Blink*, and *The Body Guard* created potent images of stalkers for public consumption. For the news media, the quintessential stalking was a violent predatory act committed by a stranger (Bochove, 1992). An innocent (Hallman, 1992) was hunted and terrorized for months by a fiendish, deranged predator bent on sexually assaulting or killing his victim.

Perhaps the media depiction of Gary Wilensky best captured the fear and sensationalism surrounding stalking. Wilensky was a tennis coach at several exclusive New York City schools. In 1988, he was arrested for stalking three children while wearing a black leather "sex" mask and videotaping them at bus stops (Leavitt, 1993). The charges against Wilensky were eventually dropped. According to Jean Arena, one of the victims' mothers: "It's like in the movies: You have to wait for someone to do something really bad before you can get them" (p. 3A). Years later, according to the police, Wilensky took his own life after attempting to abduct a 17-year-old woman. Police reported that he was intent on kidnapping the woman and taking her to a secluded hideout that was

Table 5.1
Selected Stalkers and Their Victims

Stalkers	Victims
Joni Penn	Sharon Gless, actress
Mark David Chapman	John Lennon, musician
Arthur Jackson	Theresa Saldana, actress
	John F. Kennedy, president
	Tesesa Berganza, singer
John Hinckley, II	Jodie Foster, actress
Tina Ledbetter	Michael J. Fox, actor
Stephen Stillabower	Madonna, musician
	Sean Penn, actor
Ken Gause	Johnny Carson, TV host
Nathan Trupp	Michael Landon, actor
	Sandra Day O'Connor, Justice
Ralph Nau	Olivia Newton-John, singer
	Marie Osmond, singer
	Cher, singer
	Farrah Fawcett, actress
John Smetek	Justine Bateman, actress
Robert Bardo	Rebecca Schaeffer, actress
Billie Jackson	Michael Jackson, singer
Margaret Ray	David Letterman, TV host
Roger Davis	Vanna White, TV star
Brook Hull	Teri Garr, actress
Ruth Steinhagen	Eddie Waitkus, baseball player
Daniel Vega	Donna Mills, actress
Robert Keiling	Anne Murray, singer

Reprinted from: Holmes, R. M. (1993). Stalking in America: Types and Methods of Criminal Stalkers. *Journal of Contemporary Criminal Justice*, 9(4):319.

equipped with restraints, muzzles, masks, women's wigs, and a police badge. What the media failed to mention in its reporting of the Wilensky incident was that in 1988 there were no statutes against stalking. The media had effectively redefined Wilensky's behavior and arrest as a stalking five years later. The media were silent as to whether Wilensky stalked his last victim. In essence, the media retrospectively labeled his crime to fit our latest crime panic.

Various media characterizations shape the public's conception of stalking. According to most popular accounts, the classic stalker is a cunning stranger who has targeted an innocent victim for prey. The stalker's behavior demonstrates an identifiable, systematic and sustained progression that, without official intervention, ultimately culminates in the commission of a hideous crime—typically sexual assault, child molestation, or a brutal murder. This conception of stalking has crept into some of the academic literature. One academician remarked: "Unbalanced persons send letters and make phone calls to athletes and targeted strangers for purposes of terrorizing and even sexually assaulting and murder. There may be no one truly safe from a predatory stalker" (Holmes, 1993, p. 317). In other academic accounts stalking has been linked, through selective sampling, to serial crimes like sexual assault, rape, and murder.

> Methods within the stalking process become an important and integral part of the act. Norris discusses the process of the stalk as it concerns the sex offender. It appears as a starting point in the selection process of the serial predator. Holmes has also examined the stalking of the sexual predator. He lists "the stalk" as one of the five steps in the selection and the execution of serial murder. Hazelwood extends a similar discussion with the serial rapist. (citations omitted; Holmes, 1993, p. 318)

The crime of stalking is constructed to accentuate the helplessness of the innocent victim, the calculated and systematic behavior of the stranger-offender, and the inability of current laws to cope with this new criminality. Others have characterized it as widespread and growing (Hoshen et al., 1995, p. 31). Legal scholars have also drawn on the fear-generating and very speculative prey-predator conception of stalking; the innocent victim orientation to the problem; and the unsupported assumption that stalking ultimately culminates in violence. "Victims of stalking must wait and hope the stalker will not actually follow through with threats or go beyond mere pursuit. Many victims live in fear, forced to alter their lives dramatically. Victims may suffer substantial and lasting emotional trauma from such an ordeal" (Guy, 1993, as cited in Sohn, 1994, pg. 205). At the heart of the stalking problem is the powerlessness of the police to take action until the ultimate event takes place—an act of violence. The solution is the creation of new criminal laws that allow early, formal intervention. "The criminalization of stalking attempts to protect victims by identifying the various stages of stalking and providing for intervention by law enforcement at a time that sufficiently anticipates its culmination in violence" (p. 205). Of course, their image of stalking is a myth, and the typical "stalking" is far less sensational than the media and some academics would have us believe.

◇

OFFICIALIZING THE MYTH

As stalking captured the media's attention, it also captured the attention of legislators across the country. Within two years of the media stories about the Schaeffer murder, almost every state legislative body was circulating proposals for the creation of antistalking laws. Some characterized the inordinate amount of state attention to stalking as a "legislative frenzy" (Kolarik, 1992). This characterization may have been chillingly accurate given the speed, scope, and lack of thoughtfulness that characterized legislative action.

In 1990, California became the first state to enact an antistalking law. Two years later 29 other states followed suit. By late 1993, 48 states and the District of Columbia had followed California's lead by enacting legislation to prohibit stalking (for lists see National Criminal Justice Association, 1993; Sohn, 1994; Thomas, 1993). Only two states, Maine and Arizona, had not enacted stalking statutes. By 1997 every state and the federal government had enacted legislation making stalking a crime.

In 1993 the federal government entered the picture with Senator Cohen's chilling statements that mirrored the media construction of stalking.

> Unfortunately, the victims of stalking find it impossible to be left alone, and they feel as if there is no place to turn when they become the prey of stalkers. . . . The crime of stalking is insidious, frightening, and, as I indicated before, it is on the rise. . . .
>
> About 5% of women in the general population will be victims of stalking at some time in their lives. Nationally, an estimated 4 million men kill or violently attack women they live with or date and as many as 90% of women killed by their husbands or boyfriends were stalked prior to the attack. . . .
>
> They tell me that stalking is a crime that does not discriminate, it is not gender specific, and it affects people from all walks of life. . . .
>
> I think we cannot begin to imagine the kind of fear that a mother may have as she sees a stranger stand at the corner of her home or her lot, or watch somebody follow her children to a school and stand there and just wait. It may be a celebrity or someone else, who has a man—or it could be a woman, if the situation is reversed—standing watching her movements, day in and day out, doing nothing but simply standing there waiting for what she believes to be the right moment to attack her. . . .
>
> Stalking is also unique because it is often a series of acts that escalate into violence. Therefore, it is important to develop State legislation which identifies the various stages of stalking and provides for intervention by law enforcement at a time that sufficiently anticipates its culmination in violence. . . . (S.12901)

Turning rhetoric into reality, Congress directed the National Institute of Justice to develop model antistalking legislation. The act mandated that

> The Attorney General, acting through the Director of the National Institute of Justice, shall: (1) evaluate existing and proposed antistalking legislation in the States, (2) develop model antistalking legislation that is constitutional and enforceable, (3) prepare and disseminate to State authorities the findings made as a result of such evaluation, and (4) report to the Congress the findings and the need or appropriateness of further action by the Federal Government by September 30, 1993. (U.S. Congress, Pub L. 102-395, Sec. 109b, 1993)

The National Institute of Justice in conjunction with the National Criminal Justice Association undertook the project. Project participants interpreted this Congressional mandate to require the development of "a model antistalking code to encourage states to adopt antistalking measures and provide them with direction in formulating such laws" (National Criminal Justice Association, 1993, p. 5). The extent to which the legislation was intended to encourage state legislative action is open to debate. The fact remains, however, that stalking had become politicized; governors and state legislators used the issue to attract media attention and personal exposure.

Vermont's governor, for example, selected Brattleboro for the signing of that state's new stalking bill because reporter Judith Fournier was stalked and killed there by her former boyfriend. Similarly and with some ceremony, Nevada's governor signed legislation that allowed police monitoring of telephone conversations to investigate stalkers. While political grandstanding was clearly evident, the scope of politics was even more obvious in legislative debates surrounding applicability of the statutes to abortion protestors and labor union activists as well as provisions that would exempt law enforcement officers from civil liability for failure to notify stalking victims that an arrested suspect had been released. Clearly, legislators were concerned about both the social position of certain activists and the distribution of responsibility for failure to protect victims.

In 1997, President Clinton signed into law the National Defense Authorization Act for Fiscal Year 1997, which included the Interstate Stalking Punishment and Prevention Act, that creates the felony offense of "interstate stalking" (18 U.S.C. Section 2261A). The new law provides:

> Whoever travels across a State line or within the special maritime and territorial jurisdiction of the United States with the intent to injure or harass another person, and in the course of, or as a result of, such travel places that person in reasonable fear of the death of, or serious bodily injury . . . to, that person or member of that person's immediate family . . . shall be punished. . . .

As state legislators were crafting stalking statutes and allowing the issue of stalking to drive other legislation, questionable statistics concerning stalking were being circulated. There were estimates that some 200,000 people are stalked each year (Guy, 1993), that 5% of women will be stalked at some point in their lives (Cohen, 1993; *Congressional Record*, 1993), and that 90% of the women killed by their spouses or former boyfriends were stalked prior to their murder (Beck, 1992; Cohen, 1993). Much of the data that was used in Congressional consideration of legislation came from the media. In fact many of the numbers can be traced to an article that appeared in *USA Today*. The newspaper article reported figures that were later described as "guesses" made by a Los Angeles psychiatrist studying an unrepresentative sample of celebrity stalkers (see Dietz et al., 1991; Puente, 1992; Tjaden & Thoennes, 1998, n.14).

The government panic over stalking virtually ignored the claim that 90% of stalking victims were women (Cohen, 1993; *Congressional Record*, 1993). The government's project to develop a model code for stalking as well as legal treatises attempted to neutralize the possibility that this crime might be conceptualized as gender based. The following instruction appeared in a prominent location in the government's report and was emphasized in bold: "Stalking is a gender neutral crime, with both male and female defendants and victims" (National Criminal Justice Association, 1993, p. xi). One legal writer remarked that "there are both female and male stalkers" (Sohn, 1994, n.9) and an academician notes that "husbands and wives seek out their former mates to terrorize" (Holmes, 1993, p. 317).

Certainly there are occasional cases of women who stalk men, just as there are male victims of domestic violence and serial murder. This possibility obscured the obvious gender differential and domestic aspects of the problem. However, it also extended support for proposed legislation by broadening considerably the number of persons who could now view themselves as potential victims. In other words, it established a necessary requirement for myth production that no group is insulated from stalkers. Such a gender obfuscation of the issue also lent political power to the criminalization movement by appealing to those who would ultimately determine whether or not stalking would be criminalized—male legislators. Additionally, constructing stalking as a gender neutral crime detracts from its domestic nature and allows the predatory stranger conceptions to flourish. Reason as well as extrapolation from existing research would suggest that the vast majority of stalkings, like serial murder and domestic violence, are perpetrated by men against women.

Whether the project participants were influenced by the stereotypic image of the fiendishly clever stalker who could foil any constraint, or whether they could not specify precisely what behavior defined stalking, the end result was ambiguous, imprecise phrasing. The participants intentionally did not enumerate prohibited acts, rationalizing "that ingenuity on the part of an alleged stalker should not permit him to skirt the law" (National Criminal Justice Association, 1993, p. 44). Of course, the failure to specify what particular acts constitute stalking leaves the power of interpretation and application to law enforcement officials.

As with missing children and serial murder panics, legislative action was taken before the development of an adequate definition of stalking. Six years after Rebecca Schaeffer's death thrust the term into the nation's conscience, there was "no widely accepted definition of 'stalking'. Although stalking is against the law in almost every state, the term is not defined in *Black's Law Dictionary* nor is it discussed in major legal treatises such as *American Jurisprudence* or *Corpus Juris Secundum*" (Sohn, 1994, pp. 204–205). Similarly, there existed no reliable and empirically based criminological definition of stalking. "Nevertheless, the term 'stalker' arouses certain common images in most people's minds. . . . The term brings to mind a wide range of harassing behaviors that frighten or terrorize the victim" (pp. 204–205). Despite the lack of a clear definition of stalking and admitting to the absence of any empirical evidence as to its frequency, severity, or demographic characteristics, the federal government had a model code developed, encouraged states to adopt it and enacted antistalking legislation.

States either followed California's model or heeded the encouragement of the federal government by enacting statutes that prohibited everything from being "present" (5 states) to "approaching" (4 states), "following" (43 states), "pursuing" (43 states) through "non-consensual communications" (20 states), "surveillance" (3 states) and "lying in wait" (3 states)—all designed to allow the police to take enforcement action before the ultimate crime (National Criminal Justice Association, 1993).

Consider the breadth of antistalking statutes. California's stalking law, for example, prohibits any "willful course of conduct directed at a specific person which seriously alarms, annoys, or harasses the person, and which serves no legitimate purpose" (Cal. Penal Code, 1990, p. 646). At least 14 states do not require intent to cause fear on the part of a suspect. In 18 states an explicit threat or act is not required to satisfy the elements of the crime of stalking. The California statute defines a course of conduct as "a pattern of conduct composed of a series of acts over a period of time, however short, evidencing a continuity of purpose" (p. 646). Most state statutes, however, only require two incidents to satisfy the "course of conduct" requirement. In 1993, Iowa amended its stalking statute to allow police to intervene after a single incident. After enactment of the stalking statute, following a person is criminal in California, although "following" is left undefined in the statute as well as in the laws of other states (see Thomas, 1993). In some states, Florida for example, following someone even without an accompanying threat is considered a misdemeanor (Fla. Stat. Ann., 1992). By 1998 at least a dozen states had had challenges to the constitutionality of these statutes raised in the courts and the stalking law in Texas was struck down as so vague that it violated the constitution (*Long v. State*, 1996).

What is interesting about such a rapid and widespread adoption of so many broad and vague statutes is that almost every state already had laws on the books that prohibited the acts most frequently described as stalking (for list see Sohn, 1994). Admittedly, following someone was not criminal before the stalking panic, but trespass, vandalism, terroristic threatening, harassment, assault and battery, or variants of these behaviors were illegal in almost every state. More specifically, 46 states had criminal trespass laws, 28 had harassment statutes, 19 prohibited terroristic threatening (National Criminal Justice Association, 1993) and, needless to say, every state had a prohibition against assault.

The existence of these statutes coupled with the availability of civil protections undermines the claim that existing laws were inadequate to handle this newly discovered criminality. Recourses of a noncriminal nature available to victims of stalkings include civil protection orders, restraining orders, civil contempt, mental heath commitments, emergency detentions and tort actions. In short, the characterization of existing laws as inadequate was a myth. Likewise, portrayal of the police and victims as powerless against stalkers was pure fabrication.

The more plausible explanation of any ineffectiveness of existing law was a lack of willingness by law enforcement officers to expend the energies necessary to educate and to assist domestic victims of stalking with existing legal remedies. Despite easily identifiable legal restrictions on behaviors identified with stalking, the official position on stalking closely matched the expression of one writer: "*lax or non-existent laws* give stalkers of women (and of men) repeated opportunities to *play with their prey*—to follow or harass, terrorize or beat them—to make them afraid to live their lives" (our emphasis, as cited in Sohn, 1994, p. 203).

MEASURING THE REALITY OF STALKING

In the later part of the 1990s the topic of stalking had made its rounds through the media and had begun to lose its sensational appeal. At about this same time serious research into the actual incidents and nature of stalking had begun. This research, however, was directed in part by the legal and media-based conceptions of stalking. Researchers adopted the far reaching and broad definitions of stalking advocated by political leaders and interest groups devoted to addressing the stalking problem. One important twist to the stalking issues was the recognition of the linkage between stalking and domestic violence. Joel Best (1999), for example, remarks that

> The link between stalking and domestic violence had become apparent in state legislative proceedings. . . . The National Victim Center lobbied in more than a dozen states, and Theresa Saldana (a former stalking victim and founder of Victims for Victims) campaigned in behalf of the laws. . . . Stalking attracted influential sponsors—advocates who not only kept the issue alive, but extended its boundaries . . . The media's eagerness to cover stories about celebrities undoubtedly helped. . . . The crime victims' movement and the battered women's movement characterized stalking as a common problem, a form of domestic violence, that threatened ordinary people—particularly women. Linking its cause with the visible problem of stalking gave the battered women's movement a fresh look. . . . Coupling long-standing stalking complaints about ineffective restraining orders to the lethal menace of stalking turned a tired topic into a hot issue. . . . Antistalking programs and legislation gave government agencies a way to earn credit with the victims' rights and battered women's movements by being responsive. (pp. 55–56)

Drawing on this newly constructed alliance of images but still holding to the conception of stalking as a gender neutral crime, the National Institute of Justice and the National Center for Injury Prevention funded a study that wedded violence against women and stalking (Tjaden & Thoennes, 1998a; 1998b). The researchers' findings were startling. Based on phone interviews with some

8,000 men and 8,000 women, the researchers found that 1% of women and
.04% of men had been the victims of stalking in the last year. These figures
translate to 1,006,970 women and 370,990 men being stalked annually. These
figures far exceed the guesses make by claims makers involved in the early
development of the stalking issue. Additionally, the researchers inferred that
these figures translate to 8% of women and 2% of men in the United States
being the victims of stalking at some time in their lives. The national media
quickly seized the opportunity to report on the study's findings, reporting that
one in 12 women are the victims of stalkers (Associated Press, 1997, p. 8).
Although the media and claims makers had constructed the stalking issue as
gender neutral, the survey found that 78% of stalking victims were women and
that 87% of stalkers were men. Men who experienced stalking were more likely
to be stalked by a man rather than by a woman. In fact, 90% of the stalkers who
stalked men were male. These statistics paint a very different picture of the gen-
dered nature of stalking in the United States.

The research also calls into question the psychopathic stranger conception of stalking. Results of the survey found only about 20% of female victims
were stalked by strangers. The vast majority of women victims were stalked by
former or current husbands, current or former cohabiting partners, or former
dates or boyfriends. In fact a majority of these incidents started before a relationship ended, and 80% of the victims of stalking had experienced physical
abuse in the relationship. The research also found little support of the mental
illness link to stalking. Fewer then 7% of victims reported being stalked
because of a mental illness on the part of the stalker. The reported behavior of
stalkers was not in keeping with media and political constructions of stalkers as
dangerous, sex crazed predators bent on committing some form of horrific violence. In fact, the vast majority of stalkers never made an overt threat to the victim, and 75% were reported to have merely spied on the victim.

How then did researchers reach such alarming totals of people being
stalked in America? A number of issues in the construction of the research
shed light on the large numbers generated. First, the researchers used a definition of stalking that did not include a requirement that the alleged stalker
present a realistic threat to the victim. Sending an unwanted letter or making
two or more unwanted phone calls was sufficient to be included as stalking
behavior. Second, half of the sample used by the researchers was made up of
people between the ages of 18 and 39—those people at the greater risk of being
victims of this crime. Third, stalking does not always last a only few months. It
can span several years; therefore, it is likely that the sample included incidents
from previous years. Fourth, the information presented in the report is unclear
about whether respondents were aware that the two or more incidents of
alleged stalking had to be made by the same person. Finally, the researchers fail
to report sufficient demographic characteristics of the sample, making it impossible to determine if it is truly representative of the U.S. population—particularly in terms of socioeconomic characteristics. Perhaps the most damaging
omission of the study is the failure to ask the simple question of whether the

alleged stalking resulted in any serious injury to the victim. In fact nearly half the female victims of stalking failed to report the stalker's behavior to the police, and a majority of these people indicated that the behavior was not considered a police matter. These characteristics of the study cast doubt on the findings about the number of victims of violent stalker behavior.

◇

CONSEQUENCES OF CRIMINALIZATION

Given the range of existing criminal and civil laws available to both police and stalking victims, what motivated law enforcement to support the enactment of these new statutes? The results of the National Criminal Justice Association's (1993) survey of police shed light on the utility of statutory change as well as on law enforcement's motivation. Their survey of police found that "Intervention options available to police with or without stalking laws are many and varied. Survey respondents' answers indicate that departments in states with antistalking laws depend on alternative responses as much as states without such laws" (p. 40).

This finding raises questions as to whether the stalking statutes were necessary, since law enforcement officers in jurisdictions with the new statutes used them in conjunction with existing laws. In other words, stalking is a reconstituted crime used by law enforcement officers as an add-on charge. In states with stalking laws, 81% of agencies charged offenders with trespassing, while 74% of agencies without such laws included trespassing. Seventy-four percent of agencies with stalking laws charged offenders with assault compared to 60% of states without the laws.

The utility of these statutes was essentially to increase the punitiveness of the criminal law and to grant law enforcement officers greater powers of arrest. Law enforcement agencies in jurisdictions that did not yet have the statutes wanted them, and law enforcement agencies with the statutes wanted more power.

> Eighty-six percent of respondents with antistalking laws in place felt that the intervention options available to them were adequate; only 43% of agencies without stalking laws felt their intervention options were adequate . . . Still others thought that an antistalking law that did not require a third-party witness or police presence at the time of the crime would be helpful. (National Criminal Justice Association, 1993, p. 40)

In essence, the police wanted the power to arrest as they saw fit. They sought arrest decisions based solely on police discretion not on judicial review or actual observation of a crime. The power of law enforcement officers to arrest had previously been curtailed to those incidents where they observed a crime or, in the alternative, were forced to seek judicial review of their case and secure a warrant before making an arrest. Now law enforcement officers are no longer hindered by these inconveniences. Antistalking laws were created to give law enforcement an "immediate cause to make an arrest and the state an immediate reason for prosecution" (Comment, 1992, p. A20).

It is almost impossible to distinguish the difference between the types of behavior addressed by the new statutes and those that have been prohibited in the past. The important distinction, of course, is that the new statutes grant the police extraordinary powers to arrest before a common crime has occurred. The statutes are so broad and vague that violating their provisions will most likely be determined based on victim abilities to convince the police that they were afraid or annoyed and on police willingness to view suspects as those in need of state control.

Another consequence of the new antistalking laws was an increase in the punitiveness of the criminal justice system. Reconstituting common crime as stalking allowed the media-generated characterization of the phenomenon to shape penalty provisions of the statutes. Arguing that a vandal, trespasser or mere harasser should be denied bail and, if convicted, be sentenced to a 10-year prison term could meet strong objections. A "stalker," however, is another matter entirely. These statutes impose a greater penalty on the same types of behaviors than their counterpart statutes provided. While the typical stalking statute defined the crime as a misdemeanor subject to a one-year incarceration, at least nine states allowed felony charges. Some states that classify stalking as a felony permit terms of imprisonment of 10 to 20 years, and all states have penalty enhancement provisions. In some states, felony charges mean the accused may be ineligible for bail. For example, the Illinois stalking statute allows courts to hold a stalking suspect without bail while facing a felony sentence that may be punishable by three years of incarceration. Several of the new stalking statutes specifically prescribe the denial of bail. Other statutes allow the courts to qualify pre-trial release; for instance they may require suspects to be placed on electronic monitoring.

Finally, the effects of being labeled a "stalker" rather than a trespasser, harasser, or vandal carries the stigmatization associated with the media depiction of the classic stalker. The label is infused with negative connotations that could affect family, friends, and business associates. A conviction for stalking would undoubtedly color any subsequent arrest. One can only speculate on the full range of social consequences of being labeled as a stalker.

How these statutes will be enforced in the future remains to be seen, but two of the first cases prosecuted in Florida following enactment of its stalking statute offer grim warnings of the consequences of laws passed in haste. A 12-year-old boy who had left a threatening note in the locker of one of his seventh grade classmates ("Florida," 1992) was arrested and detained. A 66-year-old man was arrested, despite the "victim's" own assertion that he never threatened her but merely called on several occasions and showed up at her home without an invitation (Friedberg, 1992). One hopes these cases are just as much aberrations as the mythical strangers who stalk innocent victims for months—always eluding the police and always killing their victims.

◇
CONCLUSION

Faulty premises are more likely to be accepted if the audience is fearful and if the premises coincide with common thinking, such as, no one should be fearful in their own home. Public attention is produced by a crisis—particularly one that disturbs the expected routine. How the public defines the situation after their attention has been focused determines the response. False premises or expectations, such as "existing laws are inadequate for enforcement" or "the police can control or prevent random violence," prompt inappropriate responses. As Robert Merton (1949, p. 80) has pointed out: "To seek social change without due recognition of the manifest and latent functions performed by the social organizations undergoing changes is to indulge in social ritual."

Ancient fears about humanity, fear of the dark, fear of strangers, and fear of the unknown all contribute to our social construction of crime problems. The strength of such fears is a sobering warning about attempts to point out contradictions in the "evidence" of a particular crime. "For all the science and quantification used to substantiate a new problem, its true momentum will be located in its appeal to deep-rooted anxieties that respond poorly to rational inquiry, still less rebuttal" (Jenkins, 1994, p. 229).

The media construct a reality of epidemic violence in which victims are selected at random. In an age of control, the lack of prediction is terrifying. Giving irrational behavior a name, like stalking, offers the illusion of control; it allows us to fill the frightening, unexplainable void with words and hollow action. The relentless push for legislation against every possible attack presents a soothing fiction that the problem is understood and has been addressed. The action of passing laws against predatory strangers belies society's helplessness in the face of that threat. Draconian punishments theoretically balance the terror inspired by random violence. One irony is that the very randomness of the behavior limits the possibility that perpetrators will be caught and controlled. Another irony is that catapulting certain behaviors into a new category will not eliminate irrational acts but instead results in equally irrational fears and expectations. Turning tragic misfortunes into the potential for injustice raises unrealistic expectations about our ability to control violence.

Blue Smoke and Mirrors
The "War" on Organized Crime

Organized crime has been the subject of countless novels, magazine articles, movies, newspaper reports, criminal investigations, congressional hearings, and public inquiries by criminal justice agencies. Fascination with the covert world of organized crime has created a popular view of this phenomenon that has elevated it to legend.

For more than half a century, law enforcement agencies have pursued, prosecuted, imprisoned and even executed crime figures. Professional, well-funded agencies have been established to investigate organized crime and to expose its many intricate conspiracies. Billions of dollars have been spent on "closing the borders" to the drug trade, on "stinging" labor racketeers, and on auditing the tax returns of gamblers. Yet organized crime continues to conduct business as usual. There is little or no evidence to show that organized crime activities have been or are being significantly disrupted. In fact, most of the available evidence points to the contrary. With all of the time, effort, and money expended in this area, we are still confronted with two basic questions. What can be done about organized crime, and how will we know if we have been successful?

The answers to these questions are contingent on a more basic question: what is organized crime? For the most part, policymakers have answered this question by pointing to a myth of organized crime in the United States.

◊

THE OFFICIAL MYTH OF ORGANIZED CRIME

What do we know about organized crime? How much empirically verified information do we have and how much data is simply based on myth and misconceived belief?

> During the medieval ages Christian theologians pondered the question, How many angels can dance on the point of a needle without jostling one another? Although we might argue the subject's importance, we must at least marvel at any attempt to solve such a problem. After all, there is little evidence on angels' width and dancing abilities. The modern-day equivalent of angel counting is "syndicate structuring." Today's Mafia watchers have about as much data as the angel counters did as they debate the nature of organized crime's organization. (McCaghy & Cernkovich, 1987, p. 205)

Many federal law enforcement officials and some scholars think they know how many angels are dancing on the point of organized crime's needle. For them the answer is simple. Organized crime in the United States is a conspiracy of outsiders, ". . . a group of men motivated by criminality and a sense of loyalty foreign to an open, democratic society" (Smith, 1978, p. 168). Organized crime was imported to the United States during the late nineteenth and early twentieth centuries in the wave of Italian immigration. With these foreign immigrants came secret, outlaw, feudal societies such as the Mafia and the Camorra, the seedlings planted on U.S. soil from which organized crime sprouted (Bequai, 1979). In 1931, these secret, feudal societies went through a catharsis, the Castellamarese War, which successfully wiped out the last vestiges of feudal Sicilian rule in the mob, removed illiterates from power, and placed business-oriented, Italian gangsters in charge of organized crime. By 1932 organized crime, years ahead of the business world, had become a sleek, modern, bureaucratized Italian crime corporation, made up of about 24 "families" based on Italian lineage and extended family relationships, governed by a national commission.

This massive, alien conspiracy was first called to our attention in a systematized manner by the Federal Bureau of Narcotics in 1946 (Smith, 1976). In later years, Senator Kefauver's committee on interstate gambling (1951), Senator McClellan's committee on labor racketeering (1957), investigations of the "Apalachin Meeting," and the testimony of Joe Valachi (1963) formed the cornerstones of the alien conspiracy theory. Following the lead of the law enforcement community, ambitious politicians, presidential commissions, journalists, academics, and writers of novels and screenplays eagerly advanced the theory. The President's Crime Commission (Task Force on Organized Crime, 1967) and Donald Cressey's *Theft of the Nation* (1967) gave the theory scholarly credibility and presented it in terms useful to policymakers. Since then, virtually every journalistic account and a host of academic treatises have championed the myth of an alien conspiracy (see, for example: Chandler, 1975; Cook, 1973; Demaris, 1981; Pace & Styles, 1975).

The myth of alien conspiracy is relatively simple. First, organized crime groups are criminal equivalents of legitimate corporate sector enterprises—exhibiting similar structural features and bureaucratic organization. Instead of president, vice-president, chairman of the board, general managers, personnel directors and the like, we have "bosses," "underbosses," "counselors," "captains," and "soldiers" (Salerno & Tompkins, 1969, pp. 84–85). Authority and discipline in the organization are based on violence, bribery, and a clan-based feudal hierarchy. Second, organized crime "families" exhibit an inexorable tendency toward monopoly and the formation of massive international cartels to dominate illicit goods and services (Task Force on Organized Crime, 1967). Third, group membership is determined by ethnic identity. As the Task Force Report on Organized Crime tells us, "their membership is exclusively men of Italian descent" (1967, p. 6). If anyone else, unlucky enough not to have been born Italian, wishes to engage in the provision of illicit goods and services, they do so only at the sufferance of the Mafia. And finally, organized crime groups attack the very foundations of democracy by their corrupting of otherwise upstanding and loyal public servants. They are an alien force perverting sound economic and political institutions (Pace & Styles, 1975).

As times change, myths must be adjusted to new realities. In the case of the alien conspiracy theory, drug trafficking by non-Italian groups presented a particularly thorny problem. The official depiction of organized crime in the United States underwent a pluralist revision. Federal, state, and local law enforcement organizations began noticing a growing number of new organized crime groups. The "traditional" Mafia was joined by "forceful new competition from Asian and Latin American underworld groups that specialize in heroin, cocaine, and marijuana" (Rowan, 1986, p. 26). Jamaicans, Colombians, Cubans, Japanese, Irish, Vietnamese, Mexicans, and Russians were added to the list (Pennsylvania Crime Commission, 1986; President's Commission on Organized Crime, 1984).

What is most intriguing about this shift in the official myth of organized crime is not how much it has changed but how steadfastly it clings to the fundamental assertions of the alien conspiracy myth. The pluralist revision is true to the conspiracy myth in that all of the new groups are defined as racially, ethnically, or culturally homogenous. They are all described in terms of some type of culturally delineated "family" structure that resembles a corporate bureaucracy, but which is rooted in the foreign customs of their homelands. They are rabidly expansionist in their marketing strategies and are "more violent," "more secretive," and "more closely knit" than the traditional Mafia. In fact, the primary explanation used for the decline of Mafia power is that it has been Americanized. That is, younger Italians have adopted mainstream American values—presumably making them less violent, less secretive, and less closely-knit (Ianni, 1974; 1972).

According to this view, the Mafia has lost its edge because of the declining interest in high-risk ventures by new leadership and moderation in the use of violence.

> The leadership is old, and the next generation of managers seems to lack spirit, dedication, and discipline. "Today you got guys in here who have never broken an egg," a New Jersey Mafia leader complained in a conversation bugged by the FBI. (Rowan, 1986, p. 24)

So, in the tradition of corporate America, at least as interpreted by law enforcement officials, Italian organized criminals have elected to make deals in lieu of using intimidation.

This is the federal law enforcement version of Darwin's theory of natural selection. Old groups give way to new and better adapted ones. The new groups assume the old Mafia functions, and the Mafia moves on into new enterprises such as the disposal of toxic wastes, securities fencing, and fraud. Essentially, the same alien conspiracies remain; the only difference is that occasionally they involve new aliens.

It is interesting to note that as federal law enforcement agencies scramble to account for new forces in illicit markets without seriously impairing their myth of organized crime, they still rely on the tenets of an old myth and on old tactics. In the early twentieth century alcohol was viewed as the vice of cultural enemies, an alien conspiracy that would ruin the country. The temperance movement was spurred by a panic over the diminution of traditional rural, middle-class, white, Protestant, lifestyles in the United States. As Joseph Gusfield (1963) comments:

> Increasingly the problem of liquor control became the central issue around which was posed the conflict between new and old cultural forces in American society. On the one side were the Wets—a union of cultural sophistication and secularism with Catholic lower-class traditionalism. These represented the new additions to the American population that made up the increasingly powerful political force of urban politics. On the other were the defenders of fundamental religion, or old moral values, of the ascetic, cautious, and sober middle class that had been the ideal of Americans in the nineteenth century. (pp. 122–123, 124)

So, like organized crime in the 1990s, liquor in the 1890s was a foreign, alien impingement on an otherwise righteous society.

The same fear of alien influence can be seen in discussions surrounding early narcotics legislation. Despite the fact that the 250,000 addicts in the United States at the turn of the century were predominantly middle-aged, middle-class, white women (Brecher, 1972), the problem of drugs was laid squarely at the feet of aliens.

> In the nineteenth century addicts were identified with foreign groups and internal minorities who were already actively feared and the objects of elaborate and massive social and legal restraints. Two repressed groups which were associated with the use of certain drugs were the Chinese and the Negroes. The Chinese and their custom of opium smoking were

closely watched after their entry into the United States about 1870. At first, the Chinese represented only one more group brought in to help build the railroads, but, particularly after economic depressions made them a labor surplus and a threat to American citizens, many forms of antagonism arose to drive them out, or at least to isolate them. Along with the prejudice came a fear of opium smoking as one of the ways in which the Chinese were supposed to undermine American society.

Cocaine was especially feared in the South by 1900 because of its euphoric and stimulating properties. The South feared that Negro cocaine users might become oblivious of their prescribed bounds and attack white society . . .

Evidence does not suggest that cocaine caused a crime wave but rather that anticipation of black rebellion inspired white alarm. Anecdotes often told of superhuman strength, cunning, and efficiency resulting from cocaine. One of the most terrifying beliefs about cocaine was that it actually improved pistol marksmanship. Another myth, that cocaine made blacks almost unaffected by mere .32 caliber bullets, is said to have caused southern police departments to switch to .38 caliber revolvers. These fantasies characterized white fear, not the reality of cocaine's effects, and gave one more reason for the repression of blacks.

By 1914 prominent newspapers, physicians, pharmacists, and congressmen believed opiates and cocaine predisposed habitués toward insanity and crime. They were widely seen as substances associated with foreigners or alien subgroups. Cocaine raised the specter of the wild Negro, opium the devious Chinese, morphine the tramps in the slums, it was feared that use of all these drugs was spreading into the "higher classes." (Musto, 1973, pp. 5–7, 65; cited in McCaghy & Cernkovich, 1987)

The fear of immigrants and repressed racial and ethnic groups in the United States was used to construct a conspiracy myth of drug use, just as it was used to construct a conspiracy myth of organized crime. The argument has always been the same: forces outside mainstream U.S. culture are at work to pervert an otherwise morally sound, industrious, and democratic people. It is a convenient and easily understood argument. It is, in fact, the only depiction of organized crime that could gain widespread popular appeal. To suggest that righteous citizens are being perverted, intimidated, and forced into vice by alien forces is far more palatable than suggesting that public demands for illicit drugs, sex, and gambling invite the creation of organized crime groups. Despite the minor alterations in the alien conspiracy myth, its revisionist form is only a slight variation of the Mafia myth.

◇

HISTORICAL MYTHS OF ORGANIZED CRIME

The "constructed proofs" used to justify the alien conspiracy myth range from the dubious to the preposterous. The assertion that the Sicilian Mafia was transplanted to the United States in the waves of Italian immigration is open to question. Research on the Mafia in Sicily indicates that it was never a highly structured criminal conspiracy; rather, it was an intermediary and fragmented force of mercenaries providing local control of the peasantry for absentee landlords (Blok, 1971). In addition, it is more than a little curious why other nations that received waves of Italian immigrants at the same time as the United States failed to develop anything even close to the U.S. version of the Mafia (Potter & Jenkins, 1985). The importation myth derives from a combination of press sensationalism and nativist sentiments in the United States (Smith, 1976, p. 1975).

The great revolution in organized crime, the Castellamarese War, never happened. Rather than the forty assassinations credited to the "young turks" led by Lucky Luciano, only four possibly related murders have been identified after extensive research efforts. In addition, serious questions have been raised about the logistical improbabilities of such an uprising (Block, 1978; Nelli, 1976). The Kefauver Committee heard a great deal of testimony about organized crime and its role in gambling. However, it failed to produce a single knowledgeable witness who even mentioned the Mafia (Smith, 1975). The investigation of the Apalachin conclave was so tangled in New York state politics that no one really knows what happened there, who was there, or what they were doing. The sparse information which is available is amenable to many more credible explanations than that of an international Mafia conclave (Albini, 1971). Finally, the 1963 testimony of Joe Valachi and subsequent statements by alleged Mafia turncoat, Jimmy "the Weasel" Fratianno, have been shown to be riddled with contradictions, factual errors and uncorroborated assertions. Neither of these informers was in any position to provide the insights credited to them (Albanese, 1996; Morris & Hawkins, 1970). As another "informer" commented:

> I remember when Joe [Valachi] was testifying before that Senate committee [McClellan] back in 1963. I was sitting in Raymond Patriarca's office [New England mob boss] . . . and we were watching Joe on television. I remember Raymond saying: "This bastard's crazy. Who the hell is he? . . . What the hell's the Cosa Nostra?" Henry asked, "Is he a soldier or a button man? . . . I'm a zipper." "I'm a flipper." It was a big joke to them. (Teresa, 1973, pp. 24–25, 28)

Rather than substance, the alien conspiracy myth is supported by the testimony of a few government-sponsored informants and public release of heavily edited and carefully selected police files and surveillance transcripts—all tied together by official speculation. Peter Reuter (1983), in his meticulous research on organized crime, has questioned both the knowledgeability of the government (pointing to problems and inaccuracies in the monitoring of legal, open, and public industries) and the inherent bias in the data collection process utilized by law enforcement agencies seeking evidence to support their own assumptions about organized crime. If other groups had been subjected to the same level of wire-tapping, surveillance, interrogation, arrest and comprehensive investigation as groups of aged Italians, federal officials would no doubt have been startled to learn that "new" organized crime groups were not new at all—some have been active for the past century.

◇

EMPIRICAL EVIDENCE AND ORGANIZED CRIME

Virtually every empirical study of organized crime has reached conclusions diametrically opposed to those in the official myth. Studies have demonstrated that rather than being a tightly structured, clearly defined, stable entity, organized crime operates in a loosely structured, informal, open system. Organized crime is made up of a series of highly adaptive, flexible networks that readily take into account changes in the law and regulatory practices, the growth or decline of market demand for a particular good or service, and the availability of new sources of supply and new opportunities for distribution. It is this ability to adapt that allows organized crime to persist and flourish. The inflexible, clan-based corporate entities described by law enforcement agencies could not survive in this turbulent environment.

It makes far more sense to conceive of organized crime as a partnership arrangement, or a patron-client arrangement, rather than as an immutable bureaucratic structure with a clearly defined hierarchy. Mark Haller's (1987) research reveals that organizations such as those surrounding the Capone gang and Meyer Lansky's extensive operations were in reality a series of small-scale business partnerships, usually involving several senior "partners" (Capone, Nitti, Lansky) and many junior partners who sometimes conducted business in concert with one another and often conducted business separately. Organized crime was not directed by Lansky or Capone in any bureaucratic sense but was merely a series of investment and joint business ventures.

After his study of organized crime in Detroit, Joseph Albini (1971) concluded that organized crime was made up of certain criminal patrons who traded information, connections with government officials, and access to a network of operatives in exchange for the clients' economic and political support. The roles of client and patron fluctuated depending on the enterprise; combinations were formed, dissolved and reformed with new actors. William Chambliss' (1978) study of organized crime in Seattle depicts an overlapping series of crime networks with shifting memberships highly adaptive to the economic, political and social exigencies of the community—without a centralized system of control. Alan Block's (1979) study of the cocaine trade in New York concluded that the drug trade was operated by "small, flexible organizations of criminals that arise due to opportunity and environmental factors" (pp. 94–95). John Gardiner's (1970) study of corruption and vice in "Wincanton," Ianni's (1974, 1972) two studies of organized crime in New York, and a study of organized crime in Philadelphia (Potter & Jenkins, 1985) reach similar conclusions. Peter Reuter's (1983) study of Italian organized crime in New York found that no group exercises control over entrepreneurs in gambling and loansharking. Reuter concludes that rather than the officially depicted view of organized crime as a monolithic conspiracy, it is in fact characterized by conflict and fragmentation.

The empirical research clearly reveals that organized crime is made up of small, fragmented, and ephemeral enterprises. There are very practical reasons for this. First, small size and segmentation reduce the chances of getting caught and prosecuted. Since employees in illicit industries are the greatest threat to those operations, and make the best witnesses against them, it is an organizational necessity for organized crime groups to limit the number of people who have knowledge about the group's operations. This is achieved by small size and segmentation so that employees only know about their own jobs and their own level of activity in the enterprise. Such arrangements are clear in the gambling and drug industries. In gambling, runners and collectors are distanced from the bank itself (Potter, 1994). In drug trafficking, the production, importation, distribution, and retail activities are kept as discrete functions, often performed by completely different organized crime groups, most of which are both temporary and small (Hellman, 1980; Wisotsky, 1986).

For the same reasons that organized crime groups choose to limit the number of employees, they also tend to limit the geographic areas they serve. The larger the geographic area, the more tenuous communication becomes, requiring either the use of the telephone (and the threat of electronic surveillance) or long trips to pass on routine information in person, a most inefficient means of managing a business. In addition, the larger the geographic area served, the greater the number of law enforcement agencies involved and the higher the costs of corruption (Wisotsky, 1986). In his study of New York, Reuter (1983) found no evidence of centralization in gambling and loansharking, and he argues persuasively that in drug trafficking even less permanence and centralization is found.

The evidence also calls into question the assumption in the official myth that organized criminals act as the corrupters of public officials. Available evidence indicates that a more accurate perspective is that organized criminals, legitimate businessmen, and government officials are all equal players in a marketplace of corruption. Each brings to the market things wanted by the others, and routine series of exchanges occur. The purveyors of illicit goods and services wish to exchange their products, money, and influence for protection, selective enforcement against competitors, and favorable policy decisions by government authorities. Public officials put their policy-making and enforcement powers on the market. Who initiates such a deal depends upon circumstances, and the initiator is as likely to be the "legitimate" actor as the "criminal."

It is not uncommon for a series of exchanges between the under- and upperworlds to develop into a long-term corrupt relationship. Studies have shown that in some cases those who occupy positions of public trust are the organizers of crime (Block & Scarpitti, 1985; Chambliss, 1978; Gardiner, 1970; Gardiner & Lyman, 1978; Potter & Jenkins, 1985). Investigations of police corruption in Philadelphia and New York have demonstrated how thoroughly institutionalized corruption can be among public servants. In the private sector, respected institutions such as Shearson/American Express, Merrill Lynch, the

Miami National Bank, Citibank, and others have eagerly participated in illicit ventures (Lernoux, 1984; Moldea, 1986; *Organized Crime Digest,* 1987; President's Commission on Organized Crime, 1984). For example, a study of the savings and loan "scandals" found that "these conspiracies more closely approximate organized crime than corporate crime" (Calavita & Pontell, 1993, p. 519). Public officials are not the pawns of organized crime; they are part of its fabric—the part found in America's respected institutions.

The investigations of the Bank of Credit and Commerce International (BCCI) and its illegal activities around the world provide ample confirmation of the cozy relationship between drug traffickers, white-collar criminals, the intelligence community, and leading politicians in the United States.

> It offered full banking services to facilitate transactions that no one else would touch. It was the bank for drug dealers, arms dealers, money launderers—indeed whoever had an illegal project and money to hide . . . [BCCI was] a kind of Federal Express for illicit goods . . . ready to move currency, gold, weapons, drugs for anyone who wanted them moved. (Meddis, 1991, p. 9A)

BCCI's illegal activities covered the gamut of organized crime, white-collar crime and political crime:
- laundering at least $14 million in narcotic profits for the Colombian cocaine cartels, shifting money to banks in the Bahamas, Britain, France, Uruguay, and Luxembourg to avoid detection (Schmaltz, 1988).
- playing a major role in the Iran-Contra scandal by acting as a conduit for weapons deals involving international arms merchant Adrian Khashoggi and drug deals (which funded the arms purchases) involving Panamanian president Manuel Noriega (Waldman et al., 1991). It is alleged that BCCI also served as a conduit for CIA funds destined for the Contras to support illegal arms deals and Contra-backed cocaine trafficking (Cauchon, 1991).

While the full extent of its criminal activities may never be known, BCCI was a major criminal enterprise operating within the corporate sector with cooperation from other "legitimate" financiers and businesses and with, at the very least, the acquiescence of those government agencies charged with ferreting out drug trafficking, terrorism, and business corruption. In fact organized corruption can become so entangled with the normal operations of government that it creates organized crime activities of its own, activities labeled as state-organized crime. State-organized crime consists of acts described by law as criminal and committed by state officials in pursuit of their jobs as representatives of the state (Chambliss, 1989).

James Mills (1986) charges that the United States government is a major player in international drug crime networks. "The largest narcotics conspirator in the world is the government of the United States whose intelligence agencies conspire with or ignore the complicity of officials at the highest levels in at least

33 countries" (p. 160). Presenting evidence that clearly contradicts the idea of an underground criminal conspiracy and strongly supports Chambliss' model of "state-organized crime," Mills describes organized crime in the drug trade this way:

> The international narcotics industry could not exist without the coopera-
> tion of corrupt governments. Our own government leans over backward
> to conceal this from the public—to recognize it would cripple foreign re-
> lations . . . The highly connected, tuxedo-clad criminal is left in place to
> provide intelligence to the United States—and drugs to its citizens . . . To
> assuage the public, politicians will continue to wage a civil war, one
> above-ground sector of the government attacking the drug traffic on
> front pages and the seven o'clock news, another underground sector se-
> cretly permitting the traffic, at times promoting it. (pp. 1140–1141)

As Mills suggests, the reason why some drug traffickers prosper and grow powerful while others are caught and incarcerated may depend more on their political protection than on their ruthlessness. Since World War II, one of the most critical sources of institutional protection for the drug trade has been the Central Intelligence Agency (CIA) (Marshall, 1991).

Finally, the role of ethnicity in determining the structure of organized crime is misinterpreted and overstated by the alien conspiracy myth. There is ample evidence that many organized crime groups are made up of individuals of varied ethnic backgrounds or those who cooperate on a regular basis with individuals of various ethnic backgrounds (Abadinsky, 1997; Block, 1979; Pennsylvania Crime Commission, 1986; Potter & Jenkins, 1985). As Haller's (1987) study of Lansky's and Capone's enterprises makes clear, organized criminals who wish to survive and prosper quickly learn the limits of kinship, ethnicity and violence and proceed to form lucrative business partnerships on the basis of rational business decisions and common needs.

In those cases where organized crime networks do demonstrate ethnic homogeneity, it is merely a reflection of the exigencies of urban social life, not the machinations of a secret, ethnic conspiracy. It makes sense that vice in an African-American neighborhood is going to be primarily delivered by an Afri-can-American crime network. Similarly, illicit goods and services in an Italian neighborhood will probably be delivered by entrepreneurs of Italian lineage. This is not an organizational design but merely a reflection of the constituency of small, geographically compact, organized crime networks.

HEADHUNTING

The alien conspiracy myth has dictated an enforcement strategy based on its precepts. Since Prohibition, the federal effort against organized crime has involved identifying and prosecuting group members for *any* available offense. Many times, these offenses are unrelated to illicit entrepreneurship and are often comparatively minor infractions. This strategy is predicated on the assumption that the actual conspiracy is too complex and well organized to be proved in court. As we shall see, this rationale is also part of the myth; the actual structure of organized crime operations is not as complex as the myth asserts.

The myth of conspiracy actually becomes an excuse for a lack of success in controlling organized crime. In the headhunting strategy, success is calculated in the form of a body count. Arrests, indictments and convictions are used to justify budgets and to ask for new enforcement powers. Because the conspiracy myth places a high premium on position in the hierarchy, the assumption has been that the farther up that hierarchy an arrest goes, the more disruptive it is to the business of organized crime. The most prized catch is the "boss" of a Mafia family. If the alien conspiracy myth is correct, and these groups are tightly structured and disciplined, the incapacitation of a "boss" should be debilitating to the organization.

Of course, because of the myth of an insulated hierarchy, the culture of violence, the code of silence, and the fidelity of clannish conspirators, successful headhunting requires a massive arsenal of law enforcement powers—powers that must be continually augmented and expanded. In addition, new laws creating new criminal categories (i.e., "drug kingpin," "racketeer") must be created so that heavy sentences and fines can be imposed on those convicted. Simply convicting them of the crimes with which they are charged would not be a sufficient deterrent; additional penalties must be included.

All of this and more was provided by the Racketeer Influenced Corrupt Organization Act in 1970. RICO provided for special grand juries to look for evidence, created a more potent immunity law, eased requirements for proving perjury, provided for protective custody of government witnesses, weakened the defense's capacity to cross-examine and exclude illegally obtained evidence, expanded federal jurisdiction to cover conspiracy to obstruct *state* law, and increased prison sentences. It is a curious but seldom noted fact that the Nixon administration, which was responsible for the passage of RICO, chose to ignore organized crime and used the provisions of the act to prosecute anti-Vietnam war protesters (Chambliss & Block, 1981). In addition, RICO has civil provisions that allow the government to pursue what the Justice Department has called a "scorched earth" approach to organized crime—seizing assets and "leaving the mobster with nothing but a return address in federal prison" (Kahler, 1986).

As is the case with many law enforcement programs, rigorous assessments of the headhunting strategy are not available. When organized criminals are successfully prosecuted, this is used as evidence that the strategy is working. When convictions are not forthcoming or when the penalties imposed seem mild, law enforcement complains that "its hands are tied"—that it lacks sufficient resources or legal authority to implement the headhunting strategy. Each of these rationalizations once again reenforces the original myth that organized crime is a highly complex and well structured operation.

Despite the fact that comprehensive statistics are not kept on how many organized criminals have been put away, some fragmentary data is available to suggest the scope of the headhunting effort. A 1986 *Fortune* magazine article listed the "top 50" Mafia bosses (based on interviews with law enforcement officials). The article showed that fifteen of the fifty were in jail, ten were indicted or on trial, and one was a fugitive (Rowan, 1986). This included eight of the top ten. Since the publication of that article twenty-four of the remaining "free" crime leaders have been indicted or jailed. If we look specifically at the fabled five families of New York, we find that all of the top leaders of the Colombo, Bormano, and Lucchese groups have been incapacitated, along with half of the Genovese group's leaders. From 1981–1985, seventeen of the twenty-four alleged Mafia bosses across the country were indicted or convicted (President's Commission on Organized Crime, 1984). In 1984 alone, organized crime indictments totaled 2,194, almost exclusively alleged Mafia group members.

In addition, conviction rates and sentences have also been going up. The General Accounting Office (GAO) estimated that the conviction rate rose from 56% to 76% in the period from 1972 to 1980 (Albanese, 1996). The GAO also noted a concomitant increase in prison terms handed down for convictions.

The problem with all of this is that the government has failed to produce any evidence that these prosecutions have resulted in a diminution of organized crime's illicit ventures. The federal government simply has no means to measure the impact of its efforts against organized crime (Potter, 1994). There are, however, indicators that suggest that organized crime is alive and quite healthy despite the prosecutorial efforts.

For example, prosecutions of one major gambling syndicate in Philadelphia in the early 1980s spawned at least two dozen other criminal networks in the same neighborhood to replace the targeted group (Pennsylvania Crime Commission, 1986). Major enforcement efforts directed at "syndicate heads" in Seattle and "Wincanton" resulted in minimal restructuring of street-level operations and no discernible impact on the provision of illicit goods and services (Chambliss, 1978; Gardiner, 1970). Major prosecutions in New York directed at labor racketeering and drug trafficking have had the effect of weeding out inefficient and highly visible operators, leaving more viable organized crime groups in their wake (Chambliss & Block, 1981). Recent prosecutions aimed at the pornography syndicate have resulted in the creation of at least six new groups and the revival of another that had been closed down ten years earlier by successful prosecution (Potter, 1986). Studies of the organization of vice have demonstrated consistently that prosecutions have only negligible impact on the provision of illicit goods and services and the operation of organized crime groups (Albini, 1971; Reuter et al., 1983).

The reason that no impact on organized crime can be demonstrated as a result of the headhunting approach is that it is based on myth. Organized crime groups learned long ago that to be successful in a threatening legal environment they must be prepared to adapt their structures and practices. The irony of the situation is that the more successful federal prosecutors become in incarcerating organized crime leaders, the more the industry responds by decentralizing and maintaining temporary and ephemeral working relationships. Because the headhunting approach never disables more than a small proportion of the total number of organized crime entrepreneurs at any given time, it actually strengthens and rewards some organized crime groups by weeding out their inefficient competitors.

It should also be pointed out that headhunting often involves targeting the easiest cases. Public prosecutions of highly visible (not necessarily highly skilled) crime figures is good press, but has very little impact. The selection of "Little Nicky" Scarfo for federal prosecution had left the field open for far more powerful and dangerous crime figures. While Scarfo had been designated as the head of organized crime in Philadelphia by federal investigators and the press, his actual role and influence were highly suspect. The differences between Scarfo and his associates who were prosecuted (with mixed success) and those who have been left more or less alone illustrate the failure of the federal enforcement effort.

Scarfo was a small-time hood who lacked political influence and had a minuscule share of the illicit market (considerably less than the 25% of the gambling market credited to his vastly more competent predecessor Angelo Bruno) (Potter & Jenkins, 1985). In addition, Scarfo's vision of criminal enterprise was decidedly limited, highlighted by capers such as an extortion scheme directed at hot dog vendors in Atlantic City (Demaris, 1986).

Active in Philadelphia during the same time as Scarfo were individuals identified by a variety of sources as controlling a great deal of political clout and a large share of the illicit market. At least one gambler had run a $35 million a year numbers bank virtually unmolested for three decades. An attorney, identified several times in print as the emissary of Meyer Lansky and later of Alvin Malnik, continued to grant favors from his plush offices, allegedly as the sole license-granting authority for illicit activities in Atlantic City (Demaris, 1986). A local realtor whose cocktail parties for judicial candidates were among the premier events of the political season continued to be the primary landlord for the pornography syndicate (Potter, 1986). Not to belabor the point, there were at least two dozen other operatives of similar stature who operated with relative immunity, while the federal government pursued "Little Nicky" with a vengeance far in excess of his importance or his capacity for future importance. It is the relative immunity of major figures in organized crime, such as money launderers, corrupt public officials, and other individuals who serve as bridges between the underworld and the upperworld, that so clearly demonstrates the deficiencies in the myth of organized crime on which headhunting strategies are based.

A relatively recent case that captured headlines was the conviction of John Gotti on murder and racketeering charges. Federal prosecutors were quick to capitalize on the Gotti conviction by calling him "the most powerful criminal in America" and predicting that his conviction would bring chaos to the well-structured world of the Cosa Nostra. A quick review of the facts of the Gotti case as revealed in testimony from the trials and the transcripts of wiretaps presented at those trials offers a very different picture.

No one will quarrel with John Gotti's involvement with criminal activities. He has a "rap sheet" that includes hijacking, public intoxication, drug charges, assault, theft, burglary, gambling, and murder. Gotti is heard on the wiretaps alternately threatening, boasting, bragging and whining about the state of his criminal career. It is precisely this view of John Gotti, however, that is most troubling. For a man being touted as "the most powerful criminal in America," he has had a conspicuously troubled career, marked by a series of arrests and a string of unsuccessful criminal acts. John Gotti's career as an organized criminal has been somewhat limited. It is true that he ran a very large dice game in Manhattan. On the other hand, the wiretaps reveal that he was a notoriously bad gambler, frequently losing $60,000 to $70,000 a day. At one point on the tapes he complains that his luck was so bad he would "have to go on welfare." It is also true that Gotti provided leadership to a den of thieves operating out of the "Bergin Hunt and Fish Club." It is equally true that the members of his "crew" frequently complained about his inability to come up with targets for scores and his inability to create income-producing opportunities in other illicit ventures.

While in past trials prosecutors have alleged that Gotti had connections to several drug operations, most of the schemes hatched by his associates failed and resulted in the loss of money. While the wiretaps show Gotti to be a man who thought nothing of using intimidation or threats, they also clearly demonstrate that he was frequently out of control in this regard. He threatened to kill people with regularity—a very dangerous and costly action for a criminal entrepreneur to engage in repeatedly. He also pursued a series of personal, non-business-related vendettas, allegedly including the disappearance of a neighbor. His bail was once revoked because of an incident resulting from a fight over a parking space. While prosecutors have been successful in portraying Gotti as a dangerous sociopath, they have not been successful in portraying him as a major organized crime figure.

Simply put, John Gotti is no Meyer Lansky, no Sidney Korshak, no Alvin Malnik. It is simply inconceivable that someone in Lansky's position would have resorted to physical violence over a parking space. It is equally inconceivable that Lansky would be arrested with shocking regularity for nearly every venture he undertook. And, of course, it is inconceivable that Lansky would be tape recorded threatening to "whack" every other punk with whom he came in contact. The evidence presented against John Gotti portrays him as a hood and a criminal. A hoodlum with a long criminal record and frequent press notices does not qualify one as the head of organized crime. It does, however, make one an excellent target for a headhunting campaign. John Gotti is another in a long list of careless, boastful, somewhat unsuccessful pretenders who are easy prey for public prosecution. The simple fact is that there are hundreds of John Gottis out there.

Men like John Berkery of Philadelphia's K&A gang, Buster Riggins of Washington, DC's sex rings, Jimmy Lambert of Kentucky's cocaine trade, and

José Battle of the "Cuban Mafia" are every bit as formidable, powerful, and dangerous as Gotti. Every one of them, if we used John Gotti as a model, is a model candidate for "the most powerful criminal in America." To single Gotti out for a leadership role is to misunderstand organized crime and to confuse real power with notoriety. Gotti's alleged heroin operation, for example, was really headed by Mark Reiter and Angelo Ruggerio. They engaged in a series of opportunistic (and unsuccessful) drug deals involving amounts of drugs and money minute in comparison to the activities of dozens of other drug merchants.

There is no indication of a monopoly or even dominance in the New York drug market by these actors; in fact, there is considerable evidence that they were fairly small operators. The "Bergin crew" was just that. It was not an offshoot of a powerful syndicate; it was an informal, social network of hoods. The "Members" came together to run a dice game, to do some "muscle work" for a loanshark, or to rob a drug dealer. They never formed a cohesive criminal organization. They were a group of individuals forming and reforming a series of criminal partnerships, some of which involved John Gotti. Even Gotti's most successful criminal venture, his crap game, involved a constantly changing series of participants from a number of crime networks.

While the evidence may have been strong enough for federal prosecutors to allege a criminal organization for RICO purposes, it was not strong enough to suggest anything beyond an informal, loosely structured, ephemeral criminal network. Evidence presented in the case suggested that almost all of New York City was bugged by one agency or another. Literally thousands of hours of conversations were recorded, most of which were irrelevant to the carefully edited versions presented as evidence of a criminal conspiracy. Testimony in the Gotti case described in detail the careers of the informers the government used against Gotti, men like James Cardinale, "Willie Boy" Johnson, Matthew Traynor, and "Crazy Sally" Polisi. It is not a pretty picture. Stories of drugs being supplied in prisons, sexual impropriety by informers and prosecutors, and outright deals allowing the continuation and furtherance of criminal activity by government witnesses were repeated in detail. The impression left is that the government sometimes authorizes one set of criminal activities in order to trap other crime figures doing precisely the same thing.

One other issue needs to be discussed before moving on—headhunting does not always result in successful prosecutions. For example, charges against Jack Nardi, Jr., a Teamsters Union official, were dismissed on October 9, 1985. In May 1986, all six defendants in the celebrated trial of "Matty the Horse" Ianniello were acquitted in a RICO prosecution in New York. The defendants had been charged with trying to defraud Con Edison. The jury found that charge either laudable or impossible and acquitted the defendants. It took the government five very expensive tries to convict Gotti. In the previous four trials he was acquitted because, as prosecutors admitted, the jury simply refused to believe turncoat criminals who had been given very lenient sentences in return for testimony. And on December 12, 1987, "Little Nicky" Scarfo and four of his alleged "family" members were acquitted in a drug case. The summation from the jury was simple: "the jury looked at this case that they put on and it stunk" (*Organized Crime Digest*, 1987). The point of this litany of defeats is not to suggest that federal prosecutors are incompetent but merely to demonstrate that the credibility of the alien conspiracy myth is weakening with juries around the country.

The idea that vigorous prosecution and stiff criminal penalties will win the war against organized crime is at variance not only with current research on organized crime but with historic precedent as well. Literally thousands of cases in which organized crime figures have been arrested, convicted, and imprisoned in the last fifty years could be cited here. The fundamental question remains—so what? There is no evidence that these successful prosecutions have in any way negatively impacted or altered the activities of organized entrepreneurial groups in illicit markets.

◊

CONTROLLING ORGANIZED CRIME

Our efforts to control and eradicate organized crime have failed. They have failed for two basic reasons: the headhunting strategy is predicated on false assumptions about the importance of "bosses," and the alien conspiracy myth is bankrupt in its understanding of illicit enterprises. Organized crime groups operate in a complex web of interrelated and tangled environments. They are impacted by the opportunities and constraints of the market, the legal system, politics, "upperworld" commerce, and the community in which they operate. Most attempts to analyze organized crime focus almost exclusively on *criminal* actions. Traditionally, analyses of organized crime have concentrated attention on the deviant aspects of organized crime rather than on its institutionalized and normative aspects. In Chambliss' (1978) words this emphasis has "obscured perception of the degree to which the structure of America's law and politics creates and perpetuates syndicates that supply the vices in our major cities" (p. 6).

Empirical research on organized crime suggests that in order to understand it, we must understand its social context. That social context is defined by two consistent threads running through the organization of crime: official corruption and the exigencies of the political economy. The evidence is compelling that organized crime should not be conceptualized as a dysfunction in society, nor as an alien force impinging upon society. Rather, organized crime is part and parcel of the political economic system. Once again, Chambliss (1978), in commenting on the organization of vice in Seattle, makes the degree of integration clear:

> Working for, and with, this cabal of respectable community members is a staff which coordinates the daily activities of prostitution, gambling, bookmaking, the sale and distribution of drugs, and other vices. Representatives from each of these groups, comprising the political and eco-

nomic power centers of the community, meet regularly to distribute profits, discuss problems, and make the necessary organizational and policy decisions essential to the maintenance of a profitable, trouble-free business. (p. 6)

This point of view has compelling implications for policy. The argument advanced here suggests that policymakers have been attacking the wrong targets in their battle against organized crime.

Dwight Smith (1978) observes that law enforcement strategy traditionally "has rested on the belief that acts of crime are the sole responsibility of the perpetrator, and that as a consequence of removing him from society, the criminal acts would disappear" (p. 162). However, the evidence suggests that the existence of illicit drug dealers, loansharks, gamblers, and other illegal entrepreneurs is due to the fact that the legitimate marketplace leaves a number of potential customers for these services unserved. The control of organized crime can be achieved only with a greater understanding of organizational and market behavior, by "learning how to reduce the domain of the illicit [entrepreneur] . . . and a wider appreciation of the entire market spectrum, and a deeper analysis of the dynamics that nurture its illicit aspects" (pp. 175–176). Smith argues that an understanding of the "task environment" of particular enterprises will promote a better and more comprehensive understanding of how such illicit enterprises emerge, survive, and make a profit from crime.

In rethinking strategies to control organized crime, we must begin by conceptualizing organized crime as a business, not an alien conspiracy. Doing so will direct us to efforts that will improve our understanding of the causes of organized criminal behavior and the means used to organize illicit enterprises. In addition, this view directs our attention toward the elimination of arbitrary distinctions between legal and illegal goods and services (particularly in gambling, lending, drug distribution and sexual services) and the importance of corruption in the ability of organized crime to prosper. Chambliss (1978) supports this view in his study of organized crime in Seattle.

Money is the oil of our present-day machinery, and elected public officials are the pistons that keep the machine operating. Those who come up with the oil, whatever its source, are in a position to make the machinery run the way they want it to. Crime is an excellent producer of capitalism's oil. Those who want to affect the direction of the machine's output find that the money produced by crime is as effective in helping them get where they can go as is the money produced in any other way. Those who produce the money from crime thus become the people most likely to control the effectively working political economy. Crime is, in fact, a cornerstone on which the political and economic relations of democratic-capitalistic societies are constructed.

In every city of the United States, and in many other countries as well, criminal organizations sell sex and drugs, provide an opportunity to gamble, to watch pornographic films, or to obtain a loan, an abortion or a special favor. Their profits are a mainstay of the electoral process of America and their business is an important (if unrecorded) part of the gross national product. The business of organized crime in the United States may gross as much as one hundred billion dollars annually . . . the profits are immense, and the proportion of the gross national product represented by money flowing from crime cannot be gainsaid. Few nations in the world have economies that compare with the economic output of criminal activities in the United States. (pp. 1–2)

So, rather than directing control efforts in an enforcement direction aimed at specific individuals or groups, a realistic view of organized crime points to the importance of the market and the political arrangements which sustain organized crime.

The way we conceptualize and understand organized crime dictates the means selected to control it. While detailed policy alternatives are beyond the scope of this discussion, several thematic departures from present policy are dictated by what we know about organized crime. The most important of those policy departures may well be consideration of steps necessary to shrink and control the market for the goods and services of organized crime.

◇
REDUCING MARKET DEMAND

The largest and most profitable organized crime enterprises are those that provide illicit goods and services to a significant segment of the public eager to obtain them. Among the most important services are drug trafficking, gambling, prostitution, and loansharking. One approach to limiting the demand for these goods is to punish the consumer. In addition to being practically and politically unpalatable, we have also seen that historically (especially with regard to drugs) such tactics have had precisely the opposite effect of the one intended.

Another approach is available, however. The first objective of control policies aimed at organized crime should be reducing the size of the illicit market and the profits emanating from that market—in other words, decriminalization. Laws against consensual crimes create remarkable opportunities for criminal entrepreneurs. The laws against vice are almost unenforceable. All of these behaviors require cooperation between buyer and seller. There is no victim to call the police; there is no complainant to instigate an investigation. As a direct result, these laws are enforced in a highly selective and discriminatory manner. Individuals who are unlucky enough to be arrested under the gambling, drug, and prostitution statutes are almost always the most visible and the easiest to catch.

Enforcement of the laws fills the prisons with junkies and streetwalkers. Ironically, the enforcement of these laws strengthens organized crime rather than controlling it. Those who will be apprehended are the smallest operators—those with the least organization, the least power, and the least expertise. Organized crime groups find that the law weeds out the inefficient and small operators. Enforcing the law leaves the entire illicit market open to exploitation by better organized, more successful criminal enterprises.

The law helps organized crime in a number of other ways as well. Since these types of goods and services are in demand but illegal, organized crime groups can charge dearly for their services. The profits reaped in the heroin and cocaine markets alone are staggering, and it is only the illegality of the drug that makes these profits possible. The immense sums of money realized from entrepreneurship in the illicit market facilitate the purchase of a web of police and political protection.

In view of the fact that the laws are dysfunctional and the markets enormous, it makes sense to end arbitrary distinctions between legal and illegal activities. Organized crime scholars have long argued that decriminalization or legalization is one way to reduce the market domain of organized crime (Albanese, 1996; Albini, 1971; Anderson, 1979; Luksetich & White, 1982). Merely removing the criminal label from gambling, loansharking, prostitution, and drug trafficking—and even legalizing and regulating them—would not eliminate organized crime's involvement entirely.

Legalized off-track betting in New York did not drive bookmakers out of business. It did, however, constrain their activity. They must offer odds within the limits of those being offered by the state. They must be restrained in their collection methods. Most importantly, bookmaking profits appear to have stabilized at between 5 and 10% (Reuter, 1983). Decriminalization would similarly constrain commerce in the most profitable enterprises in organized crime's portfolio. As long as the profits are high and the risks diffuse, criminal entrepreneurs will continue to engage in these activities. It simply makes sense to take some of the profit out of these markets.

Decriminalization of the illicit goods and services which are at the core of the business of organized crime may be difficult to achieve. The same forces that gave rise to the alien conspiracy myth make decriminalization a difficult option for policymakers to exercise. Americans have historically been unwilling to acknowledge their own role in creating a market for prostitution, gambling, loansharking, drugs, and the like—preferring to label certain acts deviant and criminal rather than accepting them as social constants in society. Decriminalizing, or even legalizing, such activities might be viewed as condoning them or as catering to moral "defects" in the "weaker" members of society. If the political reality remains such that the laws cannot be changed to shrink organized crime's market, then the focus of current law enforcement efforts must be changed to address the problem of organized crime more effectively. Specific policies should be formulated to address the "laundering" of illicit funds, corruption of officials, and improved intelligence and surveillance to target those in control of illegal operations.

◈

FIGHTING CORRUPTION

It is axiomatic to organized crime that it cannot flourish without a favorable political environment—meaning systematic abuses of the public trust. While there is no reason to believe that the customers of organized crime can be deterred from seeking illicit goods and services, there is every reason to believe that corruption can be deterred. Instead of wasting valuable resources on surveillance of criminals with a "bad reputation," government should focus attention on finding individuals who serve as links between the underworld and the upperworld. Bribery, campaign contributions, delivery of votes, and other favors are used to influence legislators, city council members, mayors, judges, district attorneys, and others (Potter, 1994).

It is not possible to place organized crime in a social context without exploring its relationships with the political system. Politicians can guarantee that organized crime is able to continue uninterrupted operations with a minimum of official governmental interference. At a minimum, increased and more comprehensive reporting of assets and sources of income should be required of public officials in key decision-making positions. Closer supervision of public officials and strengthening of conflict of interest laws are required. Obviously, greater restrictions on contributions to political candidates could be enacted—for example, limiting private contributions to $100 or adopting public financing of political campaigns.

◈

CLEANING UP THE MONEY LAUNDRIES

The recent increase in drug-trafficking profits has focused attention on the critical role of financial institutions in laundering illicit incomes. Organized crime groups have become dependent on bankers, stockbrokers, lawyers, realtors, and others close to the financial community (Demaris, 1986; Lernoux, 1984; Moldea, 1986). As a first step, there should be a standardized federal requirement for corporate reporting in order to avoid the great variance in state regulations. At a minimum, sufficient information should be required so that investigators will be able to follow money trails with greater ease. Second, the enforcement of existing reporting regulations should be increased in areas involving large sums of money transferred between and among banks. Interbank transfers and wire transfers to foreign banks and corporations should be reported. Foreign currency transactions should be subjected to reporting requirements detailing where the money is going and why.

Certainly crimes committed by financial institutions and corporations as part of organized crime operations should be treated with the same severity as other crimes. If the federal government can justify putting labor union locals into receivership based on the criminal records of their officers, the same justification should hold for brokerage houses. Federal prosecutors should recognize that a corrupt organization is a corrupt organization whether it is the Mafia or Merrill Lynch. The seizure of corporate assets under the RICO statute should become as common as the confiscation of a drug dealer's Cadillac.

◇
IMPROVING INTELLIGENCE

Following the money, rather than the perpetrator, should be the hallmark of effective organized crime investigations. By tracing the path of illicit profits, law enforcement agencies would gain valuable information on cash deposits, property transactions, fund purchases, real estate ownership, and foreign currency transfers. It is a reality of organized crime that the point at which illicit wealth accumulates is also the point closest to the most powerful underworld operators.

The alien conspiracy myth translates into law enforcement intelligence gathering limited to preparing a "rogue's gallery" of ethnics with bad reputations. Obtaining useful intelligence on organized crime is admittedly difficult, but law enforcement agencies can vastly improve their understanding of organized crime by focusing on the development of an accurate picture of organized crime markets. Intelligence operations should follow the processes of distribution, supply, manufacturing and financing—regardless of who is involved—or whether they reside in the under- or upperworlds. This approach to intelligence means that analysts should be more concerned with assessing market, production, and social conditions that shape the patterns of organized criminals' interactions.

In addition, intelligence-gathering operations must be separated from operations designed to produce arrests and convictions. Intelligence gathering, when done correctly, is unlikely to result in quick arrests and certain convictions. Agencies under pressure to show results calculated by numbers of arrests tend to choose the easiest cases and to arrest the most obvious (and usually the least important) criminal operatives. These arrests inflate statistics and contribute little to our knowledge about organized crime. Intelligence gathering must be recognized as important on its own merits, and success must be measured by the quality of data produced, not prosecutors' batting averages. Reactive intelligence-gathering strategies must be replaced by intelligence operations sensitive to shifts in law, enforcement patterns, technology, markets and social trends.

None of these suggestions for changes in policy are new, nor are they likely to be embraced by policymakers. Attacking white-collar criminals is not as politically satisfying, nor as easy, as jailing highly visible and reasonably unimportant purveyors of vice on the street. The very fact that law enforcement agencies continue to base their control strategies on mythological characterization and continue to reject a comprehensive attack on organized crime clearly demonstrates the poverty of present policies of control.

Myths that Justify Crime
A Look at Corporate Crime in the United States

Myths of crime and criminal justice, for the most part, revolve around two central themes. First, there is a criminal act or behavior. That behavior is seized upon by the media, law enforcement bureaucracies, and politicians as a way to attract public attention and to win support for policy issues related to crime. The behavior is exaggerated through political rhetoric, sensational reporting, and misrepresentations to create a distorted view of the threat to society and to individuals in that society. The burgeoning myths frequently target minority populations or groups with unpopular beliefs. Thus, we have had crime scares about women and witchcraft, homosexuals and molested children, satanists and ritual murders, people of color and drugs, and immigrants and political subversion.

The second recurring theme in myths of crime and criminal justice is a massive law enforcement response to the behavior in question. New laws are passed outlawing certain aspects of the behavior, prison sentences are increased, new powers are granted to investigating agencies, and a proactive campaign of enforcement is launched in an attempt to control the perceived danger. In taking these steps we frequently overreact and make the problem we are trying to solve much worse than it was originally.

In this chapter, we explore a very different type of myth. This myth *downplays* the importance of criminal behavior and justifies a policy of *lax* enforcement. This myth mitigates responsibility and excuses misconduct. This myth argues for less enforcement, fewer laws, and less stringent punishment; it protects those with political and economic power. The mythology of

121

corporate crime consists of three myths that neutralize and explain this type of crime.

The first of these myths is that corporate criminality causes less damage, both economic and physical, than traditional "street crimes." Government officials have tried to present the issue of corporate crime in terms of individual misconduct and fraud, ignoring the more pervasive and dangerous criminality of corporations. The second myth is that corporate crimes are accidents or oversights—that they are unintended crimes lacking the criminal intent found in crimes of violence and theft (see Benson, 1996). The third myth is that current laws and enforcement efforts are more than sufficient to deal with the problem. This argument is frequently carried a step further to suggest that present laws are too stringent and severe and out of proportion to the danger of the behavior.

◈

"REAL" CRIME AND CORPORATE CRIME

When most people think of crime, they think of acts of interpersonal violence or property crimes. In the popular imagination, a crime is an act committed against an innocent victim by an uncaring perpetrator. A crime occurs when someone breaks into your house and steals your television set and stereo. A crime occurs when an anonymous mugger knocks you to the ground and steals your wallet and watch. A crime occurs when a gunman goes on a rampage and shoots innocent victims.

These images of crime are perpetuated by the media and by the law enforcement establishment. News reports carry nightly features on robberies at convenience stores, assaults, drug crimes, and murders. Television movies and police shows emphasize crimes of violence, particularly the sensational (but rather rare) crime of murder. Police departments, the FBI, and other law enforcement agencies monitor the amount of street crime and gauge the threat of crime in society in that context. When politicians engage in their ritualistic calls for law and order, they are careful to stress crimes of violence and theft. We spend billions of dollars a year and employ over 900,000 police and thousands of other government officials and prosecutors in the battle against street crime.

While murder, rape, robbery, and other violent crimes in society are appalling, our exclusive emphasis on these crimes is fundamentally misleading. It conceals two fundamental truths about crime in the United States. The first is that the criminal justice system can do very little to control street crimes—and next to nothing to prevent them. The second basic truth is that all the violent crime, all the property crime, all the crime we concentrate our energy and resources on combatting is less of a threat to society than the crime committed by corporations. As Bertram Gross has commented:

We are not letting the public in on our era's dirty little secret: that those who commit the crime which worries citizens most—violent street crime—are, for the most part, products of poverty, unemployment, broken homes, rotten education, drug addiction, alcoholism, and other social and economic ills about which the police can do little if anything. . . . But, all the dirty little secrets fade into insignificance in comparison with one dirty big secret: Law enforcement officials, judges as well as prosecutors and investigators, are soft on corporate crime . . . The corporation's "mouthpieces" and "fixers" include lawyers, accountants, public relations experts and public officials who negotiate loopholes and special procedures in the laws, prevent most illegal activities from ever being disclosed and undermine or sidetrack "overzealous" law enforcers. In the few cases ever brought to court, they usually negotiate penalties amounting to "gentle taps on the wrist." (cited in Hagan, 1998, p. 301)

◈

THE COSTS OF CORPORATE CRIME

In simple dollar terms, there is no question that corporate crime does significantly more damage to society than all street crimes put together. The economic losses resulting from street crimes are generally estimated to be nearly $13.3 billion a year. The yearly cost of antitrust violations alone is about $250 billion; the Internal Revenue Service estimates an annual loss of $150 billion (Coleman, 1998). The total monetary damage from corporate crimes was somewhere between $174 billion and $231 billion annually according to a 1980 estimate (Clinard & Yeager, 1980). Other estimates are even higher. A *U.S. News & World Report* (1982) analysis set the annual cost of price fixing, false advertising, tax evasion, and other corporate frauds at $200 billion. That would be over $300 billion in 1999 dollars. In addition, the General Accounting Office sets the cost of health-care fraud at an additional $70 billion (Andrews, 1994). The savings-and-loan collapse, largely a product of both organized and corporate crime, cost $500 billion or about $25 billion a year spread over 20 years. Based on these estimates it would be safe to conclude that economic losses from corporate crime exceed losses from street crime annually by a ratio ranging from 17 to 1 to 32 to 1.

These rough estimates themselves illuminate the very different treatment of street crime compared to corporate crime. As Jeffrey Reiman (1998) points out, the government publishes an avalanche of statistics on street crimes, but no private or public institution—not the FBI, not the U.S. Department of Commerce—keeps up-to-date statistics on the cost of white-collar crime (p. 112). The last public record was issued by the Department of Commerce in its 1974 *Handbook on White-Collar Crime*.

Some commentators are quick to point out that these economic losses are spread across millions of victims, the damages are diffuse, and the trauma to the victim less than in the case of street crimes. They are also quick to point out that crimes of violence entail losses that far exceed monetary damages in terms of injury and even death. However, corporate crimes kill and maim as well, and in staggering numbers. Consider the following:

- Annually 100,000 workers die from diseases contracted in the course of their occupations (McCaghy et al., 2000).
- It is estimated that 140,000 people die each year from air pollution alone, most of which is the result of a violation of governmental regulations by corporations.
- Unsafe and defective merchandise produced by corporations and sold to consumers results in an additional 30,000 deaths and 20 million serious injuries a year (Coleman, 1998).

Compare this record of corporate carnage to the approximately 20,000 murders and 800,000 assaults a year committed in the United States; you can then begin to appreciate the extent of victimization from white-collar crimes. A conservative estimate from these examples would be that corporate crime is 13.5 times more deadly than homicide in the United States.

◊

CORPORATE CRIME AND CRIMINAL INTENT

Despite the damage to society resulting from white-collar crimes, government officials, corporate executives, and even some law enforcement experts argue that these crimes differ from street crimes in several important respects. They attempt to mitigate the impact of corporate crime by pointing to a lack of *mens rea* (criminal intent) (Clinard & Yeager, 1980). They say that unlike muggers, rapists, and murderers, corporate violators do not set out to commit crime. Violations simply happen in the context of occupational environments. They result from oversights, occasionally from negligence, and from the pressures inherent in the business world. These crimes and violations are not the result of a conscious decision to do harm or to inflict injury.

The argument that corporate offenders lack criminal intent is one of a series of neutralizing myths employed by white-collar criminals to excuse their conduct. Unfortunately, the facts simply belie the myth. Studies have shown clearly that injuries and deaths caused by corporate violations are not simply a matter of carelessness or neglect; many are the direct result of willful violations of the law. James Messerschmidt (1986), in a comprehensive review of research studies on job-related accidents, determined that somewhere between 35 and 57% of those accidents occurred because of direct safety violations by the employer. Laura Shill Schraeger and James Short, Jr. (1978) found that 30% of industrial accidents resulted from safety violations and another 20% resulted from unsafe working conditions. For example, Chrysler Corporation was fined $1.5 million for over 800 health and safety violations—including knowingly exposing its workers to poisons such as lead and arsenic (Eitzen & Zinn, 1997). The Environmental Protection Agency (EPA) estimates that of the 292 million tons of toxic waste produced annually by U.S. companies, 90% of it is disposed of improperly and in violation of the law (Coleman, 1998).

Anecdotal evidence, while often hard to come by in considering corporate crime, further supports the contention that many of these crimes are willful and deliberate. Consider the case of the asbestos industry in the United States. Major asbestos manufacturers were aware as early as 1934 that asbestos-related diseases (commonly referred to as "white lung") were a distinct threat to their workers (Carlson, 1979). Two of the largest manufacturers, Johns-Manville and Raybestos-Manhattan, covered up company-funded research findings. The Philip Carey Company went so far as to fire its medical consultant when he warned of the dangers of asbestos-related diseases. Rather than taking steps to protect workers in the asbestos plants, the companies engaged in a policy of quietly settling any death claims. When medical checkups at the company revealed the presence of white lung, Johns-Manville did not notify employees—despite the fact that asbestosis is a progressive disease that can be treated successfully in its early stages but is fatal if left untreated.

The Ford Pinto case provides a similar and equally chilling example of a corporate decision to commit an act of violence against consumers. It is estimated that nine hundred people were incinerated due to the engineering of the Pinto gas tank, which could burst into flames in rear-end collisions (Cullen, 1984; Dowie, 1977). The decision to market a potentially deadly product was a calculated one based entirely on profit motivations. Ford had rushed the Pinto into production in the 1960s in an attempt to compete with cheaper, smaller, more efficient Japanese imports. The company had made a substantial investment in modifying its assembly line to produce this new model when it learned, as a result of its own crash tests, that the gas tank would explode in rear-end collisions. Ford was faced with a dilemma: it could stop production and lose the money it invested in the Pinto; it could make a modification to the gas tank that would cost roughly eleven dollars per car and would correct the problem; or it could say nothing and allow a deadly automobile to be manufactured and sold. They chose the latter. Ford calculated that it would save about $87 million by settling death and injury claims rather than by making the modification in the gas tank. It was not until 1978 that the Department of Transportation finally got around to recalling the Ford Pinto.

Ford is not the only auto manufacturer guilty of producing unsafe automobiles. General Motors (GM) had a similar experience in the 1980s (Hills, 1987). GM began production of a new line of cars in 1980, known as X-cars. Its own tests indicated clearly that these X-cars had a tendency for the rear-wheel brakes to lock prematurely, causing the car to spin out of control. Even after fifteen people died in X-cars and at least seventy-one were injured, GM continued to fight government attempts to recall the cars for needed repairs.

GM had previous experience with defective vehicles. They had produced school buses with dangerous defects and delayed as long as possible in making the necessary repairs. When Ralph Nader, the well-known consumer advocate, raised the issue of dangerous school buses with GM, the company responded by hiring private detectives to investigate Nader's personal life in an attempt to blackmail him into silence (Heilbroner, 1973).

United States corporations produce unsafe cars and school buses; they also produce unsafe tires to put on those vehicles. Firestone produced a series of steel-belted radials in the 1970s known as the "500" series. The company received complaints from consumers about sudden blowouts occurring in these tires. Even after forty-one deaths related to the defective product, Firestone was still fighting to keep the tire on the market and to prevent the public from learning the truth.

While highways are acknowledged as dangerous places, particularly if you drove a Ford Pinto with Firestone steel-belted radials, the air is not much better. General Dynamics was warned by one of its engineers in the early 1970s that the cargo doors in its DC-10 aircraft were defective. The warning was ignored and 346 people were killed in a plane crash in France, when the cargo door on their plane opened during flight (Nader et al., 1976). In another case, B.F. Goodrich falsified test records and laboratory reports in an attempt to sell defective air brakes to the United States Air Force, which would have endangered the lives of thousands of fighter pilots (Heilbroner, 1973).

Other industries provide similar examples of deliberate criminal conduct. Utah Power and Light Company was cited for 34 safety violations in one of its company-owned coal mines. An underground fire in that mine killed 27 miners, and the subsequent investigation determined that 9 of those violations were directly linked to the start of the fire and its spread throughout the mine shaft. The Beech-Nut Nutrition Corporation mislabeled its baby food, claiming that a substance that was primarily colored sugar water was apple juice for babies. The company entered guilty pleas to 215 criminal counts charging that it had intentionally defrauded and misled the public (Eitzen & Zinn, 1997). Hormel, one of the nation's largest meat-packing companies, bribed a Department of Agriculture inspector to ignore violations in their production and packaging of meat (McCaghy et al., 2000). If customers discovered the faulty products, Hormel had an answer.

> When the original customers returned the meat to Hormel, they used the following terms to describe it: "moldy liverloaf, sour party hams, leaking bologna, discolored bacon, off-condition hams, and slick and slimy spareribs." Hormel renewed these products with cosmetic measures (reconditioning, trimming, and washing). Spareribs returned for sliminess, discoloration, and stickiness were rejuvenated through curing and smoking, renamed Windsor Loins and sold in ghetto stores for more than fresh pork chops. (Wellford, 1972, p. 69)

Other examples abound in virtually every industry. Consider the following examples from the pharmaceutical industry (Braithwaite, 1984; Coleman, 1998):

- William S. Merrell Company submitted false test results and records to the Food and Drug Administration (FDA) in order to avoid losing the money they had invested in developing what turned out to be a dangerous and defective drug.
- Eli Lilly and Company failed to report illnesses and at least fifty deaths associated with their arthritis medication Oraflex.
- The Richardson-Merrell Company, during testing for a cholesterol inhibitor called MER/29, noted serious vision problems caused by the drug and the deaths of laboratory animals. The company not only lied to the FDA about these findings but told the researchers to falsify their data to make the drug look safe and effective.
- Three executives of C.R. Bard, Inc., a manufacturer of balloon tips used in angioplasty, pled guilty to 391 counts of fraud. Bard had concealed from the FDA malfunctions in its products including balloon ruptures, deflations, and breakages that caused serious heart injuries resulting in emergency coronary bypass surgery (Simon, 1999, p. 120).
- Warner-Lambert, a Fortune 500 drug company, pled guilty to a felony count related to its production of an anti-epileptic drug named Dilantin. The charge against Warner-Lambert was that the company failed to notify the FDA of "stability failures" in the production of Dilantin. Adulterated shipments of the drug had been shipped and FDA efforts to determine the potency of the drug shipments had been obstructed ("Shameless," 1995).
- Not even the smallest of children are safe from corporate crime. Manufacturers of the "Luv'N'Care" baby pacifier pled guilty to 14 violations of federal law because their products put babies and very young children in danger of suffocation and choking ("Shameless," 1995).

In addition to unsafe products, major corporations also regularly expose workers to unsafe working conditions, killing as many as 14,000 workers a year and injuring another 2 million. A classic case is provided by one of the largest U.S. agribusiness corporations. Decoster Egg Farms is one of the country's largest egg producers. At its facility in Turner, Maine, over three million chickens produce almost fourteen million eggs a week. Migrant workers at the plant worked ten to fifteen hours a day, with no safety equipment. They had to pick up dead chickens with their bare hands and handle salmonella-infected manure with no gloves. In addition, they were exposed to life-threatening electrical hazards, and workers injured on the job were routinely left untreated. One worker lost three fingers in a machine used to scrape chicken manure from the barns. As many as 12 people lived in one 10-by-60-foot trailer. Living quarters featured live electrical connections, inoperable smoke alarms, and a septic system so overtaxed that toilet content backed up several inches into shower tubs. In 1997 the company settled Labor Department charges by paying $2 million in penalties and agreeing to pay full restitution and back wages to workers ("Beat," 1997).

Another example of brazen disregard for the welfare and safety of workers occurred in Hamlet, North Carolina. Twenty-five workers died in a fire that destroyed a chicken-processing plant. The doors of the plant were locked "to keep out insects and to keep employees from going outside for coffee breaks, or stealing chickens" (cited in Best, 1999, p. 127). The owner of the plant accepted the charge of involuntary manslaughter and was sentenced to 19½ years in prison (eligible for parole after serving 2½ years).

While corporations regularly endanger U.S. workers, their track record abroad is even more horrifying, exemplified by Nike. Nike came under scrutiny in 1996, when CBS News' *48 Hours* ran an exposé on working conditions at its Vietnam plant. Nike workers in Vietnam were being paid 20 cents an hour. Fifteen of the women who worked at the plant were struck on the head by their supervisor as a means of discipline, and 45 women were ordered to kneel on the ground with hands in the air for 25 minutes in another disciplinary incident. One of the women's supervisors returned to Korea when he was accused of sexually molesting female workers.

In an effort to improve its image, Nike hired the auditing firm of Ernst & Young to assess working and environmental conditions in its Vietnamese plants. While Nike was no doubt looking for vindication from a firm well known for "responsible" auditing of major corporations, they were in for a surprise. Even a major corporate player like Ernst & Young couldn't turn a blind eye to carcinogen levels 177 times higher than local law allowed and more than 100 workers at the Nike plant with various respiratory ailments. On September 15, 1997, the Hong Kong Christian Industrial Committee issued a report on Nike's factories in China, finding conditions even worse than those reported in Vietnam ("Beat," 1997; Glass, 1997).

Dangerous working conditions are not the only type of workplace offense corporations can inflict on their workers. The demeaning and brutalizing impact of sexism and racism is another part of the polluted work environment in the United States. In 1996, the Equal Employment Opportunity Commission filed a sexual harassment lawsuit against Mitsubishi Motor Manufacturing of America. The EEOC suit charged that hundreds of female workers had been victimized, and those who had complained had been forced to quit. Among the specific actions cited by the EEOC were (1) a practice by male employees of grabbing female employees' breasts, buttocks, and genitals, including one instance where a male worker put a gun between a female coworker's legs and pulled the trigger; (2) drawings of various acts of sexual intercourse that included female employees' names placed along the assembly line; (3) a practice by supervisors of calling female employees sluts, whores, bitches, and other names; and (4) routine questioning of female employees about their sexual habits and preferences ("Ten," 1996).

The curtain of racism can be drawn tightly in executive offices. In November 1996 *The New York Times* ran a front-page story exposing racist comments and discussions by the highest ranking executives of Texaco, a major oil producer. The comments were made at an August 1994 meeting about minority employees who had brought a discrimination lawsuit against the company. Among the comments made by Texaco executives at that meeting were: "This diversity thing. You know how black jelly beans agree." "All the black jelly beans seem to be glued to the bottom of the bag." "I'm still having trouble with Hanukkah. Now we have Kwanzaa." The lawsuit had alleged that Texaco fostered a racially hostile environment. Tapes of the meeting, turned over to *The New York Times* by Texaco's former senior coordinator for personnel services in the finance department, proved there was a basis for the allegations. The tape also contained comments from executives about the destruction of company records subpoenaed by the plaintiffs' attorneys ("Ten," 1996).

Not all white-collar and corporate crime endangers our health, our lives, or our dignity. Some of it merely endangers our finances. There can be little doubt that when corporations engage in price fixing and restraint of trade, they are engaged in deliberate and premeditated criminality. Estimates on the overall cost to the public from restraint of trade are difficult to calculate, but there is a general consensus that the price we pay for this corporate misconduct is around $20 billion a year (Bequai, 1978). When we consider individual cases, it becomes clear that each violation places an enormous economic burden on society.

In a recent price fixing case, Archer Daniels Midland (ADM), which bills itself as the "supermarket to the world," was fined $100 million (the largest criminal antitrust fine in U.S. history) in 1996 after pleading guilty to fixing the prices of several commodities essential to the production of processed food. While the fine was substantial, ADM executives were protected from prosecution under the plea agreement. ADM's price fixing cost consumers at least $500 million in added costs ("Beat," 1997).

There have been countless examples of price fixing. The Federal Trade Commission estimated that the public paid $128 million a year in higher prices because of an agreement among four cereal companies to minimize competition, a conspiracy that had been in effect for over 30 years (Mayer & Bishop, 1976). Southland Corporation and Borden, Inc. rigged bids on contracts on milk to schoolchildren in Florida (Hagan, 1998). Even local conspiracies to fix prices and limit competition are enormously costly. In Seattle and Tacoma, a local price-fixing conspiracy among bakers added four cents to the price of every loaf of bread, resulting in consumer losses of $35 million over the ten-year period the conspiracy was active. In 1975 the Justice Department filed an antitrust suit against three of the largest plumbing fixture producers in the United States (Borg Warner, American Standard, and Kohler) for conspiring to fix prices in the amount of $1 billion on bathroom fixtures (Hagan, 1998). Everest and Jennings engaged in an illegal price-rigging conspiracy which raised the price of wheelchairs four times over the market value (McCaghy & Cernkovich, 1987).

The impact is even more pronounced in the automobile industry, where consumers paid $1.6 billion in higher prices because of collusion to limit competition among the major automobile manufacturers (Green et al., 1972). Chrysler Corporation was charged by the federal government with selling 60 thousand vehicles as new cars, even though they had been driven by company employees. They simply disconnected the odometer so consumers would be unaware of the real mileage on the vehicles (Hagan, 1998).

Price-fixing is only one mechanism of theft utilized by corporate America. Out-and-out fraud is also not uncommon. For example, Smith Kline Beecham, one of the country's largest drug companies, paid $300 million to resolve federal charges that it had defrauded Medicare for unneeded blood tests; Corning, Inc. paid $6.8 million to settle a federal case involving Medicare billings for blood tests that hadn't been requested by physicians (Simon, 1999, p. 120). In 1992 California officials accused Sears and Roebuck department stores of fraud in auto repairs by both overcharging customers and making unnecessary repairs. Sears paid auto repair personnel a commission on work they did, thereby accelerating the fraud. In the end Sears agreed to pay $50 million to about 900,000 defrauded customers (Kelly, 1992). These two cases resulted in taxpayer and consumer losses of over $350 million, and they represent only the tip of the iceberg. In 1999 a jury found State Farm Insurance Company liable for breaching its contract with policyholders. The nation's largest auto insurer had made arrangements with body shops and repair centers to use substandard parts in the repairs of policyholders' vehicles. *CNN News* reported in October 1999 that the court was also considering a charge that State Farm committed fraud to the tune of $5 billion. Perhaps the actual extent and scope of corporate fraud becomes obvious when we consider the conduct of one of the largest health-care corporations in the United States.

Columbia/HCA is one of the largest hospital chains in the United States, controlling more than 340 hospitals. Columbia/HCA has a simple strategy for growth: cut costs, cut staff, and cut patient services. One of Columbia/HCA's managers put it simply in an interview with ABC's *20/20*. He said, "I committed felonies every day." He went on to say, "Let me tell you this—this company is a ruthless, greedy company—period. Employees are the largest operating expense. Cut that to the bone. Cut nursing to the bone. I mean, cut it to as low as your conscience will allow." *20/20* interviewed workers at Columbia's Las Vegas facility. One telemetry technician said she had to watch 72 monitors of heart patients at once. The employees told the story of a homeless man who was brought to the hospital by paramedics. Because the man had no health insurance, "No tests were run. No blood tests. No x-rays. Nothing. He was given a glass of juice and dismissed, discharged." The man died 30 feet outside the hospital's door. Federal officials raided Columbia hospitals in Tennessee, Georgia, Texas, and Florida, charging that the company was involved in a systematic effort to defraud federal health programs ("Beat," 1997).

Corporate lying, particularly about the quality, genesis, price, and utility of their products, is also common practice. False advertising costs consumers billions of dollars each year; it is one of the most common corporate crimes. Coors beer claimed that they had captured a "taste of the Rockies" in their products by using Rocky Mountain spring water. Apparently the water had to travel some distance, since Coors was actually using water from Virginia (Simon, 1999, p. 116). Montgomery Ward was fined for false advertising in 1993. The company consistently listed regular retail prices of its products as sale prices (Simon, 1999, p. 118). Other examples of false advertising include crude deceptions similar to the practices of small-time hustlers. For example, in 1996 the FTC reached consent decrees with General Motors, Mitsubishi, Honda, Isuzu, and Mazda, after determining they engaged in deceptive advertising with regard to car leases (Simon, 1999, p. 117).

Sometimes the devastating effects of corporate crime are harder to quantify and even more difficult to see. Consider the current crisis with regard to environmental pollution. Estimates by the EPA and the Harvard School of Public Health identify 50,000 to 60,000 deaths each year in the United States as the direct result of particle pollution from manufacturing plants. Particularly at risk are children, the elderly with respiratory diseases, and workers living near those plants (Simon, 1999, p. 11). In 1990 EPA identified 149 manufacturing plants in 33 states where the air pollution levels in the surrounding communities were considered dangerous (Simon, 1999, p. 11).

Almost everyone is aware of the Three-Mile Island incident in Pennsylvania, which involved a nuclear accident that released radioactivity into the atmosphere and required the evacuation of children and pregnant women from the area around the plant. The company involved, Metropolitan Edison, pleaded guilty to using inaccurate testing methods and pleaded no contest to charges of destroying records and five other criminal counts (Hagan, 1998). Other environmental disasters have included the dumping of toxic chemicals at Love Canal, New York by Hooker Chemical. At the end of 1980, 239 families were evacuated and their homes demolished. "Another 311 homes were eventually condemned and the Love Canal disaster ended up costing the American taxpayer about $200 million" (Coleman, 1998, p. 70). In fact, the EPA estimates that there are 34,000 dump sites with "significant problems" where toxic wastes have been buried in the United States (Brown, 1982). Other cases of environmental crime by corporations abound:

- Olin Corporation illegally dumped thirty-eight tons of mercury, a chemical which causes damage to the human reproductive system and nervous disorders, into the municipal sewage system of Niagara Falls, New York, between 1970 and 1977 (McCaghy & Cernkovich, 1987).
- Kentucky Liquid Recycling, Inc. forced the shutdown of the entire Louisville sewage system in 1977 by dumping toxic chemicals into that system (McCaghy & Cernkovich, 1987).

- Allied Chemical Company dumped Kepone in Virginia's James River and in 1976 pleaded *nolo contendere* to 153 criminal charges (Hagan, 1998).
- The Adolph Coors Co. had to pay over $600,000 to settle criminal charges that carcinogenic pollutants were illegally dumped by the company into Clear Creek in Colorado (Eitzen & Zinn, 1997).
- In 1997, federal judge Rebecca Beech Smith fined Smithfield Foods and two of its subsidiary companies $12.6 million for discharging illegal pollutants into the Pagan River in Virginia. Smithfield's subsidiaries operate two hog slaughtering and meat processing plants. The ruling found that Smithfield had committed more than 5,000 violations of permit limits for phosphorous, fecal coliform, ammonia, cyanide, oil, and grease. Fecal coliform is an organism found in animal and human waste that is associated with bacteria known to cause serious illness in humans. These violations occurred over a five-year period and seriously degraded the Pagan River, the James River, and Chesapeake Bay. In addition, the judge's ruling found that Smithfield has routinely falsified documents and destroyed water-quality records ("Beat," 1997).

The list of major corporate polluters doesn't stop here. Many of the largest and most respected corporations in the United States are serial polluters. Dupont, the largest U.S. chemical company, is also the leading emitter of toxins, releasing about one million pounds of poison a day into the atmosphere. Rockwell Corporation operates the Rocky Flats nuclear-weapons plant outside of Denver. The EPA has identified 166 hazardous-waste dumps at this facility. In 1992, Rockwell pled guilty to five felonies in the operation of the Rocky Flats facility. General Motors is responsible for 200 Superfund toxic clean-up sites. General Electric plants discharged 500,000 pounds of PCBs into the Hudson River in New York State; regularly released radioactive waste at its Hanford Nuclear Reservation in Washington State without warnings to residents; and produced and sold deficient nuclear-containment vessels to its customers. Georgia Pacific, one of the largest paper product producers in the world, has not complied with air pollution standards for fifteen consecutive years. Cargill, one the largest grain, meat, flour, and seed producers in the world, has been cited for 2,000 OSHA violations since 1987 and has dumped 40,000 gallons of toxic phosphoric solution into the Aliifia River in Florida (Simon, 1999, pp. 157–159).

Occasionally, corporations commit their crimes against the state. In the case of crimes such as defense contract fraud and trading with the enemy, there can be little doubt of the criminal intent of the actors involved. Corporate fraud committed in relation to defense contracts is almost legendary, and the cases are too numerous to recount in detail. A few examples are instructive. Swift and Company, one of the largest meat packers in the United States, sold hams contaminated with rat manure to the Walter Reed Army Medical Center. General Electric pleaded guilty in 1985 to overcharging the Air Force

$800,000 on a $47 million contract. General Dynamics corporation charged the Air Force $9,609 for a twelve-cent wrench. In other cases, the Pentagon was charged $659 for an ashtray, $425 for a hammer, $7,622 for a coffee maker, $400 for a socket wrench, and $640.09 for toilet seats (McCaghy & Cernkovich, 1987).

While these overcharges in defense contracts are outrageous and clearly deliberate examples of attempts to defraud the government by major corporations, they pale in comparison to charges of collaboration by United States corporations with the enemy during World War II. Charles Higham (1982), in his study of corporate misconduct during World War II, charges that executives of Ford Motor Company authorized the production of trucks for German troops occupying France; that Chase Manhattan Bank continued to do business with the Nazis throughout the war; and that while gasoline and oil was stringently rationed in the United States to support the war, Standard Oil of New Jersey was shipping fuel to the Nazis through Switzerland.

◈

THE CRIMINOGENIC CORPORATION

As shocking as these cases may be, it is important to understand they are *not* aberrations. These are not a collection of incidents that deviate from the norm. Everything we know about corporate and white-collar crime leads us to believe that crime is a way of life for many corporations. While it may be fashionable for government officials and corporate executives to claim that corporations behave responsibly and that these cases are simply isolated incidents, the data conclusively indicate otherwise.

Edwin Sutherland (1949) broke new ground with his research on white-collar crime over fifty years ago. He searched the records of federal, state, and local courts looking for adverse decisions handed down against the seventy largest corporations in the United States over a twenty-year period. His findings were revealing:

> Each of the 70 large corporations has 1 or more decisions against it, with a maximum of 50. The total number of decisions is 980, and the average per corporation is 14.0. Sixty corporations have decisions against them for restraint of trade, 53 for infringement, 44 for unfair labor practices, 43 for miscellaneous offenses, 28 for misrepresentation in advertising, and 26 for rebates. (p. 15)

Sutherland found that major corporations engage in widespread violations and that these corporations are recidivists, committing their crimes both frequently and on a continual basis (97.1% of the corporations in his study were recidivists). These numbers are even more compelling when one considers that little effort is put into discovering and prosecuting corporate violations; therefore, adverse decisions represent only a tiny portion of the actual crime committed. Later studies have confirmed Sutherland's conclusions.

In 1980, Marshall Clinard and Peter Yeager published their findings with regard to crimes committed by the 477 largest manufacturing corporations and the 105 largest wholesale, retail, and service corporations in the United States in 1975 and 1976. In that two-year period, these 582 corporations were the subjects of 1,553 federal cases initiated against them. Because these numbers include only cases brought against the corporations, they once again represent a major underestimate of the total amount of crime committed by these corporations. Clinard and Yeager (1980) suggest they had uncovered only "the tip of the iceberg of total violations" (p. 111). They found that in just two years, 60% of the corporations had at least 1 action initiated against them, 42% of the corporations had 2 or more actions initiated against them, and the most frequent violators were averaging 23.5 violations per corporation (Clinard & Yeager, 1980). Sociologist Amatai Etzioni found that 62% of the Fortune 500 companies were involved in at least one act of bribery, price fixing, tax fraud, or environmental crime between 1975 and 1984. A similar study by the *Multinational Monitor* found that the twenty-five largest Fortune 500 corporations had all been convicted of a criminal act or fined and required to make civil restitution between 1977 and 1990 (Donahue, 1992, pp. 14–19). In the face of these numbers, it is extremely difficult to argue that corporate criminality is random, isolated, and lacking intent.

These findings also suggest that there is a double standard of justice operating in the United States. Consider the outrage that would be expressed by the public, politicians, and law enforcement officials if they identified a community of people in which 60% of the residents were convicted of a crime, 40% were repeat offenders, and a substantial number were committing almost a dozen crimes a year. There would be calls for preventive detention (lock them up before they commit more crimes), automatic add-on sentences for being career criminals (keep them in jail so they can't commit crime), as well as for stepped-up law enforcement efforts (increased patrols, sting operations, career criminal profiling). But does this happen when the criminal justice system confronts white-collar crime? Are there calls for a massive crackdown on corporate violence? Do the police break down the front doors of Ford and General Motors in midnight raids? The answer is no. We make little effort to enforce the law against these criminals. When we do manage to catch them at their nefarious deeds, we tap them on the wrist, make them say they are sorry and send them about their criminal business. As Bertram Gross pointed out, the "big, dirty secret" about crime in the United States is that judges, prosecutors, police, and "law and order" politicians are soft on corporate crime.

◊

LAW ENFORCEMENT AND
WHITE-COLLAR CRIME

What has been the response of the Federal government to the thousands of
deaths and injuries and the billions of dollars in damage caused by white-collar crime? The official response has essentially sanctioned continued
criminality. The Reagan administration declared a "war on crime." What
effect did that declaration have on corporate crime? Instead of stepped-up
law enforcement, more money for investigations, and harsher penalties, the
government responded with precisely the opposite (Isaacson & Gorey, 1981).

- The Consumer Product Safety Commission's budget was slashed by
  30%, imperiling consumers more than ever;
- The number of inspectors in the Occupational Safety and Health
  Administration (OSHA) was cut by 11%. OSHA has less than three
  thousand inspectors to "regulate" four million workplaces;
- The Federal Trade Commission's antitrust division had its funding,
  personnel, and enforcement powers cut, making restraint of trade
  easier than ever;
- The federal government repealed requirements that companies tell
  workers when they are exposed to dangerous chemicals on the job;
- The requirement that pharmaceutical manufacturers list the possible risks of their medicines to consumers was canceled by the Reagan
  administration as unnecessary interference with business;
- The requirement that auto manufacturers produce cars that were
  safe at 5 miles per hour was changed to a requirement that they demonstrate safety at 2.5 miles per hour, making us much safer in an
  automobile as long as it is not moving.

Subsequent budget constraints enacted by the Bush and Clinton administrations have left most of these agencies at the same level of inadequate—
or more accurately, inoperative—funding. The official response to corporate
crime enforcement has been roughly the equivalent of a city experiencing a
wave of homicides and firing homicide investigators to prevent interference
with the exercise of free will.

While there are fewer regulators and enforcers available to combat corporate crime, it is even more disturbing to learn who those regulators are and
how the laws that govern corporate crime are written. One of the most frequently repeated canards associated with white-collar crime is that business
is overregulated and that laws designed to control pollution, the quality of
consumer products, and worker health and safety are unwarranted interfer-
ences in the free enterprise system. Corporate officials and government officials are unrelenting in their claims that laws designed to prevent corporate
crime adversely impact profits and, by implication, jobs. They charge that

environmentalists, consumer advocates, and other "do-gooders" conspire to regulate the free enterprise system out of existence. But the facts suggest otherwise. So powerful is the myth that the Clinton administration had to argue that both the environment and jobs could be reconciled.

The simple fact is that business has no objection to regulation and government interference when it benefits corporate objectives. The history of government regulation of business in the United States is one of business regulating itself for its own benefit. The earliest controls on corporate crime were the antitrust acts of the late 1800s. These early controls were in fact initiated and supported by the very businesses they ostensibly regulated (Pearce, 1976; Weinstein, 1968). Government regulations were used by the robber barons to stabilize the market and to make the economy more predictable. At the same time, they were useful for driving smaller competitors out of business by denying them the use of the same unsavory and illegal tactics that the large corporations had used with such skill in creating their dominant economic positions.

The 1906 Meat Inspection Act is a classic case in point. Ostensibly, the act was passed to protect consumers from contaminated meat products. In fact, this "government interference" had full support from the large meat-packing companies because it kept imported meat off the U.S. market at government expense, and the new regulations hindered smaller meat-packing companies by making it hard for them to survive and to compete with the major corporations (Kolko, 1963). The situation today is no different. Industry welcomes governmental meddling with price competition, such as the Interstate Commerce Commission's fixed rates on rail and water freight charges and distance (or "long-haul") charges on highway transportation that keep transportation costs artificially high (McCaghy & Cernkovich, 1987). It is simply impossible to reconcile business complaints of overregulation with demands for more controls on foreign imports, requests for government bailouts, and demands for government assistance to "beleaguered" U.S. companies.

Corporations in the United States have made the most of the protections provided them by regulatory statutes. They have used government regulations, which they help write and help enforce, to create what Mark Green, Beverly Monroe, and Bruce Wasserstein (1972) have called "shared monopolies"—markets controlled by four or fewer firms. Shared monopolies can now be found in the tire, aluminum, soap, tobacco, cereal, bread and flour, milk and dairy products, processed meat, canned goods, sugar, soup, light-bulb, and computer chip industries. One hundred corporations, out of 200,000, control 55% of all industrial assets in the United States. The largest 500 industrial corporations control 75% of all manufacturing assets (Dowd, 1993, pp. 113–115). In the transportation and utilities industries 50 of the 67,000 corporations control two-thirds of the assets in the airline, railroad, communications, electricity, and gas industries. Only 50 of the 14,763 banks in the United States control 64% of all banking assets (Simon, 1999, p. 14).

And in the insurance industry fifty of 2,048 companies control 80% of all insurance assets.

The few corporations that control most of the manufacturing capacity and wealth in the United States have interlocked their management in such a way as to guarantee that they work in relative harmony with each other in pursuing both market objectives and government protections. Chief executive officers of 233 of the 250 largest U.S. corporations sit on the board on at least one other of those 250 largest corporations, many of them sitting on the boards of ostensibly competing corporations, a clear violation of the Clayton Antitrust Act of 1914 (Simon, 1999, p. 15).

In addition to benefitting from the "regulations" that they helped to write, corporations have other programs to help boost the profit margin. Corporate welfare, consisting of tax deductions, tax exemptions, and tax-free investments, amounts to about $448 billion a year, almost four times as much as the United States spends on social programs for the poor (Simon, 1999). Archer Daniels Midland (ADM) is a primary beneficiary. As a result of federal protections provided to the sugar industry, ethanol subsidies, and subsidized grain exports, ADM has cost U.S. taxpayers $40 billion between 1980 and 1995. For every dollar in profits made on ethanol sales, ADM costs taxpayers $30. For every dollar in profits made on corn sweetener, ADM costs consumers $10 (Bovard, 1995).

"Overregulation" has not necessarily led to overtaxation. During the Roosevelt administration, in the 1940s, corporate income taxes made up one-third of all federal tax revenues; by 1996 corporate income taxes made up only 15%. In fact, about 90,000 corporations pay absolutely no taxes each year (Simon, 1999, p. 62). In the 1991–1992 tax year, Chase Manhattan, one of the largest banking conglomerates in the world, paid a tax rate of 1.7% on its $1.5 billion in income. Texaco paid only 8.8% of its $2.7 billion in income in taxes (Simon, 1999, p. 62).

The few regulators and enforcers that the government employs to enforce laws against corporate misconduct are hardly in an adversarial relationship with the industries they regulate. Those in charge of many of the regulatory agencies and commissions are people who have come to government service from the same corporations they are supposed to regulate. Contacts between the regulators and the regulated have been cordial and frequently collaborative. Regulators who have come to the government from private enterprise are often more concerned with the needs of corporations than with the safety or economic health of the public. Likewise, many agency employees leave government service to work for the companies they regulated—compelling evidence of a very cozy relationship (Hagan, 1998).

This conflict of interest has been apparent in several cases, but the most blatant example can be found in the EPA during the Reagan administration. Rita Lavelle was appointed by the president to oversee the government's "Superfund" program, designed to clean up the most threatening cases of corporate pollution from improper disposal of toxic waste. She had previously been employed at Aerojet-General Corporation in California. During her tenure at the EPA, she participated in decisions relating to her former employer (a clear conflict of interest), entered into "sweetheart deals" with major polluters, and used the Superfund allocations for political purposes. In 1983, Lavelle was convicted on four felony counts (Hagan, 1998).

Government actions can occasionally facilitate corporate and white-collar crime. The classic example is the savings-and-loan scandal. The Reagan administration deregulated the savings-and-loan industry in order to stimulate growth in the banking industry. In addition, they increased insurance protection for depositor's accounts at these institutions from $40,000 to $100,000. The administration argued that deregulation would make S&Ls more competitive. What it did was make them more criminal. Following deregulation, S&L executives began using institutional funds for their private expenses, thereby robbing their own banks (Calavita & Pontell, 1993). In addition, the new federal regulations allowed the S&Ls to engage in such practices as accepting deposits contingent on loans being made to the depositors. The depositors then defaulted on the loans. Not only did those depositors essentially obtain interest-free money to invest in high-risk speculations, but go-betweens were paid very generous "finder's fees" for arranging the loans. The S&Ls profited because the deposits artificially inflated the assets of the bank, which resulted in higher dividends being paid to stockholders and extravagant bonuses being paid to S&L executives (Calavita & Pontell, 1990). In the end neither the businesspeople who got the phony loans nor the S&L owners and executives (with a handful of exceptions) were held accountable for the billions in missing cash. The bill was presented to the taxpayers.

◈

UNDERENFORCEMENT AND NONPUNITIVE JUSTICE

The lack of staff and resources—along with the pervasive conflicts of interest in those agencies—makes the risk of apprehension for white-collar criminals very low. The Federal Trade Commission (FTC) offers an excellent example (Hills, 1971). On an annual basis, the FTC receives about nine thousand complaints. Of those nine thousand complaints, one is referred for criminal prosecution. Of those referred for criminal prosecution, some have been delayed as long as twenty years in going to trial by the corporations involved. The FTC only rarely uses its power to conduct hearings and has been extremely reluctant to use any of the enforcement mechanisms granted to it by law. This laxity in enforcement is not unique to the FTC but has been documented for other agencies as well (Benekos, 1983; Clinard & Yeager, 1979; Hagan et al., 1980; Snider, 1982).

In order to make a successful case against a corporation, defendant cooperation is almost always necessary (Hagan et al., 1980). Unmotivated, understaffed, underfunded agencies are not able to litigate even those few cases of corporate crime that actually come to their attention. The result is one of the most bizarre remedial measures found in law, the consent decree. Under the terms of a consent decree, a defendant corporation negotiates with the government over the violations the corporation has committed. It agrees to alter its pattern of conduct. In return, the government agrees that the company will not have to admit guilt. The company does not have to admit its culpability with regard to a crime, but it does have to promise to stop committing the crime, thereby ending the prosecution. The irony of this "sanction" is made clear by Peter Wickman and Phillip Whitten (1980):

> Corporations that have been involved in polluting the environment sign consent decrees with the EPA and announce that they are working on the problem. Imagine the public reaction if a common street criminal were to be dealt with in this fashion. Here's the scene: Joe Thug is apprehended by an alert patrolman after mugging an eighty-five-year-old woman in broad daylight on the streets of Paterson, New Jersey. Brought down to police headquarters, he holds a press conference with the assistant police chief. While not admitting his guilt, he promises not to commit any future muggings and announces that he is working on the problem of crime in the streets. (p. 367)

No matter how serious the crime or how flagrant the violation, the fact is that criminal sanctions are rarely applied in the case of corporate criminals. In their study, Clinard and Yeager (1980) found that the actual sanctions applied to corporate criminals were weak at best. The most common sanction was a warning, issued in 44% of the cases. Following warnings, corporate criminals were assessed fines 23% of the time, although those fines were negligible. In 80% of the cases, they were for $5,000 or less—hardly a significant sanction to corporations earning billions of dollars a year. The Senate Governmental Affairs Subcommittee (1983) noted an even more disturbing fact. Over a 31-month period, 32,000 fines levied against white-collar crime offenders had gone uncollected by the government. Not only are the fines minuscule in size, but offenders seem to feel free to ignore them altogether. In only 1.5% of the cases was a corporate officer convicted of a crime, and in only 4% of those convictions did the offender go to jail. Even so, their terms of incarceration were very light—averaging thirty-seven days (Clinard & Yeager, 1980). This pattern appears to be consistent throughout U.S. history. Albert McCormick, Jr. (1977) studied antitrust cases brought by the Department of Justice from 1890–1969 and found that only 2% of the corporate violators served any prison time at all.

◊

A DUAL SYSTEM OF JUSTICE

This survey of corporate crime is cursory and incomplete at best. There are numerous other patterns of criminality, briefly mentioned below.

- *Corporate Bribery.* There has been a pervasive pattern of bribes by corporations to foreign governments in return for preferential treatment and contracts. Such activities compromise national security abroad and threaten the foundation of democratic government at home.
- *Bank and Financial Institution Fraud.* There is a growing literature on crimes committed by banks, savings-and-loan institutions, and stock brokerage houses. Common offenses include insider trading, money laundering, or financial fraud. The scandal in the savings-and-loan industry alone will keep researchers busy recording the enormous numbers of crimes committed for years.
- *Fraud and Insider Trading.* There is conclusive evidence of widespread criminality in the financial industry. For example, Salamon, Inc. agreed to pay $190 million in fines in 1992 for its attempt to manipulate the $2.2 trillion market in government securities. Drexel Burnham Lambert paid $600 million in criminal fines in 1989 for insider trading (Coleman, 1998).

The available evidence on corporate crime leads to several clear conclusions. Criminality in the corporate sector is widespread and pervasive, and few corporate criminals are ever caught or prosecuted. Corporate criminals are recidivists; they commit crimes over and over again with great frequency. The label career criminal applies. When apprehended, these criminals are treated with kid gloves, warned, given small fines, or allowed to bargain out of prosecution altogether. In those very rare cases where they are convicted of a crime and sentenced to prison, they are treated with far more consideration and leniency than traditional offenders.

This evidence leads us inexorably to one more myth about the criminal justice system in the United States. Contrary to popular notions and official pronouncements, in opposition to slogans chiseled in marble on courthouses across the country, we do not have an equal system of justice. There are two very different justice systems. One is for the poor and defenseless, and the other is for the rich and powerful. As Ralph Nader (1985) has commented:

> The double standard—one for crime in the streets and one for crime in the suites—is well known. A man in Kentucky was sentenced to 10 years in jail in 1983 for stealing a pizza . . . Dozens of corporations have been caught illegally dumping toxic wastes. Yet, only small fines followed. (p. F3)

The double standard prevails in the Justice Department, which has no corporate-crime equivalent to the Federal Bureau of Investigation's Uniform Crime Reporting System. The Bureau has its updated list of the 10 most wanted criminals but has no high-visibility listings for the most wanton corporate recidivists. All other forms of criminal behavior in society do not begin to equal the costs, in terms of both dollars and lives, of corporate crime. Yet government officials, from the president on down, continue to protect wanton acts of criminality as long as they are committed by "respectable society." Over 40 years ago, C. Wright Mills (1952) labeled this condition "the higher immorality," arguing that there was a peculiar and pathological moral degeneracy among the most powerful in American society. Mills argued that corrupt, unethical, and illegal practices by the wealthy and powerful were institutionalized in U.S. society. Clinard and Yeager (1980) echo his findings:

> Corporate crime provides an indication of the degree of hypocrisy in society. It is hypocritical to regard theft and fraud among the lower classes with distaste and to punish such acts while countenancing upper-class deception and calling it "shrewd business practice." A review of corporate violations and how they are prosecuted and punished shows who controls what in law enforcement in American society and the extent to which this control is effective. Even in the broad area of legal proceedings, corporate crime is generally surrounded by an aura of politeness and respectability rarely if ever present in cases of ordinary crime. Corporations are seldom referred to as lawbreakers and rarely as criminals in enforcement proceedings. Even if violations of the criminal law, as well as other laws are involved, enforcement attorneys and corporation counsels often refer to the corporation as "having a problem": one does not speak of the robber or the burglar as having a problem. (p. 21)

The evidence speaks clearly. Our political institutions and our criminal justice system, in helping to perpetuate these myths about white-collar crime, have indeed institutionalized this "higher immorality."

Drug War Cowboys

The metaphor of declaring war on a social problem is a common tool of politicians and activists.

> Declarations of war on social problems are dramatic events: they call for society to rally behind a single policy, against a common foe. Typically, the initial pronouncements receive favorable attention in the mass media; the press details the nature of the problem and outlines the efforts designed to wage war against it. Usually, the enemy . . . has no one speaking on its behalf. There is the sense that society is united behind the war effort. Declaring war seizes the moral high ground. (Best, 1999, p. 144)

The mythology of the war on drugs hides the tangled weave of facts about an intractable problem. Worse, current policy creates new problems while failing to ameliorate the original problem. War rhetoric uses language such as "collateral damage"—a euphemistic reference to casualties used to mask the unsavory aspects of waging war. In the war on drugs, collateral damage is devastatingly high.

For years a debate has raged in the medical, sociological, and law enforcement communities over whether drug use and abuse was a problem for the criminal justice system or for the public health-care system. Despite the rhetoric and sensationalism of today's anti-drug campaigns, that question remains unresolved.

> The energy that has given impetus to drug control and prohibition came from profound tensions among socioeconomic groups, ethnic minorities, and generations—as well as the psychological attraction of certain drugs. The form of control has been shaped by the gradual evolution of federal police powers. The bad results of drug use and the number of drug users have often been exaggerated for partisan advantage. Public demand for

action against drug abuse has led to regulative decisions that lack a true
regard for the reality of drug use. (Musto, 1973, p. 244)

Narcotics addiction is an obdurate problem. It is a problem fueled by
politics and the bureaucratic needs of law enforcement. The natural reaction
for politicians to the drug problem is to pander to popular fear and to frame
the issue in the starkest, most unyielding terms. The "safe" political response
to the issue of drugs is to call for more law and more order. The law enforcement bureaucracy responds to this by accepting the challenge. After all, there
are very few issues on which public opinion and the rhetoric of decisionmak-
ers so closely coincide with opportunities for bureaucratic expansion. A "war
on drugs" offers the opportunity for more money, more personnel, and most
importantly, greater police powers. It is a very attractive offer most police
executives and others in the criminal justice system find impossible to refuse.

Is the war on drugs having any positive impact on the problems associated with drug abuse? And if it is not, what are the alternatives? We will
explore some of the issues related to these questions. First, we will look at the
question of drugs and related harm. What exactly do drugs do? What do we
know about the potential of illicit drugs to kill and injure users? We will try to
put the discussion of harm in context and to separate the harms resulting
from the illegality of drugs from the harms resulting from the abuse of drugs.
Second, we will look at the connection between drugs and crime. One of the
most effective tactics of today's drug warriors has been to create a mythical
link between drugs and crimes against innocent citizens. This portrayal of
drug users as "drug fiends" plays a key role in the popular conception of the
drug problem. But is this view justified? Once again, we will try to put the
issue of drugs and crime into context and to separate those dysfunctions
caused by drugs from those dysfunctions caused by the illegality of drugs.
Third, we will look at the drug war itself, the strategies employed, and their
impact on the drug problem. Finally, we will consider the viability and importance of noncriminal justice approaches to the problem of drugs.

◆

THE DEMONIZATION OF ILLICIT DRUGS

Central to the case for drug prohibition and for pursuing a drug war is the
idea that drugs are dangerous to users. The images presented in the media
are stark and frightening. Fried eggs are used to simulate "your brain on
drugs"; addicts are shown writhing in corners suffering the pains of withdrawal; earnest actors portray cocaine users who have lost their houses, jobs,
and wives to this chemical seductress. No one disputes that drugs can be dangerous. People die of heroin overdoses, and some people die from cardiac
and respiratory failure related to cocaine. People also die from lung cancer as
a result of smoking tobacco; they can die from a variety of diseases related to

the consumption of alcohol. People can die and suffer injury from any drug, legal or illegal—even aspirin and penicillin.

The question is not whether illegal drugs are dangerous, but whether they are dangerous enough to justify legal prohibition and the social outrage associated with their use. As with all other issues in the drug debate, the issue of harm has to be put in context. To gain some perspective, we will examine the three drugs that have elicited the strongest reaction from lawmakers and law enforcers: heroin, cocaine, and marijuana.

Heroin

In the 1960s, most public attention was focused on heroin, a direct derivative of the opium poppy. Heroin users snort, smoke, or inject the narcotic. Mainlining (injection into a vein) produces an immediate euphoric reaction (a "rush") followed by a period of sedation. Heroin is highly addictive; repeated use creates a physical need. In addition, the drug has a high tolerance level. The more often it is used, the greater the quantity and frequency of use required to reach a "high." The net effect of this cycle of need and tolerance is addiction. Like all narcotics, heroin suppresses both respiratory and cardiovascular activity, meaning that an overdose can lead to death. However, heroin is responsible for little direct or permanent physiological damage if properly used under supervised conditions (Inciardi, 1992). The real dangers in the use of heroin are attributable to the potential for overdose and the fact that users on the street do not engage in standard practices of good hygiene, resulting in infection from hepatitis and more recently AIDS.

Cocaine

In the 1980s federal drug enforcers, while still raising the specter of heroin, had shifted public concern to the use of cocaine. Cocaine is the most powerful natural stimulant available. Like heroin it produces a "rush" when used, but unlike heroin it is a stimulant that awakens and enlivens users. Most cocaine users snort cocaine hydrochloride (a white, crystalline powder) into their nasal passages. Snorting cocaine allows for rapid absorption of the drug into the bloodstream creating an intense but rather brief "high."

During the 1970s it appeared that cocaine would become the new drug of choice for the wealthy. It was an expensive drug, selling for over $100 a gram on the street. Because of its expense, it had a limited market of upper middle-class and upper-class users. Cocaine developed the reputation of being a glamour drug associated with sports figures and with Hollywood stars. During 1985–1986, however, cocaine appeared in a new form that made it accessible to everyone, even the poor. "Crack" is simply cocaine hydrochloride powder mixed with baking soda, ammonia, and water; dried; and subsequently smoked. "Crack" sells for $10–$15 a "hit," making it far more affordable than cocaine hydrochloride. It was the advent of "crack" that heralded much of the concern about cocaine.

Prior research on the use of cocaine had indicated that it was a relatively safe drug. Surveys of medical examiners and coroners representing 30% of the population of the United States and Canada had revealed only 26 cases of drug-induced deaths between 1971 and 1976 where cocaine had been the sole drug found in the body (McCaghy & Cernkovich, 1987, p. 454). With the advent of "crack," and the subsequent increase in the smoking of cocaine, the numbers of cocaine-related deaths quadrupled. It is important to note that 92% of cocaine-related deaths result from smoking the drug, an activity confined to about 10% of all cocaine users (Goode, 1999). Moderate use of cocaine is relatively safe, although heavy cocaine users, particularly those who smoke the drug in the form of "crack," exhibit a wide variety of symptoms such as nervousness, fatigue, irritability, and paranoia (Ray, 1999).

Central to concerns about cocaine has been the specter of addiction. Addiction is a frightening concept that has both medical and social contexts. Traditionally, addiction was defined as physical dependence—a process that involves using a drug, developing a level of tolerance, increasing dosage or frequency of use, and withdrawal symptoms if the user attempts to stop using the drug. In strict medical terms addiction is, for the most part, limited to heroin and other opium derivatives. Medically speaking, cocaine is not addictive.

The sizeable increases in cocaine usage and the introduction of crack to the drug market led to claims that cocaine and its by-products were addictive. Because it does not produce physical dependence, cocaine does not fit the traditional definition of addiction. Panic about cocaine use and the subsequent draconian laws passed to control it created a revision in the concept of addiction. The psychological model of dependence replaced physical dependence.

Throughout the 1980s and 1990s it became relatively standard fare for psychiatric hospital advertisements, tabloid television programs, television talk shows and even the nightly news to showcase alleged cocaine addicts discussing in graphic detail the anguish of their cocaine "addiction" and the horrifying consequences for their lives. This socially created view of cocaine addiction was largely uncontested. This was the view sanctioned by the government, which had declared war on a dangerously addicting drug that threatened to enslave users. The only data then available came primarily from alleged cocaine addicts in treatment or seeking treatment (Johanson & Fischman, 1989). The cocaine addiction argument went unchallenged for such a long period of time and was repeated with such ferocity by the media and the state that it became an accepted "truth." As we have seen with many other accepted "truths" related to crime and criminal justice, the substance of the claim may be more myth than fact.

The preponderance of the evidence shows that cocaine, no matter what the mode of administration (snorted, smoked, or injected) is not especially addictive for human beings (Erickson, 1993; Fagan & Chin, 1989). The government's own drug use surveys seem to make the point. For example, the 1990 NIDA household survey of drug use found that 11% of Americans reported they had used cocaine. But only 3% had used it in the past year, and only 0.8% had used cocaine in the past month (NIDA, 1991). Only about one-quarter of cocaine users showed a consistent pattern of use, let alone addiction. Even more instructive, only one in ten current users used cocaine once a week or more. This means that roughly 2.7% of cocaine users had patterns of use that might fall into a category of addictive behavior. A similar Canadian study found that only 5% of current cocaine users used the drug monthly or more frequently (Adlaf et al., 1991). So the vast majority of current cocaine users use the drug only infrequently.

It is also fair to point out that monthly and weekly use, even when it occurs, is still a long way from addiction. The studies demonstrate that only a very small proportion of cocaine users are persistent abusers, much less addicts (Erickson & Alexander, 1989). In a study of 50 people who used cocaine persistently over a ten-year period, only five demonstrated the characteristics of compulsive users at any point in those years (Siegel, 1984). These users, even during periods of heavily increased use, did not progress to habitual patterns of cocaine use. Similar studies in Canada, Scotland, Australia, and Holland all found controlled use to be the common pattern (Cohen, 1989; Ditton et al., 1991; Mugford & Cohen, 1989). All of these studies showed the level of use and problems associated with use came and went during the study period. The most frequent response to any problems that surfaced in using cocaine was to quit or greatly cut back use—hardly the characteristics of addiction (Erickson, 1993; Erickson et al., 1987; Siegel, 1984).

Craig Reinarmann and Harry Levine (1989) have carefully researched the media and state efforts to create the crack scare. Reinarmann and Levine define a "drug scare" as a period when all social difficulties—whether crime, health problems, or the failure of the education system—are blamed on a chemical substance. As outlined earlier, "drug scares" are routine in U.S. history. Problems of opiate addiction at the turn of the century were blamed on Chinese immigrants; African Americans were portrayed as "cocaine fiends" during the 1920s; violent behavior resulting from marijuana consumption was linked to Mexican farm laborers in the 1920s and 1930s. The construction of the crack scare was similar in that it linked the use of crack-cocaine to inner-city blacks, Hispanics, and youths. In the 1970s, when the use of expensive cocaine hydrochloride was concentrated among affluent whites, both the media and state focused their attention on heroin, perceived as a drug of the inner-city poor. Only when cocaine was democratized by the availability of inexpensive crack to minority groups and the poor did the social construction of crack as a demon drug begin.

The media hype, which began in 1986, was intense. *Time* and *Newsweek* ran five cover stories each on crack during that year. The three major television networks quickly joined the frenzy; NBC did 400 news stories on crack between June and December. They ran 74 drug stories on their nightly news in July. These stories universally repeated highly inflated and inaccurate estimates of crack use and issued dire warnings about the dangers of crack that were out of proportion to the available evidence.

Ironically, research from the National Institute of Drug Abuse showed that the use of all forms of cocaine had reached its peak four years earlier and had been declining ever since. Every indicator showed that at the height of the media frenzy crack use was relatively rare (Beckett, 1994; Orcutt & Turner, 1993; Walker, 1998). Surveys of high school seniors clearly showed that experimentation with cocaine and cocaine products had been decreasing steadily since 1980. The government's own drug use statistics showed that 96% of young people in the United States had never even tried crack. If there had been an epidemic, it was long over in 1986. Reinarmann and Levine argue convincingly that the intense coverage of crack may have created new markets for the drug and slowed the decline in use that had already been underway for almost a decade (Reinarmann & Levine, 1989).

Although the crack scare was a chimera, the results were serious and immediate. New state and federal laws were passed increasing mandatory sentences for crack use and sales. These laws resulted in a situation where someone arrested for crack faced the prospect of a prison sentence three to eight times longer than someone sentenced for possession of cocaine hydro-chloride—the substance needed to produce crack (Walker, 1998). The drug laws had been turned on their head, with drug wholesalers now treated more leniently than retailers and users. In addition, the crack scare resulted in the racialization of the drug war (a topic explored in detail later in the chapter). Blacks represent 48% of all individuals arrested on drug charges, roughly three-and-a-half times their actual rate of use (Walker, 1998).

"Crack Babies"

One other cocaine-related scare needs to be examined before we move on. The introduction of cocaine in smokeable form raised concerns about the potential impact of cocaine use on pregnant women and their fetuses. The use of any drug, whether alcohol, tobacco, or "crack," is risky during pregnancy (Martin et al., 1992). However, the panic that resulted from early research claims about cocaine's damage to fetuses and the laws passed by the state and federal governments in response to that research created policies that did far more damage to mother and fetus than the drug itself (Coffin, 1996). A 1985 case study suggested that prenatal cocaine use could result in several health problems related to fetal development, the health of the newborn, and future child development. Quickly thereafter, several other studies linked prenatal cocaine use to maternal weight loss and nutritional deficits; premature detachment of the placenta; premature birth; low birth weight; reductions in infants' body length and head circumference; rare birth defects, bone defects, and neural tube abnormalities (Coffin, 1996).

The media, of course, widely repeated these research findings, creating the impression that an epidemic of "crack babies" was plaguing the medical community. The intense publicity and an already demonstrated proclivity for dealing with drug issues with harsh measures led politicians to introduce laws in response to the "crack baby crisis." Laws were passed that required doctors and nurses to report pregnant drug users to child welfare authorities. Other laws quickly passed that required child welfare agencies to take children away from mothers who had used drugs while pregnant. Many states criminalized drug use during pregnancy. In July 1996 the South Carolina Supreme Court upheld a law which allowed women to be imprisoned for up to ten years for prenatal drug use (Coffin, 1996).

In the furor over the perceived dangers to the nation's most defenseless citizens, few took note of continuing research on prenatal cocaine use that challenged the foundation of the scare. Subsequent reviews of the early studies found serious methodological difficulties, including: the absence of any control groups; not distinguishing cocaine from other substances in the studies; and lack of follow-up studies noting the health and development of the newborn (Coffin, 1996).

One of the most serious problems with the early studies that had suggested a "fetal cocaine withdrawal syndrome" was that they were "nonblind," meaning that the individuals making the observations were told in advance which infants had mothers who had used cocaine during pregnancy. This biased the research and the results contradicted previous observations from doctors and nurses who had reported that cocaine-exposed children were indistinguishable from other children. In subsequent blind studies, observers were unable to detect the presence of fetal cocaine withdrawal syndrome (Coffin, 1996). In addition, research using control groups found no increased risk of Sudden Infant Death Syndrome (SIDS) among cocaine-exposed infants. Earlier studies had suggested a possible relationship between SIDS and maternal cocaine use, but they had failed to control for one of the most important variables in SIDS deaths, the socioeconomic status of the mother (Bauchner et al., 1988; Coffin, 1996).

Most of the scientific evidence points to the lack of quality prenatal care, the use of alcohol and tobacco, various environmental agents, and heredity as primary factors in poor fetal development and birth defects. Inadequate prenatal medical services have been positively associated with prematurity and low birth weight. The provision of quality prenatal care to cocaine-using mothers and to non-cocaine using mothers significantly improves fetal development. The use of alcohol, resulting in fetal alcohol syndrome, is responsible for the most severe birth defects. Tobacco use has also been strongly associated with low birth weight, prematurity, growth retardation, SIDS, low cognitive achievement, behavioral problems, and mental retardation. Lead exposure and poverty also have negative impacts on fetal and newborn development (Coffin, 1996).

The legal responses to the "crack baby scare" harmed both mothers and children. Making substance abuse during pregnancy a crime kept mothers from prenatal medical care, further endangering the fetus. It discouraged them from seeking drug treatment, which would have benefited both mother and child. When babies were removed from maternal care as a result of alleged drug use, social service agencies found it very difficult and often impossible to find homes for infants labeled as "crack babies" because of the alleged behavioral problems that might occur during infancy and early childhood. In addition, enforcement of maternal drug abuse laws was clearly and blatantly racist. Over 80% of the women subjected to prosecution under those laws were African-American or Latina women (Coffin, 1996; Polan et al., 1993).

Illicit Drugs and Death

Before discussing the most common illegal drug, we need to gain some perspective on the ultimate harm of using heroin or cocaine. If one were to listen to speeches of politicians and the warnings in anti-drug ads on television, it would appear that we are in the midst of a massive epidemic of illicit drug-related deaths. While any death is tragic and certainly should raise concern, there are two points to be made about drug-related deaths. First, they are relatively infrequent, despite popular impressions. And second, when they do occur, they are more directly attributable to drug laws than to the drugs themselves.

It is very difficult to estimate the total number of drug-related deaths because of definitional problems. For example, some estimates include the drive-by shootings of drug dealers as drug-related deaths. We are inclined to define such deaths as bullet-related. If multiple drugs (most commonly alcohol and an illicit drug) are found in an autopsy, which substance "caused" the death? In addition, autopsies often pinpoint congenital health conditions as well as the presence of an illicit drug. Once again, is the death drug-related? The Department of Justice estimates that 7,500 people die each year from the consumption of illegal drugs (Byrne, 1994). Others estimate that there are about 3,600 deaths (Nadelmann, 1989, p. 943).

The first and most obvious point is that in a country where 217 million people are over the age of 12, 7,500 is a very small number. That's about 1 drug-related death for every 29,000 people over the age of 12. This pales in comparison to the number of deaths on an annual basis from two legal drugs, alcohol and tobacco. There are 150,000 alcohol-related deaths each year. Add to that figure the estimated 390,000 people each year who die from illnesses related to the consumption of tobacco and you arrive at a figure 72 times larger than the deaths related to consumption of all other illicit drugs. Yet there is no equivalent hysterical reaction to these legal drugs comparable to the campaign against heroin and cocaine.

The Drug Abuse Warning Network estimates there are an average of 400 heroin deaths a year and 200 cocaine deaths a year. There are about 3.5 million heroin users in the United States, so the number of deaths per 100,000 heroin users is about 11. Looking at the estimated 500,000 heroin addicts, the number of deaths per 100,000 heroin addicts is about 80. There are roughly 22 million cocaine users in the United States. The number of deaths per

100,000 cocaine users is about 0.9. Of the 5 million regular cocaine users, the death rate per 100,000 is about 3.

While the numbers belie the urgency of the "drug war," it is even more troubling that most of these deaths occur as a result of the drug *laws*—not as a result of the drug itself. Take the case of heroin. As was pointed out earlier, heroin is a relatively benign drug; "there is no evidence conclusively establishing a link between heroin and disease or tissue degeneration such as that which has been established for tobacco and alcohol" (Reiman, 1998). Why then do people die from using heroin? The answer is that the drug laws create an unsafe market. Consumers of heroin and other illegal drugs purchase substances produced under unregulated conditions. Often the drugs are mixed with other dangerous substances or have potencies far in excess of that which the user expects (Nadelmann, 1989). Most drug overdoses result from the ingestion of adulterated drugs, not from misuse or abuse. In addition, the clandestine nature of drug use necessitated by drug prohibition often results in unsanitary practices that can cause death and injury. Heroin addicts share needles, spreading disease and illness. One-quarter of all the AIDS cases in the United States can be directly attributed to the unsafe and unsanitary conditions in which illicit drugs are used (Nadelmann, 1989).

Finally, the drug laws encourage misuse of illicit drugs. Consider the case of cocaine. Of the 22 million users, only about 3% will become problem cocaine abusers (National Institute on Drug Abuse, 1987). The real danger from cocaine is a direct result of the drug laws that encourage users to seek a more intense and cheaper high by smoking the drug rather than snorting it. The drug laws drive the price of cocaine up, and users innovate to compensate for the added expense. They freebase and use crack; as we have seen, there is a much greater risk when the drug is smoked.

Marijuana

The most commonly used illegal drug in the United States comes from the flowers and leaves of the *cannabis sativa* plant. The dried leaves and flowers are smoked, like tobacco, in cigarettes ("joints") or pipes. All the available evidence we have on marijuana indicates that it is not addictive, nor does a tolerance to the drug develop. "Most experts believe that death as a result of a marijuana 'overdose' is next to impossible" (Goode, 1997, p. 163). As early as 1972, the National Commission on Marihuana and Drug Abuse found that:

> Marihuana's relative potential for harm to the vast majority of individual users and its actual impact on society does not justify a social policy designed to seek out and firmly punish those who use it. This judgment is based on prevalent use patterns, on behavior exhibited by the vast majority of users and on our interpretations of existing medical and scientific data. This position also is consistent with the estimate by law enforcement personnel that the elimination of use is unattainable. (Shafer, 1972: Ch. V)

Yet in 1996, 641,642 people were arrested, 85% for simple possession (FBI, 1997).

Even the Drug Enforcement Administration has trouble making marijuana look like a dangerous drug. In September 1988, Francis L. Young, the chief administrative law judge of the DEA, reviewed all the medical and scientific evidence on marijuana and came to some startling conclusions (Trebach, 1989):

- There has never been a single documented cannabis-related death.
- About 70 million Americans have used marijuana and there has never been a reported overdose, a striking contrast not just with alcohol but with aspirin.
- Marijuana, in its natural form, is one of the safest therapeutically active substances known to man.
- In strict medical terms marijuana is far safer than many foods we commonly consume.

The real danger to marijuana smokers comes from marijuana that has been tainted by government drug control programs, such as the spraying of paraquat and other herbicides on marijuana crops. While some problems are associated with marijuana use, such as injury to the mucous membranes and interrupted attention spans (Murray, 1986), it scarcely appears to deserve the attention it gets from law enforcement authorities, especially when compared with the dangers of using tobacco, alcohol, and even aspirin.

Despite scientific findings that marijuana poses very little danger, drug warriors rekindled panic in the mid- and late-1990s, with a new, frightening portrait of the "killer weed." In this modern version of "Reefer Madness," marijuana causes brain damage, impairs reproduction, is a gateway to the use of "hard" drugs, and can "flatline" users. As discussed in other chapters, frightening stories were used to spin a wholly inaccurate mythology of marijuana to scare citizens into supporting criminal penalties against marijuana in the 1930s. In the 1990s, the myths of marijuana usage were repeated in television public service ads and in DARE classes all across the country. The facts are quite different from the propaganda. Let us take a brief look at the most common myths that constitute 1990s "Reefer Madness."

Marijuana causes brain damage. The study most frequently cited to "demonstrate" brain damage is seriously flawed. That study was conducted on four rhesus monkeys. The methodology failed to control for experimental bias, and the researcher incorrectly identified a perfectly normal monkey brain as "damaged." A review panel made up of scientists associated with the Institute of Medicine of the National Academy of Sciences strongly disputed the study results. Subsequent studies of human populations, including a study of heavy users, have never shown evidence of brain damage resulting from marijuana use (Co et al., 1977; Institute of Medicine, 1982; Kuehnle et al., 1977).

Marijuana is a "gateway" drug. There is probably no more enduring myth than the argument that marijuana serves as a "gateway" drug and leads to use of heroin, cocaine, and other "hard" drugs. There is no real evidence to support this claim; there is strong evidence, from the actual experiences of real people in actual settings, that it is entirely untrue. Take the example of Holland. The Dutch, during the 1970s, partially legalized the sale and use of marijuana. Since that time rates of heroin and cocaine use in Holland have declined substantially and continue to decline. Studies done in the United States in the 1970s, after several states "decriminalized" marijuana possession, showed a strong negative correlation between marijuana use and alcohol use. A RAND Corporation study in 1993 also measured the "gateway" effect in the United States. The RAND study showed that in states where marijuana possession had been decriminalized and marijuana was more available than in other states, drug-related emergency room visits actually decreased. Rather than being a "gateway" drug it appears that marijuana is a substitute for more dangerous drugs like alcohol, heroin, and cocaine (Dennis, 1990; Rand Corporation, 1993).

Marijuana is more carcinogenic than tobacco. It is true that marijuana, if smoked, contains about the same amount of carcinogens as tobacco. But this has to be qualified in two ways. First, tobacco smokers consume much more tobacco than marijuana smokers consume marijuana. Tobacco has a 90% addiction rate and is the most addictive of all drugs. Second, paraphernalia laws, passed as an adjunct to drug laws, make safe marijuana smoking much more difficult. Water pipes and bongs which remove many of the carcinogens in marijuana smoke are illegal in most states. Additionally, if marijuana were legal it could be consumed in cannabis drinks like *bhlang* (cannabis tea), which is totally non-carcinogenic (Dreher, 1982; Franklin, 1988).

Legalizing marijuana would lead to a massive increase in highway accidents. No one can argue that marijuana, when used to the point of intoxication, does impair psycho-motor functioning. But the truth is that marijuana is much less of a hazard on the roads than alcohol. Studies of traffic accidents have shown that people intoxicated on alcohol and people intoxicated on marijuana and alcohol have about the same number of accidents. But when people using marijuana only are studied, the accident rate is much lower. In fact, research in states that have reduced penalties for marijuana possession and experienced an increase in marijuana use have shown a decline in alcohol usage and a decline in fatal highway accidents (Chaloupka & Laixuthai, 1992; Gieringer, 1988).

Marijuana and "flatliners." In one of the most famous anti-marijuana television commercials, the Partnership for a Drug-Free America (a private organization supported heavily by contributions from the tobacco industry) presented a picture of what they claimed was a normal human brainwave and compared it to what they claimed was a "flat" brainwave from a fourteen-year-old on pot. The Partnership had to pull the ad after complaints from medical researchers. The Partnership had "faked" the marijuana intoxicated brainwave. The truth is that marijuana actually increases alpha wave activity. Alpha waves are associated with relaxation and human creativity (Cotts, 1992; Dornbush et al., 1971).

Today's marijuana is more potent. This myth isn't just the result of bad research, it's the result of lazy research. Researchers mistakenly compared the baseline THC content of marijuana seized by police in the 1970s with contemporary marijuana samples. The problem is that in the 1970s marijuana was stored in hot evidence rooms for long periods of time before it was tested for potency. The result was a deterioration and decline in potency before the chemical assay was performed. Independent chemical assays performed under scientific conditions on 1970s marijuana shows a potency equivalent to contemporary "street" marijuana (Mikuirya & Aldrich, 1988).

Marijuana can be lethal. Animal research on high doses of cannabinoids have found a lethal dose, but the ratio of cannabinoids necessary to cause death is 1 to 40,000. Simply put, you would have to smoke 40,000 times the dose of marijuana necessary to get high to overdose. The lethal ratio for alcohol is 1 to 4, making it very easy to understand how over 5,000 people a year die from alcohol overdoses.

The data appear to tell us that the danger from the consumption of illicit drugs, while real, does not justify the panic reaction that the media and government have created. In fact, the dangers of illicit drugs appear to pale in comparison to the dangers from drugs that are tolerated and even endorsed in everyday life. While exaggerating the dangers of using drugs, the mythology surrounding them also blocks the constructive use of proscribed substances (Nadelmann, 1989; Trebach, 1989). Marijuana, for example, is useful in treating disorders such as multiple sclerosis and glaucoma and in relieving the side effects of chemotherapy for cancer patients. In fact, the Drug Enforcement Administration itself has argued for the medical legalization of marijuana. Heroin is a particularly useful and very safe pain reliever, as is cocaine, both of which are widely used outside of the United States for medical treatment. It appears that in yet another way the drug laws create more problems than they solve.

◈

DRUGS AND CRIME

One of the most compelling questions raised in the debate on drug policy is whether drug use and drug addiction lead to an increase in crime in the United States. Those who favor drug prohibition point to several important research findings as indicators of a relationship between drugs and crime. For example, James Inciardi's study of narcotics users and non-narcotics users in Miami during the period 1978–1981 showed that narcotics users committed more crimes, engaged in a greater diversity of offenses, and committed the more serious crimes of robbery and burglary (Inciardi, 1992). Other findings have seemingly pointed to similar relationships between drugs and crime. For example, it appears that the degree of drug use is directly related to the degree of criminality. Drug addicts tend to commit substantially fewer crimes prior to the beginning of addiction and after the cessation of addiction than they do during addiction (Gropper, 1985). Among heroin users this effect is pronounced. Daily heroin users seem to commit twice the number of property crimes as regular users (those who use the drug three to five days a week) and five times as many property crimes as irregular (those who use the drug two days a week or less) heroin users. As the level of drug usage decreases, the involvement in crime decreases as well. In addition, research indicates that a history of drug abuse is one of the best predictors of involvement in serious offenses (Gropper, 1985).

These data do raise concern, but they must be put into context. While there is an apparent relationship between the use of drugs and the amount of crime committed by users, there is little evidence that drugs *cause* crime. A majority of heroin users have been involved in criminal activity *prior* to their use of heroin (McGlothlin, Anglin, & Wilson, 1978). As Erich Goode (1997) points out, most addicts and abusers "are involved in crime as a way of life; very few have a legitimate job; very few have enough education to make them[selves] marketable. Most commit crimes just to stay alive" (p. 126). While it is easy for policymakers to make the emotional claim that drugs cause crime, research indicates "that portraying addicts as persons in constant, frantic pursuit of drugs is an inaccurate stereotype" (McCaghy et al., 2000, p. 310).

The only drug for which a clear causal link with crime has been established is alcohol—a legal drug. Columbia University researchers found that alcohol is associated with far more violent crime than all illegal drugs combined. Of all prisoners incarcerated in state prisons for violent offenses, 21% committed their crimes under the influence of alcohol. In contrast, only 1% were high on heroin, and only 3% had used cocaine or crack (Califano, 1998). That research is confirmed by federal statistics showing that 30.7% of all crimes are committed "under the influence of" alcohol, while 16.1% of all crimes are committed under the influence of alcohol and other drugs; only 8.8% are committed under the influence of illegal drugs alone (Rasmussen & Benson, 1994, p. 106).

While there is no causal link between drugs and crime, the same cannot be said for drug laws. Drug laws adversely affect the market for drugs and the conditions under which drugs are purchased and consumed. As a result, the drug laws create a great deal of serious crime with very real victims.

> Prohibition causes what the media and police misname "drug-related violence." This prohibition-related violence includes all the random shootings and murders associated with black market drug transactions: ripoffs, eliminating the competition, killing informers and suspected informers. Those who doubt that prohibition is responsible for this violence need only note the absence of violence in the legal drug market. For example, there is no violence associated with the production, distribution, and sale of alcohol. Such violence was ended by the repeal of Prohibition. (Ostrowski, 1990, p. 650)

Illegal markets—markets created by the criminal law—breed violence for many reasons. The profits realized from the sales of illegal drugs are so high that competition becomes intense, and turf wars result. Illicit drug entrepreneurs have no recourse to legal institutions to resolve disputes over turf, quality of merchandise, and "brand" names. Because drugs are illegal, the law itself makes violence the only dispute resolution mechanism available to drug dealers. The importance of drug laws in creating violence-prone illegal markets was clearly established in a major research project looking at the crack market in New York City. The researchers found that 85% of "crack-related" crimes were the direct result of market-related issues, primarily territorial disputes among crack dealers (Goldstein et al., 1997).

The terminology "drug-related crime" implies that the pharmacological effects of drugs cause violent and criminal behavior. Research shows that "drug-related crime" is related only tangentially to drugs themselves. The actual cause of "drug-related crime" is the illicit market created because of drug laws. Research conducted by the New York City Police Department makes this clear. Researchers analyzed homicides in New York in which cocaine or crack use had played a role and identified five specific types of relationships between drugs and murder (Salekin & Alexander, 1991):

- **Psychopharmacological** homicides were murders in which the ingestion of a drug or withdrawal symptoms related to addiction caused individuals to become angry, aggressive, irrational, or violent, resulting in them committing a murder or being the victim of a killing. This relationship is the one usually thought of when the term "drug-related crime" is used.
- **Economic-compulsive** homicide describes situations in which a drug user engaged in a violent crime in order to obtain money to buy drugs. Illicit drug users commit crimes such as robbery, burglary, prostitution, and drug dealing as a means of raising funds to support their drug habits. These crimes are rarely violent and rarely result in homicide, but occasionally they do.
- **Systemic** homicides were instances of a drug dealer using violence as a competitive business strategy in the drug black market. Prime examples are competition over turf and infringement of street-brand names for drugs.
- **Multidimensional** homicides were murders that contained several events, making it difficult to discern what really precipitated the violent act.
- **Homicides with drug-related dimensions** were murders where either the perpetrator and/or the victim were using drugs but reasons other than drugs were considered the primary explanation for the murder.

The researchers concluded that the psychopharmacological model (the model usually identified with the concept of "drug-related crime") and the economic compulsive model (also sometimes identified as a major source of drug-related crime) were very rare. Competition in the drug business caused most of the homicides. Systemic homicides do not involve consumption of drugs; rather, drug laws create the competition for enormous profits.

Another study of New York City homicides estimated that 40% of the 414 homicides studied were the result of business competition in the drug market (Galiber, 1990, pp. 831, 849). In Los Angeles, police discovered a similar relationship. Highly lucrative turf wars between street gangs were linked to the drive-by shootings. The exigencies of the illegal cocaine market and the profits to be realized in that market created the danger (FBI, 1992).

Violence in the illicit drug market is a replication of precisely the same kind of violence that accompanied the prohibition of alcohol as newly created organized crime groups competed for "turf" related to illicit alcohol sales. Violence was only one outcome of Prohibition.

> Prohibition was a clear-cut failure—very possibly the biggest domestic legal mistake in the federal government's entire history. . . . It may have switched millions of drinkers from beer, a less potent beverage, to distilled spirits, a far more potent—and more harmful—beverage; encouraged the consumption of harmful, poisonous substitutes, such as methyl alcohol; it certainly gave organized crime an immense boost, pouring billions of dollars into the hands of criminal gangs, consolidating their power, and effectively capitalizing their other illegal enterprises; it encouraged corruption and brutality on the part of politicians and the police on a massive scale." (Goode, 1997, pp. 104, 105–106)

Similarly, today's drug laws are criminogenic. Because drugs are illegal, purchasers are forced into a criminal underworld to buy drugs, thereby making them potential victims of crime and bringing them into contact with criminal actors with whom they would ordinarily never have contact (Kaplan, 1983). Crimes ancillary to drug use take place because of this relationship, a relationship entirely attributable to the illegality of drugs. While no one can guarantee that repeal of the drug laws would make the underground market disappear entirely, common sense should indicate that reduced profits resulting from legal drugs would shrink the size of that market and reduce the incentive for violence in direct proportion to the reduction in market size and profit.

◈

LAW ENFORCEMENT STRATEGIES IN THE WAR ON DRUGS

Criminologist Charles McCaghy provides a concise and direct evaluation of the war on drugs:

> In baseball a player with three strikes is out. But after three dismal failures in trying to stop the use of alcohol, opiates, and marihuana, the U.S.

government still stands at the plate determined to smash the hell out of the drug problem. Unlike ballplayers, who adjust to the peculiarities of various pitchers and who put past experience to use, U.S. presidents and legislators subscribe to a single-minded philosophy—if you don't hit it, you're not swinging hard enough. (McCaghy et al., 2000, p. 323)

The costs of drug-related law enforcement and incarceration in the United States was approximately $59 billion in 1998 (NIDA, 1998, pp. 1–6). At the state and local levels, law enforcement agencies spend more than 20% of their total budgets on drug enforcement (Nadelmann, 1989, p. 940). In 1973, there were 328,670 arrests for drug law violations; in 1996, the number was 1,506,200. The 80% increase in the federal prison population from 1985 to 1995 was almost entirely due to drug convictions (Bureau of Justice Statistics, 1997b). In 1980, 8% of all inmates were in prison for drug law violations. In 1997, 23% of all adults in state prisons and an astounding 59.5% of all adults in federal institutions were convicted of drug charges (BJS, 1997b, pp. 10–11). Drug law violators receive much longer sentences than most other convicted criminals. For example, the average time served in a federal prison for a drug law violation is 78 months, compared to 67 months for rape, 51 months for burglary, 50 months for aggravated assault, and 37 months for auto theft (p. 476). In 1997 it cost about $8.6 billion a year to incarcerate convicted drug law violators (pp. 10–11).

◈

Measures of Success in the War on Drugs

With all of this law enforcement activity, has anything changed? In 1989 there was ten times as much cocaine on the streets as there was in 1977. During the same period, the purity of cocaine on the streets quintupled, and the profits from its sale climbed to an estimated $50 billion a year (Benoit, 1989, p. 33). Precisely the same effects were noted with regard to heroin. The international drug trade generates about $400 billion annually. That constitutes about 8% of all international trade, making it an industry equal to the international textile and automobile industries. The drug trade appears to have survived the drug war quite nicely.

Drug Use and the Drug War

Has the war on drugs reduced drug use? Those who support a punitive approach to drug enforcement argue that the large numbers of arrests, significant increases in incarceration rates, and long prison terms should cause a decline in drug use. But the facts do not support this claim.

The number of heavy drug users in the United States remains unchanged at about 4 to 6 million (Jehl, 1994, p. D20). Marijuana use continues to rise in all regions of the country; cocaine use is stable; and heroin use is rising markedly in the Southwest, West, and Southern regions of the country. The total number of monthly drug users is about 11.4 million, and people still spend about $49 billion a year on drug consumption (Drug Use, 1994, p. 16A).

Recent surveys of use patterns among high school students show increasing numbers of students using marijuana (up from 21.2% in 1992 to 26%) and LSD (up from 5.6% in 1992 to 6.8%) (Treaster, 1994, pp. A1, A14). About half of all high school students in 1995 tried an illegal drug prior to graduation (Johnson et al., 1996, p. 42). The percentage of high school seniors who say they find marijuana "fairly easy" or "very easy" to obtain has remained at 82% each year since 1975 (Johnson et al., 1996, p. 270).

Even the most ardent supporters of the war on drugs admit that it has not and cannot eliminate drug abuse or addiction (Kleber, 1994). Fagan and Spelman (1994) have argued persuasively that market forces, not law enforcement efforts, impact patterns of drug usage. Legal institutions have almost no impact on drug markets. In fact, there is a credible argument to be made that the existence of drug laws and the intensive enforcement campaign accompanying them may stimulate drug use and may be responsible for the production of larger numbers of addicts than we might otherwise have had. Mishan (1990), for example, suggests that the crucial factor in spreading addiction is the enormous profits in the drug trade. As long as drugs are illegal, virtually every addict becomes a drug salesperson in order to raise sufficient funds to pay for his or her habit (Zion, 1993). In addition to the profits that can be realized from the sale of illegal drugs, illegality also stimulates experimentation, particularly among adolescents, by raising the specter of the "forbidden fruit" (Ostrowski, 1989).

We know that 75 million Americans (37% of the population over the age of twelve) have used illegal drugs. Six percent of these people are current users (Walker, 1998). Three million Americans have used cocaine in the last 30 days (Eitzen & Zinn, 1997). There are about 18 to 35 million regular marijuana users in the United States and five million regular heroin users (Trebach & Engelsman, 1989, p. 40). Furthermore, it is probable that these are gross underestimates of drug use because the instruments utilized to reach these conclusions miss a sizeable segment of society altogether. High school dropouts, the homeless, and inner-city youth simply slip through the researchers' nets.

Why has there been so little progress? As McCaghy (2000) suggested, it is because present drug enforcement policies do not work and cannot be made to work even with dramatic increases in resources and personnel. The government's strategy in the war on drugs hinges on three basic policies: eradication, interdiction, and street-level drug enforcement associated with domestic drug crackdowns.

Chapter Eight

The Failure of Interdiction

The first strategy assumes that with sufficient resources drugs can be stopped from entering the United States by controlling the borders. Using the most optimistic claims of interdiction, approximately 10–15% of heroin shipments and 30% of cocaine shipments are seized. For there to be any impact on the drug market, about 75% of these shipments would have to be interdicted.

The difficulty with interdiction strategies can be illustrated by taking a quick look at the cocaine market. The entire U.S. demand for cocaine, the largest demand in the world, can be satisfied by 13 truckloads of cocaine a year. Considering that the United States has 88,633 miles of shoreline, 7,500 miles of international borders with Canada and Mexico and 300 ports of entry, finding 13 truckloads of anything is virtually impossible (Frankel, 1997, p. A1). Consider this simple fact: the criminal justice system cannot keep drugs out of maximum security prisons, much less seal the nation's borders to drug trafficking.

The only minor success that the interdiction campaign can claim is with marijuana, a bulky commodity that is difficult to transport. The net effect of that success has been an even bigger problem. Marijuana smugglers and growers in other countries have simply moved to cocaine and heroin as substitutes for marijuana, meaning even more of those drugs are being imported to the United States, and U.S. marijuana production has increased dramatically in the last 10 years.

Erich Goode provides an excellent summary of the ineffectiveness of interdiction.

> Stamping out drugs at their source is a fatally flawed policy for four reasons, each of which is related specifically to the illegality of the drug trade. *First*, an almost infinite number of entrepreneurs are willing to take a risk to earn a profit; arresting one results in another's stepping in and taking over the business. *Second*, logistically, growing, transporting, and selling drugs are impossible to detect and eradicate because the drug trade does not require much space and can be easily shifted around when necessary. *Third*, the drug business contributes to the wages even of low-level workers and the economy of regions, even entire countries; hence, it is deeply entrenched and widely supported. And *fourth*, the enormous profits of the drug business translate, for distributors, into enormous resources which enable them to evade detection, corrupt officials, and purchase personnel and equipment to combat law enforcement. (Goode, 1997, p. 88)

Goode refers to the "push-down/pop-up" factor (Nadelmann, 1988, p. 9). If drug production is halted in one location, new suppliers pop up in another to fill the gap.

The Failure of Crop Eradication Policies

Efforts directed at crop eradication in countries producing illegal drugs have failed miserably, for reasons very similar to interdiction. Drugs like heroin, cocaine, and marijuana can be grown and processed in a wide variety of locations. If one particular locale is targeted and eradication programs successfully carried out there, growers in other locations will make up for the deficit in supply. If heroin supplies in the Golden Crescent (Afghanistan, Iran, Pakistan) are targeted, opium growers in the Golden Triangle (Thailand, Burma, Laos) or in Mexico will increase production and supply the demand.

The case of cocaine is even more instructive. In theory, cocaine should be the easiest of the illicit crops to subject to an eradication strategy. It grows only in South America and principally in Peru and Bolivia (with Colombia, Ecuador, and Brazil making small contributions to the supply). At the moment the world's entire cocaine supply is grown on 700 square miles of land. Even if eradication efforts were more effective, there are 2.5 million square miles of land in South American where the crops could be relocated (Nadelmann, 1989, p. 945).

In the countries that produce the crops there is well-organized political opposition to crop eradication. The production of cocaine and opium brings in billions of dollars in hard currency to impoverished countries and puts money in the pockets of millions of cultivators, processors, and smugglers.

Efforts to eradicate the marijuana crop in the United States have made the marijuana industry stronger and more dangerous than ever before (Potter, Gaines & Holbrook, 1990). Kentucky participates in a federally-funded program to find and burn marijuana crops. The net effect of the eradication program has been to spread marijuana cultivation throughout the state, to increase the quantity of marijuana being produced, and to increase the quality. In addition, the eradication program has taken what was essentially a "Mom and Pop" industry a few years ago and turned it into a highly organized criminal cartel.

In attempting to comply with U.S. demands for domestic control of drugs, source countries engage in programs that are environmentally disastrous. The Colombian government initiated a program of aerial spraying that drops herbicides on over 100,000 acres of land each year ("White paper," 1998). Colombian peasants who depend on the coca crop as their only source of income then moved into the Amazon rainforests, clearing 1.75 million acres of rainforest (Trade and Environment Database, 1997, pp. 4–8). This is important because Colombia's forests account for about 10% of the world's biodiversity. In addition to causing this displacement, the aerial fumigation program is a failure. In 1994 coca production consumed 111,000 acres; by 1998 that production had *expanded* to 195,000 acres ("Colombia," 1998).

The illegality of cocaine adds to the environmental damage. Cocaine manufacturers hide their laboratories deep in the Colombian forests. There are no regulated means of disposing of the hazardous wastes associated with the refining of cocaine. As a result some 10 million liters of sulfuric acid, 16 million liters of ethyl ether, 8 million liters of acetone, and 40–770 million liters of kerosene are poured directly into the ground and into streams (Trade and Environment Database, 1997).

The Failure of Domestic Drug Crackdowns

Street-level drug enforcement efforts in the United States have had little success in the drug war. Intensive street-level law enforcement efforts are very expensive. Although they result in the arrests of thousands of low-level drug dealers and users, they have little impact on the other elements involved in illicit drug supply. While some of these enforcement efforts have been able to claim "temporary and transitory success," they have not impacted the availability of illegal drugs at all (Chaiken, 1988).

Let us be very clear about who is arrested in drug crackdowns. Although drug war rhetoric claims that it targets "drug kingpins," large-scale smugglers, and organized crime figures, in 1996, 75% (1,131,156) of the drug arrests in the United States were for possession and only 25% (374,044) were for the sale or manufacture of a drug (Office of National Drug Control Policy, 1998). The latter number is highly misleading. The average drug "pusher" is not a "kingpin." In fact the average dealer holds a low-wage job and sells drugs part-time to fund his or her own drug use (Reuter et al., 1990, pp. 49–50). "Little fish are getting jailed while big fish walk free. A 1995 Sentencing Commission report found that only 11.2% of drug-trafficking defendants are big-timers, while 52% were low-level street dealers and couriers" (Page, 1999, p. 17).

The militarization of U.S. law enforcement is another consequence of the drug war. Today, the National Guard has more drug agents than the DEA has special agents. The National Guard is involved in 1,300 drug-related operations daily (Munger, 1997). In addition, 89% of U.S. police departments have created paramilitary units, and 46% have been trained by active-duty armed forces members. These units are primarily used in serving no-knock search warrants—in other words, breaking into private homes. Today, about 20% of the U.S. police departments use paramilitary units to patrol urban neighborhoods (Kraska & Kappeler, 1999).

Finally, there is a "civil" side to street-level drug enforcement: asset forfeiture. In theory, asset forfeiture laws allow the state to seize "ill-gotten" gains from criminals so that they are denied the spoils of their crimes. The theory behind the laws threatens civil liberties. In a forfeiture case a "civil action" is initiated against the *property*, not the individual. Therefore constitutional protections do not apply. For example, there is no presumption of innocence, no exclusion of hearsay, and no right to an attorney. In addition, the burden of proof is reversed in a forfeiture case. The government only has to establish probable cause that the property involved is subject to the forfeiture laws. The property owner must prove that the property is "innocent."

There is no legal requirement that the property owner involved be prosecuted for any criminal act. Eighty percent of the people who forfeit property were never charged with a crime (Schneider & Flaherty, 1991). Forfeiture can move ahead even if the property owner is arrested, tried, and acquitted of the charges. In fact, property may be seized even if its owner had no knowledge of illegal activities.

In 1994, federal forfeitures totaled $730 million (Association of the Bar, 1994). Forfeiture has become a high priority in the drug war, and the ability of law enforcement agencies to profit from their enforcement activities has seriously compromised the due process goals of the criminal justice system. As a result of large federal block grants for forfeiture activities and the profits from forfeiture itself, law enforcement agencies have begun targeting potential assets rather than probable crimes. Police department policies often link salary levels, continued employment, new equipment, and total budget dollars for drug units to forfeiture activities. This has changed the nature of law enforcement and the basic relationship between the police and the public (Blumenson & Nilsen, 1998).

◇

RACISM AND THE DRUG WAR

The drug war, particularly intensive street-level drug enforcement, has been blatantly racist. African Americans represent 37% of all drug arrests. Forty-two percent of drug law violators in federal correctional facilities and 60% of those in state prison are black. Yet only 11% of the nation's drug users are black (Substance Abuse and Mental Health Services Administration, 1997, p. 19).

In addition to being subject to arrest in disproportionate numbers to their use of drugs, blacks are also far more likely to get prison sentences for drug law violations. Overall, 54% of African Americans get sentenced to prison as opposed to 34% of whites for the same drug offenses. In drug possession cases 44% of blacks get prison time as compared to 29% of whites, and in trafficking cases 60% of blacks go to prison as opposed to 37% of whites. Between 1990 and 1996 the number of blacks in the federal prison system for violent and property crimes decreased by 726, while the number of blacks in prison for drug offenses increased by 12,852 (BJS, 1998a, p. 13).

Much of this disparity results from federal laws specifically targeting crack. Crack cocaine is the only controlled substance for which a first-time offense of 5 grams (about the size of a pack of sugar) triggers a federal mandatory *minimum* sentence of 5 years. In contrast, an offender must be convicted of possession of at least 500 grams of powdered cocaine to receive the same mandatory five-year sentence (Alter, 1999, p. 6). In 1986, prior to mandatory minimums, the average federal drug sentence for African Americans was 11% higher than that of whites. By 1990, the average federal sentence for blacks was 49% higher than for whites (Meierhoefer, 1992, p. 20). Under federal mandatory minimums, first-time crack offenders and low-level crack dealers receive an average sentence of 10 years and six months. That sentence is 59% longer than the average prison sentence for rapists; 38% longer than the average prison sentence for those convicted of weapons offenses; and only 18% shorter than the average prison sentence for those convicted of murder (U.S. Sentencing Commission, 1995, p. 150). At present levels of incarceration, a newborn black male has a 1 in 4 chance of being sentenced to prison during their lifetime compared to a 1 in 23 chance for a newborn white male (Bonczar & Beck, 1997).

◇

THE WAR ON DRUGS AS WAR AGAINST WOMEN

The collateral damage of increased enforcement has impacted women in general and minority women in particular. Between 1985 and 1996, female drug arrests increased by 95%, while male drug arrests have increased by 55.1% (UCR, 1997). Between 1989 and 1994, the group suffering the greatest increase in correctional system control was black women between the ages of 20 and 29. The increase in incarceration, parole, and probation rates for these women totaled 78%. Between 1986 and 1991, black women of all ages suffered an 828% increase in state incarceration on drug charges, the highest rate of all ethnic and gender groups (Association of the Bar, 1994, p. 523).

The arrests and prosecutions of "drug mules" in Queens, New York, illustrates the scope of this problem. One study found a drastic increase in the number of women arrested and subsequently charged with felony narcotics offenses. Many of these women were first-time offenders arrested for attempting to smuggle drugs through JFK International Airport, a major entry point for international travelers. Women suspected of being drug couriers faced mandatory sentences ranging from 15 years to life on their first felony arrests. If they were also charged under federal laws they faced a 50 years to life federal sentence ("Injustice," 1992).

Investigations determined that many of these women were either unwitting agents of drug smugglers or were women only marginally involved in drug smuggling operations. Because of the severe sentences they faced, most of these women did not go to trial. Instead they accepted plea bargains carrying sentences of 3 years to life, a sentence totally out of proportion with other first-time felony sentences. Many of these women were mothers who could not risk the longer separation from their children that the original charge entailed. The study found that many women charged as drug couriers pleaded guilty even if they had valid defenses or were innocent of the charges ("Injustice," 1992).

Women are disproportionately impacted by restrictions on judicial discretion in mandatory sentencing. The inability of the defendant to present evidence of mitigating circumstances in such cases is particularly crippling (Letwin, 1994, p. 2). Women are further disadvantaged by drug laws that fail to make a distinction between major participants in drug organizations and minor or ancillary players; drug laws that fail to recognize first-time offender status; and drug laws that fail to account for individual characteristics of defendants. As a result, the rate of incarceration for women has grown dramatically, increasing by 275% from 1980 to 1992 in the U.S. as a whole, and increasing by 433% (from 2,370 to 12,633) between 1986 and 1991 for drug defendants incarcerated in state prison. By 1991, 1 out of every 3 women incarcerated in a state prison was there as the result of a drug conviction, up from 1 in 8 in 1986 (Mauer & Huling, 1995).

But the impact of the drug war on women does not end with women as drug defendants. With drug policy emphasizing enforcement and punishment rather than education and rehabilitation, the impact on families is profound. When fathers are incarcerated, women are left as single heads of households to raise the children. When male children are arrested for drug sales, their mothers face the brunt of the civil forfeiture laws—losing possessions, whatever funds they may have accumulated in bank accounts, and facing almost certain eviction from their domiciles. When male addicts share needles because of a policy that makes the provision of clean needles a criminal offense, their partners face the risk of acquiring the HIV infection.

Female users with addictions also confront legal discrimination. The threat of arrest for possession is always present; in addition, mandatory reporting requirements can deprive them of access to medical care and drug counseling and treatment. Pregnant and new mothers face the danger of criminal prosecution on charges ranging from drug distribution to assault and murder. This discourages any effort to seek pre- or post-natal care for their babies. This problem is even greater for African American women. In cases where levels of drug use are similar or equal during pregnancy, black women are 10 times more likely than white women to be reported to child welfare agencies (Neuspiel, 1996).

Drug War Blowback

Drug war strategies have created a number of problems that would not exist if it were not for the intensive enforcement efforts against drugs. The corruption of law enforcement and other criminal justice personnel is a primary example. The immense amounts of money generated by the drug trade makes it possible to offer substantial inducements to enforcement personnel to overlook activities. Half of all police officers convicted as a result of FBI-initiated corruption investigations between 1993 and 1997 were involved in drug-related offenses (GAO, 1998, p. 35). "Although profit was found to be a motive common to traditional and drug-related police corruption, New York City's Mollen Com-mission identified power and vigilante justice as two additional motives for drug-related police corruption" (p. 3).

While we usually think of corruption in relation to police officers on the street and local prosecutors, the drug war has managed to offer incentives for corruption that reach to the highest levels of the United States government. It is indeed ironic that the very agencies of government who are beating the drums loudest in the war on drugs have also established a record of accepting assistance from and providing logistical support to some of the largest drug trafficking syndicates in the world. (See Lyman & Potter, 1998; Simon, 1999).

Closely related to the spread of drug-related corruption has been the added impetus the drug war has given to organized crime. Drug laws and intensified enforcement strategies have strengthened organized crime and created a whole new generation of organized crime groups (Lyman & Potter, 2000). Drug enforcement is by its very nature highly selective and discriminatory. It targets those most visible to the police. Those few dealers who are arrested are the least important, smallest operators—the easiest to catch. The net effect of drug enforcement is to weed out the inefficient drug dealers, paving the way for organized crime to rake in profits of $78 billion a year from drugs, conducting their business with virtual immunity. Compare that figure with organized crime's profits of about $200 million in the bootlegging of tobacco (a legal drug) and it is easy to understand the benefits of drug prohibition to organized crime (Nadelmann, 1989). The only reason organized crime can realize such enormous profits in the drug market is the fact that drugs are illegal. The actual cost of growing and producing illegal drugs is modest, but the criminal surcharge that organized crime can add to the cost of drugs because it competes with no legitimate suppliers is staggering. The drug laws, in effect, act like a government-sponsored subsidy to organized crime, a subsidy worth billions of dollars a year.

Finally, the war on drugs is beginning to spill out of its inner-city boundaries. The zeal to win the war against drugs has caused the courts to abrogate the Fourth Amendment protections against unreasonable search and seizure. In June 1995, the Supreme Court decided that school administrations should not be bound by presumption of innocence if drugs are the issue. A seventh-grader in Vernonia, Oregon refused to sign a form agreeing to submit to random urine tests to detect drug use by members of the football team.

> To search a 13-year-old's room, or his pockets, the police need probable cause to think he's broken the law. But to inspect his urine, the court now says, school officials need nothing beyond a vague fear of drugs . . . The policy may not have a great effect on drug abuse among adolescents, but it will teach them that they have no rights of privacy that the government is obliged to respect." (Chapman, 1995b, p. 27)

The vigorous enforcement of drug laws has created social problems far more serious than any caused by drug use alone. Let us state the point very clearly. Drug control policy has not failed for lack of resources, funding, legal powers, or adequate personnel. It has failed because the problem is not amenable to a criminal justice solution.

◇

MAKING PEACE IN THE WAR ON DRUGS

The list of failures of our present drug control initiatives could go on endlessly. We could talk about the inconsistency in the drug laws. The two most dangerous drugs in America—tobacco and alcohol—are freely available, while less dangerous drugs lead to felony convictions. We could talk about the threats to our basic constitutional rights created by questionable police tactics emanating from the difficulties of drug enforcement. We could talk about the disrespect for the law bred by drug enforcement. We have allowed the drug problem to be framed by political leaders and law enforcement officials as strictly a criminal justice system problem. As we have seen, the problem of drugs is far more complex than this simple approach. There are a number of alternatives to the mythology that has been constructed around the issue of drugs.

Drug Treatment

Drug addiction and drug abuse are health problems that can be treated and managed through programs exponentially more effective than the criminal law or law enforcement strategies. Research points to great successes in drug rehabilitation and drug counseling. The problem is that these programs are not available where they are needed (particularly the inner city), and they are not available in sufficient numbers (most drug rehabilitation programs targeted at lower-income groups have long waiting lists). In the United States 48% of the need for drug treatment, excluding alcohol abuse, is unmet (Woodward et al., 1997). Only 7% of the drug-control budget goes to treatment; the remaining 93% is spent on the ineffective control programs discussed above (Rydell & Everingham, 1994, p. 5). Since the early 1980s, treatment has been a declining priority in federal drug budgets. In 1981 treatment made up 25% of the federal drug budget; by 1991 that percentage had dropped to 14%, while federal spending on law enforcement approaches increased by 737% (Adams, 1994, p. 1). Trying to solve a public health problem with punitive enforcement policies antagonizes the problem and ignores policies that show great promise in actually doing something about drug use and its ancillary problems. This is an enormously foolish waste of resources.

Drug treatment can break patterns of addiction and abuse. More importantly, drug treatment positively impacts every ancillary social problem linked to drug abuse. Drug treatment is 10 times more cost effective than interdiction programs in reducing the use of cocaine in the U.S. (Rydell &

Everingham, 1994). Studies that have evaluated programs ranging from methadone treatment to inpatient residential programs to outpatient drug-free programs have found dramatic and positive results. What is even more remarkable about the evaluations of the three most common drug treatment modalities is that researchers have found them effective despite the many personal problems impacting clients, their long histories of deviant lifestyles, their long absences from medical care, and a lack of support for clients' rehabilitation efforts in their communities (Hubbard et al., 1989).

The Treatment Outcomes Prospectives Study ("TOPS"), funded by the National Institute on Drug Abuse, is the most comprehensive evaluation study of the effectiveness of drug treatment done in the United States. TOPS found drug treatment programs to be extremely effective in reducing drug use (Hubbard et al., 1989). The researchers tracked 10,000 drug abusers for a five-year period following their admission to one of the 37 treatment programs being evaluated. Heroin and cocaine use declined markedly. After only one year in methadone maintenance programs, heroin use by patients had declined by 70%. Heroin and cocaine use has dropped by 75% for patients in outpatient drug-free programs and by 56% for patients in residential treatment. By the end of the five-year tracking period less than 20% of the patients used any illegal drug except marijuana, and 40 to 50% of the patients abstained from all psychoactive drugs, legal or illegal. Every dollar invested in substance abuse treatment programs saves taxpayers $7.46 in social costs.

Drug treatment is cost effective for society. The National Treatment Improvement Evaluation Study found that effective treatment costs ranged from $1800 to $6800 per client per year. The average cost of incarcerating a drug user is $23,406 a year (Center for Substance Abuse and Treatment, 1996). Yet in 1997 only 15% of state and federal inmates received substance-abuse treatment during their current terms, down from one-third getting help in 1991 (Alter, 1999, p. 27). The National Center on Addiction and Substance Abuse determined that a proven and effective program of drug treatment, education, job-training, and health care costs about $6,500 per inmate. The economic benefit to society at large is calculated at $68,800 (National Center on Addiction and Substance Abuse at Columbia University, 1998).

Moreover, according to a Bureau of Prisons study, inmates who have received treatment are 73% less likely to be re-arrested in the first six months after release than those who have not (Alter, 1999, p. 27). A 1997 Rand Corporation study found that "treatment reduces about ten times more serious crime than conventional enforcement and 15 times more than mandatory minimums" (Alter, 1999, p. 27).

Drug Education

Education that deglamorizes drugs might be the single most important component of any national drug control strategy. Deglamorization programs should provide useful and realistic portrayals of drugs and the potential for drug abuse. The ultimate goal is to convince potential drug users to exercise extreme caution in making their choices. Education has been an effective tool in preventing the initiation of tobacco use. The mythology surrounding this aspect of drugs is that any form of "education" must be good. That assumption is incorrect; not all forms of drug education are equally effective (OSAP, 1991).

One form of drug education that clearly does not work is the Drug Abuse Resistance Education (DARE) program popular with police and school officials. A federally sponsored study of DARE found that the "effect on drug use relative to whatever drug education (if any) was offered in the control schools is slight and, except for tobacco use, is not statistically significant" (Ennett, 1994). Similarly, a California study of 5,000 students found that the Los Angeles DARE program was entirely ineffective in reducing drug use among school children (Brown et al., 1997). In the most comprehensive study of DARE, Dennis Rosenbaum, a professor at the University of Illinois at Chicago, studied 1,798 students over a six-year period and found that: (1) DARE had no long-term effects on drug use; (2) DARE did not prevent the initiation of drug use by adolescents; and (3) DARE is counterproductive in that, among students in suburban schools, students who were DARE graduates had higher rates of drug use that students in the control group with no exposure to DARE (Rosenbaum, 1998).

Successful drug education programs recognize that the need for education goes beyond simple warnings about the dangers of drugs and alcohol. The most successful programs provide support structures that assist children in resisting the pressures of peer drug use. In a major study by the U.S. Center on Substance Abuse Prevention, the researchers pointed to a primary precipitator for adolescent drug use. Adolescents reject the conventional and traditional authority figures. Almost all adolescents engage in any number of "risky" behaviors as part of this process. Drug use becomes a "default" activity when no other opportunities exist to demonstrate their independence (Carmona & Stewart, 1996, p. 5).

Long-term programs that emphasize the "social influences" that lead to drug, alcohol, and tobacco use are the most successful in diverting potential users (OSAP, 1991). Such educational programs are typically conducted in concert with community prevention and home education programs involving children, parents, and teachers.

Drug Maintenance

After the passage of the Harrison Narcotics Act, there were at least 40 clinics operating in the United States that distributed morphine and heroin to thousands of opiate addicts between 1919 and 1923. Later experiments with drug maintenance included a New York City experiment with methadone maintenance in the 1960s. Methadone is a heroin substitute that does not cure addiction but allows addicts to function normally in society despite their addiction. Despite criticisms of how maintenance programs were administered and the moral objection that methadone panders to addiction, methadone maintenance is the most successful approach to U.S. drug control in the history of drug policy. As Drug Czar Barry McCaffrey (1998) has indicated:

> Methadone is one of the longest-established, most thoroughly evaluated forms of drug treatment. The science is overwhelming in its findings about methadone treatment's effectiveness. The National Institute on Drug Abuse (NIDA) Drug Abuse Treatment Outcome Study found, for example, that methadone treatment reduced participants' heroin use by 70%, their criminal activity by 57%, and increased their full-time employment by 24%. . . . Clearly many more people could be freed from the slavery of heroin addiction if only this proven effective therapy were more widely available.

Methadone treatments don't make patients high and don't interfere with daily family or work obligations. Methadone is cheap, costing about $4,000 a year per patient compared to the cost of incarceration ($23,500). Methadone maintenance programs dramatically reduce high-risk health behaviors like sharing needles, and it reduces involvement in crime (Rosenbaum et al., 1996). As McCaffrey pointed out, the problem is that there are not enough methadone maintenance programs in the United States.

One difficulty is that methadone programs are tightly controlled by state and federal regulations. State bureaucrats decide medical questions, such as dosage levels, and restrict times when the drugs can be picked up. As a result, few doctors want to work in these programs, and many addicts decide that the hassles of the clinic are worse than the hassles of the streets. Other nations take a very different approach to addiction problems. About 25% of all general practitioners in Europe prescribe methadone to patients. In Amsterdam, Frankfurt, and Barcelona, methadone buses travel to the patients who need treatment.

In Switzerland, the government tried several unique and successful experiments to deal with the problem of heroin addiction. First, the Swiss set up legal *fixerraume* (injection rooms) so junkies could inject their drugs in relatively safe and hygienic environments. "Fixerraume" have proven effective in reducing drug overdoses and the spread of AIDS. The Germans have followed the Swiss example, opening their own version called a *Gesundheitsraum* ("health room").

The Swiss, following the lead of British physicians, started a heroin prescription program in January 1994. There are heroin maintenance programs in Zurich, Bern, Thun, and Basel. Government evaluations of the program have been positive, showing that when addicts can control their dose and take it in a safe, clean place, the drug causes few health problems. The evaluation study also notes that these programs have not resulted in a black market of diverted heroin, and the health of addicts in the program has clearly improved. In the Liverpool-Mersey area of England, health professionals have worked with the police and educators to develop a series of interrelated projects designed to free addicts from both their addiction and the social environment of drug users. Elements of the program include dispensing heroin or methadone to addicts as part of a regular program of drug maintenance; a needle-exchange program; detoxification counseling; and the provision of general health care to drug abusers (Trebach, 1989).

Decriminalization and Legalization

Some political leaders like George Schultz (former Secretary of State) and Kurt Schmoke (the Mayor of Baltimore) have braved public opinion and called for drug legalization. Senator Arlen Specter of Pennsylvania has declared himself to be in favor of shifting funds for law enforcement to drug treatment and prevention. The conservative chairman of the House Judiciary Committee, Henry Hyde, says mandatory minimum sentences and drug-related asset forfeitures have gone too far, and the latter may be unconstitutional. Richard Riordan, the mayor of Los Angeles, has declared that he is looking for alternatives to the failed policies of the past. They have been joined by conservative political theoreticians, like economist Milton Friedman and columnist William F. Buckley. Most surprisingly, the legalization issue has been raised by some law enforcement officials, such as organized crime expert Ralph Salerno, former New York City Police Commissioner and Police Foundation Head Patrick Murphy, San Jose Police Chief Joseph Mac-Namara, Federal Judges Rufus King and Whitman Knapp, and former Minneapolis Police Chief Anthony Bouza.

As difficult as it may be to raise the issue of legalization in the present environment of drug war hysteria, there are a number of possible benefits that should be researched and debated:
- Repealing drug prohibition would save at least $17 billion a year in enforcement costs. These savings could be redirected to more promising approaches such as education and rehabilitation.
- Repealing the drug laws could result in a reduction of crime, particularly in the inner city where the quality of life might well improve; homicide, burglary and robbery rates would fall.
- The large-scale, systemic corruption that threatens our system of criminal justice would be reduced.
- Organized crime groups, particularly those newer groups dependent on the drug trade, would lose the incentive of enormous profits.
- The quality of life for hundreds of thousands of drug abusers and millions of drug users would improve significantly (Nadelmann, 1989).

Supporters of the drug war argue that drug use would escalate if less vigorous law enforcement efforts were adopted or if less draconian sentences were handed down (Califano, 1993, p. A27; Courtwright, 1993). Admittedly legalization is a dangerous policy alternative. No one knows how such a system would operate. No one knows if there would be a subsequent increase in drug use. Certainly we do not want to create a situation in which heroin and cocaine are as prevalent and freely used as tobacco and alcohol are today. But there are some encouraging indicators that should at least stimulate the debate.

- An overwhelming majority of Americans have indicated they would not use illegal drugs if they were legalized. In fact, only 2% of those who do not use cocaine said they would try it if it were legalized, and 93% vehemently stated they would not (Grinspoon & Bakalar, 1994, p. 358).
- Declines in experimental or recreational drug use have been clearly linked to concerns about health, social pressures, and education, not drug enforcement (Erickson & Cheung, 1992).
- In the eleven states that decriminalized marijuana during the 1970s there was no significant increase in the level of marijuana usage. In fact, marijuana consumption declined in those states (Grinspoon & Bakalar, 1994, p. 358).
- Arizona offers treatment instead of jail to all nonviolent drug offenders. Early results are promising, with 70% of those on prohibition testing clean (Alter, 1999, p. 26).
- Government data report that about 75 million Americans have used illegal drugs; about 40 million continue to use illegal drugs. These are very high numbers, yet the number of drug-related deaths is very small. According to the Drug Abuse Warning Network, there are about 4,242 such deaths or about 0.01% of all users (Bureau of Justice Statistics, 1992, p. 26; NIDA, 1992, p. 50). The simple fact is that the vast majority of Americans who use illegal drugs do not abuse them.

◊

CONCLUSION

The many myths about drug use and drug users make constructive policy choices difficult. A realistic drug policy requires that we look beyond myths. While there may be moral objections to drug policy reform, questions about how best to proceed, and disagreements over the dangers of new initiatives, there are no questions about the law enforcement approach to drug control. It is a failure—a failure that exacerbates a difficult problem. In an editorial entitled "The Casualties of War," Ellis Cose (1999) warned that using prisons to solve the drug problem hurts not just the black and Latino communities that have suffered the most, but all of America. "America needs desperately to break its addiction to this witch's brew of angry language, absurd (often dishonest) assumptions and ineffective policy that is poisoning the nation from within" (p. 13). The public cannot continue to respond to the "whoops of bloodthirsty generals waging war with a strategy that will never win." The war on drugs has

> left us with overcrowded prisons, and with hundreds of thousands of people who have lost the right to vote, and have little chance at a job and a slim prayer of being reconnected to the larger society. It has also left many Americans, particularly black Americans, with the sense the judicial system is "the new Jim Crow." (p. 29)

Salim Muwakkil (1999) made similar points in a commentary about the reality of drug use. He noted that people use drugs for many reasons and that the public needs to "transform their perceptions of drug users from stereotypes of depraved sociopaths to something closer to reality." Acknowledging that some drug abusers have made their own and their families' lives miserable, he stated:

> But as one who has witnessed the social carnage of the imbecilic war on drugs, I find it increasingly difficult to tolerate the simple-minded propaganda employed for that war . . . In order to justify our punitive treatment of those who use illicit substances, our cultural media demonizes them and wildly exaggerates the dangers of the drugs. This "bogeyman strategy" not only insults the intelligence . . . it also does little to discourage substance abuse . . . It's clear that youth are more likely to pay heed to our anti-drug lectures if our "facts" have some connection to reality . . . We are presented with kindergarten stories about the demonic evils of drugs and the despicable characters who purvey them. (p. 13)

Barry McCaffrey, the nation's drug czar, has stated that we cannot arrest our way out of the problem. Until the public and policymakers recognize that fact, the enforcement of drug laws will remain one of the glaring injustices of the criminal justice system. As Marc Mauer of the Washington, DC-based Sentencing Project states: "When it's a low-income kid, it's a criminal-justice problem. When it is a suburban kid, it's a health issue" (Alter, 1999, p. 6). To eliminate the "collateral damage" of the drug war, we need to investigate the reality behind the myth.

Juvenile Superpredators
The Myths of Killer Kids, Dangerous Schools and a Youth Crime Wave

One hundred years ago [July, 1899] the first "children's court" in the United States was convened in Chicago. It was grounded in two fundamental truths: that children, by virtue of their age and inexperience, require special protections under the law, and that with proper rehabilitation they can be restored to society as productive individuals.

Today, as the century that saw the development of the juvenile justice system draws to a close, those protections no longer exist or are seriously imperiled, to the detriment not just of the children and adolescents the system was meant to serve but also of a society that has written them off as not worth saving.

It didn't take a long, slow century for the tide to shift from protecting and rehabilitating those kids to locking them up and throwing away the key; it took less than half a decade . . .

In a frenzied few years, the basic philosophy of the children's court was trampled in a panic over pint-sized superpredators . . . For the last half of this decade, public policy on juvenile justice has been based on panic peddling and factual error. ("Children's Court," 1999, p. 16)

If the legislative prescriptions of politicians, the incessant chatter of talk show hosts, and the clamor of community leaders is to be believed, U.S. society is under siege by an army of violent juvenile criminals. The myth that the numbers of teen criminals are growing; that they are becoming more violent; and that they are disrupting our streets and schools gains more credence with each repetition. The specter of youth violence has spread from the inner cities to the heartland. Places like West Paducah, Kentucky, Jonesboro, Arkansas and Littleton, Colorado are now well-known crime locations. In the most sensational constructions, teens are depicted as dangerous *Doom*-playing psychopaths who wear trench coats, pack guns, make pipe bombs, and spew hate over the Internet while plotting senseless acts of mass violence. These teenaged threats to civilized society are marked by their anarchist music, unconventional dress, and a militant lack of respect for authority.

Media accounts of juvenile crime would have us believe that at the turn of the century juvenile crime is engulfing society. Television and the print media are filled with stories about children who commit horrible crimes, and politicians rush to produce legislation to protect us from children. Barry Glassner (1999), professor of sociology at the University of Southern California, discusses "Making Scary Kids" in his book *Culture of Fear*. He lists the findings of various studies about the media and its reports about children. In one study, 40% of the stories concerning children in major newspapers were about crime and violence; the percentage on the evening newscasts of the three major networks was 48 (p. 70). A study of local newscasts found that 55% of stories about young people contained violence. Glassner reports that these types of stories have two common elements: (1) depictions of the youths and their crimes in vivid language and (2) numbers showing some type of dramatic increase. Those numbers are usually percentages. It is far more dramatic to say that the number of homicides grew by 200% than to say that the number of homicides increased from 1 to 2.

The obsession with juvenile crime has not been limited to media sensationalism or to the law-and-order prescriptions of politicians. Social scientists have contributed to the atmosphere of hysteria surrounding juvenile crime. We are warned to prepare for a surge of violence by "a new breed of superpredators that would soon be reaching their teens" (Steinberg, 1999, p. 4). Much of the responsibility for sounding the false alarm on juvenile crime rests with a group of criminologists who compiled a report for the Council on Crime in America in 1995. This report discussed a "ticking time bomb" that was set to explode as the juvenile population increased over the next few years (Butterfield, 1996, p. 6). Princeton's John Dilulio worked hard to promote the view, insisting that the nation was threatened with a new generation of "superpredators." Playing to the surge of media interest in furthering a news theme depicting a youth culture turned violent, he put on a leather jacket and posed before a graffiti-covered wall for a *Time* magazine story (Schiraldi & Keppelhoff, 1997, p. 24A). This sensational version of juvenile crime has had a remarkable impact on our image of crime and the direction of public policy.

Not surprisingly, politicians soon took up this theme, using much of the same overblown rhetoric and sinister depictions. Consider the remarks of Arizona's Assistant Attorney General:

A tidal wave of juvenile crime and violence is gathering force. Criminologists have variously called it an epidemic, a ticking time bomb, the calm before the storm and a long descent into night . . .

Over the next ten years, the population of 14- to 17-year-olds will grow 23%, and the current generation of juveniles has already brought us the worst juvenile crime rates in recorded history . . .

The increasing juvenile murder rate coincides with an increase in "stranger murders" . . . now four times as common as killings by family members.

Experts say the coming crime wave is not so much due to poverty as to a poverty of values. While more police and prisons may help, the cure, they believe, is a renaissance of personal responsibility, and a reassertion of responsibility over rights and community over egoism. (Thomas, 1995)

In 1996, a bill to revamp the juvenile justice system introduced in the United States House of Representatives was initially called the Violent Youth Predator Act (Schiraldi & Keppelhoff, 1997, p. 24A). Although this proposal was later renamed, the views expressed by Dilulio were often repeated in congressional hearings on juvenile crime. Testifying before a Senate Subcommittee on Youth Violence, James Wootton, President of the Safe Streets Coalition (an anti-crime advocacy group) described young people in the following manner:

They live in an aimless and violent present; have no sense of the past and no hope for the future; and act, often ruthlessly, to gratify whatever urges or desires drive them at the moment. They commit unspeakably brutal crimes against other people, and their lack of remorse is shocking. They are what Professor Dilulio and others call urban "superpredators." They are the ultimate urban nightmare, and their numbers are growing. (Federal Document Clearing House, 1997)

To some extent, the views of Dilulio and other criminologists who share this perspective were not original. They merely reinforced a perception of young people that had become quite common in recent years. As television and newspaper stories about violent youngsters proliferated, many states became so alarmed by the perceived surge in violent juvenile crime that they totally transformed their systems of juvenile justice. These transformations were not the products of quiet, reflective deliberation but rather as Franklin Zimring (cited in Mills, 1999) observed, they "bordered on hysteria—not just public hysteria. It was official hysteria" (p. 3). Increasingly, the proceedings in juvenile court resembled those used with adult criminal offenders.

The nation began a "war" on juveniles—incarcerating youths in unprecedented numbers with little thought to the consequences of the crackdown on juvenile crime or even a realistic picture of the extent and frequency of juvenile crime. The totally unwarranted fear of crime by juveniles was fueled by a highly stylized picture of a violent juvenile culture. The myth of a juvenile crime wave resulted in suggested reforms that in all likelihood would have fostered rather than deterred future crime. The crime wave that the media and politicians prophesied never took place, and the idea that the

United States is under siege by an explosion of juvenile superpredators is a myth. The reality of juvenile life is that teens are much more likely to be the victims of crime than to be society's victimizers.

◊

CRACKING DOWN ON JUVENILE CRIME: TRANSFORMING THE JUVENILE JUSTICE SYSTEM

For over 100 years U.S. society has treated juveniles who commit crimes very differently than adults who commit crimes. The idea that societies need a distinct juvenile justice system is "a universal in the developed world. European and Commonwealth countries have juvenile courts. Japan has a juvenile court. And in almost every instance, the vocabulary and the philosophy of the juvenile courts elsewhere is the same as in America" (Zimring, cited in Mills, 1999, p. 3).

Since the beginning of the twentieth century, young people who commit delinquent acts have been subject to the jurisdiction of the juvenile court. This institution has been guided by the principle that it should act "in the best interests of the juvenile." To achieve this end, the juvenile court judge was granted a great deal of discretion in determining the appropriate disposition of a juvenile case. Except for a handful of very serious offenders who were transferred to the adult system, judges in most cases had a range of options—from granting probation to placing the juvenile in a secure detention facility until he/she reached the age of majority. To protect the reputation of juveniles, these proceedings were closed to the public and the names of young people who had been adjudicated delinquent could not be released. Sensitive to the effects of tagging juveniles with the label of "criminal," the courts avoided words like conviction, arrest, and crime. Furthermore, state statutes generally required that juvenile records be expunged after a specific period of time had passed. Contemporary changes to the juvenile justice system, however, promise to transform youthful indiscretions into criminal records that will haunt children into adulthood.

There has been a trend in recent decades to transform the juvenile justice system. In response to a perceived tidal wave in the level of violent juvenile crime, almost all jurisdictions have enacted statutes that contradict the historical guiding principle of the juvenile court—the notion of rehabilitation and acting "in the best interests of the child." There has been an avalanche of legislation since 1992 (Torbet, Gable, Hurst IV, Montgomery, Szymanski & Thomas, 1996). Many states have passed laws designed to increase the number of juveniles who are tried by adult criminal courts and to insure that these individuals receive more punitive dispositions. Other changes that

contradict the historical mission of the juvenile court have also been instituted. Although a full discussion of all these changes is outside the scope of
this chapter, some of the more significant are discussed below.

Traditionally, three mechanisms have been utilized to try juveniles in
adult criminal court: (1) judicial waiver; (2) concurrent jurisdiction; and (3)
statutory exclusion. Judicial waiver involves a determination by the juvenile
court judge that the case should be handled by the adult system. Typically,
this is made after reviewing such factors as the age of the offender, the seriousness of the offense, prior record, and the young person's amenability to
treatment. Under concurrent jurisdiction, the prosecutor has the discretion
to decide whether the case will be filed in adult or juvenile court. Finally,
statutory exclusion is used to automatically exclude (usually based either on
age or offense) an entire category of juveniles from the jurisdiction of the
juvenile court.

According to a recent survey, legislation has been enacted in a number
of jurisdictions to make it easier to waive juvenile offenders to adult criminal
court. Between 1992 and 1995, 11 states passed statutes that lowered the age
limit for at least one offense at which juveniles could be waived. Ten states
added crimes to the list of offenses for which waiver could occur, and 2 states
added provisions that make it easier to transfer a juvenile with a prior record
to the adult court (Torbet et al., 1996, p. 4). In fact, only 4 states (Connecticut, Nebraska, New Mexico and New York) continue to have provisions in
their code that do not allow for the waiver of any juvenile offenders. Within
a period of three years, most states had transformed this aspect of their juvenile justice systems.

Historically, allowing prosecutors to file cases directly in either juvenile
or adult court ("concurrent jurisdiction") has been a much less common
practice than judicial waiver. Nonetheless, 10 states and the District of
Columbia utilized this procedure in 1995 (Torbet et al., 1996). More importantly, 5 of these states either enacted these statutes or expanded their scope
between 1992 and 1995. For example, Wyoming now allows prosecutors to
make this determination for any child 14 years of age or older who is charged
with a violent crime.

The juvenile justice system is being transformed in other ways as well.
One of the defining characteristics of the juvenile court is the ability of the
judge to individualize justice to fit the needs of the particular offender. To
accomplish this goal, judges historically have had a range of dispositional
alternatives that they could utilize after an adjudication of delinquency (Torbet et al., 1996). Increasingly, this is not the case. In response to a perception
that public safety requires a more punitive approach, there has been a dramatic shift in disposition (i.e., sentencing) practices in many jurisdictions
across the United States. These include: (1) the imposition of sentences that
blend adult and juvenile punishments; (2) greater reliance on mandatory
sentences; and (3) the extension of juvenile court jurisdiction for dispositional purposes beyond the age of twenty-one (Torbet et al., 1996).

Although there are a variety of blended sentence models, they are all designed to insure that certain offenders are treated more harshly. These dispositions are generally based on either the offender's age or a combination of age and the nature of the offense. The scope of a number of these statutes is rather broad. For example, blended sentencing applies to any person 14 years or older in Virginia who is charged with an offense that would be a felony if committed by an adult (Torbet et al., 1996, p. 24). What is unprecedented about these statutes is that young people who are adjudicated in juvenile court can actually receive punishment in adult correctional facilities.

Sentencing policy is being altered in other ways. For much of its history, mandatory minimum sentences have not been associated with the juvenile court. Judges were given the discretion to place a delinquent on probation when this was in the best interests of the juvenile. Between 1992 and 1995, 15 states and the District of Columbia enacted or modified statutes that require certain offenders to receive a mandatory minimum period of incarceration (Torbet et al., 1996, p. 14). For example, judges in Texas must now sentence juveniles to 3 years incarceration for first-degree felonies or serious drug felonies; second-degree felonies mandate 2 years and third-degree felonies require one year (p. 14).

Legislatures are also extending the maximum age at which the juvenile court can exercise jurisdiction over adjudicated delinquents. Traditionally, juvenile court judges could commit young offenders to the state juvenile correctional department until the age of 21. However, this is no longer the case in some places. Between 1992 and 1995, 11 states and the District of Columbia raised their maximum age. As a consequence, jurisdiction now extends until age 25 in California, Oregon and Wisconsin. In Colorado, Connecticut, Hawaii and New Mexico, it may continue indefinitely for some offenses until all court orders have been satisfied (Torbet et al., 1996, p. 15).

Finally, legislatures have been making changes in the way that information regarding juvenile offenders is handled. As mentioned earlier, the original aim was to protect young people from reputation damage and stigma. It was believed that a youthful discretion should not be allowed to harm an individual's prospects of employment as an adult. In order to achieve this goal, juvenile courts proceedings were closed to the public and the names of juveniles were not released to the media. In addition, juvenile court records were generally not made available to other agencies and these records were expunged when an adolescent reached the age of majority.

There have been changes in this area as well. By the end of 1997, 42 states permitted the release of a juvenile's name, address and/or picture to the media or general public under certain circumstances; 30 states permitted or required that juvenile hearings be open to the public in certain cases; and many states had opened juvenile court records to school officials (Torbet & Szymanski, 1998, pp. 8–12). These steps ostensibly have been taken to protect community safety. However, little thought has been given to the consequences of burdening a young person with a criminal record that will follow her/him into adulthood. It is hard to believe that this will enhance the prospect for reintegration into the community.

Despite all these measures, some politicians are lobbying for even harsher practices. In 1997, the Violent and Repeat Juvenile Offender Act was introduced in Congress (S. 10). This legislation would: (1) allow teenagers arrested for crimes to be housed in adult jails for indefinite periods of time; (2) allow status offenders (e.g., runaways) to be jailed with adults for 24 hours or longer periods on weekends and holidays; (3) make juvenile felony arrest records available to colleges, even if the arrest did not result in a conviction; (4) require states to expel teenagers from high school for up to six months for regular use of tobacco and; (5) give federal prosecutors sole, nonreviewable discretion to try juveniles as adults for all felonies (Schiraldi & Soler, 1998, pp. 590–591).

The consequences of this legislation would be to reverse decades of progress in removing juveniles from adult jails. Research demonstrates that juveniles housed in these facilities are eight times more likely to commit suicide than those placed in a juvenile detention center. Studies have also indicated that juveniles placed in adult institutions are five times more likely to be sexually assaulted, twice as likely to be beaten by staff, and 50% more likely to be attacked with a weapon (Schiraldi & Soler, 1998, p. 593). Furthermore, although this legislation is ostensibly designed to deal with the problem of violent and serious juvenile offenders, it would impact most heavily on status offenders (i.e., young people who have committed an act that would not even be a crime if they were an adult). The reason for this is that there are far more juveniles arrested for status offenses than for violent crimes. According to the National Center for Juvenile Justice, it is estimated that 123,400 juveniles were arrested for a violent index crime in 1997 whereas there were approximately 196,000 juveniles arrested for running away and 182,700 arrests for curfew violations during the same time period (Snyder, 1998, p. 3).

There are other provisions of this legislation that are likely to produce more harm than good. For example, providing juvenile arrest records to prospective colleges will make the admission process more difficult. Criminologists have long recognized that restricting legitimate opportunities results in more crime, not less. There can be little doubt that this change in public policy will result in more juveniles being denied access to higher education. In a world where persons without appropriate educational training face limited prospects for employment, the consequences of this policy are not difficult to predict.

Probably the most pernicious aspect of this legislation is the provision regarding juveniles who are regular users of tobacco. Under this bill, local school districts would be required to expel students for up to six months for the "regular use" of tobacco. The Centers for Disease Control and Prevention reported that in 1993, 30% of high school students had smoked tobacco within the last 30 days and 11.5% had used chewing tobacco (Schiraldi &

Soler, 1998, p. 598). As a consequence, more than one-third of U.S. high school students could face a six-month suspension under the provisions of this proposed statute (Schiraldi & Soler, 1998, p. 598). The question that remains unanswered is how these students would occupy their time during this period away from school. Does anybody really think that this policy would make it less likely that they would spend their days on street corners abusing tobacco, alcohol, and other drugs? Legislation forcing juveniles out of the schools and onto the streets hardly seems like effective crime control policy.

Schiraldi and Soler (1998) report that the public does not support many of the harsh provisions of the Violent and Repeat Juvenile Offender Act. Perhaps this is one reason why this bill has not yet been enacted into law. Nonetheless, the changes made and those proposed in recent years clearly indicate a change in focus from rehabilitation and treatment to punishment. In fact, many of the provisions of proposed federal legislation would create a permanent underclass of uneducated, unemployable people prone to the commission of crime. Whether it is mandatory minimum sentences, procedures that make it easier try juveniles as adults, or making confidentiality requirements less stringent, the professed goal is the same: to protect society from a tidal wave of violent and serious juvenile offenders. Few policymakers, however, have raised the question of whether these changes are justified. Has there really been a dramatic rise in serious juvenile crime? Before we examine that issue, it is important to touch on some of the consequences that have resulted from this transformation of the juvenile justice system.

◊

LOCK 'EM UP AND THROW AWAY THE KEY

Between 1975 and 1995, the number of juveniles in custody increased by 45%, from 74,270 to 107,637 (Smith, 1998, p. 533). The rate of custody during the same 20-year period increased from 241 to 381 for every 100,000 juveniles in the general population (Smith, 1998, p. 534). The change in rate indicates that the increase in the number of young people held in juvenile correctional facilities cannot be explained by an increase in the number of juveniles in the population.

For minorities, the increase has been dramatic. Between 1979 and 1995, there was more than a threefold increase in the number of African-American youths held in juvenile correctional facilities (from 13,752 to 43,268) and more than a fourfold increase in the number of incarcerated Hispanic youths (from 4,395 to 18,653). Whereas African Americans constituted 28% of the population of juvenile facilities in 1979, by 1995 this proportion had grown to 40%. The corresponding figures for Hispanic youths are 9 and 17% (Smith, 1998, pp. 535–536).

It is important to note that most of the juveniles held in custody have not been charged with a violent crime. Although the proportion of violent offenders among this group has increased in recent years, the overwhelming majority of these individuals are not dangerous, gun-packing psychopaths. Data for 1995 indicate that 31% of the males and only 13% of the females were being held for a violent offense (Smith, 1998, pp. 536–537). Even without pursuing the defining elements of "violent" offense (which often includes "playground" assaults), these statistics indicate that the majority of young people housed in juvenile correctional facilities are not "superpredators."

The number of juveniles held in locked facilities (versus "in custody") has also increased. Between 1979 and 1995, the proportion of juveniles confined in secure public facilities rose from 68 to 86% (Smith, 1998, p. 531). During this same time period, funding for education, treatment, and rehabilitation declined. More young people are being placed in institutions where their physical movement is restricted, and opportunities for remediation are decreasing. Compounding the problem, many young people are confined in facilities operating above design capacity. Whereas 36% of juveniles held in public facilities faced overcrowded conditions in 1983, this proportion was 68% by 1995 (Smith, 1998, p. 532). As a consequence, many more young people are being double bunked in quarters that were originally constructed for a single individual or being forced to sleep in a room that was designed for another purpose. In all, we are incarcerating greater numbers of juveniles than at any period in U.S. history; we are disproportionately confining minority youths; and we are placing juveniles in harsher places of confinement. This situation holds little promise of curbing an alleged future juvenile crime wave.

◈

The Myth of a Juvenile Crime Wave

We have discussed how fear of violent juvenile crime has led policymakers to revamp the juvenile justice system in the United States. One of the consequences of this transformation has been a dramatic rise in the number of young people held in custody. Were these policies necessary? Are juveniles really committing more violent offenses? Is there any evidence to support the view that a tide of "superpredators" is attacking our society?

Before we examine the evidence in detail, let's state a criminological truth. Juvenile crime is related to age, a fact that seems pretty simple and indisputable. If there are more juveniles, there is more juvenile crime. This obvious truth is the sole basis for claims by the state, the media, and criminologists that there is a juvenile crime wave. In the 1990s the United States experienced a small increase in its juvenile population as the result of a "baby boomlet" (Lotke, 1997). It is a basic demographic fact of criminology that young people commit more crime than older people, with crime peaking at ages 17 or 18 and declining thereafter (Barkan, 1997, p. 78). Therefore, more juveniles means more crime. Remember that increased numbers do not translate into an increase in juvenile crime *rates*.

So, how do we get from this simple, obvious fact to a crime wave of superpredators? The reasoning is as follows. If we have more toddlers now than a few years ago, in ten years we will have more juveniles than we do now and more crime. This is hardly a cause for panic. In fact, it takes some statistical gymnastics to create a crime wave out of a few extraneous births. According to John DiIulio of Princeton University, the "swelling legion of Godless, Fatherless, valueless kids" will result in an additional 270,000 superpredators roaming our streets by the year 2010. He reaches that conclusion by assuming that 6% of all our newly conceived children will become superpredators. It goes without saying that there is no data that would support such an extravagant claim.

Franklin Zimring cautions us about believing claims of a storm of violence. "Congress and professors and others can make catastrophic errors in statistical projections. Not little ones. Whoppers" (cited in Mills, 1999, p. 3). But we don't even have to look for data to know the claim is nonsense. Look around you. Are 6 of every 100 children you know roaming the streets, killing strangers at random? To the best of our knowledge the FBI has yet to come up with a juvenile serial killer despite their best efforts. If DiIulio were correct in his estimation, we would already have 1.9 million of these superpredators on the streets, enough to make the whole country look like one of Quentin Tarantino's nightmares. We do not. In fact only about 2,900 juveniles committed a homicide in 1994 (Donziger, 1996).

Between the years 1987 and 1994, the violent crime arrest rate for juveniles rose by 70% (Sickmund, Snyder & Poe-Yamagata, 1997, p. 18). Even a higher arrest rate does not necessarily indicate an increase in the types of crimes being committed. In the last decade, many police departments were much more aggressive and more resources were being devoted to the war on crime and drugs. The rate increase could have been the result of increased detection. Whatever the reason for the upsurge, the trend is now in the opposite direction. Between 1994 and 1997, the juvenile violent crime arrest rate declined by 23%. Assuming that each arrest of a juvenile for a violent offense involved a different individual (which is a highly implausible assumption), approximately one out of every 250 juveniles aged 10 to 17 was arrested for a violent index crime in 1997 (Snyder, 1998, p. 5).

There is other evidence that violent juvenile crime is not increasing. Uniform Crime Report (UCR) data indicate that the proportion of violent crimes that are cleared by an arrest of a juvenile has been decreasing in recent years. Whether we examine the categories of murder, forcible rape, robbery or aggravated assault, the pattern is the same. In each case, the proportion of juvenile arrestees has declined. On the other hand, the proportion of property offenses cleared by a juvenile arrest has remained unchanged (Snyder, 1998, p. 4).

As discussed in chapter 2, the UCR only includes reported crimes and is subject to a variety of methodological limitations. For this reason, the National Crime Victim Survey (NCVS) is a far better indicator of the level of street crime in the United States. Thomas Bernard (1999) has utilized this data source to examine whether there has been an increase in juvenile crime. Much of the discussion in the following section draws on his analysis.

According to the NCVS, the rate of crime declined substantially in the United States between 1975 and 1992. In 1975, there were 128.9 personal crimes for every 1,000 people. This had declined by 30% to 91.2 in 1992. Household crimes also decreased during this period from 236.5 to 152.2 for every 1,000 households, a decline of 35%. Furthermore, these declines have continued and even accelerated in the mid-1990s.

It is possible, as Bernard notes, for crime to be declining and yet to have juvenile crime increase. This would be the case if juveniles were committing a larger proportion of offenses than in prior years. Victims who actually see the perpetrator are asked by the NCVS to estimate the age of the offender(s). These data indicate that the proportion of offenses being committed by young people has changed little since the late 1970s. In 1977, 33.4% of lone offenders and 44.7% of multiple offenders were perceived by victims as being less than 20 years old. By 1993, the respective percentages were 32.6% and 48.7%. Clearly, little change has occurred in these categories. Based on these findings, Bernard is able to conclude that since overall crime declined by one-third between these years, juvenile crime also decreased by about one-third.

The major exception is for the crime of homicide. Criminologists are in agreement that the juvenile homicide rate increased during the 1980s and early 1990s. Between 1984 and 1994, the proportion of homicides that involved a juvenile offender almost tripled. However, even with this increase, only 16% of homicides involved a juvenile (Sickmund, Snyder & Poe-Yamagata, 1997, p. 13). By 1998 that percentage had dropped to 12 (UCR, 1999). In addition, the increase was associated with the use of firearms by juveniles as reflected in the fact that non-gun related homicides by juveniles actually declined during this period.

Recent years indicate this pattern is also reversing. Between 1994 and 1997, homicides by juveniles dropped by 40% (Snyder, 1998, p. 8). Furthermore, the data indicate that juvenile homicides are not a national problem. Instead, they are heavily concentrated in specific urban locations. Eighty-four percent of the counties in the United States reported no juvenile homicide offenders for 1995. Another 10% of the counties reported only one. On the other hand, 5 counties accounted for 25% of all known juvenile homicide offenders. These counties contain the cities of Chicago, Detroit, Houston, Los Angeles and New York. (Sickmund, Snyder & Poe-Yamagata, 1997, p. 11). In fact, most youth homicides take place in select parts of these cities with large areas unaffected by youth homicide at all. In short, if there was a juvenile crime wave in U.S. society, it lasted only two years, was relatively small, was limited in geographic location, and was specifically related to the availability of firearms. The facts about violent youth crime do not present an image that warrants sweeping reforms of the juvenile justice system or the schools where children spend their days.

◊

Dangerous Schools and Violent Students

The tragedy at Columbine High School in Littleton, Colorado where 15 students and one teacher were murdered, two children committed suicide, and numerous others were injured is one of a number of incidents that have shocked the nation in recent years.

> Littleton—the one-word shorthand for a complex horror—has provided as big a mirror on American culture as any single event in decades. In that mirror, we've glimpsed a little of almost everything that defines us at the end of the millennium. . . . Littleton was nothing new. It was time-less trouble decked out in contemporary clothes. It was a story of adoles-cent alienation and maybe just plain evil. We've heard that tale before. We just never heard it in quite this way. . . . What the mirror shows us is too confusing to look at for long. . . . Everything there is real, but some-how the shapes are distorted, the perspective warped, the image hard to fathom and so you look away." (Schmich, 1999, p. 1)

Mythology helps us look away; it reshapes the reality that is sometimes too painful to view. Unfortunately, it also dooms us to hearing the same tale in yet another incarnation—perhaps made worse by "solutions" that don't fit.

In the aftermath of this tragedy, journalists scrambled to collect stories about every incident of a child bringing a gun or knife to school or to report locations where a bomb threat had been called in to a school. The massive media coverage creates the impression that schools in the United States are dangerous places where children and teachers are no longer safe. Over-looked are the tendencies of youthful irresponsibility. Calling in a bomb threat to avoid an exam is reckless and immature, but it is, unfortunately, not a new teen behavior that will lead irrevocably to tragic events like Littleton. Now "all bomb threats, at one time sifted for credibility, are taken seriously at most schools" (Cloud, 1999, p. 39).

In 1999, *Newsweek* issued a special report, "America under the Gun." The lead story was entitled "In the Line of Fire," and the journalist opened his story with the following sentences: "The scene—of a gunman, police and terrified children—was all too familiar. Yet another shooting in a usually placid American place, this time a day-care center in Los Angles, raises the urgent question: Is no one safe?" (p. 20). The article is complete with a fold-out section that presents the pictures of 14 offenders who shot multiple victims as well as a 16 x 8"picture of a 9mm Uzi (despite the fact that only one of the gunmen used an automatic weapon). The caption on the section reads: "In a *terrible season of killing*, suspects have been driven by hate, rage and inexplicable *demons*" (Angell, 1999, italics added).

The *Newsweek* article had all the prerequisites for myth construction. It took three years for the reporter to uncover a dozen incidents (two incidents had multiple gunmen); fewer than half the incidents reported occurred at school. Yet this time span was labeled a "season of killing." Another article in the special issue concludes with: "No one is safe anymore. That's the lesson . . . learned last April at Columbine High School" (Kantrowitz, 1999, p. 40). But are U.S. schools really killing fields?

The Departments of Education and Justice (1998, p. 9) report that the number of such events involving multiple homicide deaths increased from two during the 1992–93 school year to six in 1997–98. These tragedies have led many people to believe that our educational institutions are becoming dangerous places that students enter at their own peril. Indeed, the mass media "bombard citizens regularly with accounts of assaults, sex crimes, robberies, murders, and vandalism, and the public response to such crime" (Arnette & Walsleben, 1998, p. 1). Frequently, we hear reports that children are afraid to go to school and that in some cases they are arming themselves with weapons, fearful that they will become the victim of a senseless crime.

Fortunately, the reality of school life is far different than that projected on our television screens. Despite perceptions, homicide at school is a very rare event. The odds of a child dying as a result of a school-associated violent incident is less than one in a million. Fewer than 1% of the children murdered in 1992 and 1993 were killed on school property (Departments of Education and Justice, 1998, pp. 8–9); substantially more were killed at home. According to the National School Safety Center, out of approximately 52 million students in the United States, about two dozen are killed each year at school. On the other hand, the National Commission on Child Abuse and Neglect reports that between 2,000 and 3,000 children are murdered by parents annually (Males, 1998). Furthermore, most crime directed at young people at school involves theft, not violence. Students aged 12 through 18 are more likely to be victimized by serious violent crime away from the school (Departments of Education and Justice, 1998, pp. 8–9). Unlike the pronouncements of political and media criminologists, the data suggest that children are far safer in school than in their homes or on the streets. Certainly they are safer in school than in U.S. prisons.

These facts do not address the question of whether the nation's educational institutions are becoming more dangerous places than in years past. Fortunately, a couple of recent surveys provide insight into this issue. The first study was a collaborative effort of the United States Departments of Education and Justice. It examined the self-reports of students aged 12–19 who were interviewed regarding their experience with violent and property crimes at school. The interviewers also asked children whether they perceived a problem with respect to street gangs, illegal drugs, or firearms at their schools. This survey was initially undertaken in 1989 and repeated in 1995, so it is possible to draw comparisons between the two years (Chandler, Chapman, Rand & Taylor, 1998, pp. 1–3). The findings indicate that there was little change in the total level of victimization. In 1989, 14.5% of the students reported that they had been the victims of a crime compared with 14.6% in 1995. Although there was a small increase in the level of victimization for violent crimes (from 3.4 to 4.2%), the percentage of students who told interviewers that they were the victims of violence remains quite small. Furthermore, this increase occurred primarily among females, who went from 2% (1989) to 3.3% (1995). Among males, 4.8% reported a violent incident in 1989 compared to 5.1% in 1995.

Clearly, there is no evidence from these data that the level of school violence has increased substantially. Furthermore, it should be noted that violent victimizations include incidents of both a serious and nonserious nature. Students were classified as having experienced a violent victimization if they told the interviewer that they were physically attacked or had property taken by force, threats, or the use of a weapon (Chandler et al., 1998, p. 32). Whether some of these victimizations were actually fistfights or shoving matches among students that did not result in any injury cannot be determined from these data. We suspect that the majority were minor incidents of this nature.

The data on property offenses also do not support the notion that there has been an increase in the level of victimization at school. In 1989, 12.2 of the students surveyed indicated that they had been victims of a property crime at school. This proportion actually declined to 11.6% in the follow-up survey conducted in 1995 (Chandler et al., 1998, p. 3). One must also keep in mind the potential nature of these thefts. Certainly the majority are misdemeanor thefts resulting in small economic losses. In any case, the survey indicates that thefts of student property at school are going down, not increasing.

In a second study, public high school principals were surveyed regarding their experience with violence and disciplinary problems. According to this research, 43% of the public schools reported that they experienced no crime whatsoever (not even playground assault or simple theft), and 47% reported that they experienced only a nonviolent crime during the 1996–97 school year. Just 10% of the public schools experienced a crime of violence during this period. This study also examined physical conflict among students, weapons possession, and vandalism. The findings indicated that the proportion of respondents who reported that these were serious or moderate problems in their schools had not changed dramatically, and in some cases had decreased slightly in 1996–97 from the previous survey that was undertaken during the 1990–91 school year (School Crime, 1998, p. 2).

The findings of this research are consistent. Both reports lend no support to the notion that the nation's public schools are becoming more dangerous places. Clearly, the sentiments expressed by politicians and in the media are exaggerated. Only one out of 10 public schools in the United States reports any violence at all. Furthermore, only a small fraction of students report being the victims of violence at school.

> If crime in the classroom is an epidemic, it's like tuberculosis—one we basically control, with a few flare-ups every once in a while that beat the inoculation. Overall, school violence is not going up. Just 10 of every 1,000 students were the victims of serious violent crime at school in 1996. And while that's 10 too many, more than twice that number (26) were victims off campus. (Cloud, 1999, p. 38)

◈

THE IMPACT OF TREATING JUVENILES AS ADULTS

We have observed that many states have made it much easier to adjudicate juvenile offenders as adults. One of the goals of this policy is to reduce the level of violent crime through deterrence. This can take the form of either general or specific deterrence. The former takes place when tougher statutes discourage juveniles who might be tempted to break the law to refrain from doing so. The latter involves punishing juvenile offenders more harshly in order to reduce the likelihood that they will commit additional crimes in the future. Several studies have examined whether there is actually a deterrent effect associated with the treatment of juvenile offenders as adult criminals.

One such study was undertaken in Idaho by Jensen and Metsger (1994). In 1981, this state changed its juvenile statute and mandated that offenders between the ages of 14 and 18 years of age charged with murder, attempted murder, robbery, forcible rape, and aggravated assault be tried in adult court. Jurisdiction in these cases was automatically transferred to the adult criminal court; the requirement that the juvenile court hold a waiver hearing was eliminated. Jensen and Metsger examined whether this legislation impacted the crimes that resulted in automatic transfer in Idaho. Using unpublished data from the FBI, they used Montana and Wyoming as comparison jurisdictions. In the latter two states, waiver decisions continued to require a juvenile court hearing. The researchers calculated mean arrest rates in each state for the five-year period prior to and following the enactment of the Idaho statute. The analysis indicated that rates of serious juve-

nile crime increased in the post-statute period only in Idaho. Both comparison states reported a decrease. Consequently, Jensen and Metsger "conclude
that the Idaho legislative waiver did not have a deterrent effect on violent
juvenile crime" (p. 102).

In 1978, New York State enacted one of the most punitive juvenile statutes in the United States. People as young as 14 years of age would be tried
in criminal court for a variety of offenses. For murder, the age limit was set
at 13 years of age. Furthermore, the statute stipulated that juveniles were to
receive penalties comparable to those given adults and that all sentences
were to be served in secure facilities. Singer and McDowall (1988) reported
that an extensive effort was made by the media to inform young persons
about this new law. Although the New York statute allows the judge to send
the case back to the juvenile court (what is often called "reverse waiver"),
their data indicate that its provisions were widely used in New York City to
try serious juvenile offenders as adults. The statute was not applied as frequently in upstate New York. The researchers also used an interrupted time
series design to assess the general deterrent impact of this legislative exclusion. Despite the fact that the number of juveniles in secure confinement in
New York State had increased dramatically, their analysis indicates that this
legislative exclusion did not affect the level of juvenile crime.

There are numerous differences between these two states. New York is
large, urban and eastern; Idaho is small, rural and western. New York has a
high crime rate and a population that is heterogeneous in terms of race, religion, and ethnicity. Idaho has a low crime rate and is far more homogeneous
with respect to these characteristics. In addition, the circumstances under
which the statute was implemented varied considerably among these jurisdictions. New York's legislative change was accompanied by a great deal of
media publicity. This was not the case in Idaho. Nonetheless, both studies
reached a similar conclusion—there is no evidence to indicate that treating
young people as adult criminal offenders has any impact on serious juvenile
crime.

As noted earlier, the traditional approach by which juveniles fall under
the jurisdiction of the criminal court is through a waiver decision by the juvenile court judge. Although there is evidence that increasing numbers of
young people are being waived to adult courts (Champion, 1989b), relatively
few studies have examined the question of whether juvenile offenders who
are tried and sentenced as adults are less likely to refrain from future criminal activity. One of the few studies to address this issue was conducted in
Florida by Bishop, Frazier, Lanza-Kaduce and Winner (1996). These
researchers compared the recidivism rates of youths retained in the juvenile
system with a matched sample of young people who were transferred to the
adult criminal court. In order to deal with the threat of selection bias and
achieve equivalence across groups, individuals in this study were matched in
terms of seriousness of offense, number of charges, number of prior offenses,
severity of prior offenses, age, race and gender. The analysis employed sev-

eral indicators of recidivism including: (1) the probability of rearrest; (2) length of time until rearrest; and (3) the relative severity of the rearrest charge. The data indicated that juveniles who had been treated as adult offenders were more likely to be rearrested, that they were likely to be rearrested sooner, and that a greater proportion of these rearrested individuals were charged with felonies. These findings strongly dispute the claims of those who maintain that treating juvenile offenders as adult criminals will have a positive impact on violent crime. "Overall, the results suggest that transfer in Florida has had little deterrent value" (Bishop et al., 1996, p. 183).

The only other study to examine this issue was conducted by Fagan (1995). This researcher compared the recidivism rates "for 15- and 16-year-old adolescents charged with first- and second-degree felony offenses in juvenile court in New Jersey with identical offenders in matched communities in New York State whose cases [were] adjudicated in criminal court" (p. 239). The goal of this research design was to select a region that, although socially and economically homogeneous, differed in terms of how serious juvenile offenders are handled by the legal system. The analysis indicated that for burglary offenders, there was no relationship between the court of jurisdiction and recidivism. However, robbery offenders whose cases were adjudicated in juvenile court consistently had lower rates of recidivism than those youths who were tried in the adult system. For this reason, the author concludes that "rather than affording greater community protection, the higher recidivism rates for the criminal court cohort suggest that public safety was, in fact, compromised by adjudication in the criminal court" (p. 254).

Critics might charge that the results of the Fagan study were influenced by differences in the legal culture between New York State and New Jersey. Similarly, despite the attempt at matching by Bishop et al., significant differences might have remained between juveniles in Florida who were transferred to adult criminal court and those who remained in the juvenile system. Nonetheless, the majority of the evidence points in the same direction. There appear to be few benefits from treating juvenile offenders as adults. No general deterrent impact on juvenile crime has been observed as a result of statutes that legislatively exclude certain offenders from the juvenile justice system. In addition, the research suggests that young persons tried and sentenced as adults are more likely, not less, to commit future crimes.

Treating juveniles as adult offenders is not only a failure in terms of deterrent effect, but there are likely to be other negative consequences. Incarcerated young persons will carry the stigma of a felony conviction after release from the institution. Prior research indicates that this is likely to limit their labor market participation (Fagan, 1995). Juveniles housed in prisons are less likely to receive counseling than those who are held in juvenile facilities. In fact, Reddington and Sapp (1997) found that the overwhelming majority of adult prisons do not provide any additional treatment for incarcerated juvenile offenders. Most damaging of all, younger persons in this environment are vulnerable to physical and sexual victimization by older, more experienced inmates (Reddington & Sapp, 1997).

Differential association theory predicts that juveniles placed in adult institutions are likely to be exposed to individuals who hold values and attitudes that are not consistent with a law-abiding lifestyle (Sutherland & Cressey, 1970). This view is supported by Eisikovits and Baizerman (1983), who surveyed a number of juveniles incarcerated in an adult facility and concluded that "youth who are committed to prison for violent acts become violent youth. Violence becomes a way of life" (p. 16). "Attorneys, criminologists, and the youths themselves point out that in adult prisons kids learn to survive by intimidating others. They tend to lose whatever respect they had for authorities and for themselves. Once released, they engage in more or worse crimes" (Glassner, 1999, p. 74). These are only a few of the negative consequences resulting from policy based on the myth of superpredators.

◇

BLAMING THE VICTIMS: CRIME AGAINST JUVENILES

We have observed that many of the programs instituted to punish juvenile offenders are ill conceived. There is no evidence that juvenile crime is increasing or that students are facing an increased risk of victimization at school. Furthermore, a number of practices designed to crack down on serious juvenile crime have been shown to be ineffective. Therefore, the question must be posed: should we continue to view juveniles as violent predators who pose a danger to American society, or are juveniles in fact more likely to be the victims of crime? If the latter is true, shouldn't we be concerned with insuring that young people are not victimized by others?

The National Crime Victimization Survey (NCVS) enables us to compare the victimization rates of juveniles and adults for all violent offenses with the exception of homicide. Data for 1994 indicate that juveniles aged 12–17 were victimized by crime at a rate nearly 3 times that of adults. Regardless of whether rape, robbery, or assault victimizations are examined, the rate is far higher for juveniles than adults. This is the case regardless of the type of community (i.e., urban, suburban or rural). Furthermore, juveniles are almost three times more likely to experience a crime-related injury than adults (Sickmund, Snyder & Poe-Yamagata, 1997, p. 4).

Young people are victimized in other ways as well. These include neglect and various forms of abuse (i.e., physical, sexual, and emotional). The National Incidence Study of Child Abuse and Neglect is designed to measure the extent of these problems. The data indicate that between 1986 and 1993, the number of children abused or neglected in the United States almost doubled. The increase is dramatic in many of the categories. For example, the number of incidents involving physical abuse rose from 311,500 to 614,100 during this period. The same is true with respect to sexual abuse where there was an increase from 133,600 in 1986 to 300,200 incidents in 1993 (Sickmund et al., 1997, p. 7).

During 1994, there were an estimated 2 million reports of child abuse and neglect. In 37% of these cases, a follow-up investigation revealed either that the allegation was substantiated or that there were reasonable grounds to suspect that the child had been mistreated or was at risk of mistreatment. This translates into hundreds of thousands of cases of juveniles victimized by adults in a single year. Furthermore, "over 1,000 children died as a result of maltreatment in 1994" (Sickmund et al., 1997, pp. 9–10). Clearly, it is time to recognize that the victimization of juveniles by adults is a problem that deserves far greater attention than it has received. Perhaps the media should focus less on so-called "juvenile superpredators" and more on young people who are the victims of various types of adult misconduct.

Possibly the most baffling aspect of the myth of superpredators is the ease with which the public transforms the alarm discussed in chapter 3 about crazed predators hiding in the dark of night. Ironically, the fear about every child being at risk seemingly translates to every child (or at least everyone else's) as a violent threat with the passage of a few years. The myth takes the same stance that "it can happen anywhere" but shifts the perpetrator. Sensational stories of multiple-victim, video-game rampages have raised the level of hysteria to the point that public distrust threatens to become our greatest social evil. The harms of such attitudes are enormous.

In 1998 police in Chicago arrested two boys, aged 7 and 8, for the murder of an 11-year-old girl. Questioned by three detectives and two youth officers, they had "confessed" to the crime. The state protects the underaged from buying cigarettes, alcohol, or seeing X-rated movies because it assumes children don't have the maturity, knowledge and experience required to make responsible decisions. Whether the two little boys were even capable of understanding their Miranda rights and the consequences of waiving their constitutional protections is a moot point. Miranda rights must be read only if children are in custody. Evidently the police believed that the two little boys would feel that they were free to walk out of the interrogation room; i.e., to understand that they were not in custody, so they didn't bother with the Miranda warning. The two boys were eventually cleared, but the public's instant willingness to believe their guilt is the truly frightening aspect of this terrible mistake. "The exculpation of these two kids led people all over the country to say that maybe we've become too quick to impute adultlike savagery to kids of that age" (Kiernan, 1999, p. 9).

Unfortunately, there had been previous instances in Illinois that primed the pump for the mistaken arrest. On August 28, 1994 Robert Sandifer, 11 years old, shot to death a teenage girl and was found dead days later, killed by members of his own gang. Less than two months later, two boys aged 10 and 11 dropped a 5-year-old to his death out of a fourteenth-floor window. The General Assembly reacted by passing a series of laws to deal more harshly with young criminals, including one measure that would allow children as young as 10 to be sent to a youth prison rather than to a residential treatment facility and another to authorize construction of such a facility. Politics delayed construction of the facility until 1997, by which time it became obvious that there was no need for one. Nonetheless, the original intention "illustrates the risks of fashioning public policy from political outrage and demonstrates the gap between the perception of juvenile crime and its reality" (Kiernan, 1999, p. 1). Steven Drizin, supervising attorney for the Northwestern University School of Law's Children and Family Justice Center, stated, "There was no need to build that facility, and many people who recognized that at the time are turning out to be prophetic. There was never more than a handful of very young kids charged with serious crimes" (p. 9).

Illinois has reversed course completely, and The Commission on Juvenile Competency appointed by the State's Attorney recommended in 1999 that children younger than 10 accused of crimes be handled in a civil process that would provide intensive social services rather than detention or incarceration; that option would be available to children between the ages of 10 and 12 at the discretion of prosecutors.

> It would be altogether fitting for Illinois to lead the way again, lead the way *back* to a rational, compassionate and just set of laws for dealing with young suspects. Laws that require minors to be represented by counsel during questioning. Laws that allow judges, not prosecutors, to decide whether a kid belongs in juvenile court. Laws that assume the innocence—and the potential—of youth. ("Children's Court," 1999, p. 16)

CONCLUSION

There is no empirical evidence to support the view that American society is under siege by a tidal wave of "youthful superpredators." Although this fear has led to a radical transformation of the juvenile justice system, the data indicate that juvenile crime is decreasing. The National Criminal Victimization Survey reports that juvenile crime has decreased substantially since the 1970s. In addition, arrest rates for juveniles have also declined since the early 1990s. Furthermore, there is no evidence to suggest that crime is becoming a more serious problem at school. Despite a small number of tragic incidents in which students armed with firearms killed multiple individuals, the likelihood of a child becoming the victim of a violent crime at school has increased only slightly. The overwhelming majority of schools continue to report no violent crimes whatsoever.

We have also observed that there is no evidence that the "get-tough" approach is having a positive effect on the crime rate. In fact, the studies available report the opposite: juveniles tried as adults are more likely to become repeat offenders, not less. The data also call into question the stereotype of juveniles as offenders. The NCVS indicates that young people are substantially more likely to be the victims of crime than adults. Furthermore, this survey does not include the multitude of children who are abused and neglected each year in the United States. Superpredators are a myth. Rather than policies designed to protect society from a mythical danger, we need policies to shield us from unintended consequences of society's fears.

Battered and Blue Crime Fighters
Myths and Misconceptions of Police Work

The public and media have long been fascinated with police officers and their work. This fascination is reflected in books, newspaper and magazine accounts, as well as television documentaries. Movies and television series have frequently depicted the police and their work. From the *Keystone Cops* of the early cinema to *RoboCop*, many of us have grown up with media portrayals of policing. These images usually coalesce around recurrent themes that promote and shape our view of the nature of police work in U.S. society. Two media characterizations of police work prevail: policing as an exciting yet dangerous profession and the stress experienced by police officers in the conduct of their duties.

The danger and glamour of police work is revealed in movies like *Dirty Harry, Lethal Weapon* and its sequels, *Nighthawks, Silence of the Lambs,* and *Die Hard with a Vengeance.* These movies and other television accounts of policing show the autonomous police officer, single-handedly or sometimes with a minor partner, fighting diabolical, sophisticated, and well-armed criminals. These are not run-of-the-mill criminals like the drunk driver, the thief, or the check forger. More often than not, police officers are pitted against psychosexual killers, serial murderers, and international terrorists. In almost every depiction of Hollywood policing, officers are shown shooting it out with armed criminal suspects while simultaneously being locked in conflict with the police department they work for—as well as the unenlightened criminal justice system that is unwilling to understand the unique demands of police work.

Movies like *Blue Knight* and television serials such as *NYPD Blue* and *Homicide: Life on the Street* have painted portraits of police officers and their work as exciting but personally destructive. These presentations focus on the effects of being a police officer—how policing destroys officers' personal lives. Media portrayals often chime the theme of mental distress because of a growing dissatisfaction and frustration with the criminal justice system's emphasis on criminal rather than victim rights. Stress is rampant among television cops, and suicide is always a possibility. Each side effect is presented as commonly experienced by all members of the profession. Media fascination with policing has even extended to what police officers and policing might be like in centuries to come. Movies like *RoboCop* show policing in terms of its crime-fighting role and allude to the almost superhuman qualities needed by modern law enforcement officers.

Media depictions are, of course, not the only sources from which we draw our images of policing and police work. The law enforcement community and political leaders alike reinforce perceptions of danger, glamour, and stress. The "war against crime" and the renewed "war on drugs" reinforce an image of police officers locked in mortal combat with sophisticated, high-tech international criminals and drug dealers who will use all means available to them to succeed in their nefarious activities and to avoid arrest. These arch-criminals are portrayed as more numerous and better armed than the police—and willing to use deadly force in an instant.

In an attempt to become more open with the public, police executives have given the media access to police operations, allowing them to film drug raids, gang sweeps, and other high profile operations. Television shows like *Cops* reinforce the notion that police work is dangerous and exciting; camera crews selectively move from call to call filming officers' unique activities. The image is projected that police officers—our most visible symbols of justice—are under siege by drug-dealing kingpins, youth gangs, occupational stress, and even their own police departments.

The allure to study the negative side of police work has not gone unnoticed by scholars. Virtually hundreds of articles have been written about the dangers and stresses in police work, and almost every introductory text in criminal justice or policing contains a section devoted to these topics. One work on policing has even been entitled *The Custer Syndrome*, alluding to the way police are severely outnumbered by their criminal counterparts and the "belief that not losing ground [in the war against crime] can be counted as success" (Hernandez, 1989, p. 2).

How accurate are the depictions of policing presented by the media and reinforced by the government and law enforcement community? How conclusive is the research on the dangers and stress of policing in America? This chapter will address a few of the common myths and misconceptions of crime fighting. We will conclude with a consideration of how the disjuncture between perceptions, expectations, and reality shapes the police as an occupational group as they live the myth of crime fighting.

◊

REAL POLICE WORK

Despite the images and claims that police officers are outnumbered by their criminal counterparts and despite the political rhetoric of waging war on crime, police officers do considerably less "crime fighting" than one might imagine. Citizens invariably equate police work with pursuing criminals. Whether they are being depicted in a police series on television or in a current movie, police officers are portrayed almost solely as crime fighters. Citizens spend hours of leisure time watching cops engage in such activities as high-speed pursuits of wanted felons, questioning persons suspected of having committed serious crimes, shooting it out with dangerous criminals, and in other law enforcement tasks requiring precision skills and often under threatening conditions.

Crime Fighting

Unfortunately, this media image is erroneous. It is a myth to believe that the police spend the majority of their time involved in crime-fighting activities. In fact, the average cop on television probably sees more action in a half-hour than most officers witness in an entire career. As a general rule, most police work is quite mundane. Police spend a considerable part of their time on such routine tasks as writing traffic citations, investigating automobile accidents, mediating disputes between neighbors and family members, directing traffic, and engaging in a variety of other service-related and order-maintaining activities. If television were to create a program that realistically depicted police work, it would soon go off the air due to poor ratings. It would offer little in the way of "action" and would quickly be tuned out by bored viewers.

Since the 1960s, a variety of research techniques have been employed to study police workloads (Greene & Klockars, 1991). Radio calls from dispatchers to patrol cars (Bercal, 1970), telephone calls by citizens to the police (Cumming et al., 1965), dispatch records (Reiss, 1971), observational data (Kelling et al., 1974), self-reports from police officers (O'Neill & Bloom, 1972) and telephone interviews of citizens (Mastrofski, 1983) have all been utilized in an attempt to learn what the police actually do and how much time is spent on various activities. Despite the fact that these studies relied on different methodologies and were conducted in different communities and during different time periods, all determined that relatively little of an officer's day is taken up responding to crime-related activities. Although the proportions varied, only between 10 and 20% of the calls matched public perceptions of police officers as crime fighters.

The findings from the various studies indicate that a substantial proportion of an officer's time does not involve any contact with the public. Police spend many hours engaged in preventive patrol, running errands, and performing a number of administrative tasks that consume a considerable part of their workday. In their 1991 study, Jack Greene and Carl Klockars excluded from their analysis time that was spent by the police in activities not involving direct contact with the citizenry. When officer workload is reconceptualized in this manner, the proportion of time that is classified as crime-related activity does increase. However, almost all this work involves taking crime reports from citizens. The authors conclude that the:

> findings in no way lend support to the headline news vision of police work as a violent running battle between police and criminals. It bears emphasis that our data show that the average police officer spent about one hour per week responding to reports of crimes in progress. When the officers arrive, they often find that what was described as a crime in progress was, in fact, not a crime or that the perpetrator is gone. (Greene & Klockars, 1991, p. 283)

Police Shootings

Both television and film frequently portray law enforcement officers as engaged in shoot-outs with dangerous criminals. Although this type of entertainment may produce high ratings for television programs and large profits for movie studios, how does this view of police work compare with reality? How often do police officers in real life fire their weapons at suspects? How many persons are shot and/or killed by the police each year in the United States?

Unfortunately, there are no national statistics published that address this issue. As a consequence, it is not a straightforward matter to determine how many people are killed and/or wounded by police bullets each year. Researchers have had to rely on data that have been collected for other purposes (*Vital Statistics of the United States*) and information that has voluntarily been supplied by police agencies to determine the annual number of killings attributable to police officers.

Vital Statistics records the birth and death records that are collected and published by the United States Public Health Service. Because they contain a category that notes deaths due to legal intervention, they have been useful to researchers who study killings of citizens by the police. According to *Vital Statistics*, there was an average of 360 deaths due to legal intervention in the United States each year between 1970 and 1975. Because judicially ordered executions did not take place during this period, it can be assumed that almost all these persons died at the hands of police officers. Unfortunately, *Vital Statistics* may underreport the number of police killings by as much as 51% (Sherman & Langworthy, 1979). Therefore, there may have been as many as 735 killings by police each year during this period.

Data supplied by police departments would give a more complete assessment than the information on killings extrapolated from *Vital Statistics*. Unfortunately, no national survey based on police records exists. The most comprehensive study to date was undertaken by Lawrence W. Sherman and Ellen G. Cohn (1986), who utilized a variety of data sources, including information elicited from police departments, to examine the rate of police killings during a fifteen year (1970–84) period in the fifty largest cities of the United States. They report that in no year did the police in these cities kill more than 353 people. Although these researchers report enormous variation in the *rate* at which police officers kill citizens, such incidents are relatively rare. Jacksonville (Florida) ranked at the top with respect to one measure of police homicide between 1980 and 1984, yet the average officer in that community would have to work 139 years before taking anyone's life. Honolulu, on the other hand, ranked at the bottom during this same period. A police officer in that community would kill a citizen once every 7,692 years. The study concludes that these rare events are becoming even more infrequent. The number of persons killed by big-city police officers declined from 353 in 1971 to 172 in 1984; law enforcement personnel were killing about half as many people in 1984 as they were in 1971. Despite a perception on the part of many citizens and the media that the streets are becoming more dangerous, the number of citizens mortally wounded by the police has clearly declined.

There are several explanations for this phenomenon. First, almost all police departments that serve large communities have adopted firearms policies that prohibit the use of deadly force against certain fleeing felons (Fyfe & Blumberg, 1985). Both James J. Fyfe (1979) and Sherman (1983) have reported that a change to a more restrictive policy is followed by a decline in the number of shootings by police officers. Second, training has improved and the level of discipline has tightened in many departments. Third, there has been an explosion of civil litigation. The net effect of this has been a substantial increase in the number of lawsuits that are filed as a result of shootings by police. Municipalities now have a strong financial incentive to prevent unjustifiable incidents and thus avoid financial liability.

In order to gain an idea of how frequently police officers shoot citizens, nonfatal incidents must also be examined. Once again, there is no national data that addresses this issue. However, Arnold Binder and Lorie Fridell (1984) reviewed the various studies that had been conducted by researchers in individual departments. Based on their review, they concluded that approximately 30% of persons shot by the police will die. Based on this ratio of woundings to fatalities, a police officer in Jacksonville (the city with the highest rate of homicide by police officers) would have to work an average of forty-two years before shooting a citizen. In many other communities, the time period would be appreciably longer. Because a police career rarely lasts more than 35 years, the majority of police officers will go their entire career without shooting anyone.

The Dangers of Police Work

One of the most pervasive myths about police work is that it is a dangerous occupation. Scenes of officers attacked and killed by ruthless criminals are staples of film and television. This perception is reinforced by the occasional real-life incident in which a police officer is gunned down. When such a tragic event occurs, the evening news includes footage of the deceased officer's funeral and scenes of the hundreds of officers from other departments paying their last respects to the slain officer. Invariably, the story includes a commentary to the effect that police officers are on the frontline in the war against crime, facing the possibility of death from a crazed assailant at any given moment.

The message that policing is a dangerous occupation is routinely reinforced, and often the danger is portrayed as escalating precipitously. After all, our cities have become plagued with gangs, drugs, and automatic weapons. Police must deal with problems that did not even exist a decade ago, such as the epidemic of crack cocaine and the proliferation of high-powered weapons on the street. Obviously, being a cop today must be more dangerous than was the case in years past—or so we are told.

How accurate is this picture? Clearly, police officers are murdered by suspects. This is an undeniable fact, and each one of these killings is a terrible tragedy for the officer, the officer's survivors, the department, and the community. However, there are some questions that must be addressed: How pervasive is the danger that law enforcement officers face? Is policing really a dangerous occupation? Has it become more so in recent years?

Fortunately, these are relatively easy issues to resolve. The Uniform Crime Reports (UCR) publishes data each year with respect to the number of law enforcement officers who have been feloniously killed in the United States. It is believed that this is one of the most comprehensive and complete sections of the UCR (Konstantin, 1984). These data indicate that the killing of law enforcement officers is a rare event (Vaughn & Kappeler, 1986).

The data also indicate that these relatively rare events have declined dramatically in recent years. From a high of 132 in 1974, police killings declined to 61 by 1998. In fact, when the period 1974–76 is compared to the years 1986–98, the average annual number of killings drops from 124 to about 70. It is noteworthy that this risk associated with police work has declined despite the restrictions that have been placed on police use of firearms, the alleged increase in the rate of violent crime, the proliferation of semi-automatic weapons on the streets of U.S. cities, the war on drugs, and the increase in the level of gang-related violence that has occurred in many communities.

To some extent, these statistics on police killings mask the reduction in risk that has occurred because the number of law enforcement personnel has increased substantially during this period. "Because the number of officers has actually *increased* significantly in the last two decades, the *rate* at which officers have been killed has declined quite significantly as well" (Fridell & Pate, 1997, p. 581). There were 594,209 persons employed full-time in law enforcement at all levels of government in 1974 (Hindelang et al., 1977). Today it is estimated that over 922,000 people are employed in law enforcement. Because there were 132 killings of police officers in 1974, the aggregate risk per officer was approximately one chance in 4,501 that year. With 61 deaths in 1998, each officer stood one chance in 15,129 of being slain. This is the aggregate rate of risk for all law enforcement personnel. Some officers patrol neighborhoods or perform assignments that place them in somewhat greater danger. Overall, the number of law enforcement personnel killed on the job declined by more than 46% in twenty-five years.

Another way to examine the question of danger is to compare the fatality rate of police officers with that of persons working in other occupations and professions. Richard Holden (1991) examined the mortality data published by the Bureau of Labor Statistics for the years 1984–1986. The analysis indicates that police officers consistently face a lower fatality rate than persons employed in mining, construction, transportation, and agriculture. However, the author cautions that a number of methodological problems make this comparison somewhat problematic. For example, the death rate for law enforcement personnel excludes officers who die as a result of traffic accidents unless they were in direct pursuit of a suspect. Therefore, this analysis must be considered somewhat tentative. Nonetheless, there is no support for the myth that policing is one of the most dangerous occupations.

The myth that policing is a dangerous occupation has a number of consequences for law enforcement. First, this misperception results in an increased level of public support. A belief that law enforcement personnel routinely confront danger generally leads citizens to give the police the benefit of the doubt when it comes to various controversies involving the propriety of certain actions. Second, the public perception that the police are armed and ready to deal with danger twenty-four hours a day can be beneficial when it is time to engage in contract negotiations (Fyfe, 1982). Third, the belief that being a law enforcement officer is akin to the work of a soldier on the frontlines can have a deleterious effect on the officer's spouse (Niederhoffer & Niederhoffer, 1978). Finally, the pervasive sense that their mission is dangerous affects the way that police officers deal with the public. One can only speculate about how many times officers use excessive force or are abrupt in their dealings with citizens because they perceive a world that is more dangerous than is actually the case.

Myth of Danger in Domestic Violence Incidents

There is perhaps no myth more widely ingrained in police folklore as the belief that the domestic violence call is the most dangerous for an officer. William K. Muir (1977) reported that it was the "unanimous sentiment" of the officers he studied that more police are killed in these situations than in any other type of call. Family violence researchers have also emphasized the danger that lurks for police in domestic violence encounters (Straus et al., 1980). However, the fact is that the risk of felonious death is far less in domestic violence situations than in many other types of assignments.

This myth was seriously undermined by David Konstantin (1984), who analyzed the situational characteristics of all police killings that occurred in the United States between 1978 and 1980. He found that only 5.2% of the fatalities occurred in situations where officers had responded to domestic disturbances. This was substantially less than the proportion who died intervening in robbery situations, pursuing suspects, making traffic stops, investigating suspicious persons, or as a result of assaults (Konstantin, 1984).

Although this analysis suggests that domestic disturbance calls do not present a high level of risk, it is not definitive because it does not take into account the relative amounts of time that police officers spend performing various tasks. For example, domestic violence calls would be risky if they accounted for only one percent of total police calls for service but five percent of reported deaths. Fortunately, Joel Garner and Elizabeth Clemmer (1986) have utilized several existing measures of police activity to calculate the risk of death that officers face when they respond to a domestic violence complaint. These authors conclude that domestic violence consistently ranks below both robbery and burglary as a source of danger to police. A three-year study of domestic violence calls and police injuries concluded that "for the Charlotte Police Department, domestic disturbance calls are not a major source of assaults or injuries to the officers involved in relation to other types of calls" (Hirschel et al., 1994, pp. 99, 112). In fact, the calculations resulting from one activity measure rank domestic violence situations at the bottom in terms of officer fatality and fifth out of ten types of calls for service "in the ratio of injuries to calls for service." Garner and Clemmer (1986) assert that "the available evidence strongly suggests that researchers and police managers abandon the notion that domestic disturbance calls result in a large number of police deaths" (p. 527).

How did the myth develop that many police officers die responding to domestic violence calls? Konstantin (1984) offers a number of possible explanations. The most likely explanation is that police officials and researchers misinterpreted the data that were provided by the FBI in its annual publication, *Law Enforcement Officers Killed* (LEOK). Prior to 1982, all officer deaths resulting from disturbances were lumped into one category regardless of whether they resulted from domestic violence calls or other types of disturbances (Garner & Clemmer, 1986). Many persons mistakenly assumed that all these incidents involved domestic disturbances; in fact, a substantial proportion were deaths that resulted from calls responding to bar fights, reports of a suspect with a weapon, and other types of disturbances that have nothing to do with family quarrels.

Konstantin gives other reasons why the level of danger in domestic violence calls may have been exaggerated. Responding to family quarrels can be a traumatic experience for a police officer. After all, it is the only situation where both the offender and the complainant may join forces against the officer. Second, it is possible that those who developed domestic crisis intervention training programs have overstated this danger in order to persuade police departments of the value of their programs. Finally, responding to family quarrels is likely to be perceived by police officers as "social work." Because these encounters take up so much of an officer's time, they may be viewed as demeaning to his/her image as a crime fighter. Therefore, in order to convince themselves that they are doing "real police work," the police may have exaggerated the danger from this type of assignment.

The myth that domestic violence calls represent a high level of danger results in a less effective response by police officers to these situations. Spokespersons for womens' rights organizations have often complained that the police do not take assaults perpetrated by husbands and boyfriends very seriously. As the police become educated to the true nature of the risk that this responsibility entails, it is hoped they will develop alternative strategies for dealing more effectively with this problem.

◊

MYTHS OF POLICE STRESS

Stress is a neutral term but often carries a negative connotation. Stress can have both beneficial and adverse effects. Some people may perform at their best and be highly productive when enough stress is present to encourage or motivate high levels of performance. People undergoing mild forms of stress may experience an increased sense of awareness or alertness and will thus be capable of better performance in the workplace. Sometimes excessive work-related stressors can be debilitating and hinder performance and productivity. People undergoing excessive stress may begin to falter in their jobs and personal lives. Massive amounts of stress have been linked to impairment of the immune system and can have deleterious physical consequences.

Currently, little more is known about police stress than when researchers began studying it more than a decade ago. While it is generally recognized that police stress exists, there is little agreement regarding its cause, effect or extent (Gaines & Van Tubergen, 1989; Mallory & Mays, 1984; Terry, 1983). While it is plausible to assert that police stress exists, there is little scientific research that points to a specific cause for the stress law enforcement officers experience. Instead scholars have developed several perspectives on the extent and sources of police stress.

Some researchers view stress as a problem of personal adjustment (Lofquist & Davis, 1969). From this perspective, police officers have varying degrees of ability to cope with the demands made by their profession. That is, certain police officers are not capable of performing under the strains imposed by the occupation. Since no two persons are the same, stress affects officers differently.

> External social factors may include everyday interaction with the chronic criminal, the vagrant, the prostitute, or the juvenile delinquent. The constant contact with such troubled individuals in unsavory places can bring about additional stress and can create a very negative view of the world. (Arrigo & Garsky, 1997, p. 611)

Personal needs, values, abilities, and experiences affect how individual police officers respond to the stress of their work environment.

An alternative and very different perspective views police stress as a structural problem that does not reside in personal adjustment but in the pathology of the police organization and the working environment. Scholars taking this view examine such factors as management style, role conflict, and other structural sources of stress. "The police organization itself can be viewed as an external social factor. The demanding rules of the profession, disagreeable job assignments, and limited promotion opportunities contribute to stress in the police organization" (Arrigo & Garsky, 1997, p. 611). If officers are unable to perform, if they are hindered or are having problems, the police organization and environment are at fault—not the individual officer.

Regardless of whether stress is a product of individual adjustment or a structural deficiency in the police occupational environment, what are the effects of police stress? Do police officers experience higher levels of stress than bankers, lawyers, or physicians? Are police suicides, drug abuse, divorce and mortality rates side effects of the stress inherent in the police profession?

The Myth of Police Suicide

One of the most frequently cited indicators of the high levels of stress in police work is the suicide rate of police officers. "Police suicide, like the other consequences of stress, is closely linked to the unique nature of police work" (Alpert & Dunham, 1997, p. 203).

Relatively few studies have been conducted to examine the actual cause of police suicide. Some early studies focused on comparisons between the rates of suicide among police officers and the general population. With few exceptions, they concluded that police officers suffer a higher rate of suicide than the general public (Friedman, 1967; Violanti, Vena, & Marshall, 1986). While the rate of suicide changes depending on the police population examined and the time periods covered by researchers, it was generally concluded that police officers commit suicide more frequently than members of the general public. Urban police officers are said to experience the highest rate. Some studies suggested the rate of suicide among urban police might be six times higher than that experienced by the general public. Researchers studying the records of suicide in the city of Chicago found police officers were five times as likely to take their own lives as would ordinary citizens (Wagner & Brzeczek, 1983).

Other research into police suicide compared the rate of suicide across different occupations. In these studies, researchers examined the suicide rates for numerous occupations and compared them to the police profession. One study of thirty-six occupations found that policing had the second highest rate of suicide (Labovitz & Hagedorn, 1971). Nonetheless, Lester's (1983) research into police suicide found the suicide rate was also high among the self-employed and people in manufacturing occupations. Uncritical readings of these findings are often offered as direct evidence of the stress inherent in police work.

Even though early research into police suicide has generally indicated a high rate of suicide among police officers, this myth of policing is beginning to change as researchers collect additional data and take a more critical look at the problem. A 1990 study of police officer suicide in the Los Angeles Police Department found the suicide rate of police officers remained lower than the suicide rate for other adults in the same geographic area (Josephson & Reiser, 1990, p. 227). These scholars felt that "research done at the Los Angeles Police Department (LAPD) and the data available in the literature fail to provide support for the belief of an inordinately high suicide rate among police in general."

A 1994 study examined the National Mortality Detail Files to determine whether police officers had a higher rate of suicide than members of the public. The researchers concluded that when controls are added for differences in socio-economic variables like age, race, gender, and place of employment "being a police officer is not significantly associated with the odds of death by suicide" (Stack & Kelley, 1994, p. 84). Other cautious researchers have offered alternative explanations other than stress for the seemingly high rate of police suicide.

> First, although more women are entering the field [less than 12% of the police population] police work is a male-dominated profession, and males have demonstrated a higher rate [two times greater] of successful suicide than females. Second, the use, availability and familiarity with firearms by police in their work provide them with a lethal weapon that affords the user little chance of surviving a serious suicide attempt. (Alpert & Dunham, 1997, p. 204)

There is also evidence that suggests at least some suicides by police officers may be the result of the discovery of acts of corruption or deviance rather than any inherent stress of police work. Some police officers have taken their lives after an investigation of corruption. After the New York City Police Department's probe of the "Buddy Boys," a corrupt police ring, some members whose activites were exposed committed suicide. Police officers have also taken their lives following allegations of sexual assault or child molestation. While not all or even a majority of police suicides are a product of uncovering deviance and corruption, no research has been conducted regarding the relationship between corruption and suicide.

A review of the existing literature and arguments surrounding stress and police suicide indicates that conceptual and methodological problems associated with conducting this type of research makes it difficult to draw any firm conclusion. One can say with some confidence, however, that there is no available research that conclusively proves that the rate of suicide experienced by police officers is any greater than populations with similar background characteristics. Additionally, there is no conclusive evidence that work-related stress experienced by police officers is the cause of suicide. It is largely a myth that police kill themselves because of a level of stress greater than that experienced by members of other occupations.

Drug and Alcohol Abuse

Some researchers have claimed that higher rates of alcoholism and drug abuse are a product of occupational demands and a means by which police officers deal with the stress inherent in police work (Dietrich & Smith, 1986).

> Police chiefs usually admit that alcohol is a severe problem among offic-
> ers, indicating that as many as one-half of their force drink heavily. Ad-
> ministrators often refer to the existence of alcohol-related problems in
> police departments, including the practice of officers getting together af-
> ter work and drinking heavily, drinking on the job, and absences due to
> hangovers. (Alpert & Dunham, 1997, p. 202)

The first meaningful study of police misconduct specifically examining the use of alcohol by on-duty police officers was conducted by Albert Reiss in 1971. In researching infractions of departmental rules in three cities, Reiss found that drinking while on duty occurred in all cities examined and that the extent of on-duty use of alcohol ranged from 3.2 to 18.4%. A later study indicated that as many as 25% of police officers have serious problems with drinking. Alcohol use among police is underestimated. Many officers, fearing departmental discipline, are unwilling to officially report their deviance. Police organizations appear ambivalent toward drinking problems, placing blame on the individual officer and not the police occupational structure (Kroes, 1976). A 1988 study found that approximately 20% of police officers in a single agency used illegal drugs while on duty. Furthermore, these researchers found that the rate of on-duty alcohol use among veteran police officers reached nearly 20% (Kraska & Kappeler, 1988).

Current research on police drug use was prompted by the adoption of employment drug-testing practices by police departments. This research has generally indicated a small proportion of drug use by police officers. In 1986, the New Jersey State Police tested all 2,300 members of its force for drug use. Only five officers or .2% of the agency tested positive (Burden, 1986). Similar results were found for the City of New York Police Department. The discrepancies among various studies are likely due to one of two factors. First, the media has focused a great deal of attention on the issue of police drug use. It is possible that officers have become more careful to avoid detection. Second, these drug-screening tests are often administered to probationary employees with advance warning. Officers would therefore have time to modify their behavior before taking a drug test. Since many traces of illegal drugs leave the body rapidly, little advance warning is necessary for officers to modify their behavior.

While there is fairly strong evidence to support the extensive use of alcohol and drugs by police officers, there is less support of a direct causal relationship between drug use and police stress. An equally plausible explanation for the use of drugs and alcohol is that these substances are used for recreational purposes. In Kraska and Kappeler's (1988) study, they failed to uncover one police officer reporting current use of drugs who did not have a preemployment history of drug use. If police stress was a substantial cause of the abuse of these substances, one would expect to find officers without histories of drug use turning to these substances only after experiencing the stresses of police work.

Similarly, the different proportions of officers using drugs and alcohol might suggest that officers have recreational drugs of choice. Veteran officers may be more likely to use alcohol and younger officers more likely to use other illicit drugs. Very little, if any, research has been done comparing cross-cultural/generational samples of police officers and drug use. There is a distinct possibility that the differences between the levels of alcohol and drug use is a product of police subcultural acceptance of one drug over the other. Alternatively, officers may engage in these behaviors out of boredom or peer pressure as much as from any stress inherent in crime fighting.

The Myth of Police Mortality

One myth prevalent among law enforcement officers is that they experience greater mortality rates from natural causes than do other citizens. This myth of policing can be viewed as the culmination of stress-related myths of policing. When one links the dangers, the suicide rate, and the stress myths, it is a natural inference that police officers must experience a greater rate of work-related mortality. This myth has been extended to the perception that police officers do not live long after retirement. If the stress and mortality myths were accurate, we would expect to find that officers who stayed in policing longer had shorter lives after retirement because of the toll exacted from fighting crime. Myths associated with police mortality have been given credence by misreadings of research and unsupported statements in the police literature.

Police officers appear to suffer from increased mortality risk from cancer of the colon and liver, diabetes, and heart disease than people not involved in law enforcement (Norvell et al., 1988). Danielle Hitz (1973) reported a higher rate of cirrhosis of the liver due to alcohol use by police officers. A study of 2,376 police officers in Buffalo, New York, found that while the overall mortality rate among police officers for a variety of ailments was comparable to the general United States population, police officers showed a significantly higher rate of mortality from certain forms of cancer. Officers were particularly susceptible to cancer of the digestive organs (Violanti et al., 1986).

The study also pointed out that 48% of the participants smoked, 15% had high cholesterol, 86% had very little exercise, and 25% were at least 25% overweight. Pulling out only the higher incidence of a particular disease without acknowledging the context of health factors unrelated to the profession is highly misleading. Uncritical readings of stress-related research may be passed on to recruits in the training academy, with no mention of the limitations of the research studies.

Richard Raub (1988) has pointed out that statements such as "The average police officer dies within five years after retirement and reportedly has a life expectancy of twelve years less than that of other people" and "Police offi-

cers do not retire well" are not supported by the data. These and similar statements combined with pulling unfounded conclusions from the research literature reinforce the myth that the police occupation dictates dire outcomes after
retirement. Raub found that there was no empirical support for the myth that
police officers have a shorter life expectancy after retirement than civilian populations. In his study of the life expectancies of retired officers from the Illinois,
Kentucky, and Arizona state police agencies, he found that the length of time
officers live after retirement matched mortality tables for general populations.
This research also showed that officers who retired at older ages "enjoyed a
longer life compared to those who are younger at retirement" (pp. 91–92).
Thus, some police retirees may even live longer lives after retirement than
other populations. There is little direct evidence that supports the myth that
police experience higher rates of mortality because of the stress inherent in
their work or that they experience shorter lives after retirement.

Police Divorces

Many authorities have commented on the high divorce rate that is believed to
plague police marriages (Terry, 1981). Reports of this problem have come
from a variety of sources. The media, police chaplains, departmental officials,
the wives of police officers, and even some researchers have asserted that the
stress inherent in law enforcement results in a very high level of divorce (Niederhoffer & Niederhoffer, 1978). Indeed, there are a number of features about
police work that do place a strain on family life. The schedule worked by many
officers may make it very difficult to have a normal social life. Because of
rotating shifts, spouses must adjust to being left alone at night. In addition,
police officers may be required to work weekends and holidays. Second, the
job presents many opportunities for marital infidelity. Spouses must take the
officer's word that he/she really did have to work late or appear in court. Third,
the trauma and pain that police witness as a routine part of their job can take
an emotional toll on the officer and place an added strain on the relationship.
Finally, police marriages are subject to all the same difficulties that trouble
other couples (e.g., financial concerns, disagreements over child-rearing, etc.).

Because of the high level of interest in this topic, a great deal of empirical
research has been conducted. However, the findings from various studies are
contradictory. While some researchers report a high rate of police divorce
(Durner et al., 1975), the majority conclude that the level of divorce is far lower
than commonly assumed. Unfortunately, a number of methodological problems plague this body of research. The biggest drawback is that many studies
do not distinguish between divorces that occurred prior to the time that the
officer joined the department and those that occurred afterwards. Obviously,
any stress inherent in law enforcement cannot account for a divorce that
occurred before the individual joined the department.

It is noteworthy that the most comprehensive studies have concluded that
police officers have a divorce rate that is no higher than the national average.

James P. Lichtenberger (1968) examined data from the 1900 census and found that the rate of divorce for police was lower at that time than for most other occupations including doctors, lawyers, and college professors. Jack E. Whitehouse (1965) examined records from the 1960 census and observed that police and detectives had a divorce rate of 1.7%, which compared favorably to the national average of 2.4 for males in the same age bracket. Nelson A. Watson and James W. Sterling (1969) undertook a massive study that brought responses from 246 police departments. They observed that not only was the police divorce rate lower than the national average for adult males, but that a far higher proportion of male officers were married. Finally, Arthur Niederhoffer and Elaine Niederhoffer (1978) came to a similar conclusion as a result of a questionnaire survey that elicited responses from 30 departments.

Despite all the anecdotal accounts and subjective reports detailing the horrors of police marriages, it is clear that these ideas are based on myth. The reality is that the overwhelming majority of police officers are family men who have stable marriages (Terry, 1981). In a similar vein, Niederhoffer and Niederhoffer (1978) conclude, "divorce, police style, may well be lower than divorce, American style" (p. 170).

$\Diamond$

LIVING THE CRIME FIGHTER MYTH

Myths often become interpreted as reality for the people they affect. Behavior is often built around myth and perception rather than reality. Many of the myths of policing have contributed to the development of a group perspective among members of the police occupation. This cognitive group orientation and self-perception is often referred to as a culture.

The term "culture" is used to describe differences between large social groups. Social groups differ in many aspects, and people from different cultures have varying beliefs, laws, morals, customs and other characteristics that set them apart from people of other cultures. These values and artifacts are unique to a given people and are transmitted from one generation to the next (Kappeler et al., 1998). Cultural distinctions are easy to see when one compares, for example, North American and Japanese cultures. Clearly, Americans have different traditions, laws, language, customs, religions, and art forms than do the Japanese.

There can also be cultural differences between people who form a single culture or social group. People who form a unique group within a given culture are called a subculture. The difference between a culture and a subculture is that members of a subculture, while sharing many values and beliefs of the larger dominant culture, have separate and distinct values. These differences make subcultural members unique as compared to the larger, more dominant culture.

Clearly, police officers in America share the larger cultural heritage; they speak the same language, operate under the same laws, and share many of the same values. There are also certain myths and perceptions of the police subculture that make officers different from other members of society. Therefore, some scholars have maintained that the police are a unique occupational subculture.

The Dangerous World of Crime Fighting

The self-perception of being involved in a dangerous and violent profession combined with the legal monopoly police have on the sanctioned use of violence and coercion sets police officers apart. They view themselves as a unique group in society.

Because of their perception of police work—often based on myth—officers develop a unique worldview. Worldview is the manner in which a group sees the world and its own role in relationship to that world (Redfield, 1952). This means that various social groups, including the police, perceive the world, people, and situations differently from other social groups. By way of example, lawyers may view the world and events happening as a source of conflict and potential litigation. Physicians may view the world as a place of disease and illness needing healing. The police worldview categorizes the world into insiders and outsiders. "The police, as a result of combined features of their social situation, tend to develop ways of looking at the world distinctive to themselves, cognitive lenses through which to see situations and events" (Skolnick, 1966, p. 42). The way the police see the world can be described as a "we-they" or "us-them" orientation. Police officers tend to see the world as being composed of cops and others. Anyone who is not a police officer is considered an outsider to be viewed with suspicion.

This we-they worldview is created for a variety of reasons, including the danger myth. The myth of danger is reinforced in the formal socialization processes. Police officers undergo formal socialization when they enter the academy. One author noted that in the police academy:

> Group cohesiveness is encouraged by the instructors as well. The early roots of a separation between "the police" and "the public" is evident in many lectures and classroom discussions. In "war stories" and corridor anecdotes, it emerges as a full blown "us-them" mentality. (Bahn, 1984, p. 392)

Through these "war stories" in the course of field training and after graduation from the police academy, officers relearn and experience the myths of crime fighting, particularly the potential for danger (Kappeler et al., 1998). Police officers often picture the world as dangerous. This view leads officers to see citizens as potential sources of violence or even as enemies. This crime-fighting myth fosters the we-they police worldview; police officers see themselves as a closely knit, distinct group and citizens as "outsiders" (Sherman, 1982; Westley, 1956).

The Spirit of Crime Fighting

The concept of ethos encompasses the fundamental spirit of a culture. Ethos is a subculture's sentiments, beliefs, customs, and practices. Ethos often includes the things valued most by a subculture or occupational group. When this term is applied to the police subculture, some general observations arise. First, the police value bravery. Bravery is a central component of the social character of policing. As such, it is related to the perceived and actual dangers of law enforcement. The potential to become the victim of a violent encounter, the need for support by fellow officers during such encounters, and the legitimate use of violence to accomplish the police mandate contribute to a subculture that stresses the virtue of bravery. Also, the military trapping of policing, organizational policies such as "never back down," and informal peer pressure glorify bravery in the police subculture. It is not unusual for police training officers to wait until a recruit has been presented with a dangerous situation before recommending the recruit be given full status on the department. Until new officers have been tested on the street, they are usually not fully accepted by their peers.

◊

CONCLUSION

Myths often contain postulates or statements of belief held by a group that reflect their basic orientations. Myths, in a less formal sense than academy training, reinforce expressions of general truth or principle as they are perceived by a group. Myths act as an oral vehicle for the transmission of culture from one generation to the next and reinforce the subcultural worldview. Myths are advanced in the police academy, by field training officers, and during informal gatherings of police officers. Stories are told and retold regarding the dangers of policing and the bravery of crime fighters. Through exposure to the myths, new generations of police officers interpret their experiences. Their perceptions of the world viewed through these "truths" create a belief system that dictates acceptable and unacceptable behavior. Myths are an important ingredient in the socialization process for new crime fighters.

While all occupational groups undergo a socialization process, socialization based on myth can have very negative consequences. People may be attracted to police work because of the myths of excitement and danger. When the reality of day-to-day police work is experienced, new officers may become disillusioned with their chosen career. If the myths of policing are internalized by a majority of a police force, very aggressive practices can result that have negative effects on the individual officers, their departments, and the community they serve. The alienation of the police from the community is a product of socializing based on myth and misperception.

Order in the Courts
The Myth of Equal Justice

Nor shall any State deprive any person of life, liberty, or property, without due process of law; nor deny to any person within its jurisdiction the equal protection of the laws. In all criminal prosecutions, the accused shall enjoy the right to a speedy and public trial, by an impartial jury.

Whether we recognize those excerpts as an amendment to the Constitution or are only vaguely aware of the source, we often invoke the ideal they represent: equal justice for all determined by impartial judges and juries. Is the ideal a myth or reality? Is justice blind? Are cases decided on their merits, impervious to race, gender, and socioeconomic status? If justice itself were on trial, its guilt or innocence would probably vary depending upon what peers served on the jury. This chapter looks at some of the key principles and people in the judicial process—both the popular media-based trappings and the actual practice.

What images contribute to our perceptions of jurisprudence? The figure of justice symbolizes impartiality and usually appears as a blindfolded woman with a scale in one hand and a sword in the other. The Constitution and the Bill of Rights are echoes of the former; many segments of the public know only the latter. Language embodies the dual nature, as well. "With liberty and justice for all" implies fairness, equity, and what is right. "Is there no justice for that unspeakable crime" means punishment, atonement, and redress. A third meaning is "lawful," but the other two reverberate more often in the collective conscience and contribute to mythical notions about how the judicial process functions.

◊
THE ROLE OF LAW IN SOCIETY

Public images created by movies, television, novels, newspaper stories, and radio reports play up the adversarial nature of the system. Hushed spectators listen to brilliant orators arguing opposing positions in a point/counterpoint duet. The judge dressed in black robes referees the interaction from a bench elevated above the fray, gavel at hand to maintain order, fairness, and decorum. Oaths are sworn on a Bible; the language is formal and arcane: "Your Honor," "If it please the Court," "Hear ye, hear ye." The jury's attention is riveted first on testimony presented by the state—a sovereign power rather than a mere citizen—against the accused. The defense skillfully cross-examines and then presents its own version of the facts, employing all due process guarantees.

Of course, these public, adversarial dramas do not bear any resemblance to the preponderance of cases disposed of bureaucratically. They do, however, offer images that creep into composite views of justice and contribute to the myth of equal justice under the law.

What is the relationship between law and society? The law, as the codified basis of the criminal justice system, serves as a banner to announce the values of society. It tells us where the boundaries of acceptable behavior lie and links those who violate the boundaries—criminals—with evil, pain, incarceration, and disgrace. Why are some behaviors illegal and not others? Are laws based on a culture's morality? Is every behavior considered deviant defined as illegal? As Erich Goode and Nachman Ben-Yehuda (1994) state,

> Definitions of right and wrong do not drop from the skies, nor do they simply ineluctably percolate up from society's mainstream opinion; they are the result of disagreement, negotiation, conflict, and struggle. The passage of laws raises the issue of *who will criminalize whom*. (p. 78)

By what process do crimes get defined, the criminal law created, and violators punished?

Society is composed of individuals struggling to defend their interests in interaction with others doing the same thing. According to George Vold (1997), "The whole political process of law making, law breaking, and law enforcement becomes a direct reflection of . . . fundamental conflicts between interest groups and their . . . struggles for the control of the police power of the state" (pp. 208–209). The winners decide who is in violation of the law—that is, who is criminal. In Vold's description, the contact of groups is an endlessly changing kaleidoscope of force-ratios. Laws are the peace treaties intended to safeguard the prominence of the victors.

Goode and Ben Yehuda (1994) point out that all groups in a society do not have equal access to the legal process. Some have more influence with the media, some with legislators, and some with the educational system. "Views of

right and wrong do not triumph by becoming widely accepted in a society simply because they are objectively true or because they best preserve the social
order or generate the greatest benefit for the greatest number of people" (pp.
78-79). In its most altruistic form, law is a consensus about how to safeguard
everyone's interests—as understood by particular people at a particular time.
The framers of the Constitution may have been engaged in unselfish efforts to
construct an impartial rule of law, but women could not vote, and slavery was
not legal—constraints of the worldviews at that time.

Discretion

The law, then, is not a natural, universal "truth." Law and legal institutions are
a product of the society, culture, and conflict. Even within a single culture, law
varies (Black, 1976). The myth that police officers, prosecutors, and judges are
guided solely by law, rules, and regulations falls when confronted by the
impossibility of full enforcement and the practice of selective enforcement.
Discretion affects how much law is invoked in particular situations and occurs
at every step of the process from arrest to sentencing.

In actual practice, the law is much more frequently applied to visible
street crimes. Lower socioeconomic groups are more likely to encounter the
force of the law. In addition, the amount of social diversity between offender
and victim affects how the law is applied. Donald Black (1989) uses homicide
to illustrate:

> The amount of variation in the handling of homicide cases is spectacular,
> ranging from those that legal officials decide not even to investigate (as
> frequently occur when prisoners or skid-row vagrants kill each other) to
> those resulting in capital punishment (as may happen when a poor robber
> kills a prosperous stranger). (p. 59)

Impartial application of the laws is thus a myth in the case of homicide. As
Michael Kramer (1994) notes, "Despite the many supposed safeguards, what
matters most is who you are, who you kill, and who your lawyer is" (p. 32).

The Reassuring Ideal

Some laws exist more to protect our mythical allegiance to what is right than
to provide actual safeguards to those without power. For example, there may
have been laws preventing cruelty to slaves, but if slaves could not testify in
court, what use did the law serve? (Williams & Murphy, 1999). Legal rights are
frequently insufficient. Citizens have the legal right to bring a lawsuit against
someone who has wronged them, but the reality is that lawsuits require both
time and money.

Laws prescribe and proscribe behavior; they are not philosophies.
Despite the narrowness and limitations, the law often overpowers other forms
of resolution. As soon as rules are written down, people suspend personal
responsibility for acceptable behavior and rely on the written minimum. Social

regard and concern are replaced with technical adherence to the "letter of the law." Have you ever heard someone mutter "There ought to be a law" in a situation where it would be easier to resort to some anonymous authority rather than personally devise a workable solution?

Such attitudes contribute to the myth that the law and the courts can solve all problems. Perhaps the most poignant examples come from cases involving adoptive versus biological parents. Jessica DeBoer was taken at age two and one-half from her adoptive home in Michigan and returned to her biological parents in Iowa. Baby Richard in Illinois was four years old and was removed from his adoptive home. The media seize these personal tragedies and broadcast the details incessantly; TV movies are made; books are written. The courts are criticized and judges vilified because the public refuses to recognize that the rule of law is limited. The courts do not dispense justice; at best, they administer and interpret the laws and rules as they were formulated.

The Reality

A corollary of the myth that the law can solve all problems occurs when there are disparities between behavior and values. For instance, if drug use is increasing, yet society maintains a strong anti-drug value, laws can be written to punish suppliers. The original "criminals"—those who purchase the illegal drugs—can be replaced by much more evil villains, those who flaunt society's values by enticing and corrupting its youth. Society neatly resolves the discrepancy between professed values and behavior by redefining the "real" criminal. Rather than determining *why* values are rejected and redefining its laws, society shifts the blame through more laws.

The most frequent manifestation of criminal justice is repression. As Lawrence Friedman (1993) reminds us:

> Our criminal justice system—maybe every criminal justice system—includes an aspect that is downright oppressive. Criminal justice is, literally, state power. It is police, guns, prisons, the electric chair. Power corrupts; and power also has an itch to suppress. A strain of suppression runs through the whole of our story. The sufferers—burnt witches, whipped and brutalized slaves, helpless drunks thrown into fetid county jails, victims of lynch mobs—cry out to us across centuries. (p. 462)

Once the myth that repressive laws will deter undesirable behavior takes hold, it is not easily abandoned. If two convictions were not enough to stop a criminal, "three strikes and you're out." The question about why the first two efforts at deterrence were unsuccessful is never addressed.

CELEBRITY CASES

Images of justice are derived from a number of secondary sources. American history is required of all students before graduating from high school. The introduction to this chapter reviewed some of the images embedded in our consciences about justice. Before *Court TV,* the majority of citizens had never been exposed to criminal trials. The media—and particularly the coverage of celebrity cases—have provided glimpses into a world most people don't experience firsthand.

The Media and the Courtroom

The media play an important role in shaping our perception of equal justice in the courts. Trials involving celebrities or spectacular crimes have an inherent attraction for the media. Even before the days of *Court TV,* the media focused on celebrity cases. In two instances in 1966, the media were cited by the Supreme Court in overturning convictions. Sam Sheppard's conviction for murdering his wife was overturned 9 years later in part because of the "carnival" atmosphere in the courtroom. A popular television series and later a motion picture were based on the case. Jack Ruby's conviction for shooting Lee Harvey Oswald in front of television cameras was overturned after it was determined by an Appeals Court that ten of the 12 jurors had seen the shooting on television and believed he was guilty before the trial.

In 1994, O. J. Simpson was accused of murdering his ex-wife and her friend; he was found not guilty in 1995. The case was instructive on a number of levels. It illustrates both the gulf between minority and majority attitudes toward the criminal justice system and the public's ambivalent attitude between enforcing the Constitution and "justice." It was also a prime example of the myth of equal justice.

Differing Perceptions

After the arrest, the media engaged in endless polls about Simpson's guilt or innocence. Many more whites than African Americans believed he was guilty. Poll results probably had less to do with the evidence than with opinions about differential treatment by the criminal justice system. An article in *Time* magazine (Smolowe, 1994b) described the pervasive perception among African Americans that the system discriminates against them. Many African Americans perceived Simpson "as one more victim of the white power system. There is talk of a 'white-media conspiracy' to embarrass African Americans by toppling yet another black icon" (p. 26). District of Columbia delegate Eleanor Holmes Norton expressed the opinion that "For many blacks, every black man is on trial. . . . the black man is increasingly seen as a criminal by virtue of his sex and color" (pp. 25–26).

The evidence gathered raised arguments over whether Simpson's rights were violated by unreasonable search and seizure. That, in turn, raised the recurring issue of how deeply the public believes in the rights of the defendant. The public desire to punish the guilty often outweighs the methods by which convictions are secured. The public is not alone in its waffling. Myron Orfield conducted a confidential survey of judges, prosecutors, and public defenders and found broad agreement that police frequently perjure themselves on 4th Amendment matters and that judges ignore the law to prevent evidence from being suppressed. Judges may be wary of antagonizing voters when the spotlight is on. One public defender said, "You bring a motion to quash in a heater case in the six months before a retention election and you should be cited for ineffective assistance of counsel" (Chapman, 1994, p. 3).

With Liberty and Justice for All

Finally, the Simpson case has many of the trappings of the myth of equal justice. A "dream team" of 15 defense attorneys worked on his case, at estimates of up to $60,000 per week. A hotline was established with a toll-free number and a $500,000 reward offered for tips leading to the arrest of the real killer. Simpson had no trouble finding a publisher for his book, *I Want to Tell You*, which helped pay for his defense and presented arguments to preserve his reputation. Simpson's wealth and fame helped alter the balance of power that is skewed toward the state.

> Prosecutors, who can draw on big police departments, teams of investigators and lawyers to prepare their cases, have success rates of more than 90% at trial in most jurisdictions. The typical murder defendant has little money and is represented by an underpaid, overworked public defender. (Streisand, 1994, p. 63)

Without the resources to combat the power of the state, most cases never reach the trial stage. Ninety percent of criminal cases are settled before trial. Albert Alschuler, law professor at the University of Chicago, remarked: "Compare O. J. Simpson with the defendant who's represented by a public defender who has 500 cases a year and says 'You'd better plead guilty today because you'll get out sooner'" (Callahan, 1995, p. 6). Paul Petterson, indigent defense coordinator for the National Association of Criminal Defense Lawyers stated, "There's a whole different system for poor people. It's in the same courthouse—it's not separate—but it's not equal."

The trial and acquittal of O. J. Simpson was a goldmine for the media. For months, they had an audience eagerly paying attention to every report. While some commentators in the print media used the story to explore implications about the system of justice in the United States, the major focus was on the mythical trappings of celebrity trials. Perhaps the most telling aspect of the case was the influence of money. "The Simpson case has demonstrated perhaps more starkly than ever before that in the American justice system, as in so much else in this country, money changes everything—and huge amounts of money change things almost beyond recognition" (Gleick, 1995, p. 41).

Questions of impartiality are not limited to socioeconomic bias. As reviewed earlier, laws reflect the culture of the society in which they are made and the interests of those who work to pass them. The judges elected to interpret the laws are equally subject to assorted influences, whether their own biases, public opinion, or a combination of factors. Some reports of judicial decisions are mind boggling, to the extent that one wonders how the myth of an impartial, wise, considered judgment survives. However, the few reports of this nature are usually buried in back sections of the newspaper and are limited to short columns. We include two examples to demonstrate the range of beliefs that affect decisions rendered.

In Maryland, voluntary manslaughter is an offense punishable by up to ten years, with recommended sentencing of three to eight years. Robert E. Cahill of the Baltimore County Circuit Court sentenced a man who pled guilty to voluntary manslaughter to 18 months in jail, with work release. The truck driver defendant had come home, discovered his wife in bed with another man, used a loaded rifle to chase him from the house, began drinking heavily, and shot his wife in the head several hours later as she was lying on the couch. He called 911 and said he had shot his wife because she was sleeping around. During sentencing, the judge said, "I cannot think of a circumstance whereby personal rage is [more] uncontrollable . . . I seriously wonder how many married men . . . would have the strength to walk away . . . without inflicting some corporal punishment" (Sjoerdsma, 1994, p. 21). In Michigan, a Macomb County Circuit Court judge gave custody of a young child to her father (the parents had never married) because the mother had put the child in day care while she attended the University of Michigan ("Day," 1994).

Impartiality seemingly has so many hurdles that the very concept may be mythical. The structure of equal justice in America rests on the premises of fairness and equality to legitimate the use of state power. Fairness and equality, however, are as ephemeral and mystical as the symbols of the court itself. The reality of justice in the United States is much harsher, and the reality of justice does violence to both fairness and equality.

◊

THE BIAS OF ARREST

The gateway to the criminal justice system is arrest—the point at which one is taken into official custody and charged with the commission of a crime. In a system guaranteeing equal protection under the law and equal justice to its citizens, an arrest should occur only after police and investigators have carefully gathered evidence of a crime. If probable cause exists, the suspect is taken into custody. The criteria for determining probable cause should be the same for everyone. This is the majesty of a criminal justice system that guarantees equal protection. It is also a myth.

Socioeconomic Inequities

The vast majority of people arrested and processed through the criminal justice system are poor, unemployed, and undereducated. Indeed, 33% of the individuals in our prisons were not employed prior to their arrests, 45% were not employed in full-time jobs, 47% had not graduated from high school, and 50%

made less than $10,000 a year in income (Reiman, 1998, pp. 134–135).

Does the overrepresentation of the poor, undereducated, and unemployed in arrest statistics represent a failure of equal justice or does it represent higher rates of criminality among those groups? Defenders of the justice system claim that the disadvantaged in society simply commit more crime and more serious crimes than others. If this is true then perhaps the bias of arrest noted above reflects actual criminality, not a failure of the system to guarantee equality. Note that using arrest statistics is already one step removed from a fair assessment. Arrest statistics are only useful if everyone has exactly the same probability of arrest. The figures reveal nothing about those who commit crimes but are not caught or those who are able to sidestep arrest. The filtering process begins with decisions about whom to arrest.

Research on the police clearly shows that suspects from lower socioeconomic groups and suspects who are members of minority groups are arrested more frequently, on weaker evidence, and for more crimes than their white, affluent counterparts. For example, Robert Sampson (1986) found that juveniles living in lower-class communities were far more likely than juveniles in middle-class and upper-middle-class neighborhoods to be arrested for precisely the same activities. Once arrested, those living in poorer neighborhoods were far more likely to be referred to juvenile court. In a study of the linkage between reported crimes and arrests, Liska and Chamlin found that arrest rates correlated not with reported crime, but with the degree of economic inequality in a community (Liska & Chamlin, 1984). Belinda McCarthy found that unemployed individuals were far more likely than employed individuals to be arrested, in investigations of similar crimes (McCarthy, 1991, pp. 19–29).

For precisely the same criminal behavior, there is a far greater likelihood that the disadvantaged will enter the criminal justice system. As Jeffrey Reiman (1998) states: "The image of the criminal population one sees in our nation's jails and prisons is distorted by the shape of the criminal justice system itself" (p. 102).

> One of the reasons the offender at the end of the road in prison is likely to be a member of the lowest social and economic groups in the country is that the police officers who guard the access to the road to prison make sure that more poor people make the trip than well-to-do people. . . . The *weeding out of the wealthy* starts at the very entrance to the criminal justice system: The decision about whom to investigate, arrest, or charge is not made simply on the basis of the offense committed or the danger posed. It is a decision distorted by a systematic economic bias that works to the disadvantage of the poor. (p. 110)

Racial Inequities

Race also affects the decision to arrest. A study of police discretion in six southern cities (Powell, 1990) found that officers demonstrated a clear tendency to take more punitive actions against black offenders than white offenders, especially in the three most urban research sites. These findings were confirmed by research on case-processing in Nebraska (Johnson &

Secret, 1990). In that study, race was found to be the major extralegal variable related to decisions of detention, referral to court, and sentencing. The only aspect of the justice system which seemed not to discriminate against blacks was adjudication. At that point in the process, whites were more likely than blacks to be convicted. Researchers attributed this inconsistency to the fact that blacks were more likely to be charged and processed based on weaker evidence.

Comparisons of UCR and NCVS statistics offer clear evidence of racism. The number of African Americans arrested for crimes (as compiled in UCR reports) far exceeds the number of victims who identified offenders as African Americans (in NCVS surveys) (Reiman, 1998, p. 103). In robbery cases 49% of victims identify their assailants as African Americans, yet 62% of all robbery arrests are African Americans. In aggravated assault cases 29% of victims identify their assailants as African Americans, yet 40% of all arrests for aggravated assaults are of African Americans (Maguire & Pastore, 1995, pp. 243, 388). In drug arrests the disparity is even more compelling.

There are many possible explanations for this bias in arrest (Reiman, 1998, pp. 109–110). The living conditions, housing, and lifestyles of the disadvantaged do not provide the same level of privacy as enjoyed by the more affluent. What the rich do in their dens, bedrooms, and fenced yards, the poor do in public, making arrests for drugs, drinking violations, gambling, and sexual activity more likely. Wealthier families can provide the arresting officer or the prosecutor with alternatives to a criminal justice response. The son or daughter of a well-to-do family can always get "counseling," "drug treatment," "therapy," and other forms of professional help that might correct his or her aberrant behavior. The poor cannot make such overtures. The $5,000 or $10,000 needed to get a juvenile into drug treatment is simply not available to all members of society.

It can be argued that police officers are trained in such a way that they are more likely to identify a poor youth, particularly a member of a minority group, as a potential criminal. This police stereotyping may direct attention to the disadvantaged and away from the advantaged. It can also be argued that the police operate in a bureaucratic system, and like all bureaucracies policing seeks to avoid difficult problems and handles those cases that are less troublesome. A middle-class or upper-class offender is more likely to take the case to trial, more likely to exercise political influence, more likely to afford a private attorney. The poor can offer no such resistance to the charges; therefore, arrests of the poor and disadvantaged are simply easier on the police bureaucracy. Whatever the reasoning behind disparity in arrests, the basic fact is that middle-class and upper-class offenders, participating in the same activities and engaging in a similar rate of criminality, are less likely to find their way into the criminal justice system.

◈

THE BIAS OF TRIAL

The police guard the entrance to the criminal justice system. If inequities occur because of the discretion granted officers, does the trial process right any wrongs committed? Who makes the decisions that affect the determination of guilt or innocence?

Homogeneous Participants

The judge, the prosecutor who will try the case, and the defense attorney who will represent the charged (but still innocent) defendant are all attorneys. All are members of their local, state, and probably national bar associations. Thus, a select group of people will try to determine the facts of the matter.

Prior to the 1920s, bar associations were exclusive social clubs. When they became professional associations, they set strict educational standards, testing criteria, and licensing requirements (Ladinsky, 1984). The argument for these standards was that the legal profession had a responsibility to provide well-educated, high quality attorneys for the public. The reality was that these standards virtually guaranteed that most attorneys would come from segments of society whose families could afford the costs of a quality legal education (Chambliss & Seidman, 1986; Stone, 1915). The net result is that most attorneys come from the privileged strata of society.

Although progress has been made in the last two decades, there remains substantial underrepresentation of minority groups in the legal profession when compared with total minority populations (Bonsignore et al., 1998). There is also a marked system of gender inequality in both law school admissions and in the practice of law. Most partners in law firms and most law school faculty members are still white males from middle- or upper-middle-class backgrounds. Few female lawyers have been promoted to partners, and there are few members of racial minorities who reach that level in law firms (Spire, 1990). Entrance to the legal profession is guarded not only by educational and licensing standards but by the reality of family income, gender, and ethnic background.

Once in the legal profession, this stratification process continues for most lawyers. The best lawyers from the best schools with the best experience are quickly absorbed into prestigious law firms practicing civil, and more particularly, corporate law. Those attorneys who find their way to the bar in the criminal courts are usually from less prestigious law schools, have less training, and come from lower socioeconomic backgrounds (Ladinsky, 1984).

Those attorneys who do choose to practice criminal law are soon integrated into a system of mass-produced justice. While images of Perry Mason or Ben Matlock may motivate some attorneys, they soon find that the reality of practicing criminal law is far removed from the glorified version of defense attorneys on television. Heavy caseloads preclude quality preparation for all but the elite of the profession. Most cases are mundane—tried in a blur of assembly-line proceedings.

Many attorneys in the public defenders' offices are, for the most part, putting in their time and getting experience in order to move on to a law firm and eventually enter the more lucrative practice of civil and corporate law. Their priorities are to avoid offending people in the system and to get through the public defender experience without incurring any black marks against their future acceptance into the upper strata of the practice of law (Platt & Pollack, 1975). Another option for practicing criminal law is to join the district attorney's office as a prosecutor. Many who aspire to future political office follow this path. Burnout among criminal lawyers is the rule, and it occurs early in their careers. Those who remain often view a position on the bench as the next step, and they need the support of the local legal culture to reach that goal.

In *Gideon v. Wainwright* (1963), the Supreme Court ruled that states must provide legal counsel in felony cases. Defendants who cannot afford an attorney are either assigned a public defender or a private attorney appointed by the court. Neither necessarily serves the defendant well. Public defenders carry heavy caseloads. Most don't have time to see their clients until 15 minutes or so prior to the trial, hardly time to prepare a quality defense. In addition, public defenders are employees of the court. Their professional lives depend on good working relations with prosecutors and judges.

> Because the public defender works in day-to-day contact with the prosecutor and the judge, the pressures on him or her to negotiate a plea as quickly as possible, instead of rocking the boat by threatening to go to trial, are even greater than those that work on court-assigned counsel. (Reiman, 1998, p. 118)

Court-assigned private attorneys also have little incentive to invest time or resources to represent their clients' interests. They are paid a flat fee, considerably lower than rates charged private clients. Bringing a case to a rapid conclusion, preferably through a bargained guilty plea, is very much in their economic interest.

In his classic study of the Chicago criminal courts, Abraham Blumberg (1975) found that the defense counsel was usually the first to suggest a guilty plea. Public defenders were almost twice as likely as privately retained counsel to argue for a guilty plea at the very first meeting with their client. In addition, privately retained counsel were twice as likely to get the charges against clients dismissed or to win a not guilty verdict than court-appointed attorneys or public defenders. In a study of over 28,000 felony cares in Tennessee, Virginia, and Kentucky it was found that public defenders were able to get charges dropped or an acquittal for 11.3% of their clients while private attorneys got charges dropped or an acquittal in 56% of their cases (Champion, 1989a). Clearly the quality and commitment of the defense attorney impacts the outcome of criminal cases. In essence, justice is correlated with the ability to pay by the hour.

Judges sit at the apex of the judicial system. They are charged with fair application of the rules and the blind dispensing of individualized justice. Most come from the highest strata of a highly stratified profession—families with considerable economic and political power. At the federal level the homogeneity is even more pronounced. The qualifications of a mandatory elite education, appointment by the president, and political approval from both other lawyers and powerful politicians limits the number of potential applicants and results in little social diversity on the federal bench (Chambliss & Seidman, 1986). Having crossed the portal to the criminal justice system, clients find the participants in the process of assessing guilt or innocence are people very unlike themselves.

Pretrial Detention

The very first decision made in the adversarial trial system is whether to keep the defendant in jail awaiting trial, to set bond, or to release the defendant on his or her own recognizance. Bail itself is inherently discriminatory. Most of the poor charged with a crime cannot pay even nominal bail, nor can they afford the services of a bailbondsman. As a result, those not released on their own recognizance who cannot afford bail are jailed even though they are still legally innocent. Fifty-six percent of people in local jails are unconvicted—awaiting arraignment or trial or on trial (Reiman, 1998, p. 116).

Beyond the obviously unpleasant fact of being punished before any ruling of guilt or innocence, the inability to make bail or gain release biases the entire criminal process from this point forward. First, the poor cannot afford to sit in jail. They have meager incomes from which they must support families. Unlike salaried workers, they receive no pay when they can't work—whether they are ill, in jail, or on vacation. The hardships for their families are serious and compelling. Second, they are unable to participate in preparing their own defense and seldom have the resources to hire those who could.

Unlike the television image of Ben Matlock sending his trusty private detective sidekick out to track the truth, the poor are represented in court by court-appointed lawyers or public defenders, who have no investigative staff or budget. The responsibility for getting statements from witnesses and gathering evidence falls on the defendant, who can do neither if he or she is behind bars. Private detectives, laboratory analyses, and expert witnesses are all expensive and well beyond the financial capabilities of almost all criminal defendants. All these factors create an irresistible pressure on the defendant to agree to a plea bargain.

In the rare instance that a case goes to trial, imagine the impression on the judge or jury of a defendant dressed in a jail uniform versus someone dressed in a neatly pressed suit. Somewhere between 75% and 90% of all criminal cases are resolved by a plea bargain (Reiman, 1998, p. 117). The pressures on a poor defendant to plea bargain are enormous. A guilty plea usually means he or she will get out with time served (the time already spent in jail because release was denied) or a small additional sentence. That means family support can resume and personal needs can be met. Even if the defendant believes that he or she is innocent, there is a powerful incentive working here to "cop a plea" to a lesser charge simply to end the ordeal begun by arrest. This powerful impetus toward a guilty plea, regardless of guilt or innocence, begins with the lack of quality legal representation compounded by the issue of pretrial detention.

The process of plea bargaining contributes to the bureaucracy of the court—and marks further divergence from the myth of justice through an adversarial system. Rather than a fair contest between evenly matched parties, the system becomes administrative screening: which cases are more likely to fit a profile of speedy prosecution and conviction? Plea bargaining is normally hidden from public view; discretion is more easily practiced without much scrutiny. Lawrence Friedman (1993) links the discovery process with this move toward administration. Although intended as beneficial to defendants, discovery was "also a symptom of the long-term secular shift in power away from the lay jury and the trial itself toward an administered, bureaucratic, professional system of justice. In this sense, discovery was, to a degree, a blood brother of plea bargaining . . ." (p. 387).

Most cases never reach the trial stage. The image of the jury foreman reading a verdict carefully deliberated by 12 peers is largely a myth—the dramatized image of television and movies.

> In fact, the trial is the residue of a residue: it is a mechanism for handling survivors of a long filtering process. Not all serious criminals are caught; not all those who are caught are arrested; not all those who are arrested are charged; and most of those who are charged never reach trial—their cases are dropped, or they plead guilty. (Friedman, 1993, p. 386)

Despite the rarity of trial, it is interesting to contrast the mythical aspects of trials, when they do occur, with reality. Jury tampering is a common phrase. The public knows it is illegal, but what precisely does the phrase mean? In highly publicized cases like the Simpson trial, both defense attorneys and prosecutors use the press to plant seeds in the public's—and potential jurors'—minds. Another perfectly legal resource—if clients can afford it—is the jury consultant. Clients pay up to six figures to hire experts who will attempt to predict how potential jurors will vote. They investigate the associations to which jurors belong, the cars they drive, where they live, how they maintain the lawn, and any other behavior that might give clues to predispositions or biases.

Once the trial begins, consultants monitor jurors' responses (body language and other nonverbal indicators) to opening statements, cross-examination style, and objections. The jury itself is often composed of people who could not find an excuse not to serve. In today's increasingly disparate society, what precisely does a jury of one's peers constitute? Trials where juries are sequestered from their families for months at a time call into question the requirement of a unanimous vote. Will people continue to discuss the facts of the case endlessly, or will their patience be exhausted and they'll vote the majority so they can return home?

So, the poor are more likely to be arrested for crimes than the well-to-do, more likely to be denied their freedom awaiting an adjudication, and more likely to be convicted because they cannot afford high-quality legal representation. One distinguishing characteristic separates those who go free from those who do not—money. The same characteristic separates those who go to prison from those who do not.

◈

THE BIAS OF SENTENCING

Once a defendant has been adjudicated as guilty, it falls on the court to hand down a sentence appropriate to the crime and its circumstances. The doctrine of equality, fairness, and equal protection under the law dictates that this decision not be affected by extraneous factors, such as race, gender, or socioeconomic status. The reality is that such factors play a critical role in the sentencing decision.

Racial Disparities

The empirical research done by criminal justice scholars has demonstrated with remarkable regularity that minority group members (particularly African Americans) and the poor get longer sentences and have less chance of gaining parole or probation, even when the seriousness of the crime and the criminal record of the defendants are held constant (Meierhoefer, 1992). There have been numerous studies that demonstrate bias in sentencing; we mention only a few. A study of 1,970 defendants arrested in Florida found both race and class bias. Unemployed black defendants were the most likely to be imprisoned (Chiricos & Bales, 1991). The researchers suggest that sentencing patterns demonstrate that prison serves as both a means of punishment and as warehouses for surplus labor. In a study of sentencing practices involving 8,414 Detroit-area defendants convicted of violent felonies, Spohn and Cederblom (1991) determined that African-American defendants were significantly more likely than white defendants to be sentenced to prison. Even in rural areas disparities are apparent. For example, a South Dakota study compared the severity of punishment meted out to whites and Native Americans. Race was the statistically significant variable that explained the differences in punishment severity (Feimer, Pommerstein, & Wise, 1990).

Joan Petersilia (1983), studying sentencing patterns in California, Michigan, and Texas, found:

> Controlling for the factors most likely to influence sentencing and parole decisions, the analysis still found that blacks and Hispanics are less likely to be given probation, more likely to receive prison sentences, more likely to receive longer prison sentences, and more likely to serve a greater proportion of their original time. (p. 28)

In looking at the death penalty, research has concluded that racial bias is pervasive in capital cases. Keil and Vito (1992) found systematic discrimination in the application of capital punishment, with African Americans who kill white victims far more likely to receive capital punishment than whites who kill other whites. A Florida study by Radelet and Pierce (1991) found a strong correlation between both the defendant's race and the victim's race in the application of the death penalty. In cases with white victims the defendant was six times more likely to get the death penalty than in cases with African-American victims. Moreover, African-American defendants who killed white victims were more than twice as likely to receive the death penalty than were white defendants who killed white victims. Finally, African-American defendants who killed white victims were fifteen times more likely to be sentenced to death than were African-American defendants who killed African-American victims. Radelet and Pierce conclude that racial discrimination, both offender-based and victim-based, permeates the contemporary use of capital punishment.

Gender Disparities

In looking at juvenile crime, the evidence shows that girls are disproportionately arrested or reported to the juvenile justice system for "status" offenses such as truancy, running away from home, sexual activity, and parental curfew violations (Chesney-Lind, 1995). A study of the incarceration of delinquent girls in U.S. public training schools and detention centers found that girls were more likely than boys to be confined for status offenses and less serious delinquency offenses (Schwartz, Steketee, & Schneider, 1990). While studies of gender discrimination in court processing and sentencing are still rare, those that have been done have shown a gender bias in the justice system. A study of delinquent youths in Miami (Horowitz & Pottieger, 1991) revealed that juvenile girls convicted of prostitution were more likely than any other type of offender to be adjudicated. (judged in trial)

Gender discrimination is clearest and most compelling in cases where a woman is the victim of violence, particularly in rape or battering cases. Judges influence and decide cases based on their stereotyped notions of the roles of women. Courts have consistently demonstrated a gender bias in mediating domestic violence and rape cases. Police are reluctant to arrest; prosecutors are reluctant to prosecute; juries are reluctant to convict; and judges are reluctant to sentence in any sexual assault case where: (1) a woman is perceived as precipitating her own rape or assault by her style of dress; her drinking or drug-consuming activity; or her participation in certain activities, such as going to a bar or hitchhiking or (2) there is a lack of physical evidence of a severe injury proving forced intercourse (Estrich, 1987; LaFree, 1989). The second consideration ignores the fact that many rapes do not result in visible injury, and many times women do not resist out of fear of being murdered. The first assumption precludes women from engaging in activities perfectly acceptable for a man, such as going out alone at night, going to a bar, or drinking to excess. In essence, if women engage in that behavior they automatically lose the protections of the criminal justice system (Beneke, 1998).

Similarly, in battering cases police have been remarkably slow to act if (1) the batterer claims that he was provoked in some way by his victim or (2) the woman does not immediately leave her batterer (Karmen, 1995; Pagelow, 1984; Smith, 1990). These considerations ignore the possibility that the woman has nowhere to go, other obligations in the family setting, no money to enable her to leave, and, most importantly, places herself in the greatest danger when she does leave an abusive situation.

Types of Crime Disparities

The evidence of discrimination in sentencing based on socioeconomic status and race is compelling, but it is only part of the story. If we look at crimes that only the affluent can commit—antitrust violations, embezzlement, income tax evasion, price-fixing—we find the courts "kinder and gentler." Rarely are these offenders sentenced to prison. Despite the fact that these crimes of the affluent are indeed criminal offenses, the court is given—and exercises with regularity—other options for the sophisticated criminal. Rather than prison, these offenders usually face such punishments as fines, consent decrees, warnings, and cease and desist orders (Frank, 1985). In a study of Medicaid fraud the researchers found that only 38% of health-care professionals convicted of Medicaid fraud were sentenced to prison compared to 79% of grand theft defendants, even though the Medicaid fraud defendants caused average economic losses 10 times greater (Tillman & Pontell, 1992). Despite the fact that these crimes do infinitely more damage to society in terms of economic cost, death, and injury, the criminal justice system suddenly considers the "quality of mercy" in dealing with these offenders.

BIASED JUSTICE

Crime covers an extensive range of behavior. The only unifying theme is that the behavior has been defined as illegal. The law only regulates behavior. It doesn't change attitudes, and it can't solve tangled political and social problems. Alcohol and abortion have been both legal and illegal. Attitudes about the two topics create problems which the law cannot solve, yet we continually turn to the system to accomplish a task for which it was not designed. Real solutions require rational thinking and hard choices by the public and elected officials, not tough-on-crime rhetoric mindlessly trumpeting the need for more laws and mandatory sentences.

Just as our concept of "criminal" extends far beyond "illegal," our concept of justice has become a mystical veil shielding us from the reality of unsolvable problems and a system that cannot live up to expectations. To improve the legal system, we apply the same failed formula—we pass more laws. We persist in the unfounded assumption that the legal code is similar to the cause-and-effect laws of nature. It is not. It is prescribed or proscribed behavior devised to protect and regulate interests. The law enables some interests and restricts others. It legitimates some behavior and punishes others. Behind every legal judgment is a social and political judgment. The shining ideal of justice is that it is blind; behind the ideal is the reality that the law is a social construction, not an unassailable truth.

This brings us to one additional definition of justice: justification. The reality of the legal system is not that one is innocent until proven guilty beyond a reasonable doubt before a jury of peers. The reality is that who you are, where you live, whom you know, and the assets you have to defend yourself determine what kind of justice you will receive. Those most like "us" are presumed innocent—and often, for that reason, are never charged and never enter the process. Suspicions about "others" are usually cause for arrest—which in turn results in presumptions of guilt and justifies looking the other way when constitutional rights are violated or plea bargaining is accepted because someone cannot afford any other choice. Even the concept of applying the law equally is inherently inequitable, but we cling to the cherished notion of equality to justify the established system. The gap between standards and reality—the law in theory and the law in action—is much more than a philosophical discussion for those who must experience it.

◈

CONCLUSION

Analyzing the myths about the legal system reveals a great deal about the values held by society. In the debate over freedom versus order, where does justice fit? Do we believe in defendants' rights, or does that depend on the defendant? Are protection of people and property more important than protection of constitutional rights?

From the time of arrest, through pretrial detention, through the criminal trial, and into prison, the key factor that determines the severity and harshness with which the criminal justice system treats its clients is money. Those who can commit sophisticated crimes, pay high-priced attorneys, and afford private treatment and counseling will find justice with a merciful and caring face. Those who cannot will find long sentences and prison their punishment for being poor.

Cons and Country Clubs
The Mythical Utility
of Punishment

In the previous chapter, the myth of equal justice was dissected. Who you are and who your lawyer is often determine whether you are presumed innocent or assumed guilty. Now we turn to the corrections system which oversees the results of the efforts of the police and the courts. If a verdict of guilty is returned, is the playing field finally levelled? The comforting myth tells us that fairness and equity determine punishment. But does it?

◇

WHO DOES THE CRIME DETERMINES THE TIME

In 1995 a jury returned a guilty verdict for an unspeakable crime. In this instance, the jury chose life imprisonment for Susan Smith for drowning her two young sons. For nine days in the fall of 1994, Smith told her neighbors in Union, South Carolina—and the nation—that a black man in a knit cap had carjacked her vehicle and abducted her sons at gunpoint. Richard Lacayo (1994) described it as reaching for the "available nightmare" to excuse her own deadly impulses by "recasting them in the features of some unnerving outsider" (p. 46). Despite the rage generated when the deception was revealed, ten months later the jury chose not to invoke the death penalty. The trial had revealed a tragic childhood of sexual abuse and suicide attempts. The question is would the mythical carjacker have received the same sympathy? Was the jury influenced by the fact that Susan Smith was "one of them"—not an unknown stranger, no matter how reprehensible her crime.

Do we focus on the offense when it is committed by those who are not "like us" and on the offender if we "know" them?

Equity of punishment for similar crimes is one fertile area for myths about corrections. In the preceding chapters, we have looked at myths invented to explain otherwise incomprehensible crimes and at myths devised to make us feel good about ourselves or about the system—idealized versions of a much more gritty reality. The corrections system is interesting in that the media play a reduced role in contributing to and promoting myths. The occasional article will report the latest statistics released by government sources about the number of people in the system, and Hollywood occasionally revisits the prison film genre. For the most part, the public simply isn't interested in corrections, unless a sensational event occurs such as a riot or the murder of Jeffrey Dahmer in prison. The death penalty is the only topic that receives consistent news coverage—or programs for which officials are seeking approval (and funding) such as boot camps, shock incarceration or electronic monitoring. The assumptions that helped construct the system also assume the problem is solved once this phase is reached.

◇

MYTHICAL ASSUMPTIONS:
UNRELENTING CONSEQUENCES

What are the assumptions that helped create the system? Lawrence Friedman points to the universality of punishment as a solution to undesirable behavior. Parents punish children by taking away privileges. The punishment is often characterized as "teaching a lesson." Teachers discipline students who don't follow the rules; managers penalize unproductive employees. In Friedman's (1993, p. 10) terms, punishment raises the price of undesirable behavior and attempts to control certain actions by making them more costly.

Punishment is thus a cornerstone of corrections. Beyond the concept of punishment, what is expected of the corrections system? As one group of researchers (Crouch et al., 1999) put it,

> In spite of our extensive use of prisons, we do not have a unified and widely accepted prison policy. Our failure to develop a consistent prison policy results from the many conflicting definitions of what prison can or should accomplish. For example, we expect prisons to keep honest citizens honest (general deterrence), deter offenders from additional law-breaking behavior (specific deterrence), isolate criminals from the community (incapacitation), inflict a just measure of suffering on them (retribution), and yet somehow "cure" them of their anti-social attitudes and behavior (rehabilitation). (p. 85)

As these researchers ask, are these rationales for incarceration reasonable, compatible, and/or achievable? Is the system grounded on mythical, incompatible premises masquerading as rationales?

The public appetite for more punitive sanctions including "three strikes" and "truth in sentencing" laws has taken a harsh toll on the criminal justice system. In California, for example, defendants convicted of a third felony receive a mandatory sentence of 25 years to life imprisonment. The result is overcrowded jails, courts which cannot handle the cases, and endless delays. Each month, Los Angeles County's jail releases 4,200 inmates ahead of schedule because of third-strike felons awaiting a jury trial (Brandon, 1995). Compounding the problem is the fact that California's law does not distinguish between violent and nonviolent felons for the third strike. California's costly ($55.5 billion) three strikes campaign has netted twice as many marijuana offenders as murderers and rapists combined (Lotke, 1998). In April 1995, Steven White, a drug addict who stole to support his drug habit but never committed a violent crime, was charged with his third strike—stealing a VCR. He committed suicide before going to trial. His public defender in San Diego County stated,

> It's a morally irresponsible law. Even from the most benign light, it's financially irresponsible. Do you want to pay $20,000 to $40,000 a year to house people who are essentially a public nuisance, or do you want to focus on individuals who are murderers and rapists?

Despite its 30 prisons and four more under construction at a cost of over $5.2 million, California will need more by the end of the century if the incarceration rate continues unabated.

Society does not randomly choose methods of punishment; the approach selected depends on the tenor of the times. According to Lawrence Friedman (1993), ideas about the causes and cures of crime "rattle about in the heads of good citizens. How afraid are people of crime? How high on the agenda is crime and punishment?" (p. 315).

> We throw people into prison at an astonishing rate. There has never been anything like it in American history. Penology is overwhelmed by the sheer pressure of bodies. The general public is not interested in rehabilitation, not interested in what happens inside the prisons, not interested in reform or alternatives. It wants only to get these creatures off the streets. (p. 316)

Erich Goode and Nachman Ben-Yehuda (1994) point out that during times of stress there is a collective yearning for retribution. "Punitive policies reflect the public's desire for scapegoats who are seen as responsible for society's problems, against whom anger, resentment, and anxiety can be directed (p. 130).

Also contributing to the unparalleled growth in inmates is the war on drugs. As the warden at Stateville Correctional Center in Illinois, Tony Godinez, puts it, "No one foresaw the magnitude of the drug problem. An absolute explosion. It's possible, however, that we have exacerbated the problem by making the laws as strict as they are. You put a dealer away, you make an opportunity for someone else to step in and take his job. Yesterday you had one criminal. Today you've got one criminal and one inmate. Are you safer? No. Does it cost you more? Yes" (Lindeman, 1995, p. 19).

Society Wronged Exacts a Steep Toll

While there have been periods when rehabilitation was considered an appropriate response to deviant behavior, the often revisited attitude has been that criminals deserve whatever they get—punishment is supposed to be painful. Much of the history of prisons in this country was one of abominable living conditions. One observer visited a number of jails early in the twentieth century and described them as "human dumping grounds" where inmates were left "to wallow in a putrid mire demoralizing to body, mind, and soul" (Friedman, 1993, p. 310). Another observer found massive brutality, floggings, water torture, and "minor" operations to the genitals of sodomists at the Kansas Penitentiary in 1908.

Current charges that prisons coddle prisoners are not new. They repeat a well-established myth. The Governor of Kansas responded to the observers' comments quoted above with "Kate would like to see the prisoners kept in rooms and fed and treated as if they were guests at the Waldorf Astoria" (Friedman, 1993, p. 312).

> The underlying problem of prisons, of course, was political and social: the men and women locked up were the lumpenproletariat; many of them were black; and the general public neither knew nor cared what happened to them. Indeed, people *wanted* prisoners to be treated harshly. (p. 311)

Theoretically, prisoners' rights had always been protected by the Eighth Amendment, which prohibits cruel and unusual punishment. During the first half of this century, however, courts refused to respond to complaints. Federal judges felt that they should not interfere in prison operations even if prisoners complained that their rights were violated by abuse and overcrowding (Crouch et al., 1999). The classic prison institution was viewed as a zone of power in which inmates were essentially slaves. The prison was

> a model of discipline, the prisoner was silent, isolated, cut off from the world, helpless but not hopeless—raw matter, which the prison tried to mold. The prison controlled every aspect of the prisoner's life: food eaten, clothes worn, type of haircut, books read, mail written, when to get up, and what time lights went out. (Friedman, 1993, p. 314)

Eventually, the courts ruled against some practices—sometimes against entire state systems—as violating standards of decency, being disproportionate to the offense, and as unnecessary and wanton infliction of pain. However, "court intervention to improve prison conditions and limit crowding was on a collision course with trends promoting a more punitive attitude toward offenders and greater degrees of incarceration" (Crouch et al., 1999, p. 93).

The thorny issue of prisoners' rights which the public perceived as an oxymoron spurred an emphasis on victim's rights. The public reacted against a system that was perceived as caring more for the rights of criminals than the rights of the innocent—which granted the undeserving far more than was deserved.

> While researchers have at various times declared offenders to be biolog-
> ically deficient, mentally defective, poorly trained, or lacking social con-
> trols, to most citizens they are simply evil. The public wants criminals to
> be dealt with in a way that not only controls their behavior but symbolizes
> society's anger and desire to exclude, hurt, or eliminate law violators.
> (Crouch et al., 1999, p. 98)

Despite some rulings protecting prisoners from cruel and unusual pun-ishment, the courts have also supported the belief that prison should be unpleasant. As Robert Johnson and Hans Toch (1982, p. 13) tell us, this con-cept

> has been sanctioned (one is tempted to say "sanctified") by the courts.
> The Supreme Court held that "to the extent that (prison) conditions are
> restrictive and even harsh, they are part of the penalty that criminal of-
> fenders must pay for their offenses against society. The Court's majority
> not only concluded that "the Constitution does not mandate comfortable
> prisons," but that "prisons . . . which house persons convicted of serious
> crimes, cannot be free of discomfort.

Remove and Deter

Another assumption of the correctional system is that prison serves as a deterrent both for preventing crime and for keeping criminals away from committing more crime. After all, if the promised punishment is severe enough, people will think twice about committing a crime.

> Stiffen the backbone of the system, make it more certain that criminals
> pay for their crimes, and pay hard; surely crime will dwindle as a conse-
> quence. Deterrence—that is the key. Moreover, a burglar in jail can hard-
> ly break into your house. This effect is called "incapacitation." It, too,
> seems like plain common sense. If the crooks are all behind bars, they
> cannot rape and loot and pillage. The death penalty, of course, is the ul-
> timate incapacitator.
>   Never mind . . . soft-headed worry about causes of crime; forget pov-
> erty, unemployment, racism, and slums; forget personality and culture.
> Use the steel rod of criminal justice to stamp out crime, or to reduce it to
> an acceptable level. Get rid of sentimentality; take the rusty sword down
> from the wall; let deterrence and incapacitation do their job. (Friedman,
> 1993, p. 456)

Does Deterrence Work?

Wilbert Rideau, an inmate in the Louisiana State Penitentiary, responded to a question about whether tougher sentences were a restraining influence.

> Not at all. The length of a prison sentence has nothing to do with deter-
> ring crime. That theory is a crock. I mean, I've lived with criminals for 31

years. I know these guys, and myself. That's not the way it works. When
the average guy commits a crime, he's either at the point where he doesn't
care what happens to him, or more likely he feels he is going to get away
with it. Punishment never factors into the equation. He just goes ahead
because he feels he won't get caught. (Woodbury, 1993, p. 33)

A Milwaukee gang member had the same reaction when asked about
Wisconsin's third strike law. "The law don't make no difference to me
because I ain't gonna get caught. I mean, if I really thought I was gonna get
caught, I wouldn't commit a crime in the first place, now would I?" (Smolowe,
1994c, p. 63).

So we have a number of assumptions and attitudes contributing to views
of the correctional system. The public sees prisons as a place to send prisoners to punish them and to get them off the streets; judges assume they are
responsibly discharging their duties to distribute punishment fairly, without
the emotional vengeance of the public; the police and prosecutors hope
deterrence will keep others from committing similar crimes. Finally, there are
the prison administrators who must store, feed, clothe, supply medical care,
and protect the inmates with the help of corrections officers—within the limits of the budget provided.

The second section of this chapter will look specifically at losses suffered as a result of incarceration. After discussing general deprivations in
prison, we take a look at how prison has become a more painful experience
in recent decades—contrary to popular myth. Several recent innovations in
punishment have made incarceration even more unpleasant. Next, we
explore some of the problems that inmates face after release. Finally, to gain
further insight regarding the question of whether U.S. inmates are "coddled,"
we compare their experience with that of persons incarcerated in Scandinavian prisons.

Before we move to the next section we want to mention an omission in
most of the research on life within prison walls. Most research has concentrated on inmates in male medium and maximum security institutions. As a
result, much of the discussion in this chapter is restricted to male prisoners.
This is not for reasons of exclusion but rather a recognition that more
research is needed to address the experiences of female prisoners. In 1997,
the 84,427 women incarcerated represented 6.5% of the total number
(1,302,019) of persons incarcerated. Today, women are being sent to prison in
historically high numbers. Between 1997 and 1998 the percentage increase of
the female prison population was 6.5%, while the percent increase for men
was 4.7. The total number of male prisoners has grown 67% since 1990; the
number of female prisoners increased 92%. The fastest growing segments of
the prison population are black and Hispanic females. Between 1990 and
1997, the numbers in this group increased more than 80% (Beck & Mumola,
1999). Until more research is available on female prisoners, views of the system are primarily confined to discoveries made in male prisons.

BEHIND BARS

Prison Life is a magazine for inmates. Its editor-in-chief is Richard Stratton, who spent eight years in a penitentiary before having his sentence commuted. He believes that inmates need a voice and the public needs to be set straight. "I'm not going to pull any punches. Prison is a profane place. It's a place with gritty, harsh realities and that's what I want the magazine to reflect." The magazine takes issue with the drug war, mandatory sentencing, abusive correctional officers, inhumane prison conditions and the perception that inmates are worthless animals who deserve to rot behind bars (Marx, 1995a, p. 2).

Wilbert Rideau answered a question about the effect of the get tough mood on prisons.

> Since the 1970s, they have increasingly become just giant warehouses where you pack convicts to suffer. Look around me in this place. It's a graveyard, a human wasteland of old men—most of them just sitting around waiting to die. Of the 5,200 inmates here, 3,800 are lifers or serving sentences so long they will never get out. America has embraced vengeance as its criminal-justice philosophy. People don't want solutions to crime, they only want to feel good. That is what politicians are doing, they're making people feel secure. They offer them a platter of vindictiveness. (Woodbury, 1993, p. 33)

A corrections officer at Cook County Jail's Division 1 maximum-security facility in Chicago asked: "You ever had a dream where there is a huge ball of fire and you're entering hell? Well, this is it. This is worse than hell" (Marx, 1995b, p. 2). The reporter who interviewed Warden Godinez described Stateville like this:

> It's a factory with only one product: detention, keeping these people away from you. Almost two out of three inmates are double-celled, meaning they live with another inmate in a 6-by-9 room built for one person. Two bunks and a toilet. It's like living in your bathroom with a roommate.... When the place is locked down, the inmates leave their cells—escorted— only for visits or medical emergencies. They eat in their cells. On the eighth day they get a shower. (Lindeman, 1995, p. 19)

Contrary to these portrayals, many citizens believe that our prisons do not punish offenders severely enough. Institutions are perceived as places where individuals leisurely pass their time watching color TV, oblivious to the responsibilities that persons on the outside are forced to meet. After all, inmates are provided with three meals a day and have a roof over their heads. The only problem with this view is that it is largely a myth. As Robert B. Levinson (1982) writes, "the idea of a country club correctional center is about as viable a notion as the existence of the Loch Ness monster—many people believe in it but nobody has ever seen one" (p. 242). In reality, prison is the harsh and painful experience described above that provides inmates with few amenities.

◇

THE PAINS OF IMPRISONMENT

Many years ago, Gresham Sykes (1958) noted that inmates in maximum security prisons face a number of significant deprivations. In addition to losing their liberty, inmates are deprived of heterosexual relationships, goods and services, autonomy, and security. According to Robert Johnson and Hans Toch (1982), deprivations remain basic and painful. Inmates often face manipulation, exploitation, and violence. Crowded prisons are not only uncomfortable, they are volatile. Riots often represent organizational failures, yet the public commonly views them as evidence that prisoners are incorrigible and unworthy of the rights enjoyed by the rest of us.

> Living in prison has never been easy. . . . The task of adjustment is made more difficult by the fact that simple survival or endurance is not enough. Prisoners must cope with prison life in *competent* and *socially constructive* ways if the experience of imprisonment is not to add to recurring problems of alienation and marginality. . . . The prisoner is confronted by a hostile or indifferent prison environment in which denial of personal problems and manipulation of others are primary ingredients of interpersonal life. The result is that the prison's survivors become tougher, more pugnacious, and less able to feel for themselves or others, while its non-survivors become weaker, more susceptible, and less able to control their lives. (Johnson & Toch, 1982, p. 19)

Loss of Liberty

Clearly, the loss of liberty is central to the prison experience. Inmates are cut off from the outside world, and their personal space shrinks almost to extinction. For example, a Texas prison was designed to house two inmates in a nine-by-five-foot cell, tight quarters by any standard. Because of overcrowding, a third inmate was added. Three adults shared 45 square feet. "Even when crowding does not lead to illness or violence, it undermines the already limited privacy of prison life. . . . By limiting personal space, crowding exposes prisoners daily to constant and unwelcome contact with others" (Crouch et al., 1999, pp. 86–87).

Movement within the institution is controlled. For some prisoners, their movement is almost entirely constricted. John Irwin and James Austin (1997) note that a number of states are constructing so-called "maxi-maxi" facilities to house recalcitrant inmates. These facilities are modelled on the federal prison at Marion, Illinois, where inmates remain in lock-down almost around the clock. For example, California has constructed a segregated housing unit at Pelican Bay where prisoners spend 22.5 hours each day in windowless cells built of stainless steel and solid blocks of concrete.

The loss of liberty includes separation from family members and friends. Although inmates are allowed to receive mail and have approved visitors, it is often difficult to maintain relationships. Many institutions are located in remote rural areas—far from the urban centers where most inmates and their families reside. Frequently, these facilities are not accessible by public transportation. If visitors do not have access to a dependable automobile, the funds to operate it, and time off from jobs, traveling to the institution on a regular basis can be difficult and time-consuming, if not impossible.

Enforced separation places an enormous psychological strain on the bond between inmate and family. Prisoners may become concerned about the sexual fidelity of their partner; inmates with children worry about their well-being. Many individuals become anxious that their status in the family will diminish or that they will be abandoned by their spouse.

Deprivation of heterosexual relationships is a significant pain of imprisonment that often has serious social and psychological impacts on the prisoner. Relatively few jurisdictions in the United States allow inmates to have conjugal visits. This absence contributes to the high level of sexual tension that pervades institutions.

Another pain that prisoners must confront is the loss of goods and services. The basic survival needs are met; inmates do not go hungry or die from exposure to the elements. In addition, inmates generally receive adequate health care and are provided with an opportunity to exercise. However, prisoners are confined to the bare minimum, with enormously restricted opportunity to seek higher levels of satisfaction. Their environment is stark and forbidding. Although the food meets basic nutritional standards, it is generally boring and plain. There are only a few pieces of basic furniture and inmates are allowed few personal effects with which to express their individuality. Having been reared in a society that measures the worth of an individual largely in terms of material possessions, this deprivation results in an enormous amount of psychological distress and questioning of one's self-worth.

Loss of autonomy is another pain that inmates must confront. Persons incarcerated in correctional institutions are told when they may eat, sleep, shower, leave their cells or engage in other activities. One of the characteristics of adulthood is the ability to make decisions about things that affect one's life. Because inmates are denied any opportunity to make these basic decisions, they are in effect being reduced "to the weak, helpless, dependent status of childhood" (Sykes, 1958). This problem is compounded because the prison administration generally does not give prisoners any rationale for decisions. As Sykes notes, "providing explanations carries an implication that those who are ruled have a right to know."

The most significant pain of imprisonment is the loss of security. As an inmate at the New Jersey State Prison told Sykes (1958), "the worst thing about prison is you have to live with other prisoners" (p. 77). Lee H. Bowker (1982) notes that prison victimization may be either psychological, economic, social, or physical. There are numerous negative effects for inmates: withdrawing from prison activities, "feelings of helplessness and depression, economic hardship, physical injury, disruption of social relationships, damaged self-image" (p. 69).

Victimization

Psychological victimization is extremely common in prisons. It may involve verbal manipulation designed to trick inmates into performing sex or giving up certain material goods without a fight. In other cases, inmates may be psychologically damaged by rumors circulated by other prisoners or correctional officers specifically to inflict emotional distress and to damage reputations. Claims that an inmate is homosexual or an informer and rumors alleging infidelity on the part of a prisoner's spouse are examples of psychological victimization with a variety of unpleasant consequences for the recipient (Bowker, 1982).

Economic victimization is prevalent in many U.S. prisons. Because material goods and services are relatively scarce, a sub-rosa economic system has developed in most institutions to provide inmates with a variety of items. Howard Abadinsky and L. Thomas Winfree, Jr. (1992) note that "in any high volume illegal business, there is a great deal of cash, which is itself the object of theft, extortion, robbery and blackmail; prisons are no exception" (p. 523). In effect, inmates may be victimized twice. In many cases, they not only pay a high price for illicit goods and services, but they may subsequently lose them to the predatory activity of other prisoners.

Social victimization occurs when inmates are targeted because of their membership in an identifiable social category or group. Individuals may be vulnerable as a result of their race, ethnicity, religion, ideology or type of offense (e.g., child molestation). In recent decades, gang membership has become an important factor in this form of victimization. Individuals have been assaulted or murdered because they were associated with a rival gang (Bowker, 1982).

Physical victimization is often the greatest fear—whether in the form of homicide, assault, or rape. Many prison systems have experienced a significant rise in the level of violence among inmates in recent decades. Although most jurisdictions still report no homicides, some institutions have rates that are 15 times greater than that for the nation as a whole (Klofas, 1992). The frequency of assaults is more difficult to measure since prisons do not report comprehensive statistics (Abadinsky & Winfree, 1992). Nonetheless, the available data are quite disturbing with some researchers estimating that there are 20 times more assaults per capita in prisons than on the outside (Klofas, 1992).

Several factors account for the high level of violence in American institutions. First, there are a substantial number of incarcerated individuals who are prone to violence. Robert Johnson (1996) notes the presence in many facilities of "state-raised" convicts (individuals who have grown up in orphanages, detention centers, training schools and youth prisons). Second, a number of factors in the prison environment contribute to the cycle of violence:

> 1. inadequate supervision by staff members, 2. architectural designs that promote rather than inhibit victimization, 3. the easy availability of deadly weapons, 4. the housing of violence-prone prisoners in close proximity to relatively defenseless victims, and 5. a generally high level of tension produced by the close quarters and multiple, crosscutting conflicts among both individuals and groups of prisoners. (Bowker, 1982, p. 64)

Finally, violence is facilitated by aspects of the social climate of the prison, including the high degree of social distance between inmates and correctional officers and the taboo that prevents inmates from reporting altercations to the staff (Toch, 1994).

The issue of sexual victimization within institutions is complex. There are several commonly accepted myths associated with this topic. Among these are the notion that rape is the most common type of sexual activity that takes place in prison and that this type of assault is a frequent occurrence. It is ironic that many people believe rape is endemic in institutions yet hold the view that these facilities are "country clubs."

Researchers who have examined the frequency of sexual assault in prison generally conclude that this type of victimization is a rare event. Richard Tewksbury (1989) questioned 150 individuals at a correctional facility in Ohio and did not uncover a single case. Likewise, only one prisoner out of a sample of 330 (0.3%) reported that he had been raped or sodomized in a federal facility (Nacci & Kane, 1983). Lockwood (1980) conducted extensive interviews with inmates in two facilities in New York State and could find only one case of actual sexual assault. Based on information that was provided by inmates and staff, it was estimated that between one and two incidents occur each year among the 2,000 prisoners incarcerated in the adult facility. However, this type of assault was somewhat more common in the youth prison that was examined. Although most inmates claim they have not been victimized sexually, they also believe rape is fairly common in prisons (Quinn, 1999).

Although relatively few inmates actually experience coerced sex, a substantial number are threatened, insulted, propositioned, fondled, and sometimes even physically attacked. In some cases, the harassment continues for a considerable length of time. Sexual aggression is a much more common occurrence than actual assault. Nacci and Kane (1983) note that 29% of the inmates in their sample had been propositioned in their current institution. Nine percent reported that someone had attempted to force them to perform sex against their will in a prison. Lockwood (1980) determined that 28% of the inmates in his sample had been the targets of sexual aggression. For younger white males, the risks were considerably greater.

Conduct of this type has a number of deleterious consequences for both the victim and the social climate within the institution (Lockwood, 1994). The most significant impact is fear. Inmates who have been targets of sexual aggression remain concerned long after the incident has occurred that they may be sexually assaulted or even killed. Victims sometimes experience anxiety, anger, isolation and stress. In extreme cases, these individuals may respond violently or have suicidal thoughts.

Social relations among inmates suffer if inmates become so concerned about sexual assaults that they become withdrawn and reluctant to form friendships. More serious consequences are also possible including fights between prisoners and even murder. Nacci and Kane (1983) note that 5 of 8 homicides reported over a 26-month period at the United States Penitentiary at Lewisburg had a sexual motivation and that "a quarter of the major assaults were linked to inmate homosexual activity."

Living in the Shadow of Incarceration

While life in prison is certainly not a country club existence, inmates are not the only ones affected by an incarceration. Family, friends, and co-workers of inmates are all affected by the incarceration experience. Children are often forced to grow up without fathers or mothers. Research conducted by the American Correctional Association (ACA) finds that 75% of female prisoners are mothers who often have sole custody of children. These children are often forced to live with family members or become wards of the state. About 6% of female prisoners are pregnant, and they will be forced to deliver their babies while in custody. These children too either will be forced to live in custody, live with other family members, be placed in foster care, or become wards of the state. As members of the National Center for Institutions and Alternatives (1998) remark,

> The multiple effects of maternal incarceration on the child include traumatic stress, loneliness, developmental regression, loss of self-confidence, aggression, withdrawal, depression, antisocial behavior, gang activity, interpersonal violence, substance abuse, and teenage pregnancy: exactly the characteristics associated with committing crimes or becoming a prisoner in the future. (p. 4)

Incarceration not only destroys families, it destroys economic stability and opportunity. Families are often faced with the loss of substantial income. The family has lost the potential income of the person incarcerated, and the remaining family members may be forced into an endless cycle of poverty. The spouse or loved one of a person incarcerated may lose their job, whether because of the stigma of being associated with someone who has been imprisoned or because they have no alternative for child care now that they are alone. Many families of inmates are forced onto welfare roles or other sources of public assistance. Personally, the cost of diminished self-esteem is high; socially, this adds to the costs of incarceration. "Prosecuting and imprisoning people in such high numbers destabilizes communities and robs them of human and financial resources" (NCIA, 1998, p. 10).

◈

THE MODERN PRISON

Clearly, incarceration is not a pleasant experience. Furthermore, conditions in many institutions have deteriorated in recent decades due to: (1) changes in both the demographic composition and the size of the prison population; (2) the unintended consequences of judicial interventions designed to "humanize" the prison environment; (3) the demise of the rehabilitative model of corrections; and (4) the increased tendency to use prison incarceration as a response to the social problems created by a growing underclass of socially disadvantaged individuals.

Earlier in this century, the "Big House" was the prevalent type of penal institution in the United States. Although the environment in these prisons was extremely regimented and harsh forms of discipline were often utilized by the staff, violence on the part of inmates was a relatively infrequent occurrence. Prisoners were generally guided by a code of conduct that "could be translated into three rules: Do not inform, do not openly interact or cooperate with the guards or the administration, and do your own time." The inmate with the highest status was the so-called "right-guy" (Johnson, 1996). This was an individual who stoically accepted the pains of imprisonment, did not betray the interests of other inmates and avoided causing trouble. Although there were occasional eruptions of violence in the "Big House," it was not something that inmates and staff were forced to confront on a continual basis.

Since the 1960s, a number of changes have taken place that have dramatically altered the nature of these prisons. In many cases, the repressive but comparably safe Big House has become so unstable and violent that inmates and staff no longer feel secure (Johnson, 1996). Problems that were formerly quite rare have become commonplace in many U.S. prisons. These include gangs, attacks by prisoners on correctional officers and violence by inmates directed against other inmates. The "right guy" has been replaced by the "convict" or "hog" as the most respected individual. This role has been described by Irwin (1980): "the convict or hog—stands ready to kill to protect himself, maintains strong loyalties to some small group of other convicts (invariably of his own race), and will rob and attack or at least tolerate his friends' robbing and attacking other weak independents or their foes" (p. 195).

Demographic changes in the composition of the inmate population have contributed to the institutional climate that currently exists in many facilities. Until recent decades, most southern states maintained a segregated prison system. It was common for institutions to house black and white inmates in separate units (Irwin & Austin, 1997). These practices ended as the drive to integrate society gained momentum in the 1950s. Prison integration coincided with a dramatic rise in the proportion of minority inmates. In 1950, 29.7% of the inmate population was black; in 1997, the percentage was almost 50%. Today, an increasing number of prisoners are either black or Hispanic.

Table 12.1
Demographic Incarceration Numbers per 100,000

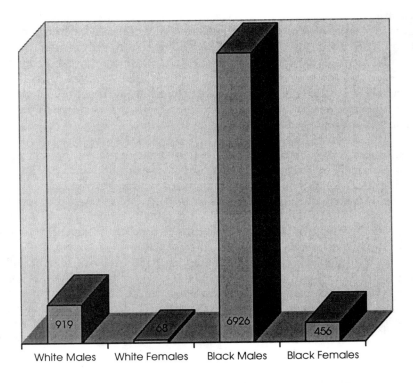

| White Males | White Females | Black Males | Black Females |
| 919 | 68 | 6926 | 456 |

Source: BJS (1998b). *Sourcebook 1997*.

According to the U.S. Census Bureau, there were more blacks in prison than whites in 1996 although only about 13% of the population is black. The incarceration rate for white citizens is 193 out of every 100,000; the rate for blacks is 1,571 per 100,000 citizens—8 times greater. At 1998 levels of incarceration black males in this country have a greater than 1 in 4 chance [29%] of going to prison during their lifetimes, while Hispanic males have a 1 in 6 [17%] chance, and white males have a 1 in 23 [4%] chance of serving time (BJS, 1999). One must keep in mind that more than 50% of the prison growth over the last decade was by the incarceration of nonviolent offenders.

There have been several consequences of the greater heterogeneity found among prison populations (Irwin, 1980). Racial tension and racial polarization have increased among inmates in many institutions. In many facilities in the large industrial states, prison gangs have formed along racial and ethnic lines, or have continued associations formed prior to incarceration. Gang members have often been involved in assaults, robberies and murders directed at rival gangs and independents. Members have also shown little reluctance to attack correctional officers. As Warden Godinez at Stateville puts it,

> Gangs are nothing more than a replacement for the family structure. We should not be shocked at how young men and women gravitate to a subcultural family if they don't get recognition and emotional support at home and in the community. All the images, all the impressions, all the lessons they get—or don't get—in those early years, how am I going to overturn all that when they get here?" (Lindeman, 1995, p. 22)

Another factor that has contributed to the development of the modern violent prison is the rapid growth in the size of the inmate population that has taken place since the 1970s. With more and more persons being incarcerated, institutions in most states have become seriously overcrowded. Although the findings from research studies that have examined the impact of prison overcrowding are mixed, some deleterious effects are unavoidable when institutions operate far beyond their designed capacity (Beck & Mumola, 1999; Irwin & Austin, 1997).

Double-celling is one consequence of overcrowding. Richard Sluder (1995) reports that double celling and overcrowding are associated with a number of problems. These include: (1) a deterioration of sanitary conditions within the facility; (2) more rapid transmission of contagious diseases; (3) an increase in concerns regarding security; (4) difficulties in providing inmates with basic necessities; (5) a decrease in access to programs and services; and (6) feelings of helplessness and loss of privacy among the inmates. Despite these problems, double-celling continues to be utilized by many jurisdictions as a means of housing an expanding prison population.

The intervention of the courts has also had a significant impact on the prison environment. In the "Big Houses" of earlier years, discipline was sternly enforced. It was common for administrators to place severe restrictions on inmate associations and expression and to ensure compliance with prison regulations through the use of corporal punishment by correctional officers. Many of these measures were declared unconstitutional in the 1960s and 1970s, as courts gradually abandoned their reticence to monitor prison procedures.

While the judicial efforts attempted to correct violations of prisoners' rights, nothing replaced the old system of control that had been dismantled. Inmates were not given a constructive role in shaping the conditions of their confinement, and no one came up with alternative means of guaranteeing cooperative behavior. Increasingly, disorder, violence and fear replaced order, producing a climate of terror. Correctional officers often became demoralized because of a perception that their authority had been undermined. The net result was that more inmates sought protection in protective custody; many correctional officers became reluctant to enforce the rules; and eventually the most predatory convicts ruled the prison (Johnson, 1996).

Finally, the demise of the rehabilitative model of corrections had an adverse impact on the quality of life within prisons. Since the late 1960s, there has been agreement among both liberals and conservatives that the rehabilitative model is flawed and should be abandoned (Cullen & Gilbert, 1982). A consensus had developed across the political spectrum that release from institutions should not be contingent on inmate participation in a treatment program. Instead, prisoners should be required to serve a fixed amount of time under the new "justice" model of corrections. The consensus, according to Lawrence Friedman (1993), had both ambiguous roots and equivocal results. Some had supported the move to determinate sentences as a way to curb possible discriminatory practices and to make punishment uniformly consistent for like crimes. The actual results of the change from indeterminate to determinate sentencing played into the increasingly punitive tendencies discussed earlier.

Alan Dershowitz, the Harvard law professor handling the appeal of Heidi Fleiss convicted of three counts of pandering and given a mandatory sentence of three years, said about mandatory sentencing, "It reflects the worst sense of priorities of our criminal justice system. The idea that a jail cell will be taken up by Heidi Fleiss is outrageous." The case against Fleiss also points to the myth that mandatory sentencing is fair. None of the men listed in Fleiss' directory of clients were charged (Smolowe, 1994d, p. 59).

The justice model also provided correctional authorities with an ideological justification for reducing the level of services provided to inmates (Cullen & Gilbert, 1982). After all, why should money be spent to improve the quality of life for prisoners if they have been incarcerated solely for the purpose of punishment? Proponents of the "justice" model do not believe that rehabilitative efforts have been effective. As a consequence, many jurisdictions that shifted to this approach have reduced their level of funding for various programs, including educational and vocational training, designed to assist inmates (Irwin & Austin, 1997). The political and popular thinking about prisoners today has no regard for concepts such as incentives. The pervasive "get tough" mentality gives lawmakers an excuse to avoid addressing the complex problems of a huge prison population.

Dora Schriro, director of the Missouri Department of Corrections, believes prisons need support for education and job training.

> I do not want to rehabilitate inmates, which means return them to what they were. I want to *habilitate* them. My focus is on mandatory education that results in high school equivalency, and mandatory industry work to have a vocation. I want them to have the basic tools for citizenship—literacy, employability, sobriety. (Gavzer, 1995)

Another source also emphasized the benefits of providing opportunities,

> Prison officials say higher-education courses significantly reduce an inmate's likelihood of returning to prison after he has been released. And the classes make the prison population easier to manage by helping keep inmates out of prison gangs and providing incentives for good behavior. ("Lock 'em up," 1995).

Yet, increasingly inmates are warehoused in institutions that provide few activities to channel their time productively. Even if research were to contradict beneficial results of such programs in prison, the question would remain whether the programs themselves were intrinsically flawed or whether prisons are not viable rehabilitative centers.

The "justice" model has also weakened the link between institutional behavior and release. In the past, parole authorities had tremendous discretion under indeterminate sentencing statutes to hold individuals who did not conform to prison regulations or to release them for good behavior. In jurisdictions that have adopted fixed sentences, the authority to parole obedient inmates no longer exists. Because sentences have tended to become longer under this approach (Cullen & Gilbert, 1982), many prisons now contain a substantial number of inmates serving long sentences with little incentive to cooperate with authorities.

◇

RECENT INNOVATIONS IN PUNISHMENT

Despite the harsh conditions that already exist in many U.S. prisons, recent years have witnessed the rise of correctional practices designed to be even more punitive in nature. These include the development of the so-called "maxi-maxi" prison, the return of the chain gang and the move to create military-style boot camps in many jurisdictions.

Super-maximum prisons and "maxi-maxi" units within prisons have been constructed in at least 30 states to house inmates who have engaged in disruptive or violent behavior while incarcerated. While the media and some correctional officials emphasize the dangerousness of the inmates housed in such units, the institutions were clearly designed to punish. AdminMax, nicknamed Alcatraz of the Rockies, was constructed in 1994 and cost $60 million. It was designed to hold 484 high-risk inmates. These institutions are generally designed with "state of the art" technology that restricts inmate interaction and allows prisoners to receive essential services including meals without leaving their cells. In many cases, these facilities have a central control center that houses heavily armed guards who maintain constant surveillance on the units. The inmates are required to spend almost all their time in cells with fully sealed front doors (Irwin & Austin, 1997).

The federal complex outside Florence, Colorado, is called the "Hellhole of the Rockies" by inmates because of its restrictive nature (Annin, 1998,

p. 35). Inmates are housed in eight- by twelve-foot cells where even the furniture is made of concrete and windows are mere five-inch slits in the wall. Some inmates have written federal judges, pleading for "some form of human contact" (p. 35). The isolation is so extreme and the monitoring so intense that the prison can psychologically destroy an inmate.

Another practice that meshes with concerns that inmates are not sufficiently punished is the return of the "chain-gang," a feature of U.S. corrections that had disappeared in recent decades. Alabama and Arizona have reinstated the use of this type of forced labor. Typically, inmates clear brush, cut weeds, and perform similar tasks along state highways. Alabama locks inmates to each other in groups of five. In Arizona, each prisoner has his own separate chain to prevent an escape; works 10 hours per day, four days per week; and is compensated at the rate of 10 cents per hour ("Chain," 1995). "Chain-gangs" are an extremely popular form of punishment with the public, and several other states are planning to institute similar programs.

Another innovation that meets public approval is military-style boot camps. The first boot camps were opened by the states of Georgia and Oklahoma in 1983. One decade later, there were 60 facilities with a capacity of over 9,000 inmates operated by 30 states and the federal government (Dickey, 1994). These institutions attempt to create an environment for offenders that is similar to military basic training. Although there is a great deal of variation among boot camps, these facilities generally subject participants to strenuous physical exercise, hard work, and stringent discipline. In addition, many also provide education, counseling, and drug treatment. Offenders typically spend 90 to 180 days in the boot camp as an alternative to a lengthy prison sentence (Dickey, 1994). Initially, these institutions were designed for young nonviolent male offenders. However, the programs have been extended to include females as well (Gover et al., 1999).

Correctional administrators often view boot camps as a means of reducing prison crowding and conserving scarce resources. This is the case if the camps are used as an alternative to incarceration in a more traditional prison. However, if the offenders sent to boot camps would otherwise be sentenced to probation, there is no effect on prison crowding, but there is an increase in cost (Gover et al., 1999). Because offenders placed in boot camps serve shorter sentences, this is also seen as a means to alleviate some of the pressures that institutions currently face.

There is no evidence that the military atmosphere, structure, and discipline of correctional boot camps significantly reduced the recidivism of releasees when compared to other correctional sanctions (Sherman et al., 1997). Yet, boot camps are extremely popular with the public. Televised images of offenders being marched around in military formation are appealing to many citizens (Dickey, 1994). Boot camps, it is believed, will instill discipline and respect for authority in individuals who lack these values. The reality is that claims made on behalf of the long-term effects of boot camps are similar to the unfulfilled promises that accompanied the development of earlier programs such as "Scared Straight" (Finckenauer & Gavin, 1999). That program was an effort to deter juveniles from a life of crime through conversations with verbally abusive, institutionalized convicts who made threats and described their prison experience in the most graphic terms.

◊

POST-INSTITUTIONAL ADJUSTMENT

For most inmates, incarceration creates a number of obstacles that must be overcome when attempting to adjust to life on the outside. The vast majority of prisoners were seriously disadvantaged before they entered the institution. In many cases, their lives were impaired by a history of alcohol or drug abuse, strained personal relationships, a poor education, and few job skills with which to compete in a modern technological economy. With the demise of the rehabilitative model of corrections, institutions are now even less likely to provide education or vocational training than was the case in past years. As a consequence, inmates leave prison with all their previous disadvantages plus the additional stigma of a felony conviction. The latter bars former offenders from certain occupations and also makes it very difficult to obtain employment of any kind. Furthermore, should a parolee fail to disclose his status to a potential employer, this may constitute grounds for revocation and return to the institution. Research indicates that an incarceration results in a 70% decline in income even for those able to find work (Sentencing Project, 1998). Only 21% of the parolees in the state of California were employed full-time in 1991 (Irwin & Austin, 1997).

In addition to finding a job, the individual must locate a place to live. Prisoners released from custody rarely have more than the few hundred dollars that they may have earned in the institution (Irwin & Austin, 1997). Financing an apartment is only part of the problem. The former inmate may not be able to supply potential landlords with satisfactory references. Routine questions about previous addresses and requests for credit bureau reports become insurmountable hurdles for many former inmates. Relationships with friends and family are often strained. The stigma of incarceration creates situations in which friends or family members question whether this individual can be trusted.

The psychological adjustments to life on the outside are challenging. Ex-inmates face "reentry" difficulties; they pass from a highly routinized, controlled, reduced and slow-paced prison life into the complex, fast-moving, impersonal world of the streets (Irwin & Austin, 1997). The former prisoner leaves a regimented existence that offered little opportunity to exercise autonomy for an environment where stressful interactions with many people in a variety of unfamiliar settings occur at a frenetic pace. Whether it is shopping for groceries, taking the subway, crossing the street during rush hour, or performing other routine tasks that most citizens take for granted, these are activities that are alien after a prolonged period of incarceration.

Former prisoners frequently confront legal difficulties; they are often the targets of police attention. When a crime occurs in the community that is similar to the one for which they were incarcerated, it is not uncommon for the police to "round up the usual suspects" for questioning. Even if only briefly detained, this can be a very unnerving experience for an individual who is trying to readjust to life in the community.

This problem is compounded for convicted sex offenders. All 50 states have some form of registration and notification provisions mandated by Megan's Laws, named after a New Jersey girl assaulted and murdered by a convicted sex offender who lived near her home (Schodolski, 1999). The laws require individuals released from custody after serving sentences for a sex offense to register their addresses with the police. Some jurisdictions even allow this information to be released to the media or to private citizens. Courts have repeatedly ruled that notification is not an undue punishment, but others argue it belies the basic sense of justice in the United States. Myrna Raeder, professor of law at Southwest University, comments, "At the heart of our system is that once you have paid for your crime you are like any other citizen. This is kind of the scarlet letter" (p. 10).

Public disclosure is likely to lead to harassment or even violence. One example occurred when "a father and son vigilante team, acting on information gained from the application of 'Megan's Law,' broke into a Phillipsburg, New Jersey home and began beating a man they mistook for a recently released sex offender." Civil libertarians warn about just such vigilante attacks. They fear that the instinct to protect will hurt innocent people.

The bureaucracy of administering lists of names compounds the problem. A couple purchased a home in Ann Arbor, Michigan. They were perplexed when they received a phone call from the American Civil Liberties Union and were told their address was on a sex-offender registry. The son of the previous owners had registered the address, and it was not removed when the house was sold (Schodolski, 1999).

The unintended consequences of measures to protect are multiple. Perhaps the most dangerous consequence of notification laws is a false sense of security. Kim English, director of research at the Colorado State Division of Criminal Justice, says, "In doing this we are presuming that sex offenders are people hiding behind a bush. But they are not. They are our uncles, our scoutmasters, our priests." As discussed in chapter 3, the majority of sexual assaults are carried out by individuals known to the victim. Notification laws are useless in such cases.

Between 1980 and 1993, the rate of parole violations increased in the United States by 413%. Only 49% of the parolees discharged from supervision in 1992 were classified as "successful" (Irwin & Austin, 1997). The others had been returned to prison either for committing a new crime or because of a technical violation (i.e., they had violated one of the conditions of their parole supervision). The reason for this dismal trend is that the nature of parole supervision has changed in recent years:

> Instead of a system designed to help prisoners readjust to a rapidly chang-
> ing and more competitive economic system, the parole system has been
> designed to catch and punish inmates for petty and nuisance-type behav-
> iors that do not in themselves draw a prison term. (p. 122)

Basically, parole supervision has become more intrusive. Increasingly, surveillance is taking the form of electronic monitoring, intensive parole supervision, and drug testing to monitor the behavior of persons released into the community. As a consequence, officers can more easily detect situations where a violation of parole conditions has occurred. This has led to a vast increase in the number of inmates returned to prison for technical violations.

Given all these difficulties, it should not come as a surprise that many individuals who are released from prison are not successful on the outside. Ironically, the public does not view recidivism as evidence of the myth of deterrence. Rather, the character of the inmate is used as an explanation rather than seeing the faults of the system. The reality is that even releasees who

> stay out of prison do not live successful or gratifying lives. . . . They re-
> main dependent on others or the state, drift back and forth from petty
> crime to subsistence, menial, dependent living, or gravitate to the new
> permanent urban underclass—the "homeless." Many die relatively
> young. (Irwin & Austin, 1997, p. 133)

Scandinavian Prisons

The harsh nature of many prisons in the United States can also be illustrated by a brief examination of penal institutions in Scandinavia. Although these types of cross-cultural comparisons are often fraught with difficulty, it may be useful to point out some of the features that distinguish secure facilities in those societies from their U.S. counterparts.

John R. Snortum and Kare Bodal (1992) surveyed the conditions of confinement that exist within secure prisons across Scandinavia (Norway, Sweden and Finland) and in the state of California. "California's two maximum security prisons projected a particularly oppressive picture of prison life, including overcrowding, lack of privacy, lack of space, lack of cell amenities, lack of safety, long hours of confinement, prison labor at slave wages, sexual deprivation, and visiting conditions that were, for the most part, chaotic and demeaning" (p. 56).

Scandinavian institutions lack the racial polarization, the ever-present threat of violence, and the serious overcrowding that characterizes many U.S. facilities. To some extent, these differences are due to the nature of Scandinavian societies which are: (1) much more racially and ethnically homogeneous than the U.S.; (2) have far lower rates of violent crime; and (3) contain very few economically disadvantaged individuals.

Nevertheless, certain distinctive features of Scandinavian prisons are the result of deliberate policy choices. There is no double-celling of prisoners.

All inmates in Sweden and Norway are provided with a private cell that includes both a desk and a chair as well as a bed. Instead of bars, each cell has a solid door which can be closed to insure privacy. In both countries "systems have generous provisions for home leaves and both allow easy access to unsupervised privacy with prison visitors" (Snortum & Bodal, 1992, p. 55). In the words of a Swedish administrator, "sexual activity is regarded as a private matter for every person, including prisoners" (p. 52). As a consequence, the sexual tension that pervades many U.S. institutions is lacking. Prison sentences are much shorter, with more than one-half of the inmates in Sweden serving two months or less. Finally, a number of programs have been instituted in Sweden that allow inmates to leave the facility for a substantial period of time to participate in drug treatment, vocational training, or military service (Snortum & Bodal, 1992).

CONCLUSION

Prison in our society has always been and remains a harsh and painful experience. In recent decades, these institutions have become even more unpleasant. Nonetheless, legislators and the public continue to seek ways to increase the level of discomfort. Whether this entails reinstating "chain-gangs" or placing offenders in boot camps, the motivation is similar: incarceration is punishment for breaking society's rules. Many citizens focus on retribution and find any amenities that detract from the goal of punishment to be inappropriate "coddling" of inmates. They do not recognize what most correctional authorities and inmates have long understood: doing time in U.S. prisons is not now and never has been easy. The notion of a "country-club" prison is a myth.

The anger and frustration that lead to the "lock 'em up mentality" wants to pretend that we can "throw away the key." The fact is that most inmates will return to the "mean streets." In 1994, $22 billion dollars ($10 billion higher than five years earlier) was spent operating the nation's prisons. Stateville Warden Godinez explains the problem:

> You want to vote against paying an extra thousand dollars per kid to improve education, and then you turn around and give me $18,000 per inmate to watch 'em for the rest of their lives. . . . Don't get me wrong. I'm no liberal. If someone does a crime and is convicted, they deserve to do their time. I'm just saying, if you treat the symptoms and do nothing about the causes, this is what you get. You build forty more prisons thinking that's going to solve your problem, and I guarantee you you'll fill the prisons. . . .
>
> I'll tell you this. Prisons are not the answer. Incarceration should be the final, final resort. We've got a million people locked up today, more than ever. But ask yourself this: "Do I feel any safer?" When you get robbed, you're a victim twice. First, when they take whatever they take.

Second, when they're caught and you're paying $18,000 a year for them to stay here. (Lindeman, 1995, pp. 19, 22)

Wilbert Rideau (the Louisiana inmate) had similar comments about how to address the problem and how to pay for it.

Crime is a social problem, and education is the only real deterrent. Look at all of us in prison: we were all truants and dropouts, a failure of the education system. Look at your truancy problem, and you're looking at your future prisoners. Put the money there.

[Pay for education programs] by shortening sentences. Sure, that's a hot button, but the public must come to realize that it can't enjoy its full measure of vengeance and expect at the same time to reduce bulging inmate populations. The citizenry must determine the minimum amount of punishment that it is willing to settle for, and then channel the millions it has saved into schools and preventive programs. (Woodbury, 1993, p. 33)

So the myths about the corrections system that need debunking are many: punishment does not always fit the crime, deterrence is not a rationale for prisons, prisons are not country clubs, and perhaps most importantly, the more than four million people in the corrections system are not all equally reprehensible predators. Some are innocent, some are old and harmless, some are unfortunate, and some are, in fact, incorrigible. Anyone who has ever driven after drinking more than the legal limit, shoplifted, used illegal drugs, or taken something of value from work is eligible for the correctional system. Rather than ignoring (or denying) possible similarities between "us" and "them" by segregating the offenders in prisons and increasing their distance from us, perhaps we should take another look at what we want the correctional system to accomplish. The more we understand the behavior that offends and attempt to look at the offender rather than resorting to predetermined stereotypes, the better the chances of reaching rational alternatives to prisons that offer no programs, no opportunities, and no hope.

The Myth of a Lenient Criminal Justice System

The evidence is overwhelming that the United States has the highest rate of violent crime among Western industrial societies. Homicide, rape, and robbery are four to nine times more frequent in the United States than they are in Europe. Burglary, theft, and auto theft are also more frequent, but not to the same degree.

The homicide rate offers a good illustration of the differences that exist with respect to violent crime in the United States compared to other Western democracies. In 1996, there were 7.4 homicides in the United States per 100,000 people. This contrasts with a rate of 2.1 for Canada, 1.3 for England and Wales, 2.1 for Italy, 1.7 for New Zealand, and 1.4 for Sweden. In other words, if the United States had the same homicide rate as Canada, there would have been an estimated 5,575 murders instead of 19,650 in 1996 (Flanagan & McGarrell, 1997).

The homicide data for young males are even more disturbing. The *Journal of the American Medical Association* has examined the rate at which men 15 through 24 years of age were killed in various industrial democracies during 1986 and 1987 (Rosenthal, 1990). The analysis indicates that the United States is far ahead of these other nations with 21.9 murders per 100,000. Scotland is next with a rate of 5.0 killings. In fact, it is noteworthy that in 13 nations including England, France and Ireland, there were fewer than 2 young males murdered per 100,000. Austria had the lowest rate of homicide (0.3). In other words, a young man living in the United States was 73 times more likely to be the victim of a homicide than someone of the same age residing in the Republic of Austria. As Barry Glassner (1999) remarks, "For black men between the ages of fifteen and thirty, violence is the single leading cause of death" (p. 112).

Why does the United States have such a high rate of violent crime compared to other Western societies? One explanation often advanced is that the courts are too lenient with offenders. Various politicians, most police officers, and a majority of the citizenry all decry the fact that criminals do not receive the severe punishments they deserve. If judges would impose tougher sentences, then we would be able to reduce the crime rate, or so it is often suggested. According to a Gallup survey, 78% of the respondents subscribe to the view that their local courts do not deal harshly enough with criminals (Maguire & Flanagan, 1997).

This chapter examines both cross-national and longitudinal data with respect to punishment. In the first section, correctional practices in the United States are compared with those of other Western democracies. The analysis utilizes two indicators of leniency: incarceration rates and practices with respect to the use of capital punishment. In both cases, it is clear that the United States is not more lenient than other comparable societies.

The second section of this chapter addresses the data regarding various correctional populations. Included in this analysis are statistics with respect to the number of jail inmates, sentenced federal and state prisoners, probationers and parolees. When the underlying trend is examined in each of these populations, it is difficult to make the case that our system of justice has become lenient in recent years.

◈

INTERNATIONAL COMPARISON

In an attempt to determine whether the high rates of violent crime in the United States are the result of lenient criminal justice practices, it is necessary to examine correctional policies that are currently followed in other Western nations. Because these societies share our democratic political tradition and have economies that are quite similar to ours, a strong case exists for comparing correctional practices in the United States to those of Canada, Great Britain, Australia, and the other industrialized nations of Western Europe.

Incarceration Rates

Table 13.1 examines the incarceration rates for various Western democracies. It is clear from inspection of these data that the United States incarceration rate is far higher than that of any other Western nation. In 1995, the United States imprisoned 600 persons for every 100,000 residents in the population. This is a rate more than 6 times greater than that of England, France, and Germany; around 9 times greater than Sweden; and more than 9 times the rate for the Netherlands.

When we examine Western nations that lie outside Europe, the picture does not change. Canada, our neighbor to the north and a society that is remarkably similar to the United States, has an incarceration rate of around 115 persons for every 100,000 residents in the population. Australia and New Zealand are two other nations with which we share a common language and the same legal tradition. Australia incarcerates 91 out of every 100,000 residents. New Zealand has the highest incarceration rate (127 per 100,000) among the other Western nations—almost 5 times lower than in the United States.

Table 13.1
Incarceration in Democracies

Nation	Inmates	Rate*
United States**	1,585,401	600
South Africa	110,120	265
New Zealand	4,553	127
Portugal	12,150	125
Canada	33,882	115
Luxembourg	469	115
Scotland	5,697	110
Northern Ireland	1,740	105
Spain	40,157	105
England/Wales	51,265	100
France	53,697	95
Germany	68,396	85
Italy	7,323	85
Austria	6,761	85
Switzerland	5,655	80
Belgium	7,401	75
Sweden	5,767	65
Netherlands	10,143	65
Denmark	3,421	65
Finland	3,018	60
Greece	5,897	55
Norway	2,398	55
Ireland	2,032	55
Japan	46,622	37

*Per 100,000 population.
**Includes both prison and jail populations.
Source: The Sentencing Project (1997). *Americans Behind Bars: U. S. And International Use Of Incarceration*. Washington, D.C.

The United States has the second highest rate of incarceration in the entire world (Mauer, 1994). Only Russia with a rate of 690 per 100,000 imprisons more people per capita than the United States (Sentencing Project, 1998). It is ironic that our nation should share the lead in this area with its former Cold War rival. Clearly this review of cross-national incarceration rates does not lend any support to the myth that the United States is lenient with offenders.

Capital Punishment

When we inquire whether the United States is lenient with convicted criminals, it is also helpful to look at practices with respect to the death penalty. Here "the pattern is so simple, it is stunning. Every Western industrial nation has stopped executing criminals, except the United States" (Zimring & Hawkins, 1986, p. 3). Canada, Great Britain, Australia, New Zealand, and all the nations of Western Europe have halted this practice. In many societies, capital punishment was abolished long ago. The last execution for a civil crime took place as far back as 1860 in the Netherlands, 1863 in Belgium, 1875 in Norway, 1876 in Italy, and 1892 in Denmark (Zimring & Hawkins, 1986). In other cases, abolition is of more recent origin. Great Britain had its last execution in 1964; Canada abolished the death penalty for civilian offenses in 1976. Spain and France were among the last Western European societies to do away with capital punishment, in 1978 and 1981 respectively.

Most jurisdictions in the United States have not followed suit. Although no executions took place between 1968 and 1976, the trend in recent years has been in the opposite direction. The number of persons sentenced to death has increased, and executions are becoming more frequent. The United States appears to be on a decidedly different course than the rest of the Western world regarding capital punishment.

The United States also differs in its application of the death penalty. It is one of the few societies in the world that permits the execution of persons for crimes committed as juveniles. More than three-quarters of the nations have set 18 as the minimum age for execution (Streib, 1987); this policy has won the support of the United Nations. The Geneva Convention prohibits, even in wartime, the execution of civilians for crimes committed under the age of 18. Over 100 countries have laws that prohibit the execution of juveniles or have agreed to international treaties that prohibit the practice. In recent years, only 8 nations are known to have executed offenders who were juveniles at the time of their crime—Bangladesh, Iran, Iraq, Nigeria, Pakistan, Saudi Arabia, Yemen and the United States (Streib, 1998).

Since 1985, the United States has executed more juveniles than any of these counties with the exception of Iraq. Although it is not common for juveniles to be put to death in the United States, the sentence is permitted under statutes that have been enacted in approximately half the states. By 1997, 12 states allowed the execution of children 16 years of age and younger and the state of Mississippi allowed the execution of 13-year-olds (Snell, 1998).

The Supreme Court has paved the way to allowing states to execute mentally retarded offenders and the United States has not wasted any time implementing the practice. To date the United States has executed 34 mentally retarded offenders. Clearly, with respect to capital punishment and incarceration rates, there is no evidence that the United States is lenient with offenders.

Why is the United States far more punitive in its treatment of offenders than other Western democracies? Part of the explanation lies in the fact that the United States has a substantially higher crime rate than most other societies (BJS, 1987). James P. Lynch (1988) has argued that when overall crime rates are considered, United States courts do not incarcerate a greater proportion of offenders. However, crime rates alone do not explain the tremendous increase in correctional populations that have occurred in recent years.

◇

THE TREND TOWARD GREATER PUNITIVENESS IN THE UNITED STATES

As indicated above, there is strong evidence that the United States has become even more severe in its treatment of offenders in recent years. It should be noted that the trend toward increased incarceration is not a universal phenomenon. Both Denmark (Brydensholt, 1992) and England (Mauer, 1992) have developed policies that are designed to reduce the number of prison inmates. The United States is moving in the opposite direction. In this section, four sources of data are examined that highlight the trend toward more persons under the control of the criminal justice system. These include statistics regarding the number of offenders incarcerated in prison, incarcerated in jail, under supervision in the community on probation and parole, and under judicial sentence of death.

Prison Incarceration

Table 13.2 indicates that the number of sentenced prisoners in state and federal institutions increased almost seven times during the period between 1972 and 1998. In 1972, there were 196,092 prison inmates in the United States. During this period, the number increased by 1,105,927 to an all-time record of 1,302,019. Data that go back to 1925 are available regarding the number of sentenced prisoners (see Maguire & Flanagan, 1991). They indicate that this increase is unprecedented in U.S. history.

In order to determine whether population changes account for this increase, Table 13.2 presents data regarding the rate of prison incarceration per 100,000 residents during this period. Between 1972 and 1998, this rate increased over fivefold—from 93 to 461. Although the United States population increased somewhat during these years, the population increase accounted for a very small proportion of the growth in prison incarceration. In addition, there has been a decline in the number of persons in the most "crime prone" age group of 15–24 (Steffensmeier & Harer, 1991).

The rise in the number of inmates has been so dramatic that overcrowding has become the major problem in U.S. prisons. The incarceration figures

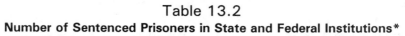

Table 13.2
Number of Sentenced Prisoners in State and Federal Institutions*

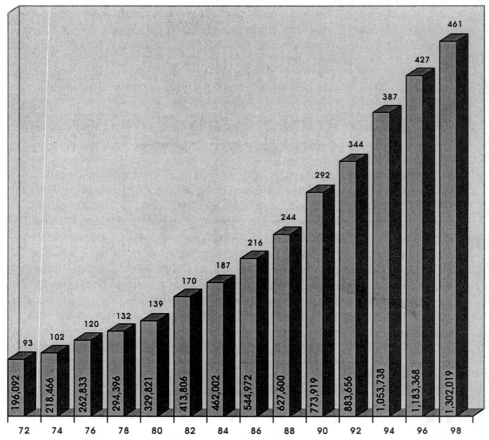

*Rate per 100,000 population on December 31; includes only prisoners sentenced to 1 year or more; 1998 estimated.
Numbers at top of columns represent rate per 100,000 population.
Source: *Prisoners*. U.S. Department of Justice, Bureau of Justice Statistics, Washington, D.C.

discussed here are the number of people in prison on a given day of the year. They do not reflect the problems of housing the 12 million new admissions to prison every year. In many states, the situation is so critical that courts have ruled that overcrowding constitutes "cruel and unusual punishment" and is in violation of the Constitution. As a consequence, correctional administrators have been ordered to reduce the number of persons in institutions exceeding the capacity for which they were built. By the end of 1994, the problem had become so serious that 22 jurisdictions reported a total of 48,949 state prisoners held in local jails or other facilities because of overcrowding in state facilities (BJS, 1995). By 1998 federal prisons were operating at 27% over capacity, and state prisons were operating at 22% over capacity (Beck & Mumola, 1999). Given this level of overcrowding, it would be very difficult to argue that the prison environment has become less harsh than in previous years.

Jail Incarceration

Generally speaking, prisons hold inmates who have been convicted of a felony and have been sentenced to serve more than one year in custody. Jails, on the other hand, house persons who are awaiting trial or have been convicted of a misdemeanor. However, Table 13.3 indicates that the situation with respect to both prisons and jails is quite similar. In 1978, the average daily population of local jails was 157,930. By 1998, there had been an increase of approximately 434,500 to 592,462. In a span of twenty years, the jail population has more than tripled.

The increase in the number of jail inmates cannot be explained by population growth in the United States. In 1978, there were 76 inmates in local jails per 100,000 residents; this proportion increased to 96 by 1983 and grew to 212 per 100,000 by 1997. During this period, the rate of jail incarceration more than doubled. Had the total population of the United States remained unchanged during this time span, there would have been at least twice as many people in the nation's jails in 1997 compared to 1978. In short, demographics cannot account for the rising tide of jail inmates.

As the number of jail inmates has skyrocketed, many jails are facing some of the same problems with respect to overcrowding as prisons. In 1990, 28% of the jurisdictions in the United States were under court order to limit population in at least one jail under their control; in addition, over 150 jail jurisdictions were operating under court directive to improve one of a number of specific conditions of confinement (Stephan & Jankowski, 1991). Clearly, it cannot be argued that jail is a more pleasant environment than in previous years.

The enormous rise in institutional populations is even more striking when the numbers of inmates in both jails and prisons are combined. In 1978, there were a total of 452,326 persons in America's penal institutions. Nineteen years later, this number had surpassed the million mark, growing to a grand total of 1,785,335 persons. The combined rate of prison and jail incar-

Table 13.3
Average Daily Population of Jail Inmates

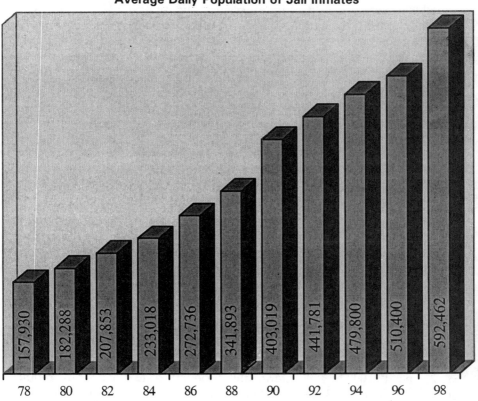

Source: *Jails and Jail Inmates*. U.S. Department of Justice, Bureau of Justice Statistics, Washington, D.C.

ceration also skyrocketed during this period, from 208 per 100,000 in 1978 to 645 in 1997. Based on these statistics, the view that the United States has become lenient with criminal offenders is clearly a myth.

Probation and Parole Populations

As table 13.4 indicates, the number of persons under community supervision is another example of a dramatic increase in recent years. In 1980, there were 1,118,097 adult probationers and 220,438 adult parolees in the United States. Eighteen years later, these populations had risen to 3,417,613 and 704,964 respectively. The number of probationers and parolees tripled in this

Table 13.4
Number of Adults on Probation and Parole in the United States*

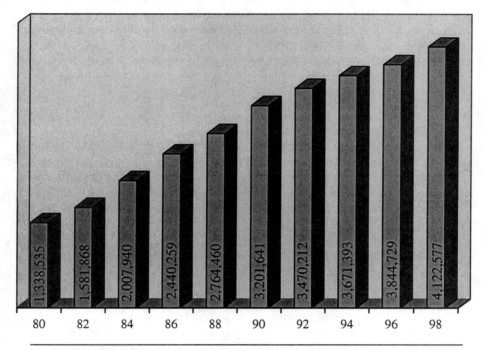

| 80 | 82 | 84 | 86 | 88 | 90 | 92 | 94 | 96 | 98 |

1,338,535 — 1,581,868 — 2,007,940 — 2,440,259 — 2,764,460 — 3,201,641 — 3,470,212 — 3,671,393 — 3,844,729 — 4,122,577

*All counts reflect the total at the end of the year; 1998 estimated.
Source: *Probation and Parole*. U.S. Department of Justice, Bureau of Justice Statistics, Washington, D.C.

time period, bringing the total to more than one percent of the United States population.

If jail and prison populations had declined during this period, a strong argument could be made that the greater number of probationers and parolees was indicative of a trend toward greater reliance on community alternatives to institutionalization. As indicated in the discussions above, this is clearly not the case.

Combining all numbers of people under correctional supervision (inmates in jails and prisons and those who have been placed under probation or parole supervision) completes the picture of the changes that have taken place in the criminal justice system in recent years. There were 1,840,400 individuals under the control of the correctional system in 1980 (Beck, 1999). Sixteen years later, this total had increased to an estimated 5,523,100. By 1997 this number had reached over 5.7 million.

The data reported indicate that the United States punishes a substantial number of its citizens, a proportion far greater than any other Western democracy. For young African-American males, the situation is even more bleak. Mauer (1999) noted that almost one in three (32.2%) black men in the age group 20–29 is either in prison, jail, on probation, or parole on any given day. In fact, the number of young black men in prison and jail is greater than the total number of black men of all ages enrolled in college. It would be quite difficult to make a case that this pattern is indicative of a criminal justice system that is soft on crime.

Persons Under Sentence of Death

Two decades ago, the United States Supreme Court ruled in *Furman v. Georgia* (1972) that the death penalty was unconstitutional because of the selective and arbitrary manner in which it was being applied. As a consequence, all the statutes authorizing capital punishment were stricken from the books. The United States seemed ready to join the other Western democracies that had halted the practice of executing citizens for crimes committed in peacetime.

The Supreme Court in its 1972 *Furman* decision did not, however, address the question of whether executions in themselves were cruel and unusual punishment. Instead, the court merely stated that the manner in which the death penalty had previously been administered violated the Constitution. The door was therefore left open for states to draft new statutes with respect to capital punishment. Within 4 years, approximately 38 states had done so. By the time the United States Supreme Court finally addressed the question of whether executions were constitutional (*Gregg v. Georgia,* 1976), the composition of the court had changed in a more conservative direction. In addition, public opinion had also shifted, with many more Americans voicing support for the death penalty. Thus, it was not very surprising when the Supreme Court ruled that capital punishment in and of itself does not violate the constitution.

Between 1968 and 1976, no one was executed in the United States. When the Supreme Court ruled in *Gregg v. Georgia* that the death penalty could be imposed as long as certain procedural standards were followed, executions resumed in 1977. At first, the pace was quite slow. The late 1970s saw only a handful of individuals put to death. As time passed, the numbers increased substantially. By the mid-1980s, executions had become relatively routine events that generated little public attention and little media publicity in most cases. Between 1977 and 1999, 576 prisoners were executed in the United States (Associated Press, 1999). In 1999, there were, on average, eight executions per month.

The number of persons actually executed is only part of this picture. Following the *Gregg* decision, the number of convicts under sentence of death also increased rather substantially. Table 13.5 indicates that there were only 134 persons on death row in 1973, the year after the United States Supreme Court gave its constitutional approval to the continued use of the death penalty. Ten years later, there were nine times as many persons under sentence of death (1,209). By 1999, the total had grown to 3,565 (Associated Press, 1999). Defendants were being sentenced to death at a pace that outstripped the ability of the courts to dispose of appeals. The number of individuals on death row was 25 times greater in 1999 than had been the case in 1973.

Table 13.5
Persons under Sentence of Death

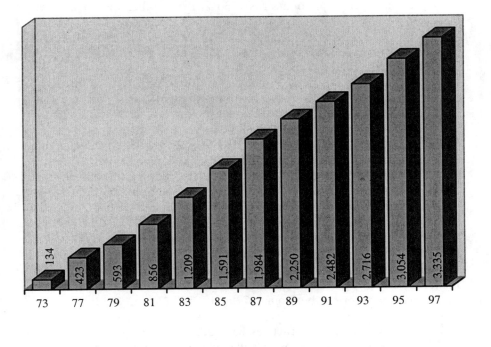

Source: *Capital Punishment*. U.S. Department of Justice, Bureau of Justice Statistics, Washington, D.C.

◊

THE CRIME RATE IN THE UNITED STATES

What factors account for the more punitive criminal justice practices that have evolved in recent years? It has already been noted that population changes do not explain the increased number of individuals under correctional supervision. Another possibility is that these changes in the jail, prison, probation, and parole populations merely reflect changes in the crime rate that have occurred during this period. If there were a dramatic rise in crime, we would expect more offenders to be incarcerated and/or released into the community under the supervision of the courts.

Despite the fact that the crime rate has declined, the number of adults arrested rose somewhat (34%—from 6.1 to 8.2 million). However, this increase was dwarfed by the dramatic rise in various correctional populations during the 1980s. Between 1980 and 1990, the number of jail inmates rose 146%, the number of prisoners rose 134%, the number of probationers increased by 139%, and the number of parolees increased 141% (Irwin & Austin, 1997). Clearly, these data suggest that the huge rise in the number of persons under correctional supervision in the United States has not been in response to an increased crime rate.

If increased crime rates do not explain the dramatic rises in various correctional populations that have occurred in recent years, what factors do account for this trend? There are several explanations. The "war on drugs" has contributed to a substantial part of the increase. A greater proportion of drug violators are being incarcerated than in previous years, and sentence lengths for this crime have increased. In the federal prison system, the number of persons serving time for drug offenses has more than doubled since 1981 and now accounts for 71% of the inmate population. On the state and local level, the impact of the war on drugs is also evident. Nearly 36% of the rise in the state prison population between 1985 and 1994 was the result of an increase in the number of inmates convicted for drug offenses (Mauer, 1997). In addition, the increased emphasis on drug testing has contributed to a higher failure rate among parolees. The United States Department of Justice reports that there was "a 284% increase in the number of parole violators returned to prison between 1977 and 1987" (Austin & McVey, 1989, p. 5).

Secondly, sentencing practices have become more punitive as many states and the federal government have enacted mandatory sentence statutes that apply to various offenses. These laws *require* judges to sentence offenders to a period of incarceration, often for a specified period of time. There is no possibility of the defendant receiving probation or a suspended prison sentence. Forty-six states now have mandatory sentence statutes (BJS, 1988). An analysis by the United States Sentencing Commission concluded that mandatory sentences have been a contributing factor in the dramatic rise of the federal prison population (Mauer, 1992).

In addition, the federal government and at least a dozen states have enacted so-called "three strikes and you're out" statutes which mandate life imprisonment without parole for certain offenders upon the conviction of a third felony (Mauer, 1994). These laws are likely to exacerbate the trend toward increased incarceration. In California, the Department of Corrections projects that over the next 5 years, this provision will cause the prison population to grow by almost 70% and force the state to spend an additional $4.5 billion on new prison construction (Claiborne, 1995). The impact is likely to be similar in other states that pass these types of overreaching statutes.

Finally, a conservative ideology has developed that asserts society can solve its crime problem by taking a hard-line approach (Marenin, 1991). One result of this philosophical shift has been a narrowing of defendants' rights. Although the impact of such changes in criminal procedure is mostly symbolic (Gordon, 1990), this attitude has encouraged politicians to offer the public other simplistic "get tough" measures for dealing with offenders instead of rational policies that seek to alleviate the root causes of crime and violence. Former Attorney General of the United States, Richard Thornburgh, opened a "crime summit" several years ago by telling law enforcement officials to leave consideration of the causes of crime to ivory-tower types (Fyfe, 1991).

Increasingly, candidates for political office appear unwilling to propose solutions that could make a difference. Instead, policymakers call for more prisons, longer sentences, and the death penalty for more offenses. Proposals to spend money on prevention programs are derided by opponents. If the get-tough approach had significantly reduced the level of crime and violence in America, a strong case could be made that it was worth the human and financial costs. However, these policies have had little impact on the crime problem.

This approach to crime control is ineffective—and very expensive. State and local government spending on correctional institutions totaled over fifteen billion dollars in 1988 (Maguire & Flanagan, 1991). Spending by state governments for corrections in the 1980s was increasing at a substantial pace while expenditures for other needs, such as education and hospitals, lagged behind (Austin, 1990). The money spent on jails and prisons produces little in the way of tangible results, and it diverts funds from programs that could have a positive impact on the lives of citizens. Elliott Currie (1985) cautioned that the get-tough approach to crime should be viewed as a conservative social experiment that failed:

> It is difficult to think of any social experiment in recent years whose central ideas have been so thoroughly and consistently carried out. The number of people we have put behind bars, for ever-longer terms, is unprecedented in American history. And unlike most such experiments which are usually undertaken with minimal funding and on a limited

scale, this one has been both massively financed and carried out on a grand scale in nearly every state of the union. If it has failed to work in the way its promoters expected, they have fewer excuses than most applied social theorists. (p. 12)

CONCLUSION

Despite the data, the myth persists that we are lenient with offenders. Public opinion surveys indicate that the proportion of Americans who believe the courts do not deal harshly enough with criminals is identical to the number who expressed this sentiment in 1980 (Maguire & Flanagan, 1991). How can one account for this disparity between the attitudes of citizens and the reality of our justice system?

To some extent, this public perception is shaped by the fact that some offenders are treated more leniently than is appropriate. Because citizens receive much of their information regarding the operation of the criminal justice system from accounts that are presented in the media, anecdotes that discuss how a serious offender escaped punishment probably play an important role in shaping perceptions about the system. Unfortunately, citizens often do not appreciate the fact that such accounts receive so much press attention precisely because they are atypical. Thus, events that are relatively rare (for example, a murder suspect who escapes punishment as a result of a legal technicality) are viewed as everyday occurrences. The reality of the situation is that most serious offenders are not treated leniently by the courts.

Another factor that may account for the false perception that the system is lenient is the perceived level of crime and violence in our society. Citizens, especially those residing in urban areas, hear and read reports in the media of murders, robberies, and rapes that seem to occur on a continuing basis. Despite the increased probability during the 1980s that a convicted offender would go to prison (Cohen, 1991), there are still a large number of crimes that do not result in an arrest. For this reason, citizens see society as inundated with crime and assume that the criminal justice system must not be doing its job. Often, the complaint is that "the courts must be soft, why else would there be so much crime?" Unfortunately, what most citizens fail to appreciate is that this is a problem which the criminal justice system cannot solve by itself and that harsh sentences do not necessarily deter crime. Without basic social reforms, there is little that the police, the courts, and the corrections system can do. Proponents of the "get tough" approach should try to explain why other democracies can achieve a far lower rate of violent crimes without incarcerating so many of their citizens.

The most harmful consequence for society of the leniency myth is that it continues to divert public attention and resources away from policies that could really make a difference in the fight against crime. As Marenin (1991) has noted, "conservatism politicized and ideologized a difficult social problem and made it harder to seek solutions which might work but which cannot be reduced to a thirty-second commercial" (p. 17). As a consequence, decision makers have been forced to pursue policies that focus on increasing the severity of criminal penalties and locking up more offenders. Programs that could have a real impact on crime (such as expanding job training, increasing access to drug treatment, or providing more economic opportunities for members of the underclass) are dismissed as too "soft." However, these measures are likely to be far more effective and less costly in the long run than a continuation of the present "get tough" approach.

Debunking the
Death Penalty
Myths of Crime Control and
Capital Punishment

Capital punishment is an issue that has generated intense public interest over the centuries. Criminologists have written volumes on this subject; appellate courts have devoted considerable time to deciding death penalty cases; and politicians have used it as an effective campaign issue. Capital punishment has even played a role in presidential elections. For example, it is widely believed that the response of Michael Dukakis during the second presidential debate to a question posed regarding the death penalty contributed to his landslide defeat by George Bush in the 1988 election. The Democratic nominee had been asked by a journalist if he would favor this sanction if his wife were raped and murdered. He replied that he would not.

As the Democrats learned to their chagrin, the question of capital punishment has deep symbolic meaning. Increasingly, crime and many other policy questions are discussed in a simplistic manner that focuses more on symbols than on solutions to complex social problems. Politicians have found that it is easier to reaffirm their support for the death penalty during a political campaign by using a thirty-second sound bite than to offer a meaningful program that seriously addresses the crime problem in America. As a consequence, support for capital punishment has become a litmus test of how tough one is on crime. At the same time, policymakers and citizens place an importance on this sanction that is disproportionate to its actual role in the criminal justice system.

Although the question of capital punishment is often debated more passionately than any other public policy question in the area of corrections, there is good reason to believe that the public is not well informed on this subject. Various opinion polls suggest that sizeable segments of the public believe that the death penalty acts as a deterrent to murder or that it is necessary to protect society. Citizens also sometimes question whether society should be forced to bear the cost of incarcerating convicted murderers for life, implying that it would be less expensive to execute these individuals. In addition, it is routinely asserted that any vigorous attack on our tremendous crime problem must include capital punishment if it is to be successful. Yet all these beliefs are based on myth. There is little empirical support in the research literature on capital punishment for any of these positions.

This chapter debunks a number of common myths regarding the death penalty. These include: (1) the myth that the death penalty is a more effective deterrent to murder than life imprisonment; (2) the myth that the death penalty is less expensive to impose than life imprisonment; (3) the myth that the death penalty is necessary to protect society from convicted killers who are likely to repeat their offense; and (4) the myth that capital punishment is necessary in order to fight crime.

◈

THE MYTH OF GENERAL DETERRENCE

In a Harris poll taken in 1997, 75% of Americans supported the death penalty, and an equal percentage supported it as a deterrent to murder (BJS, 1998b). This belief is probably due to the strong confidence that most Americans place in the ability of punishment to alter behavior. It is often reasoned that if parents are able to modify their children's actions with very mild sanctions, then the threat of execution (a very serious penalty) should deter people from committing murder (a very serious crime). However, a review of the literature indicates that this confidence in the efficacy of capital punishment is misplaced. The overwhelming majority of studies report finding no deterrent effect.

Probably no other question has received as much attention as the issue of whether the death penalty is a more effective deterrent to murder than a lengthy prison sentence. From a scientific perspective, the ideal way to address this question would be to use a lottery drawing to assign persons at birth to either life imprisonment or the death sentence should they eventually be convicted of capital murder (Zeisel, 1977). It would then be possible to ascertain whether persons who were at risk of receiving the death penalty were less likely to commit those types of murder that could land one on death row. For moral and legal reasons that require little explanation, this kind of experiment is unthinkable in a democratic society. As a consequence, scholars have been forced to rely on research designs that utilize "naturally grown" data in an attempt to approximate this impossible experiment.

Exploring the question of whether the death penalty is a better deterrent, researchers have employed a variety of strategies. This chapter examines nine approaches that have been utilized to address this issue: (1) an examination of homicide statistics in other Western democracies; (2) a comparative analysis of homicide rates in contiguous states where one jurisdiction exercises capital punishment and another does not; (3) an examination of the change in the homicide rate after the death penalty has been abolished or reinstated in a particular state; (4) the impact of an execution on the homicide rate in a specific jurisdiction where the sentence was recently carried out; (5) a comparative examination of the rate at which police officers are murdered in states that do and do not have capital punishment; (6) an examination of whether prison inmates are more likely to kill in states that have abolished capital punishment; (7) an analysis of the same question regarding the behavior of murderers who are eventually released on parole; (8) the impact of the death penalty on the level of noncapital felonies that are committed; and (9) various statistical models that have attempted to determine whether the death penalty is a more effective deterrent to murder than imprisonment.

Other Western Democracies

Very little research on the question of deterrence has compared homicides rates across various societies. One of the few international comparative studies was conducted by The United Kingdom Royal Commission on Capital Punishment (1953). Researchers reviewed the statistics on jurisdictions that had abolished or stopped using the death penalty for murder. Its review of data from seven European countries, New Zealand, and states within Australia and the United States found that "there is no clear evidence in any of the figures we have examined that the abolition of capital punishment has led to an increase in the homicide rate, or that its reintroduction has led to a fall" (p. 23). Yet the United States is the only Western democracy that retains capital punishment. At the same time, the United States has the highest homicide rate in the industrialized world. Although our high homicide rate results from many factors that have nothing to do with the death penalty, the relationship between these variables certainly does not support the notion of general deterrence. If this punishment was indeed a deterrent, why would the only Western nation that still employs it also have the highest rate of homicide?

Contiguous States

Some of the earliest work on the question of deterrence involved a comparative examination of the homicide rates in contiguous states where one jurisdiction had abolished capital punishment and the other(s) retained this penalty. The rationale underlying the use of contiguous states is that they are likely to be similar in other ways that could affect their homicide rate. If these jurisdictions share various economic, demographic, and social characteristics, any difference observed with respect to their murder rate should be attributable to the fact that they differ in the imposition of the death penalty. The classic studies utilizing this approach were conducted by Thorsten Sellin (1980). He compared Kansas (an abolitionist state) with Missouri and Colorado (retentionist states) and Maine (an abolitionist state) with the retentionist states of Massachusetts and New Hampshire. Sellin observed that the homicide rates in the abolitionist states were not higher (in some cases they were actually lower) than those reported in the retentionist states. Based on a number of comparisons of this type, Sellin (1980) was able to conclude that there is no evidence of a greater deterrent effect when a jurisdiction retains the death penalty.

On a national level, comparisons of states with the death penalty and those without it find a majority of death penalty states have murder rates significantly higher that those found in states without the death penalty. For example, in 1996 the national average murder rate in death penalty states was 7.1 per 100,000 citizens whereas the rate in states without the death penalty was only 3.6. Overall, states without the death penalty have a murder rate about one half that of states with the death penalty. While one can argue that states with higher murder rates were more inclined to adopt or retain the death penalty, one cannot realistically argue that the death penalty has a deterrent effect on murder rates.

Abolition/Retention of the Death Penalty

Another approach that was used by Sellin (1980) to study this issue was to examine jurisdictions that have either abolished or reinstated the death penalty. During the nineteenth and twentieth centuries, a number of states changed their statutes regarding this sanction. The early studies only looked at the before and after homicide rate in jurisdictions that had revised their death penalty statute. However, later studies also examined the trend in contiguous states that had not made a change (Zeisel, 1977). This research found no evidence of an increased deterrent effect in jurisdictions that retained or reintroduced the death penalty. In general, the homicide rate closely followed the trend in contiguous states (Sellin, 1980). Whether capital punishment was abolished or reinstated did not seem to matter.

When international comparisons are made, homicide rates have been found to be greater in countries that use the death penalty than those which do not.

> In an analysis of selected countries, the five abolitionist countries with the highest homicide rate averaged a rate of 11.6 per 100,000 persons. The five retentionist countries with the highest homicide rate averaged a rate of 41.6 per 100,000 persons. In other words, countries that have capital punishment appear to have higher murder rates than those countries that do not have capital punishment. (Godfrey & Schiraldi, 1995, p. 4)

Impact of an Execution

The fourth approach employed is to examine the impact of an execution on the murder rate in the specific jurisdiction where the sentence was recently carried out. The first such study was conducted by Robert Dann (1935) during a period when executions were quite common in the United States. He examined the impact of five executions in Philadelphia, which had not been followed by another execution for a sixty-day period. The rationale underlying this approach was that if capital punishment indeed deterred murder, all the publicity that surrounded an execution should cause the homicide rate to decline in the days and weeks subsequent to the execution. However, Dann observed that the murder rate actually increased somewhat in the sixty-day period that followed this punishment.

In California, a similar study was conducted by William Graves (1956). He examined the homicide records of Los Angeles, San Francisco, and Alameda counties in order to determine whether there were fewer murders in the days following an execution than was the case in the days leading up to this event. As a comparative measure, he examined the same days of the week for those periods in which an execution did not occur. Graves reported that compared with weeks when no death sentences were carried out, the number of murders actually increased the day prior to an execution and on the day of the execution. However, they declined in the two-day period that followed the execution. The result was that the slight deterrent effect was almost entirely cancelled out by the earlier brutalization effect. This finding led Graves to speculate that persons contemplating homicide may be "stimulated by the state's taking of life to act sooner" (p. 137). What Graves did not note because of the manner in which his data had been classified was "that homicides were higher in the weeks after than in the weeks before executions" (Bowers et al., 1984, p. 284).

A similar pattern is revealed when comparing the murder rates in California during its abolitionist and retentionist years.

> During the retentionist period from 1952 to 1967, when executions occurred on average about every two months, homicide rates increased from 2.4 per 100,000 in 1952 to 6.0 per 100,000 in 1967. Within this fifteen-year period, the homicide rate increased by 150%—an annual increase of 10%. Conversely, between the abolitionist period of 1967 and 1991, when no executions took place, the homicide rate increased from 6.0 per 100,000 to 12.6 per 100,000. Over this twenty-four year span, the homicide rate increased by 110% or 4.8% annually. (Godfrey & Schiraldi, 1995, p. 6)

The researchers concluded that "the average annual increase in homicides was twice as high during years in which the death penalty was being carried out than in years during which no one was executed."

Steven Stack (1987) conducted an analysis of publicized executions that took place in the United States between 1950 and 1980. He reported a small deterrent impact for executions that received national publicity. However, the number of executions in this category is quite small. No deterrent impact was observed for the overwhelming number of cases that did not generate national publicity. The author noted that "as executions become more common, the amount of press coverage tends to decline" (p. 538). As a consequence, the death penalty soon loses even the marginal deterrent impact that was observed in this study.

There are a number of research reports that suggest the death penalty may actually have a brutalizing impact on individuals (Bowers, 1988). In other words, the state does not deter homicide but in fact does the opposite when it executes a criminal. It sets a bad example, and thereby its citizens also commit murder. If this turns out to be correct, the use of capital punishment may actually be counterproductive to the goals that many supporters believe it can accomplish.

Over the last ten years research into the brutalization effect of executions has become more sophisticated and reliable. Two recent studies in Oklahoma and Arizona have found some support for the brutalization hypothesis. A study published in 1994 by Cochran, Chamlin and Seth examined the effect of a well-publicized execution in Oklahoma. The execution of Charles Troy Coleman was the state's first in 25 years. The researchers examined time series data from the UCR on the number and types of homicides committed in the state a year prior to and after the execution. Their analysis found that while the execution had no deterrent effect for homicides in general there was a brutalization effect on stranger homicide levels.

Three years later, Thomson (1997) published a study of the brutalization effect in the state of Arizona using the same before-and-after research design as the study conducted by Cochran and colleagues. He examined the effect of the 1992 execution of Donald Eugene Harding. As was the case in the Oklahoma study, Thomson found no support for the deterrence theory, but found support for several hypotheses associated with brutalization theory. The researcher reasoned that if brutalization were supported, there would be increases in "spur-of-the-moment homicides," "strangers and/or argument homicides," and "gun-related homicides." The results of his analysis found large increases in each of these types of homicides. As we learn more about capital punishment and as our research becomes more refined and reliable, there is growing evidence of the brutalization effect of capital punishment.

Killings of Police Officers

Under our legal system, not all homicides are eligible for the death penalty. In order to be convicted of first degree murder, one must act with premeditation or take a life during the commission of a felony. Killers of police officers are generally candidates for this sanction in jurisdictions that retain capital punishment. Unlike many homicides that are committed "in the heat of passion," killings of police officers usually meet the necessary legal criteria to qualify as capital offenses. In addition, the apprehension rate is very high. Persons who murder police officers can expect to be both arrested and convicted. Therefore, if the death penalty is a more effective deterrent than incarceration, criminals should be less likely to kill police officers in those states that have retained this penalty.

There have been several studies that have addressed this question (Bailey, 1982; Bailey & Peterson, 1987; Cardarelli, 1968; Sellin, 1980). Despite the fact that these were conducted by different researchers, who utilized different methodologies and examined various time periods, the results have been remarkably similar. The homicide rate among law enforcement officers is no higher in states that have abandoned capital punishment. More recently Bailey and Peterson (1994) examined police homicides and concluded, "we find no consistent evidence that capital punishment influenced police killings during the 1976–1989 period. . . . [P]olice do not appear to have been afforded an added measure of protection against homicide by capital punishment" (p. 71).

The severity of sanctions seemingly have little influence on the rate of assaults on police officers (Hunter & Wood, 1994). The job of a police officer is not more hazardous when the death penalty is abolished. In fact, some research indicates that the existence of the death penalty may create a heightened danger for police officers.

> Because the death penalty can actually be an attraction to some murderers, the crime of murder is geared toward legal qualifications. Thus, if the death penalty is limited to the death of police officers or Federal marshals, they will become targets. Similarly, if the death penalty is designed to protect prison guards or carjacking victims, these individuals will be vulnerable. (Van Wormer, 1995)

Homicides Committed by Prisoners

Another approach employed to assess the deterrent impact of the death penalty is to compare the homicidal behavior of prisoners incarcerated in retentionist and abolitionist jurisdictions. In a study undertaken by Sellin (1980), it was reported that over 90% of these killings occurred in states that retained capital punishment. Furthermore, Wolfson (1982) has concluded that "the percentage of imprisoned murderers who recidivate is approximately the same in retentionist and abolitionist jurisdictions" (p. 167). She criticizes as seriously flawed an assumption of the deterrence argument that these individuals can be deterred by the same legal threat that was ineffective in preventing them from killing before they arrived in prison.

Homicides Committed by Parolees

In the United States, a substantial proportion of inmates serving a life sentence are eventually released on parole. Because even in retentionist jurisdictions, the overwhelming majority of persons convicted of homicide receive a prison sentence, many persons convicted of murder will eventually be released from custody. Researchers have asked whether these parolees are less likely to kill again in jurisdictions that retain the death penalty. Although the data to address this issue are scarce, the tentative conclusion is encouraging. Hugh Adam Bedau (1982) observed that murderers rarely kill again: "Both with regard to the commission of felonies generally and the crime of homicide, no other class of offenders has such a low rate of recidivism" (p. 180). In addition, the post-release conduct of murderers in abolitionist states was actually somewhat better than the conduct of those released in jurisdictions that still retained capital punishment. We will return to this issue later in the chapter.

Deterrence of Noncapital Felonies

Almost all research has focused on the impact that the death penalty has on the murder rate. The only exception is a study conducted by William Bailey (1991) who attempted to ascertain whether executions deter persons from committing noncapital felonies. Drawing upon arguments offered by Johannes Andenaes (1974), Marlene Lehtinen (1977), Ernest van den Haag (1978), and Walter Berns (1979), Bailey examined three conceivable ways that the death sentence acts as a deterrent for other types of offenses. The first is that as a form of punishment, the death penalty educates people regarding the importance of obeying the law. The second is that the death penalty deters those crimes where a killing is not intended but could result nonetheless. Armed robbery is an example of this type of offense, because there is always the possibility that the victim will resist and thus be killed (whether intentionally or inadvertently). Finally, the third hypothesis is that the death penalty conserves scarce criminal justice resources that could be used to investigate and prosecute other types of crime if capital punishment had the effect of actually lowering the homicide rate.

Bailey's analysis found no support for the deterrence argument. Despite the fact that this study measured the death penalty in a number of ways (e.g., the number of executions during the year, the ratio of the number of executions to the number of homicides reported during the same year, etc.), there was no observed relationship between the use of capital punishment and the index felony rate. The author noted that

> this pattern holds for the traditional targeted offense of murder, the person crimes of negligent manslaughter, rape, assault, and robbery, as well as the property crimes of burglary, grand larceny, and vehicle theft. In other words, there is no evidence . . . that residents of death penalty jurisdictions are afforded an added measure of protection against serious crimes by executions. (Bailey, 1991, p. 35)

Multiple Regression Analysis

All the previous methodologies refute the myth that the death penalty is a more effective deterrent than incarceration for the crime of murder. Therefore, it was quite a shock when Isaac Ehrlich (1975) reported that his statistical model indicated that each execution saved the lives of seven to eight innocent victims. He had used a complex statistical technique known as multiple regression analysis to examine the impact of various factors on the homicide rate in the United States between 1933 and 1969. Multiple regression is a procedure that allows researchers to examine many variables simultaneously in order to determine the independent impact that each has on the murder rate. Theoretically at least, it should be possible to separate the impact on the homicide rate of the death penalty from other factors that also may contribute to homicide (such as the unemployment rate, the age distribution of the population, the proportion of citizens who own handguns, etc.). In practice, however, multiple regression models may give conflicting results depending on what variables are included in the analysis, how they are measured, and what period of observation is employed (Shin, 1978).

Ehrlich's study received widespread notice both in the popular media and among policymakers. Not surprisingly, it was the only study on deterrence cited by the Solicitor General (Robert Bork) in a brief before the United States Supreme Court that purported to show that executions deter homicide (Ellsworth, 1988). The work of Ehrlich also stimulated a great deal of research by other scholars who employed the same methodology. There were many attempts to replicate his findings; these were unsuccessful. Subsequent analysis revealed a number of critical flaws in the design of the Ehrlich study. In this chapter we include a brief overview of these methodological shortcomings.

Peter Passell and John Taylor (1976) reported that when the 1960s were omitted from Ehrlich's data, the deterrent effect disappeared. The 1960s were a period when executions were becoming relatively uncommon in the United States. Therefore, one is left to ponder the implausible conclusion that executions were not a deterrent when they were relatively routine but that they served as a deterrent during the entire time span studied by Ehrlich.

Another major criticism is that Ehrlich conducted a national analysis that did not distinguish between jurisdictions that did and did not execute citizens (Zeisel, 1977). Most importantly, the overwhelming majority of scholars who have utilized this methodology (and even the same data) have not reached the same conclusion (Passell & Taylor, 1976).

None of the studies that examine the deterrence question can reach the level of design that would be provided by our impossible experiment discussed earlier. Much of the research in this area contains shortcomings that have been noted by various authors (Wilson, 1983). First, the use of contiguous states may mask important differences between jurisdictions that can impact their homicide rate. Second, researchers may classify a state as retentionist because the death penalty remains on the books, even though no executions have been carried out in many years. Third, many studies utilize the total homicide rate to measure deterrence. However, not all homicides are capital crimes. A more appropriate measure would include only homicides that qualify for the death penalty. Unfortunately, these data generally do not exist. Despite these shortcomings, what is striking is that studies utilizing a wide array of different methodologies have almost always come to the same conclusion: the belief that capital punishment is a more effective deterrent to murder than imprisonment is a myth.

Why is the death penalty not a more effective deterrent? First, the majority of homicides occur between people who are acquainted with each other. Most of these killings do not involve any kind of rational calculation. Instead, the offender commits the crime in a moment of rage or passion without giving any thought whatsoever to the future consequences of this behavior. Second, in those cases that do involve premeditation, the offender generally does not expect to be apprehended. Regardless of the potential sanction, it cannot serve as a deterrent if the perpetrator does not believe that it will be applied. Finally, the death penalty does not deter more effectively than life imprisonment because these are both very harsh sentences. Douglas Heckathorn (1985) notes that no difference can be expected with respect to the general deterrent impact of two sanctions if both are perceived as severe, even if one is somewhat harsher than the other. In other words, an upper threshold is reached with respect to severity beyond which no additional deterrence occurs.

◇

THE COST OF THE DEATH PENALTY

It is commonly believed that it is cheaper to execute a criminal than to keep him/her in prison for life. In fact, the authors have often been asked by students, "why should society pay to keep convicted killers housed, clothed and fed for the rest of their lives?" However, the death penalty does not reduce the financial burden on the corrections system. However, this is not the case.

Intuitively, one would think that executions should be cheaper than supporting an offender in the penitentiary for many years. Indeed, a system of justice that executed suspected murderers on the spot would be less expensive than maintaining those individuals in prison for life. However, this is not the way that capital punishment is carried out in a democratic society. Because our justice system places a very high premium on protecting the lives of innocent persons, an extensive number of procedural burdens must be met before a defendant can be executed. These protections are extremely costly, but they are necessary to insure that only guilty persons receive the death penalty. Although these safeguards are not infallible in accomplishing this goal, their presence insures that any system of capital punishment devised by our society will be much more expensive than life imprisonment.

There are several factors that contribute to the high cost of capital punishment. First, capital cases almost always go to trial. As we learned in chapter 11, the overwhelming majority of other felony cases are resolved through plea bargaining. This option is virtually never applied in capital cases. Because the prosecutor is asking for the death penalty, the state has nothing to offer that can induce the defendant to enter a guilty plea. Very few defendants are likely to consent to a death sentence. In a few unique cases, defendants have requested that a death sentence be carried out. These requests, however, are seldom made before adjudication. Therefore, a criminal trial becomes inevitable.

Obviously, trials take considerably more time and are more expensive than simply accepting a guilty plea from the defendant at arraignment. However, capital trials are even more time consuming and involve far greater expense than do noncapital cases. The Supreme Court has stated on several occasions that death as a punishment is qualitatively different and that defendants in such cases are entitled to a higher standard of due process. This makes every aspect of a capital trial more complex and more time consuming for the parties involved. "Many issues may arise in a single case. In one multi-defendant case, for example, a judge estimated that 2,800 legal pleadings had been filed by the parties" (JCUS, 1998, p. 4).

Most cases in which the federal death penalty was sought arise under the "drug kingpin" provision of the 1988 Anti-Drug Abuse Act. These

> cases typically involve investigations stretching over years, and encompassing numerous acts of violence. They often include several homicide charges, many witnesses, and evidence in the guilt phase derived from wiretaps, video surveillance, informants, and experts. The magnitude of some of these cases is illustrated by a judge's estimate that the prosecution listed 500 potential witnesses in one case, and another judge's estimate that the prosecution disclosed 30,000 pages of documents in discovery. (JCUS, 1998, p. 8)

When the state seeks to impose the death penalty, the costs begin to accumulate even before the case is heard by the court. In a noncapital trial, prosecutors and defense attorneys routinely scrutinize prospective jurors in an attempt to gain maximum advantage at trial. However, in capital cases, the voir dire process becomes considerably more time consuming and requires that a greater number of prospective jurors be interviewed. To some extent, this results from the fact that the United States Supreme Court allows prosecutors in capital cases to exclude opponents of capital punishment from serving as jurors if they are unable to vote for a death sentence (*Wainwright v. Witt,* 1985). As a consequence, each prospective juror must be questioned at length regarding their views on capital punishment.

There are other reasons why the voir dire process takes longer in a capital case. Each side may be allowed a greater number of peremptory challenges than in a noncapital trial. More importantly, because there is a high degree of public interest in a capital case, a great amount of pretrial publicity may have been generated. Therefore, the defense attorney may be required to spend a substantial period of time questioning prospective jurors to insure that they have not formed an opinion prejudicial to the defendant. The cumulative effect of all these factors is that the voir dire process takes 5.3 times longer than in noncapital trials (Spangenberg & Walsh, 1989).

The extensive voir dire is not the only additional cost in a capital trial. Defendants are likely to raise a greater number of pretrial motions in these cases, and these motions tend to be more lengthy and more complex, involving issues unique to cases where the death sentence is a potential outcome (Spangenberg & Walsh, 1989). In addition, there is generally greater use of expert witnesses in capital cases. If the defendant raises the insanity defense (which is more likely in a capital case), psychiatric testimony will be presented by experts on behalf of both the defense and the prosecution. Because many defendants are indigent, the state will be obligated to pay the psychiatric witnesses for both sides, unlike noncapital cases. The cost of securing experts in capital cases can run 5 times higher than noncapital cases.

There is one final cost that must be considered when analyzing the trial stage of a capital case. In almost every jurisdiction in the United States, capital trials are bifurcated. This means that the issue of sentence (execution or imprisonment) is determined in a separate hearing that follows the verdict. In essence, there are two phases to the trial: conviction and punishment. Both of these allow for the introduction of evidence and the presentation of witnesses before the jury. As a consequence, both the prosecutor and the defense attorney may be forced to incur some of the same expenses twice. In the process, court time is consumed in a manner that would not occur in noncapital trials.

A recent report by the Judicial Conference of the United States (1998) examined the costs associated with the trial of capital cases that sought the death penalty. The conference concluded that the defense costs for a case where the death penalty is sought is about 4 times higher than in comparable cases where death was not sought. The cost to prosecute a death penalty case was estimated to be 67% higher than defense costs. Again, the state must pay for both expenses.

> The Attorney General has authorized seeking the death penalty in a total of 111 cases between 1988 and December 1997. The average total cost (for counsel and related services) of authorized cases in the Subcommittee's sample was $218,112, as compared to $55,772 for cases in which the death penalty was never authorized. (p. 3)

These costs are not limited to the federal government. Of the $90 million that California citizens pay each year to have the death penalty about $78 million of the cost is incurred by trials.

The trial is not the only added financial burden in a capital case. There is also an appeals process that is more drawn out than in other criminal cases.

Obviously, if the state is seeking the death penalty, the courts seek assurance that a grievous error has not been committed. For this reason, most states with capital punishment provide for an automatic review of death sentences by a state appellate court. Because appellate courts often give somewhat greater scrutiny to death penalty cases than to other appeals, prejudicial errors are more likely to be uncovered (Nakell, 1982). The result is that capital cases result not just in more trials but in more retrials as well.

The appeals process adds greatly to the cost of processing capital defendants. Both judges and prosecutors are forced to spend a considerable amount of time (both in court and out) dealing with issues that are raised by the defendant. This is a burden on defense attorneys as well. Robert Spangenberg and Elizabeth Walsh (1989) note that on average a capital appeal requires between 500 and 1,000 hours of defense attorney time. In some cases, the entire cost of the defense is paid by the state.

The final cost consideration is that capital defendants require special accommodations within the correctional system. They are not treated like other inmates. Instead, they are placed in a maximum security setting in jail upon arrest. This is followed by a move to death row after their sentence is handed down. The level of security on death row is far more elaborate than in other sections of the prison. This entails substantially greater cost in terms of staff time than would be needed to house other inmates. In addition, the stay is not brief. For persons executed during 1997, the average time spent under a sentence of death was eleven years and one month (Snell, 1998).

When all these extra costs are considered, it is not surprising that a number of empirical studies have found that a criminal justice system that includes the death penalty is more expensive than one without this sanction. For example, it costs taxpayers in North Carolina an additional $2.2 million to execute a killer as opposed to a sentence of 20 years to life. The costs for a death penalty case in Texas, a state that is among the top executioners in the United States, averages $2.3 million, about three times the cost of imprisoning an inmate in a single cell in the highest security prison in the state for 40 years (*Dallas Morning News*, 1992). Estimating the national costs based on this figure finds that since 1996 we have incurred an additional $900 million seeking the death penalty instead of life imprisonment. As Franklin Zimring of the University of California explains, "It's always more expensive to have and use the death penalty than it is not to have it, for the simple reason that lawyers are more expensive than prison guards" (Chapman, 1995a, p. 25).

Similar findings have been reported for other states as well (Tabak & Lane, 1989). In Florida, each execution cost that jurisdiction over $3 million, or approximately six times the amount that would be spent to incarcerate these individuals for life. Florida spent an estimated $57 million on death penalty cases from 1973 to 1988. The enormous expense resulted in 18 executions at a average of about $3.2 million per execution. (*Miami Herald*, 1988). The cost of executing one person in New Jersey was estimated to be approximately $7.3 million. Jim Dwyer estimated that the projected costs of executing New York's first death row inmate, Darrel Harris, at $3 million. He commented, "After spending $3 million extra for a capital case, New York will have bought itself nothing that it could not have gotten with a sentence of life without parole" (NY *Daily News*, 1998). In California, it has been reported that the taxpayers could save $90 million per year by abolishing the death penalty (Tabak & Lane, 1989).

Having observed that capital punishment is more expensive than life imprisonment, the question arises: how much weight should financial considerations carry in the debate over the death penalty? Proponents of the death penalty would argue that if justice demands this sanction for certain offenders, cost should not be a factor in the decision-making process. However, this rationale overlooks the fact that only a finite amount of resources are available to the criminal justice system. Therefore, the proper context in which to consider cost is to compare the benefits of capital punishment versus other policy options. For example, is society better protected by executing a small number of persons, or could these dollars be utilized more effectively by permanently incarcerating three times as many offenders? Perhaps it would be wiser to allocate this money for more police officers. These are the kinds of public policy alternatives that could be addressed once it is understood that the death penalty is more expensive than life imprisonment.

◈

INCAPACITATION

Another myth surrounding the death penalty is the belief that this punishment is necessary to protect both society and prison inmates from persons who are likely to kill again. Indeed, correctional administrators often express concern that if convicted capital offenders are not put to death, they will cause mayhem in the institution and place the lives of other inmates in jeopardy. Whether this concern is warranted is a question that has received some attention in the research literature.

Clearly, persons who receive the death penalty cannot commit future murders. However, the question that must be addressed is whether capital punishment performs this incapacitative function more effectively than life imprisonment. In other words, what is the marginal benefit of the death penalty in terms of protecting society from persons who have already demonstrated that they have the capacity to take human life? This is a question that has been examined from a number of perspectives.

Persons serving time for murder may have the opportunity to kill again under one of two circumstances: they may commit another homicide while in prison or in the community if released on parole. The most massive study of recidivism by parolees who had been convicted of murder was undertaken by Sellin (1980). He reported on the post-release behavior of 6,835 male convicts serving sentences for willful homicide who were released on parole from state institutions between 1969 and 1973. This study concluded that in the three-year period following their release, 310 (4.5%) of these individuals were returned to prison for committing a new crime. However, only 21 (0.31% of the total group) returned because they had committed another willful homicide. In fact, these individuals were less likely to commit murder while on parole than persons who originally had been sentenced for armed robbery, forcible rape, or aggravated assault.

Unfortunately, the Sellin study is not an examination of the behavior of persons who had been sentenced for capital murder. Many of the individuals in his study had been convicted of second degree murder or voluntary manslaughter. Thus, it may not be possible to infer from this research how persons convicted of capital murder would behave if released from prison. However, an event occurred in 1972 that made such analysis possible. The United States Supreme Court ruled in *Furman v. Georgia* that the death penalty as it had been administered up to that time was cruel and unusual punishment in violation of the Eighth and Fourteenth Amendments to the Constitution. As a consequence, all persons who were awaiting execution in the United States had their sentences commuted to life imprisonment.

At the time of the *Furman* decision, there were over 600 inmates on death row. This ruling by the Court therefore provided an opportunity to conduct a natural experiment. Researchers have been able to follow up on the activities of these commuted inmates and observe how they behave when released into the general prison population. In addition, because many of these prisoners have eventually been placed on parole, it has been possible to examine their behavior upon release into the community.

To date, several researchers have tracked the behavior of inmates whose sentences were commuted as a result of the *Furman* decision. James Marquart and Jonathan Sorensen (1988) looked at 47 inmates in Texas who were taken off death row by this decision. They compared these convicts to a control group of 156 inmates who had been sentenced to life imprisonment for either murder or rape (the same offenses for which the *Furman* inmates had been sentenced to death). Comparisons were drawn between the behavior of these inmates both in prison and following release on parole.

The study reported that despite the fact that both groups spent an average of approximately one decade in prison, 75% of the *Furman*-commuted inmates and 70% of the comparison group did not commit a serious violation of institutional rules (Marquart & Sorensen, 1988). Most significantly, no inmate in either group was implicated in a prison homicide. The authors conclude that "the *Furman* inmates, as compared with the life sentence cohort, were not unusually disruptive or rebellious, nor did they pose a disproportionate threat to other inmates and staff, as had been previously predicted by clinicians and administrators" (p. 686).

These researchers also analyzed the parole behavior of inmates who had been released into the community. Overall, only 14% of the Furman-commuted inmates committed a new felony upon release. Although this is a somewhat higher figure than the percentage for the life sentence cohort (6%), the authors attribute this finding to the somewhat longer period that the former group had spent in the community (Marquart & Sorensen, 1988). There was little actual difference upon release between the behavior of convicts who had originally been sentenced to death and those who had been given life imprisonment. Furthermore, only one of the parolees who had spent time on death row committed another homicide after being released from the institution. Clearly, fears that these individuals would be a menace to society if released turned out to be unfounded.

Gennaro Vito, Pat Koester and Deborah Wilson (1991) also analyzed *Furman*-commuted inmates. Although their focus is similar to that of Marquart and Sorensen, the cohort they examined includes all persons still living in 1987 who were removed from death row in twenty-six states by the Furman decision in 1972 (N = 457). These authors report that 177 of these inmates were eventually paroled and that eight (4.5%) committed another violent crime after release. This included three parolees who committed a new murder. Consequently, the repeat homicide rate for this group was 1.6%. Based on these findings, the authors conclude "that societal protection from convicted capital murderers is not greatly enhanced by the death penalty" (p. 96).

Although various studies found a few convicted murderers who killed again, Sellin (1980) observed that murderers on parole are less likely to kill than convicts paroled after being convicted of other violent offenses. Marquart and Sorensen (1988) noted that persons who originally were placed on death row in Texas were no more dangerous either in prison or upon release into the community than inmates sentenced to life imprisonment. In fact, many of the convicts who had their sentence commuted by *Furman* became model prisoners. Therefore, it must be concluded that the death penalty offers little additional protection to society over that which can be achieved through life imprisonment. It is a myth to believe that the safety of citizens, inmates, or prison staff depends in any way on the imposition of capital punishment.

FIGHTING CRIME

Another myth regarding the death penalty is that it is an effective tool in the battle against crime. It is true that the United States is plagued with an inordinate amount of violent crime compared to other Western nations. However, whether or not we continue to execute offenders is irrelevant in society's attempt to control crime. Despite the rhetoric that is often generated by candidates for public office, much of the discussion regarding capital punishment that takes place in political campaigns is a diversion from the real issues that must be confronted if we are to reduce the level of crime in the United States.

The United States Supreme Court ruled in *Coker v. Georgia* (1977) that the death penalty may not be imposed for the crime of raping an adult woman. Although the court did not explicitly rule out the use of capital punishment for other offenses that do not include the death of the victim, the rationale of this decision would seem to preclude this possibility. The holding was that rape is a very serious crime, but it does not involve the taking of a human life. Consequently, to execute an offender for the rape of an adult woman would constitute cruel and unusual punishment in violation of the Eighth Amendment. This decision would seem to rule out the use of capital punishment for other serious crimes that did not cause death, such as armed robbery and air piracy. Given this decision, the death penalty cannot deter these crimes.

Even in the case of murder, the death penalty applies only to specific types of murder. In jurisdictions retaining capital punishment, it is authorized only in certain instances. The crime must meet the requisite legal criteria to be classified as capital murder, and the prosecutor must also demonstrate to the jury that certain aggravating circumstances were present. As a consequence, only a small proportion of persons charged with murder can be sentenced to death. Even fewer are actually sentenced and executed.

In order to understand how infrequently capital punishment is actually carried out, it is necessary to present a few facts. Between 1980 and 1989, there were 206,710 murders reported to the police (Maguire & Pastore, 1994). However, during the same period (1980–1989), only 117 executions were actually carried out (BJS, 1994a). This translates into approximately one execution for every 1,767 murders committed during this time frame. "A killer has only a slightly greater chance of dying in the electric chair than of being struck by lightning" (Chapman, 1995a, p. 25).

Although the death penalty was applied more frequently in the nineties, it remains a relatively rare event. Murder is only part of the crime problem in the United States. In most cases, citizens are not afraid to walk the streets of our cities because they fear being murdered. What makes citizens fearful for their safety are the 1.6 million or so other violent felonies that occur each year—muggings, rapes, and assaults. These are the offenses that occur with great frequency and that diminish the quality of life in many communities. The death penalty is totally irrelevant in these cases. Therefore, it must be concluded that the notion that the death penalty is a solution to the crime problem is a myth.

Perhaps the most unfortunate aspect of the debate regarding capital punishment is that it diverts attention away from legitimate solutions to the crime problem. It is far easier for a politician to flaunt his or her support for the death penalty (especially when opinion polls indicate that this is a popular position) than to offer meaningful proposals for reducing the level of street crime.

William Rentschler (1994) notes:

> The death penalty is so widely accepted largely because it provides a mea-
> sure of seeming certainty to a society greatly frustrated by its inability to
> solve its most vexatious problems. But it is a simplistic answer, akin to the
> primitive law of the jungle. It is evidence of a society unwilling and inca-
> pable of coming to grips rationally with hard challenges. Capital punish-
> ment makes a mockery of such noble legal canons as equal justice under
> law. . . . The death penalty is reserved exclusively for society's little peo-
> ple, its powerless, its rabble, its dregs. This alone makes capital punish-
> ment wrong in a just society. (p. 19)

He points to the Simpson case as an example of the fact that wealth, fame and
community standing prove a Russian proverb: "No one is hanged who has
money in his pocket." Another commentator rephrased the concept in the
vernacular of the streets: "If you've got the capital, you don't get the punishment" (Page, 1995, p. 15). As Robert Bohm (1989) has noted, "capital
punishment offers a simplistic and believable solution to a complex phenomenon of which the public is frightened and of which it is generally
uninformed" (p. 192). A more educated public can serve as a catalyst to raise
the level of discourse in this area.

◆

THE JUVENILE DEATH PENALTY

In the United States twenty-five states allow the execution of juveniles;
twenty-one states set the minimum age for execution at 16 and four states at
17. No other Western nation, no other industrial nation, no other democracy
in the world allows the execution of juveniles. In fact, since 1990, the United
States joins only Iran, Nigeria, Pakistan, Saudi Arabia, and Yemen as nations
that have executed children. With nine executions of juveniles since 1990, the
United States criminal justice system kills more children than the rest of the
world combined. In fact, the state of Texas, with five juvenile executions since
1990, kills more children than any other country in the world (Amnesty International, 1998).

One of the major reasons for this paucity of juvenile executions worldwide is that executing children, simply put, is a war crime. Almost all nations,
even those with a death penalty, conform to the seven major international
instruments which forbid juvenile executions. Those instruments are
(Amnesty International, 1998):

1. International Covenant on Civil and Political Rights
2. Convention of the Rights of the Child
3. American Convention on Human Rights
4. Geneva Convention relative to the Protection of Civilian Persons in
   Time of War 12 August 1949

5. Protocol Additional to the Geneva Conventions of 12 August 1949, and relating to the Protection of Victims of International Armed Conflicts
6. Protocol Additional to the Geneva Conventions of 12 August 1949, and relating to the Protection of Victims of Non-International Armed Conflicts
7. Safeguards Guaranteeing Protection of the Rights of Those Facing the Death Penalty

Violations of treaties and protocols designed to maintain international civility is one of a number of problems with executing children in the United States. Research has consistently shown that the application of capital punishment in the United States is entirely arbitrary. From state to state, and even from jurisdiction to jurisdiction within states, defendants who commit similar homicides are treated differently for no apparent reason. Sometimes the state seeks the death penalty, sometimes not. Sometimes juries sentence the offender to death, sometimes not. Researchers have compared the application of the death penalty to a lottery governed by no rational process at all (Berk et al., 1993; Gross & Mauro, 1989; Paternoster 1991).

The juvenile death penalty is even more arbitrary and capricious than the death penalty for adults. About 1.8% of all persons executed in the United States were children (under 18 years of age) at the time of the crime (Capital Punishment Research Project, 1998). In the post-*Furman* era (up to December 1, 1998) there have been twelve juvenile executions, or about 2% of all executions since 1973 (Streib, 1998, p. 3). Despite significant increases and declines in juvenile homicide rates in the 1980s and 1990s, the rate of juvenile death sentences has remained constant at about 2% of all executions, raising the question of whether its use is even related to incidence of homicide (BJS, 1999).

The juvenile death penalty is blatantly racist. Over two-thirds of the 288 children executed in the United States have been African American. In addition, all of the children executed in the United States for the crimes of rape or attempted rape (40 children in all) have been black. As of October 1, 1998 65% (33 blacks and 15 Latinos compared to 26 whites) of the children on death row in the United States are minority offenders (Streib, 1998). The race of the victim is another area of bias in juvenile death penalty cases. As of October 1, 1998, 68% (n = 64) of the cases in which a juvenile was sentenced to death in the United States in the post-*Furman* era involved a white victim. Additionally, questions of age and gender bias also arise in view of the fact that 83% of the victims in these cases were adults and half were women. Ninety-eight percent of the juveniles sentenced to death were male (Streib, 1998, p. 12). Only four cases involved females.

Juvenile death sentences are subject to an extraordinarily high rate of reversal by the courts. Of the 177 juvenile death sentences imposed since 1973, only 74 (42%) remain in force. Twelve have resulted in executions (7%) and ninety-one (51%) have been reversed on appeal (Streib, 1998). For the

103 juvenile death sentences that have been resolved (excluding the seventy-four still under litigation) *the reversal rate is 88%* (91 out of 103) (Streib, 1998). The clear implication of this sobering fact is that in cases where the state wishes to execute a child, serious problems of prosecutorial misconduct, defense attorney incompetence, and judicial error appear to dominate.

The juvenile death penalty contradicts virtually every other law concerning children in the United States. The law in most states assumes that juveniles are not of sufficient maturity and judgment to exercise a wide range of rights. In most states the age of majority is 18; 21 is the youngest age at which alcohol may be bought, possessed and consumed; children may not enter into contracts until the age of 18; children may not buy cigarettes until the age of 18; children must be 18 before agreeing to donate their organs; children must be 18 before they may execute a will; children must be 18 before entering into a marriage; and, of course, the 26th Amendment to the Constitution sets the voting age in the United States at 18. The contradictions inherent in the laws that assume juveniles do not have sufficient responsibility, maturity, or judgment to make these decisions while at the same time assuming that they are fully in control of their judgments when they engage in criminal behavior is a horrific and illogical contradiction in the law. This is particularly the case in homicides where much evidence indicates that (1) children have an undeveloped and unsophisticated concept of death; and (2) children are often impulsive and reckless in their actions.

But most importantly the horror of executing children cannot be fully understood until we look at the children who have been murdered by the state in the United States. Consistently, pervasively, and invariably the children we execute have four common characteristics: (1) they were mentally ill or mentally retarded at the time they committed their crime; (2) they were victims of horrifying sexual and physical abuse; (3) they were victimized by a society that has one of the highest child poverty and infant mortality rates in the world and which consigns many children to lives of hopelessness and grinding poverty; and, (4) they were represented by inexperienced, unskilled, and incompetent counsel. So the truth of juvenile executions in the United States is that we execute the ill and infirm without providing them with any advocacy.

To say that such a policy reeks of eugenics and "ethnic cleansing" is almost an understatement. Consider the following (Amnesty International, 1998):

> Curtis Harris was one of nine children brought up in a family with an alcoholic father who regularly beat him throughout his childhood. Curtis was one of the 21% of all U.S. children raised in poverty (44% of all black children, and 37.9% of all Latino children in the U.S. are raised in poverty) (U.S. Department of Commerce, Bureau of Census, 1994). At his trial, despite the fact that Curtis was an African American, the state excluded all black jurors. Curtis had an IQ of 77 and suffered

from organic brain damage as a result of the beatings inflicted by his father. The state of Texas executed him on July 1, 1993.

At age four, Joseph John Cannon was hit by a truck. He was left with a severe head injury, hyperactivity, and a speech impediment. These conditions were enormous impediments to success in school, and at the age of six he was expelled and received no further education or care from the state of Texas. He filled his days sniffing glue and solvent. At the age of ten he was diagnosed as suffering from severe organic brain damage. Joseph attempted suicide at the age of 15 and was subsequently diagnosed as being schizophrenic and borderline mentally retarded. From the age of seven to the time he committed his murder, he suffered repeated and severe sexual abuse from a series of male relatives. So horrifying was Joseph's childhood that when he finally escaped his family after being confined on death row he was able to learn to read and write. The state of Texas had not protected him from his family, had not provided him with medical care for his chronic brain injuries, and had not treated his mental illness. Texas did, however, execute him in 1998.

Robert Anthony Carter was one of six children in an impoverished black family who grew up in one of the poorest neighborhoods in Houston, Texas. His mother and stepfather routinely beat him throughout his childhood with electrical cords. He suffered a series of childhood head injuries, including being struck in the head by a brick at age five and being hit on the head so hard with a baseball bat at age ten that the bat broke. Robert received no medical attention for either of these injuries. Shortly before the murder for which he was ultimately convicted, Robert was shot in the head by his brother and suffered thereafter from regular fainting spells and seizures. Nonetheless it took a Texas jury, who heard no mitigating evidence, only ten minutes to sentence him to death.

Dwayne Allen Wright was raised in a poor family in an economically depressed neighborhood of Washington, D.C. When he was four his father was sent to prison. His mother suffered from mental illness and was unemployed throughout much of his childhood. When he was ten his half-brother, the only person Dwayne was close to, was murdered. Dwayne developed serious emotional difficulties, did poorly at school, and between the ages of 12 and 17 spend most of his time in juvenile detention facilities and hospitals. During this period he was treated for major depression with psychotic episodes, his verbal ability was evaluated as retarded, and doctors diagnosed him with organic brain damage. Upon release, at the age of 17, Dwayne committed a murder. The American Bar Association appealed for clemency, stating that his proposed execution "demeans our system of justice" and asserting that "a borderline mentally retarded child simply cannot be held to the same degree of culpability and accountability for the actions to which we would hold an adult." Nevertheless, the commonwealth of Virginia executed him in 1998.

What conclusions can we draw about the children selected for execution in the United States? The answers are the poor, the mentally retarded, the sexually and physically abused, those with chronic and congenital physical defects, those represented by incompetent counsel, and those refused treatment for their maladies by the state that will ultimately murder them. In essence, the children who have been abandoned as social trash receive the ultimate rebuke for offending society.

◈

CONCLUSION

This chapter has attempted to debunk a number of myths regarding the death penalty. The discussion began with a broad overview of the vast literature on the question of general deterrence. Despite a wide range of methodologies that have been employed to address this issue, there is no evidence that capital punishment is more effective as a deterrent to murder than incarceration. Next we discussed the costs that capital cases entail. Contrary to what many persons believe, a system of justice that includes the death sentence is actually more expensive than one without this sanction.

Other myths were examined as well. Proponents of capital punishment often assert that executions are necessary to protect citizens from convicted killers who are likely to repeat their crimes. However, evidence suggests rather clearly that capital offenders do not present an inordinate risk to other inmates, correctional staff, or to persons in the general community. Finally, we concluded that capital punishment is largely irrelevant as a means of fighting crime.

Having observed that the death penalty is not a more effective general deterrent to murder, that it is more costly than life imprisonment, that it is not necessary to protect society or to fight crime, the question remains: is there any rational basis for supporting retention of capital punishment? Clearly, this sanction can only be defended on grounds of retribution. In William Rentschler's (1994) words:

> Many want to rid society permanently of the slavering brutes they perceive as perpetrators of violence. A sizable majority of citizens would give the state virtual carte blanche to exterminate these beasts. But wait. The "slavering brute" image embraces only a fraction of those who murder, maim and commit hideous, heinous crimes. . . . homicides are committed in greater numbers by family members, including parents and children,

friends, neighbors and business associates, than by prowling, predatory strangers. (p. 19)

The death penalty is "a punishment of perfect exactness administered by a justice system filled with imperfect human beings who often have inexact knowledge. Imprisonment leaves us moral room to correct the inevitable errors and arbitrary applications; killing does not" (Zorn, 1995a, p. 1).

Proponents should consider a number of questions before embracing the mythical aspects of the death penalty. For example, why have all other Western nations abandoned this practice? Are innocent persons occasionally executed? Is the death penalty carried out in a racially discriminatory manner? Aspects of myths cling tenaciously in the public conscious, and politicians exploit public fear to gain favor. If public policy is based on myth, areas that offer possible alternatives are often rejected or ignored.

National Drug Control Strategy

1999

Merging Myths and Misconceptions of Crime and Justice

Myths are stories that resonate within a culture. They contain charismatic heroes with whom audiences can identify—and who demonstrate virtues for the benefit of society. Myths contain villains who embody behavior society wants to eliminate. Myths order a random world; they interpret chaos and resolve conflicts and contradictions. Eventually, public focus on a particular crime wanes allowing the mythical characteristics to settle into social reality. New social problems will then emerge or old myths will be dredged up to remind us of who the criminals are and how to go about solving crime problems.

RECYCLED FRAMEWORKS

After the initial fear and panic surrounding a crime myth subsides, the conceptual residue becomes a frame of reference for determining our future views of social problems. Crime myths become mental filters through which social issues are sifted. Although crime myths fade, their effect on our conception of crime and justice linger. Once a myth becomes entrenched in thought, it takes only an occasional incident to fan the smoldering embers of the latent myth into another flame of public attention.

This process of interpreting problems to fit our myth-based notions of

crime and justice is enhanced if mythmakers construct new problems or events
within the framework of previously constructed myths. Such characterizations
and historical frames of reference insure that mythical conceptions of crime
never truly die. One of the powers of crime myth is that past conceptions blend
with present events to create future conceptions of crime. In this sense, crime
myths lend historical and conceptual continuity to our perceptions of crime and
its control.

The picture of violent crime in the United States results from a composition of panics promoted by the mythmakers of society. Moreover, these panics
tend to fold into one another, supporting the idea that society is somehow
under siege by crime (Jenkins & Katkin, 1988). As crime myths fold into one
another, they begin a recycling process that can form a single, unified, and very
popular conception of the reality of crime. Conceptual bits and pieces of the
myths of stranger child abduction, serial murderers, stalkers, organized crime
and predatory street criminals may merge to form an enveloping mythology of
violent crime. Similarly, myths of the dangers of police work, the equity of the
judicial process and misconceptions of punitive justice may fuse to create a single ideology of the proper social response to crime. Once a unified conception
of crime and its control becomes a part of popular thought and governmental
policy, the empirical reality of crime will mirror and support our mythology.

Under our mythology of crime, the police role will be limited to vigorously tracking stereotyped criminals—unfettered by constitutional restraint.
Social service aspects of policing will be reduced to rhetoric that merely masks
the core function, and crime fighting will truly become the police response to
social problems. The role of the judiciary will be similar to an assembly line with
judges moving through their dockets at great speed, unhindered by the niceties
of due process. We will fill our newly built prisons with those who are "different" (the poor, uneducated, minority members, organized criminals, and drug
offenders), and we will continue to search for new technologies that enable the
justice system to widen its net of social control. The death penalty, the ultimate
and most final solution to crime, will be carried out with greater swiftness and
frequency without constraints and delays.

The empirical reality of crime (which results from the focus we choose)
will be offered as evidence of our mythical conceptions. Stalkers kill—especially if we only study stalkers who have killed. A neat tautology but dangerously unenlightening. Consider the rise in reported child abuse. Few issues
raise more concern, fear, and the impulse to protect than child abuse. In 1973,
Congress passed the Child Abuse Prevention and Treatment Act (CAPTA)
which provides federal matching funds to states that comply with strict federal
guidelines for child-abuse detection, prosecution, and prevention programs.
From 1976 to 1993, the yearly number of child abuse reports grew from 669,000
to more than 2.9 million (Brott, 1995).

In 1995, there were proposals to dismantle CAPTA and to return child
abuse policy to the states. Opinions are sharply divided over whether the law
should be changed. It has focused attention on terrible harm, but that focus has

sometimes been skewed. Under CAPTA, states must pass laws requiring people in contact with children (such as doctors, therapists and teachers) to report all incidents of suspected abuse. If they do not, they may be fined or imprisoned; if they do, they are granted immunity from prosecution for causing false prosecutions. According to Richard Gardner, professor of child psychiatry at Columbia Medical School, "The mandated reporting and immunity provisions have created a child-abuse establishment—a network of social workers, psychologists and law-enforcement officials who actually encourage charges of child abuse, whether they're reasonable or not" (Brott, 1995, p. 10). Gardner cites figures indicating that unsubstantiated reports of abuse increased from 35 percent in 1973 to 66 percent in 1993. Therapists in San Diego testified before a grand jury that they fear removal from an approved list of mental health professionals if they oppose the recommendations of child protection agencies.

Critics of the law claim that people falsely accused or even imprisoned have little or no recourse. While the act was passed for defensible purposes, its mandates have created unforeseen difficulties and, in many cases, have "manufactured" criminals. Not only have the lives of persons unjustly accused been irrevocably changed, but the process of demonization creates more anxiety as the public unconsciously assimilates a distorted view of a world out of control.

In all myths, there resides a kernel of truth. How that kernel germinates and proliferates and the intended and unintended consequences attached to proposed solutions determine its potency. We cannot look only at reported crime, police records, court dockets, the composition of prison populations, and who is put to death to determine the characteristics of criminals or to determine if society is more dangerous today. Rather, we must examine all facets of the system and the social context in which the system operates to determine if our definitions and the processes we endorse are the problem.

◇

THE ELECTRONIC ECHO CHAMBER

Barry Glassner (1999) discusses the role of the media and the psychological phenomenon of the *availability heuristic*.

> We judge how common or important a phenomenon is by how readily it comes to mind. Presented with a survey that asks about the relative importance of issues, we are likely to give top billing to whatever the media emphasizes at the moment, because that issue instantly comes to mind. Were there a reasonable correspondence between emphases in the media and the true severity of social problems, the availability heuristic would not be problematic. (p. 133)

The media choose a theme that will resonate with the public. As Philip Jenkins (1998) points out, that often means personalizing or contextualizing an issue to make it comprehensible. He uses the savings and loan scandal as an example.

The sums are inconceivable, and that is precisely the problem. An audience overawed by bank robberies of a few million dollars had little grasp of the moneys taken from the thrifts, and still less did the ordinary public (or most journalists) ever understand the technical chicanery employed. Advocates wishing to draw attention to the disaster had to do so by placing it in a context that a lay audience would find both understandable and morally wrong. This meant drawing every possible connection with known and stereotyped criminals like organized criminals, rogue intelligence agents, and drug dealers, and a crash among Nebraska thrifts became a "real" crime only when it could be linked with the fashionable bogey of satanic sex rings. The S. and L. issue made little headway with the national audience until corporate criminality found a face (literally) in the form of Charles Keating and the senators whose support he allegedly bought; Keating promptly became the nationally identifiable scapegoat for the whole catastrophe. (p. 237)

Often, the "face" put on the problem by the media is even more personalized. The media project the images of Polly Klaas, or Megan Kanka, or Jon-Benet Ramsey, and parents everywhere are terrified. The mass media become an electronic echo chamber in which personal tragedies are magnified to a universal fear. Rational arguments cannot assuage the heightened emotions. The public grasps for the lifeline of heated political rhetoric to calm the panic. Images of crack babies who will forever pay the price for their mothers' irresponsible behavior masks the truth about crack. A by-product of social and economic distress becomes the *explanation* for the distress (Glassner, 1999).

◈

OF POLITICS AND DEMAGOGUES

Will political leaders, government officials and the media continue to promote mythical solutions to crime? The emotional furor and fear generated by myth production create a context for political grandstanding. This grandstanding often takes the form of proposing new crimes and classes of criminals. Philip Jenkins (1998) discusses the response to sex offenders by lawmakers who fervently want to treat sexual violence as an issue that can be corralled and eliminated. To accomplish this, the predator is projected as a stark symbol of evil. "Given concrete form, the problem can be met by means that legislatures understand, namely, passing ever more stringent laws and beginning a demagogic bidding war to impose the harshest penalties for the behavior" (pp. 237–238).

It is common for political leaders to advocate the use of the most severe criminal sanctions, such as the death penalty, at the pinnacle of sensationalism over a particular issue. Although few of these calls are ever transformed into formal social control, they do promote current beliefs that existing solutions to crime are acceptable and viable options for reducing both crime and the related social problems.

Joel Best (1999) explains that new crimes offer bureaucrats the same opportunities as any other new responsibility.

> New duties justify additional resources, perhaps new agencies. The FBI lobbied against the Hate Crimes Statistics Act, saying the data would be difficult and costly to collect yet not useful. However, once the bill became law, the bureau accepted the responsibility—and the budget—required to administer the program.
>
> New crimes offer government officials opportunities for media coverage; the press reports on hearings, interviews key legislators, and covers signing ceremonies. . . . Since violent crime seems dramatic, these events make good news stories as far as the media are concerned, and the coverage usually casts officials in a favorable light, making them eager to cooperate. . . . Thus, campaigns against new crimes forge strong, unusually cooperative links between the media and government. (p. 67)

Philip Jenkins discusses the symbiotic relationship of the media and bureaucracies. When the media sound the charge for a particular issue, there is a clear message to the nation that there is a major problem. A number of agencies from the police to the customs service to the postal service gear up to do their part to prevent the harm.

> These bureaucratic entities have a vested interest in justifying their "crusade" by the constant production of statistics indicating the rising frequency . . . while federal agencies are especially keen to stress the interstate and international dimensions of the problem and its conspiratorial aspects. As official actions intensify, so do the number of instances of misbehavior detected and prosecuted., which in turn increases still further the sense of a spreading epidemic. Statistics and research findings gain credibility to the extent that they fit public expectations, and they are often simplified or even distorted into some easily remembered format that is repeated until it becomes a truism. . . . After a few years, the perception of a problem becomes so well entrenched that its reality and significance seem not to brook questioning. (p. 220)

◊

FALLOUT FROM CRIME MYTHS

Starting in the 1970s and extending to today, there has been a trend in the United States toward becoming one of the harshest nations in the world in dealing with crime. Despite the myth that criminal justice is "soft" on crime, the facts are simple: we lock up more people, for longer sentences, for more offenses than any nation on the face of the earth. Not only is this incongruous in a country with a declining crime problem—and inherently brutal—but the policy is self-defeating. Mythical definitions are making the situation worse and creating more crime—the very situation the mythical solutions set out to correct.

The media, politicians, and the public all follow the human inclination to assign blame. The greater the horror of a crime, the less we are willing to attribute it to a tragic aberration. We construct an elaborate cause and effect to avoid the unsettling reality that some tragedies cannot be prevented. Yet when you declare war on an intractable problem, the alleged solution creates disastrous collateral damage—and the elevated expectations will eventually ensnare the politicians in their own promises, which cannot be kept.

Through our growing panic and concern over serial murder, missing children, stalkers, street crime and terrorist activities, we have enhanced law enforcement resources, developed task forces, implemented national programs, and created vast bureaucracies to deal with crime myths. Once created, bureaucratic machines are seldom dismantled even when their need is called into question. They take on a life of their own and have a vested interest in creating and continuing the very crime myths they were designed to eliminate.

Consider Otwin Marenin's (1991) reflections on the legacy of the law and order conservatism sweeping America:

> As rights were denounced, so were procedures which protect them. A false solution was created—if only some rights were stripped away we will succeed in fighting the scourge of lawlessness; if only the Police had a few more powers they might not have to beat on people who look as if they might insist on their rights; if only Judges were denied control of cases and evidence then guilty people could not avoid being found guilty; if prisoners could be housed four to a cell and death-row inmates killed off speedily all criminals could be taken off the street. In practice, as all who work in the system know, these changes would be minor and have little systematic impact on crime or the effectiveness of criminal justice policies. For the public, which knows how the system works from anecdotal cases and stereotyped cop-shows, such imagery hits the right note. Yet the promise made—crime will decrease and you will be safer—cannot be delivered. . . . (p. 17)

Longer sentences for repeat offenders continue to be a political panacea for crime. It is an easy solution to sell because it seems logical. According to popular folk wisdom, severe punishment and the certainty of prison will deter crime. That may be commonsense logic, but it is wrong. The simple fact is that prison does not deter crime, and severe sanctions probably increase the amount of crime in society. If prison terms deterred further criminality, we would expect that people who go to prison would be among those least likely to return there. However, the fact is that about 60 percent of everyone in prison has been there previously (Greenfield, 1985). Most prisoners eventually released from correctional institutions are rearrested, and about two out of five end up back in prison (Beck & Shipley, 1987).

Does length of time spent in prison affect future criminality? Research studies have clearly demonstrated that there is no connection between time served in a correctional institution and the likelihood that a prisoner will commit further crimes. Research shows that individuals paroled before the end of their sentences are no more likely to commit additional crimes than prisoners who serve their full sentences (Livingston, 1996). In fact, several studies have shown that the more severe the sanctions and the more frequent their administration, the greater the probability of additional criminality (Gottfredson, et al., 1973; Shannon, 1982). As discussed in chapter 14, the same lack of deterrence is clearly demonstrated for the death penalty, which not only fails to deter homicide but may well stimulate additional homicides through a "brutalization effect."

So the commonsense logic of deterrence is neither logical nor sensible. It is based on a fundamental misunderstanding of both criminals and crime. For deterrence to work, the offender must be a logical actor who understands the consequences of criminal behavior, knows the penalties, and weighs the costs of crime against the benefits of crime. Logic and calm reflection are simply not parts of the crime equation. In addition, a sizable number of offenders are people without hope, living in desperate circumstances. They are the poor, the unemployed, the uneducated, and the socially alienated. Fear of prison is a relatively minor consideration when stacked up against the dismal hopelessness of their day-to-day existence. Yet, police and politicians continue to pledge eradication of mythical crime problems through more law and order and more punishment.

An inevitable part of fighting mythical crime is a call for more police power. The mythmakers argue that if the police are unable to solve our crime problems it is only because we have failed to employ enough law enforcement officers or because we have not allowed them to be aggressive enough in fighting crime. Myths of the dangers of police work and the growing dangerousness of criminals merged to form federal legislation.

In 1988, a New York police officer named Eddie Byrne was killed while investigating a drug-related crime. This incident, in part, led Congress to enact a federal death penalty clause that allows the sentence of capital punishment to be imposed for "a defendant who kills or counsels to kill a law enforcement officer, while attempting to avoid apprehension, punishment, or sentencing for a drug violation . . ." (Williams, 1991, p. 394). The legislative history of the act indicated that "the murder of New York City police officer, Eddie Byrne, was one of the motivations for applying the death penalty section to those who kill law enforcement officers over drug-related offenses" (Williams, 1991, p. 394).

While the killing of any law enforcement officer is a tragedy that should not go unnoticed by society, it is a rare event. Law enforcement officers and their families, as well as the general public, may feel that this legislation is a necessary step to protect police officers. As noted in chapter 10, however, the number of police officers killed in the line of duty has been declining for over two decades. Very few officers are killed under the specific circumstances of the federal death penalty clause. It is ironic that the federal government created this law while the state in which the incident occurred did not deem such a law necessary.

Another factor that makes the Congressional action noteworthy is that the government has helped to promote linkage between the myths of the dangers of police work, the evils of drug use, and the viability of the death penalty.

Congress took no similar action against Miami police officers who killed drug traffickers in order to steal and later sell their drug cargo, and there are far more incidents of police drug corruption than there are cases of police officers killed by drug trafficking criminals. Nor were there calls from the citizens of New York for the death penalty for corrupt police officers like Michael Dowd. The drugs reach the same market whether sold by "criminals" or corrupt police officers. In the New Orleans Police Department corruption extended to the murder of an officer by his partner, yet there were no calls for the death penalty.

The myth that the death penalty will reduce crime is invoked whenever new laws are debated. In 1993 New Jersey legislators sought to allow prosecutors to seek the death penalty even in cases where the accused had no intent to injure or kill the victim. In 1994, Iowa's Governor announced that he would introduce a bill that mirrored the federal death penalty clause for drug-related homicides, despite the fact that Iowa abolished the death penalty in 1965. In 1995, legislators were taking another look at re-enacting the death penalty. Also in 1995, Governor George Pataki signed legislation to make New York the thirty-eighth state with a death penalty—an act all previous governors of that state had refused.

Two explanations exist for the enactment of the federal death penalty clause and New York's second look at using death. Either Congress was drawn into the myths of policing, drug crime and the death penalty, or the motivations were purely political. What better way for politicians to promote myths than to create a law that gives the impression of being tough on crime but which has little or no potential for use. Such a symbolic law does, however, reinforce myths of drug crime and police work while forging a symbolic link to the death penalty as the final solution to our crime problems. In President Clinton's State of the Union address in 1995, he proudly stated that the death penalty could be used in over sixty federal crimes. He also was careful to protect the recently passed Brady Bill by vowing not to allow automatic weapons back on to the streets so that law enforcement officers would no longer have to confront a "hail of bullets."

In the aftermath of the 1995 bombing of the federal building in Oklahoma City, the political reaction was swift, certain—and redundant. Political leaders called for the hiring of an additional 1,000 federal law enforcement officers, the passage of sweeping legal reform to grant greater powers to law enforcement officials to invade citizens' privacy, and the more frequent use of the death penalty. Law enforcement officials also added their voice to the chorus calling for the creation of a national center for tracking and monitoring "dangerous" groups.

Political leaders, law enforcement officials and the media gave scant attention to the fact that law enforcement's quick capture of a suspect was not the work of brilliant criminalists, not a product of elaborate profiling, nor was it made possible by a newly surrendered civil right, but rather it was the product of a chance encounter with a state trooper enforcing a traffic violation. Government officials, law enforcement officers, political leaders and the media were silent as to the fact that the government's own research indicates that terrorist acts in the United States and its territories have declined dramatically over the past decade. Consider Robert Wright's (1995) observations on the bombing:

> In a sense, it is natural that we worry irrationally—that we are terrified by images of Americans "just like us" dying violently. The human mind evolved to assess and address risk on the basis of such images. But that's because during human evolution, before television, such images did reflect risk—local risk. Further galvanizing us is the fact that bombings are intentional; aspiring bombers are out there somewhere, to be stopped. Death by traffic mishap, in contrast, has no plan, no perpetrator. It seems the inexorable working of fate or chance, and we accept each year's statistics, if we notice them at all, with resignation.
>
> Sounds rational, but it isn't. Whereas heading off the next bomber is a chancy business at best, we could, if we chose, adjust highway death downward with nearly the precision of a volume control knob. We could better enforce speed limits, say, or close all bars at dusk. Implicitly, society chooses not to save lives this way. Drivers and drinkers would bridle at the inconvenience. Indeed, most states have raised the speed limit to 65 mph since 1987, adding an estimated 400 to 500 deaths a year nationwide.
>
> That's defensible. Life is full of tough trade-offs between ease and safety, and we have to draw the lines somewhere. But do these trade-offs of convenience really warrant more reverence than trade-offs of civil liberty? If saving a few hundred lives—including children's lives—wouldn't justify a loss in highway efficiency, does it really justify growth of the government's power to eavesdrop and otherwise intrude on our lives? (p. 86)

◈

MASKING SOCIAL PROBLEMS WITH MYTH

Crime control bureaucracies consume an ever-expanding amount of social resources as they widen their sphere of influence and modify their missions to fit organizational and political goals. Such enforcement policies burden an already overtaxed criminal justice system and mask other social problems. We have noted that fear develops based on the notion of victimization by strangers or persons different from ourselves. Children are abducted by strangers. Serial murderers prowl, looking for innocent victims to slay. Organized crime is controlled and operated by foreign-born nationals having little allegiance to our way of life. Police officers are under assault from criminals. Such characterizations of crime, criminals and the criminal justice system, as we have seen, have little basis in reality, but they are real to the public.

People fear walking the streets; car doors are locked in dangerous parts of the city; contact with strangers is avoided—and the result is a general withdrawal from society. Fear of victimization and social isolation begins a downward spiral that can produce more crime, more victimization, and more myth. As we remove ourselves from the street and isolate ourselves from the concerns of others in our communities, we abandon society and its real problems. We are no longer willing to become involved in our communities, much less in real crime prevention and the workings of the criminal justice system. We leave matters of justice to the mythmakers.

Ethan Nadelmann (1999) discusses the problems with relying on zero-tolerance rhetoric and policies to achieve the illusory goal of a drug-free society.

> U.S. drug prohibition, like Prohibition decades ago, generates extraordinary harm. It, not drugs per se, is responsible for creating vast underground markets, criminalizing millions of otherwise law-abiding citizens, corrupting both governments and societies at large, empowering organized criminals, increasing predatory crime, spreading disease, curtailing personal freedom, disparaging science and honest inquiry and legitimizing public policies that are both extraordinary and insidious in their racially disproportionate consequences. (p. 23)

Government officials are free to spawn myths of crime and justice and to waste valuable resources on ineffective crime control practices that expand the crime control industry. One of the latest attempts to expand law enforcement and government control involves computers. FBI agents arrested 20-year-old Jake Baker at the University of Michigan for posting a fictitious story on the Internet entitled "Pamela's Ordeal." The story described the gruesome torture, rape and murder of a woman by two men. Because he used the name of a student in one of his classes and because he used interstate communication to transmit the story, Baker spent a month in a federal prison cell.

Baker was indicted for violating Section 875(c) of the U.S. Criminal Code: "Whoever transmits in interstate or foreign commerce any communication containing any threat to kidnap any person or any threat to injure the person of another shall be fined not more than $1,000 or imprisoned not more than 5 years, or both." Bond was originally denied because the judge had a "gut feeling that he wouldn't want his daughter out on the streets if Baker were set free" (Lowenstein, 1995, p. 1).

Although Baker was charged with an existing statute, the Internet offers fertile ground for mythmakers. It is an unknown territory, and "people typically react to new communication technologies by trying to reign them in" (Lowenstein, 1995, p. 1). Sen. James Exon (D-Neb.) has introduced a bill to regulate obscenity and indecency on computer communication networks that would hold providers of network services criminally liable for transmission of indecent messages. The FBI is currently lobbying Congress for unrestricted access to the information superhighway.

When crime control policy is developed based on myth or misconception, it has the effect of diverting resources and attention from real social problems. It is far easier to report issues like child abduction or stalkings than to present threats of an infinitely larger potential but decidedly more technical nature. Child abductions, stalkings, and child abuse can be immediately condensed into a personal, dramatic package that touches on universally held values. It is excruciatingly painful to read the details of a young mother killed by her ex-husband despite asking the police for help. There is immediate identification with her tragedy and an intense desire to have prevented the harm.

Each of the crime myths we have considered in this book blinds us to social problems of greater magnitude and consequence. When vast social resources are expended to hunt down mythical criminals, to prevent stranger abductions of children or to investigate foreign-born organized crime figures, resources are consumed that could be used to study and to control real social problems. While we continue to divert enormous sums of public money to law enforcement and corrections, we are failing to deal with basic problems that impact directly on crime in U.S. society.

Jeffrey Reiman (1998) points us in the right direction; social inequality and social disorganization are stimulants to street crime.

> There are many things that we do know about the sources of crime. Note that I have said "sources" rather than "causes," because the kind of knowledge we have is far from the precise knowledge that a physicist has about how some event *causes* another. We know that poverty, slums, and unemployment are *sources* of street crime. We do not fully understand how they *cause* crime, because we know as well that many, if not most, poor, unemployed slum dwellers do not engage in street crime. Yet to say that this means we do not know that such conditions increase the likelihood of an individual resorting to violent crime is like saying that we do not know that a bullet in the head is deadly because some people survive or because we do not fully understand the physiological process that links the wound with the termination of life. (p. 28)

Contrary to the often suggested alchemy of more police and stiffer punishment to combat the biological, psychological, or moral weakness of criminals, the evidence is compelling that the root of crime is more realistically found in the soil of social and economic desperation. Our priorities are in the wrong place, and our punitive response to mythical crime is a social disaster.

Because of crime myths we overlook broader social problems like teenage runaways, children abused at the hands of their relatives, and the crime "organized" in corporate board rooms and governmental offices across the country. We wage wars against inanimate objects such as drugs and pornography as if they have a life of their own—without considering the supply-and-demand equation and the spin-off crimes caused by waging crime wars and criminalizing behavior. Consider just a few of the questions and problems that are masked when we focus on mythical crime.

- What is the real extent of crime in America?
- Why is law enforcement unable to deal with crime?
- Is there true equity in our courts?
- What are the vested interests of the criminal justice industry?
- How many deaths are associated with drugs like alcohol and tobacco?
- What spin-off crimes are caused by the drug war?
- Are injuries caused by the government's drug crop eradication programs?

- How much corruption of governmental officials results from drug criminalization?
- What percentage of the public demands vice-related services and products?
- Is there a symbiotic relationship between government and corporate crime?
- Who pays the $231 billion price tag of corporate and white-collar crime?

◈

RESTRUCTURING THE STUDY OF CRIME

For the past century, social scientists have researched and argued the "causes" of crime. The debate has ranged from the sublime to the ridiculous, from the slope of one's forehead and the spacing of one's eyes to the alleged moral inferiority of some of the residents of our inner cities. No one has isolated a cause of crime. This is, of course, not surprising. Crime is a socially constructed event created by many social processes interacting over time and space. Unfortunately, crime myths undermine the scientific study and treatment of crime.

Crime myths change our perception and understanding of crime and criminal behavior. They are often "quests for evil." They sometimes use simplistic and even supernatural explanations for crime to the detriment of scientific understanding. This is especially the case with crimes that have been characterized as predatory. When crime is characterized as evil, rehabilitation is rejected in favor of harsh punishment including death.

Less sensational, but equal in effect, is the characterization of criminal behavior as a product of freely chosen behavior. When the causal and social bases of crime are rejected, punishment becomes the logical social response. Legal prescriptions are used to treat the symptoms of social problems, and science is relegated to crime detection and criminal profiling rather than understanding crime and its social causes. Offenders are stereotyped as pathological and violent, and their behavior is analyzed from a simplistic prey-predator paradigm. Challenges to the scientific study of crime often alter the empirical reality of crime. The restructured study of crime begins to mirror our mythical conceptions of crime by providing more "evidence" that is tainted by the detection, apprehension, and control paradigm of criminology.

Unfortunately, myths of crime and justice are not put to rest with the same vigor with which they are created. Debunking myths does not have the same attraction as does their construction. After clear definitions of criminal behavior have been developed and the actual frequency of the crime has been determined, there are few newspaper accounts, television documentaries, commercials, or calls by political leaders to demystify our images of crime. Often, all that exists in the aftermath of a crime myth are criminal laws, more cops, harsher punishments, misplaced social resources, a feeling of moral superiority, and a growing intolerance for human diversity.

CONCLUSION

We hope this text has challenged you to view crime myths with a critical eye—
to think about the origin of issues and to watch for patterns of myth construction. Myths can only be challenged by critically processing information.
Critical thinking must develop alternative filters through which to sift myths—
questions must be posed, stories must be challenged and simple solutions must
be questioned. We must begin to ask: Who is the mythmaker? What is the
mythmaker's motivation? What group is being targeted by the myth? What
behavior is being targeted for control and why? Most importantly we must ask:
What are the consequences of waging war against mythical crime?

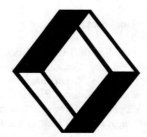

References

Abadinsky, H. (1997). *Organized crime* (5th ed.). Chicago: Nelson-Hall.

Abadinsky, H., & Winfree, L., Jr. (1992). *Crime and justice: An introduction* (2nd ed.). Chicago: Nelson-Hall.

Abrahamsen, D. (1945). *Crime and the human mind.* New York: Columbia University Press.

Abrahamsen, D. (1960). *The psychology of crime.* New York: Columbia University Press.

Abrahamsen, D. (1973). *The murdering mind.* New York: Harper & Row.

Abrahamsen, D. (1985). *Confessions of Son of Sam.* New York: Columbia University Press.

Adams, E. (1994, February 4). ABA urges additional funding for drug treatment. *New York Law Journal,* 1

Adlaf, E. M., Smart, R. G., & Canale, M. D. (1991). Drug use among Ontario adults 1977–1991. Toronto: Ontario Addiction Research Foundation.

Agopian, M. (1980). Parental child stealing: Participants and the victimization process. *Victimology: An International Journal, 5,* 263–273.

Agopian, M. (1981). *Parental child stealing.* Lexington, MA: Lexington Books.

Albanese, J. (1996). *Organized crime in America* (3rd ed.). Cincinnati: Anderson.

Albini, J. (1971). *The American mafia: Genesis of a legend.* New York: Appleton-Century-Crofts.

Allen, E. (1999). President's message [On-line]. Available: http://missingkids.com

Allison, J., & Wrightsman, L. (1993). *Rape: The misunderstood crime.* Thousand Oaks, CA: Sage.

Alpert, G., & Dunham, R. (1997). *Policing urban America,* (3rd ed.). Prospect Heights, IL: Waveland Press.

Alter, J. (1999, September 6). The buzz on drugs. *Newsweek,* 25–28.

Amnesty International. (1998, November). *Juveniles and the death penalty: Execution worldwide since 1900.*

Andenaes, J. (1974). *Punishment and deterrence.* Ann Arbor: University of Michigan Press.

Anderson, A. (1979). *The business of organized crime: A cosa nostra family*. Stanford, CA: Hoover Institution Press.

Andrews, J. (1994, August 4). Health-care industry fraud eats up billions yearly. *The Christian Science Monitor*, 3.

Angell, E. (1999, August 23). In the line of fire. *Newsweek*, 134, 20–22.

Annin, P. (1998, July 13). Inside the new Alcatraz. *Newsweek*, 35.

Arnette, J. L., & Walsleben, M. C. (1998). *Combating fear and restoring safety in schools*. Office of Juvenile Justice and Delinquency Prevention. Washington, DC.

Arrigo, B., & Garsky, K. (1997). Police suicide: A glimpse behind the badge. In R. Dunham & G. Alpert (Eds.), *Critical issues in policing* (3rd ed., pp. 609–626).

Associated Press. (1997, November 11). One in 12 women victims of stalkers, survey finds. *Chicago Tribune*, p. 8.

Associated Press. (1999, September 28). U.S. executions hit 45-year high. *Chicago Tribune*, p. 16.

Association of the Bar of the City of New York. (1994). A wiser course: Ending drug prohibition. *The Record, 49*, 5.

Austin, J. (1990, December). *America's growing correctional-industrial complex*. San Francisco: National Council on Crime and Delinquency.

Austin, J., & McVey, A. (1989, December). *The 1989 NCCD prison population forecast: The impact of the war on drugs*. San Francisco: National Council on Crime and Delinquency.

Bahn, C. (1984). Police socialization in the eighties: Strains in the forging of an occupational identity. *Journal of Police Science and Administration, 12*,(4), 390–394.

Bailey, W. (1982). Capital punishment and lethal assaults against police. *Criminology, 19*, 608–625.

Bailey, W. (1991). The general prevention effect of capital punishment for non-capital felonies. In R. Bohm (Ed.), *The death penalty in America: Current research*. Cincinnati, OH: Anderson and Academy of Criminal Justice Sciences.

Bailey, W., & Peterson, R. (1987). Police killings and capital punishment: The post-Furman period. *Criminology, 25*,(1), 1–25.

Bailey, W., & Peterson, R. (1994). Murder, capital punishment, and deterrence: A review of the evidence and an examination of police killings. *Journal of Social Issues, 50*, 53–71.

Baker, M., Nienstedt, B., Everett, R., & McCleary, R. (1983). The impact of a crime wave: Perceptions, fear, and confidence in the police. *Law and Society Review, 17*, 319–333.

Ballantyne, A. (1987, May 1). Man released in child deaths inquiry. *Guardian*. London.

Baniak, Peter. (1998, October 19). AdWatch. *Lexington Herald-Leader*.

Barak, G. (1994). Media, society, and criminology. In G. Barak (Ed.), *Media, process, and the social construction of crime* (pp. 3–45). New York: Garland.

Barkan, S. (1997). *Criminology: A sociological understanding*. Englewood Cliffs, NJ: Prentice-Hall.

Barlow, M., Barlow, D., & Chiricos, T. (1995a). Mobilizing support for social control in a declining economy: Exploring ideologies of crime within crime news. *Crime & Delinquency, 41*(2), 191–204.

Barlow, M., Barlow, D., & Chiricos, T. (1995b). Economic conditions and ideologies of crime in the media: A content analysis of crime news. *Crime & Delinquency, 41*(1), 3–19.

Bastian, L. (1992). *Criminal victimization 1991*. Washington, DC: Bureau of Justice Statistics.

Bastian, L. (1995). *Criminal victimization 1993*. Washington, DC: Bureau of Justice Statistics.

Bauchner, H., Zuckerman, B., McClain, M., Frank, D., Fried, L., & Kayne, H. (1988). Risk of sudden death syndrome among infants with in utero exposure to cocaine. *Journal of Pediatrics, 113,* 831–834.

Beat the devil: The ten worst corporations of 1997. (December). *Multinational Monitor, 18,* 12.

Beck, A. (1992, July 13). Murderous obsession. *Newsweek,* 60.

Beck, A. J. (1999). Trends in U.S. correctional populatons. In K. Haas & G. Alpert (Eds.), *The dilemmas of corrections* (4th ed., pp. 44–65). Prospect Heights, IL: Waveland Press.

Beck, A. J., & Mumola, C. (1999, August). *Prisoners in 1998*. Bureau of Justice Statistics. Washington, DC: U.S. Government Printing Office.

Beck, A. J., & Shipley, R. (1987). Recidivism of young parolees. *Bureau of Justice Statistics Special Report*. Washington, DC: U.S. Government Printing Office.

Becker, H. (1963). *Outsiders*. New York: Free Press.

Beckett, Katherine. (1994). Setting the public agenda: "Street crime" and drug use in American politics. *Social Problems, 41,* 425–447.

Bedau, H. (Ed.). (1982). *The death penalty in America* (3rd ed.). Oxford: Oxford University Press.

Beil, L. (1998, October 12). Study finds news doesn't reflect true face of nation's homicides. *Dallas Morning News*.

Beneke, T. (1998). Men in rape. In M. Kimmel & M. Messner (Eds.), *Men's lives,* (4th ed., pp. 312–317). Boston, MA: Allyn and Bacon.

Benekos, P. (1983, March). Sentencing the white-collar offender: Evaluating the use of sanctions. Paper presented at the Academy of Criminal Justice Sciences annual meeting, San Antonio, TX.

Benoit, E. (1989, October 3). The case for legalization. *Financial World*, 32–35.

Benson, M. (1996). Denying the guilty mind: Accounting for involvement in white-collar crime. In E. Goode (Ed.), *Social Deviance*. Boston: Allyn and Bacon.

Bequai, A. (1978). *White-collar crime: A 20th-century crisis*. Lexington, MA: Lexington Books.

Bequai, A. (1979). *Organized crime: The fifth estate*. Lexington, MA: Heath.

Berger, J. (1984, August 27). Traits shared by mass killers remain unknown to experts. *The New York Times*.

Berk, R., Weiss, R., & Boger, J. (1993). Chance and the death penalty. *Law and Society Review, 27,* 89–110.

Bernard, T. J. (1999). Juvenile crime and the transformation of juvenile justice: Is there a juvenile crime wave? *Justice Quarterly*.

Berns, W. (1979). *For capital punishment*. New York: Basic Books.

Best, J. (1987). Rhetoric in claims-making: Constructing the missing children problem. *Social Problems, 34*(2), 101–121.

Best, J. (1989). *Images of issues*. Hawthorne, NY: Aldine de Gruyter.

Best, J. (1999). *Random violence*. Berkely, CA: University of California Press.

Best, J., & Horiuchi, G. (1985). The razor and the apple: The social construction of urban legends. *Social Problems, 32,* 488–499.

Binder, A., & Fridell, L. (1984). Lethal force as police response. *Criminal Justice Abstracts, 16*(2), 250–280.

Bishop, D. M., Frazier, C. E., Lanza-Kaduce, L. & Winner, L. (1996). The transfer of juveniles to criminal court: Does it make a difference? *Crime and Delinquency,* *42*(2), 171–191.

Black, D. (1976). *The behavior of law.* New York: Academic Press.

Black, D. (1989). *Sociological justice.* New York: Oxford University Press.

Block, A. (1978, January 6). History and the study of organized crime. *Urban Life, 455–*474.

Block, A. (1979). The snowman cometh: Coke in progressive New York. *Criminology,* *17,* 75–99.

Block, A., & Scarpitti, F. (1985). *Poisoning for profit: The mafia and toxic waste.* New York: William Morrow.

Blok, A. (1971). *The Mafia of a Sicilian village, 1860–1960.* Prospect Heights, IL: Waveland Press.

Blumberg, A. (1975). The practice of law and a confidence game: Organizational cooptation of a profession. In W. Chambliss (Ed.), *Criminal law in action.* Santa Barbara: Hamilton.

Blumenson, E., & Nilsen, E. (1998). Policing for profit: The drug war's hidden economic agenda. *The University of Chicago Law Review, 65,* 35–114.

Bochove, D. (1992, July 26). Living in fear. *Calgary Herald,* p. A10.

Bohm, R. (1986). Crime, criminal and crime control policy myths. *Justice Quarterly, 3*(2), 193–214.

Bohm, R. (1989). Humanism and the death penalty, with special emphasis on the post-Furman experience. *Justice Quarterly, 6,* 173–195.

Bok, S. (1998). *Mayhem: Violence as public entertainment.* Reading, MA: Perseus Books.

Bonczar, T., & Beck, A. (1997, March). *Lifetime likelihood of going to state or federal prison.* Washington, DC: Bureau of Justice Statistics.

Bonsignore, J., Katsh, E., D'Errico, P., Pipkin, R., Arons, S., & Rifkin, J. (1998). *Before the law: An introduction to the legal process* (6th ed.). Boston: Houghton-Mifflin.

Bovard, J. (1995). *Archer Daniels Midland: A case study in corporate welfare.* Washington, DC: Cato Institute.

Bowers, W. (1988). The effect of executions is brutalization, not deterrence. In K. Haas & J. Inciardi (Eds.), *Challenging capital punishment: Legal and social science approaches.* Newbury Park, CA: Sage Publications.

Bowers, W., Pierce, G., & McDevitt, J. (1984). *Legal homicide: Death as punishment in America, 1864–1982.* Boston: Northeastern University Press.

Bowker, L. (1982). Victimizers and victims in American correctional institutions. In R. Johnson & H. Toch (Eds.), *The pains of imprisonment* (pp. 63–76). Prospect Heights, IL: Waveland Press.

Braithwaite, J. (1984). *Corporate crime in the pharmaceutical industry.* Boston: Routledge & Kegan Paul.

Brandon, K. (1995, July 7). Three-strike law taxing California prisons. *Chicago Tribune,* p. 3.

Bromley, D., Shupe, A., & Ventimiglia, J. (1979). Atrocity tales, the Unification Church, and the social construction of evil. *Journal of Communication, 29*(3), 42–53.

Brott, A. (1995, February 1). Major reworking of child abuse law. *Chicago Tribune,* p. 10.

Brown, J., D'Emidio-Caston, M., & Pollard, J. (1997). Students and substances: Social power in drug education. *Educational Evaluation and Policy Analysis, 1*(1), 65–82.

Brown, M. (1982). Love canal and the poisoning of America. In J. Skolnick & E. Currie (Eds.), *Crisis in American institutions* (5th ed., pp. 297–316). Boston: Little Brown.

Brydensholt, H. (1992). Crime policy in Denmark: How we managed to reduce the prison population. In M. Carlie & K. Minor, (Eds.), *Prisons around the world*. Dubuque, IA: Wm. C. Brown.

Burden, O. (1986, March 10). The hidden truths about police drug use. *Law Enforcement News*, p. 5.

Bureau of Justice Statistics. (1987, February). *Imprisonment in four countries*. Special Report. Washington, DC: U.S. Department of Justice.

Bureau of Justice Statistics. (1988, March). *Report to the nation on crime and justice* (2nd ed.). Washington, DC: U.S. Department of Justice.

Bureau of Justice Statistics. (1992). *Drugs, crime and the justice system*. Washington, DC: U.S. Department of Justice.

Bureau of Justice Statistics. (1993). *Highlights from 20 years of surveying crime victims*. Washington, DC: U.S. Government Printing Office.

Bureau of Justice Statistics. (1994a). *Capital Punishment 1993*. Washington, DC.

Bureau of Justice Statistics. (1994b). *Child rape victims, 1992*. Washington, DC.

Bureau of Justice Statistics. (1994c). *Federal law enforcement officers, 1993*. Washington, DC: U.S. Government Printing Office.

Bureau of Justice Statistics. (1994d). *Murder in families*. Washington, DC.

Bureau of Justice Statistics. (1995). *Nation's correctional population tops five million*. Washington, DC.

Bureau of Justice Statistics. (1997a). *Criminal victimization, 1996*. Washington, DC: U.S. Government Printing Office.

Bureau of Justice Statistics. (1997b). *Prisoners in 1996*. Washington, DC: U.S. Government Printing Office.

Bureau of Justice Statistics. (1998a). *Prisoners in 1997*. Washington, DC: U.S. Government Printing Office.

Bureau of Justice Statistics. (1998b). *Sourcebook of criminal justice statistics 1997*. Washington, DC: U.S. Government Printing Office.

Bureau of Justice Statistics. (1999). [On-line]. Available: www.oip.usdoj.gov/bjs

Butterfield, F. (1996, January 6). Experts on crime warn of a "ticking time bomb." *The New York Times*, p. 6.

Butterfield, F. (1998, August 3). As crime falls, pressure rises to alter data. *The New York Times*.

Byrne, C. (1994). *Fact sheet: Drug data summary*. Washington, DC: Bureau of Justice Statistics.

Cahill, T. (1986). *Buried dreams: Inside the mind of a serial killer*. New York: Bantam.

Calavita, K., & Pontell, H. (1990). Heads I win, tails you lose: Deregulation, crime and crisis in the savings and loan industry. *Crime and Delinquency, 36,* 309–341.

Calavita, K., & Pontell, H. (1993). Savings and loan fraud as organized crime: Toward a conceptual typology of corporate illegality. *Criminology, 31*(4), 519–548.

Califano, J. (1993, December 15). Battle lines in the war on drugs. No, fight harder. *The New York Times*, p. A27.

Califano, J. (1998). Forward. In J. Califano. *Behind bars: Substance abuse and America's prison population*. New York, NY: The National Center on Addiction and Substance Abuse at Columbia University.

California Penal Code (1990). Section 646.9. St. Paul: West.

Callahan, P. (1995, January 30). To O.J. or not to O.J.: That is the question at law school. *Chicago Tribune*, p. 6.

Capital Punishment Research Project. (1998, January 12). *Report*. Headland, AL: Author.

Cardarelli, A. (1968). An analysis of police killed in criminal action: 1961–1963. *Journal of Criminal Law, Criminology and Police Science, 59,* 447–453.

Carlson, J. (1995). *Prime time enforcement.* New York, NY: Praeger.

Carlson, K. (1979). Statement before the Congressional Committee on Education and Labor, Subcommittee on Compensation, Health and Safety, Hearings on Asbestos-Related Occupational Diseases, 95th Congress, Second Session. Washington, DC: U.S. Government Printing Office, pp. 25–52.

Carmona, M., & Stewart, K., (1996). *A review of alternative activities and alternatives programs in youth-oriented prevention.* Washington, DC: Center for Substance Abuse Prevention.

Cauchon, D. (1991, August 15). Head of BCCI-linked bank quits. *USA Today,* p. 8A.

Caute, J., & Odell, R. (1979). *The murderers' who's who.* London: Pan.

Cavender, G., & Bond-Maupin, L. (1998). Fear and loathing on reality television: An analysis of *America's Most Wanted* and *Unsolved Mysteries.* In G. Potter & V. Kappeler (Eds.), *Constructing crime: Perspectives on making news and social problems* (pp. 73–85). Prospect Heights, IL: Waveland Press.

Center for Media and Public Affairs (CMPA). (1997). *Media monitor.* Washington, DC: Author.

Center for Substance Abuse and Treatment. (1996). *National treatment improvement evaluation study.* Washington, DC: U.S. Government Printing Office.

Chaiken, M. (1988). *Street-level drug enforcement: Examining the issues.* Washington, DC: U.S. Department of Justice.

Chain gangs return to prisons in Alabama and Arizona. (1995, May 15). *Criminal Justice Newsletter, 26*(10), 1–3.

Chaloupka, F., & Laixuthai, A. (1992). *Do youths substitute alcohol and marijuana? Some econometric evidence.* University of Illinois: Chicago.

Chambliss, W. (1978). *On the take: From petty crooks to presidents.* Bloomington: Indiana University Press.

Chambliss, W. (1988). *Exploring criminology.* New York: Macmillan.

Chambliss, W. (1989). State-organized crime. *Criminology, 27*(2), 183–208.

Chambliss, W., & Block, A. (1981). *Organizing crime.* New York: Elsevier.

Chambliss, W., & Seidman, R. (1986). *Law, order, and power* (2nd ed.). Reading, MA: Addison-Wesley.

Champion, D. (1989a). Private counsels and public defenders: A look at weak cases, prior records, and leniency in plea bargaining. *Journal of Criminal Justice, 17*(4), 253–263.

Champion, D. (1989b). Teenage felons and waiver hearings: Some recent trends, 1980–1988. *Crime and Delinquency, 35,* 577–585

Chandler, D. (1975). *Brothers in blood: The rise of the criminal brotherhoods.* New York: Dutton.

Chandler, K. A., Chapman, C. D., Rand, M. R., & Taylor, B. M. (1998). *Students' reports of school crime: 1989 and 1995.* U.S. Departments of Education and Justice. Washington, DC.

Chapman, S. (1994, July 10). The Simpson case and the problem of the constitution. *Chicago Tribune,* p. 3.

Chapman, S. (1995a, March 2). Dead reckoning. *Chicago Tribune,* p. 25.

Chapman, S. (1995b, June 29). A freedom denied. *Chicago Tribune,* p. 27.

Cheney, M. (1976). *The coed killer.* New York: Walker.

Chesney-Lind, M. (1995). Girls, delinquency, and juvenile justice: Towards a feminist theory of young women's crime. In B. Price & N. Sokoloff (Eds.), *The criminal justice system and women: Offenders, victims, and workers* (pp. 71–88). New York: McGraw-Hill

Children's court: Back to the future. (1999, July 25). *Chicago Tribune*, p. 16.

Chiricos, T., & Bales, W. (1991). Unemployment and punishment: An empirical assessment. *Criminology, 29*(4), 701–724.

Christie, N. (1994). *Crime control as industry* (2nd ed.). London: Routledge.

Claiborne, W. (1995, March 20–26). Three strikes and you're out of wiggle room. *The Washington Post* (National Weekly Edition).

Clinard, M., & Yeager, P. (1979). *Illegal corporate behavior*. Washington, DC: Law Enforcement Assistance Administration.

Clinard, M., & Yeager, P. (1980). *Corporate crime*. New York: Macmillan.

Cloud, J. (1999, May 3). What can the schools do? *Time*, 38–40.

Co, B. T., Goodwin, D. W., Gado, M., Mikhael, M., & Hill, S. W. (1997). Absence of cerebral trophy in chronic cannabis users. *Journal of the American Medical Association, 237*, 1229–1230.

Cochran, J. K., Chamlin, M. B., & Seth, M. (1994). Deterrence or brutalization? An impact assessment of Oklahoma's return to capital punishment. *Criminology, 32*(1), 107–134.

Coffin, P. (1996). *Cocaine and pregnancy: The truth about crack babies*. New York: The Lindesmith Center.

Cohen, P. (1989). *Cocaine use in Amersterdam in nondeviant subcultures*. Amsterdam: Instituut voor Sociale Georgrafie, Universiteit van Amsterdam.

Cohen, R. (1991). *Prisoners in 1990* (May). Washington, DC: Bureau of Justice Statistics.

Cohen, W. (1993). Antistalking law. Senate—October 04, 1993, S12901.

Coker v. Georgia, 433 U.S. 584 (1977).

Coleman, J. (1998). *The criminal elite* (4th ed.). New York: St. Martin's Press.

Colombia calls drug crop eradication a failure. (1998, September 9). Reuters News Service.

Comment. (1992, June 16). Making stalking a crime. *Atlantic Journal and Constitution*, p. A20.

Congressional Record. (1993, October 4). 139, S12901– 01.

Congressional Record—Senate. (1983, October 27). Statements on introduced bills and joint resolutions, S14787.

Cook, F. (1973). *Mafia!* Greenwich, CT: Fawcett.

Corporate crime: The untold story. (1982, September 6). *U.S. News & World Report*, 25.

Cose, E. (1999, September 6). The casualties of war. *Newsweek*, 29.

Cotts, C. (1992, March 9). Hard sell in the drug war. *The Nation*.

Courtwright, D. (1993). Should we legalize drugs? History answers: No. *American Heritage, 41*(50), 44.

Cox, M. (1998, December 9). Philly police admit they fudged on crime stats. *Lexington Herald-Leader*.

Cressey, D. (1967). *The theft of the nation*. New York: Harper & Row.

Crime Control Digest (1985, January 14). Massachusetts' new missing children law requires immediate reports, 10.

Crouch, B., Alpert, A., Marquart, J., & Haas, K. (1999). The American prison crisis: Clashing philosophies of punishment and crowded cellblocks. In K. Haas & G. Alpert (Eds.), *The dilemmas of corrections* (4th ed., pp. 84–100). Prospect Heights, IL: Waveland Press.

Cullen, F. (1984). The Ford Pinto case and beyond. In E. Hochstedler (Ed.), *Corporations as criminals*. Beverly Hills: Sage.

Cullen, F., & Gilbert, K. (1982). *Reaffirming rehabilitation*. Cincinnati: Anderson.

Cumming, E., Cumming, I. & Edell, L. (1965). Policeman as philosopher, friend and guide. *Social Problems, 12*, 14–49.

Currie, E. (1985). *Confronting crime: An American challenge*. New York: Pantheon Books.

Dallas Morning News. (1992, March 8).

Dann, R. (1935). The deterrent effect of capital punishment. *Friends Social Service Series, 29*.

Darrach, B., & Norris, J. (1984). An American tragedy. *Life*.

Davis, R., & Meddis, S. (1994, December 5). Random killings hit a high. *USA Today*, p. 1A.

Dawsey, D., & Malnic, E. (1989, July 19). Actress Rebecca Schaeffer fatally shot at apartment. *LA Times*, p. 1.

Dawson, J., & Langan, P. (1994). *Murder in families*. Washington, DC: Bureau of Justice Statistics.

Day careless. (1994, August 8). *Time*, p. 28.

Decker, S. (1993). Exploring victim-offender relationships in homicide: The role of individual and event characteristics. *Justice Quarterly, 10*, 585–612.

Dee Scofield Awareness Program (1983a). Federal legislation: The first steps Tampa, Florida. (Educational Report No. 5).

Dee Scofield Awareness Program (1983b). Estimated annual-missing children (Educational Report, November). Tampa, Florida.

Demaris, O. (1981). *The last mafioso*. New York: Bantam.

Demaris, O. (1986). *The boardwalk jungle*. New York: Bantam.

Dennis, R. J. (1990). The economics of legalizing drugs. *The Atlantic Monthly, 265*, 5.

Department of Justice (1994). *Crime rate essentially unchanged last year*. Washington, DC: Bureau of Justice Statistics.

Departments of Education and Justice (1998). *Annual report on school safety*.

Detlinger, C., & Prugh, J. (1983). *The list*. Atlanta: Philmay Enterprise.

Dickey, W. (1994, March). *Evaluating boot camp prisons*. Washington, DC: Campaign for an Effective Crime Policy.

Dickson, D. (1968). Bureaucracy and morality: An organizational perspective on a moral crusade. *Social Problems, 16*, 143–156.

Dietrich, J., & Smith, J. (1986). Non-medical use of drugs and alcohol by police. *Journal of Police Science and Administration, 14*, 300–306.

Dietz, P. E., Matthews, D. A., Stewart, T. M., Hrouda, D. R., & Warren, J. (1991). Threatening and otherwise inappropriate letters to Hollywood celebrities. *Journal of Forensic Sciences, 36*(1), 185–209.

Ditton, J., Farrow, K., Forsyth, A., Hammersly, R., Hunter, G., Lavelle, T., Mullen, K., et al. (1991). Scottish cocaine users: Wealthy snorters or delinquent smokers? *Drug and Alcohol Dependence, 28*, 269–276.

Donahue, J. (1992). The missing rap sheet: Government records on corporate abuses. *Multinational Monitor, 14*, 12.

Donziger, S. (Ed.). (1996). *The real war on crime*. New York: Harper Perennial.

Dornbush, R. L., Fink, M., & Freedman, A. M. (1971, May 3–7). Marijuana, memory and perception. Paper presented at the 124th annual meeting of the American Psychiatric Association.

Dowd, D. (1993). *U.S. capitalist development since 1776: Of, by, and for which people?* New York: M.E. Sharpe.

Dowie, M. (1977, September). Pinto madness. *Mother Jones*, 18–32.

Drechsel, R., Netteburg, K., & Aborisade, B. (1980). Community size and newspaper reporting of local courts. *Journal Quarterly, 57,* 71–78.

Dreher, M. C. (1982). *Working men and ganja: Marijuana use in rural Jamaica.* New York: Institute for the Study of Human Issues.

Drug use increasing despite federal war. (1994, May 12). *Gannet Suburban Newspapers,* p. 16A.

Dumont, M. (1973). The junkie as political enemy. *American Journal of Orthopsychiatry 42*(4), 533–540.

Dunn, K. (1994, April 10). Crime and embellishment. *Los Angeles Times Magazine,* pp. 24–25, 36–39.

Durner, J., Kroeker, M., Miller, C. & Reynolds, C. (1975). Divorce—another occupational hazard. *Police Chief, 62*(11), 48–53.

Duster, T. (1970). *The legislation of morality.* New York: Free Press.

Eberle, P., & Eberle, S. (1986). *The politics of child abuse.* Secaucus, NJ: Lyle Stuart.

Egger, S. (1986, November). Utility of case study approach to serial murder research. Paper presented to ASC, Atlanta, GA.

Egger, S. (1984). A working definition of serial murder. *Journal of Police Science and Administration, 12*(3), 348–357.

Ehrlich, I. (1975). The deterrent effect of capital punishment: A question of life and death. *American Economic Review, 65,* 397–417.

Eigenberg, H. (1990). The national crime survey and rape: The case of the missing question. *Justice Quarterly, 7,* 655–671.

Eisikovits, Z., & Baizerman, M. (1983). "Doin' time:" Violent youth in a juvenile facility and in an adult prison. *Journal of Offender Counseling Services and Rehabilitation, 6*(5).

Eitzen, D., & Zinn, M. (1997). *Social problems* (7th ed.). Needham Heights, MA: Allyn and Bacon.

Ellsworth, P. (1988). Unpleasant facts: The Supreme Court's response to empirical research on capital punishment. In K. Haas & J. Inciardi (Eds.), *Challenging capital punishment: Legal and social science approaches.* Newbury Park, CA: Sage Publications.

The elusive logic of drug sentences. (1995, March 30). *Chicago Tribune,* 20.

Ennett, S. (1994). How effective is drug abuse resistance education? A meta-analysis of Project DARE outcome evaluations. *American Journal of Public Health, 84,* 1394–1401.

Erickson, P. G. (1993). Prospects of harm reduction for psychostimulants. In N. Heather, A. Wodak, E. A. Nadelmann, & P. O'Hare (Eds.), *Psychoactive drugs and harm reduction* (pp. 184–210). London: Whurr.

Erickson, P. G., Adlaf, E. M., Murray, G. F., & Smart, R. G. (1987). *The steel drug: Cocaine in perspective.* Lexington, MA: Lexington.

Erickson, P., & Cheung, Y. (1992). Drug crime and legal control: Lessons from the Canadian experience. *Contemporary Drug Problems, 19,* 247–260.

Estrich, S. (1987). *Real rape.* Cambridge, MA: Harvard University Press.

Fagan, J. (1995). Separating the men from the boys. In J. C. Howell, B. Krisberg, J. D. Hawkins & J. J. Wilson (Eds.), *Serious, violent, and chronic juvenile offenders: A sourcebook.* Sage Publications.

Fagan, J., & Spelman, W. (1994, February 11). Market forces at work. *The New York Times*, p. A34.

Fagin, J., & Chin, K. L. (1989). Initiation into crack and cocaine: A tale of two epidemics. *Contemporary Drug Problems, 17,* 247–260.

Fass, P. S. (1997). *Kidnapped: Child abduction in American history*. Oxford: Oxford University Press.

A fatal obsession with the stars. (1989, July 31). *Time*, 43–44.

Fawkes, S. (1978). *Killing time*. London: Hamlyn.

FBI says Los Angeles gang has drug cartel ties. (1992, January 10). *The New York Times*, p. A34.

Federal Bureau of Investigation. (1994). *Crime in the United States—1993*. Washington, DC: U.S. Government Printing Office.

Federal Bureau of Investigation. (1999, October). [On-line]. Available: www.fbi.gov/pressrm/pressrel/ucr98.htm

Federal Document Clearing House. (1997, April 16). Remarks made by James Wootton before the Subcommittee on Youth Violence of the Senate Committee on the Judiciary.

Feimer, S., Pommerstein, F., & Wise, S. (1990). Marking time: Does race make a difference? A study of disparate sentencing in South Dakota. *Journal of Crime and Justice, 13*(1), 86–102.

Finckenauer, J., & Gavin, P. (1999). *Scared straight: The panacea phenomenon revisited*. Prospect Heights, IL: Waveland Press.

Finkelhor, D., Hotaling, G., & Sedlak, A. (1992). The abduction of children by strangers and non-family members: Estimating the incidence using multiple methods. *Journal of Interpersonal Violence, 7*(2), 226–243.

Fishman, M. (1998). Crime waves as ideology. In G. Potter & V. Kappeler (Eds.), *Constructing crime: Perspectives on making news and social problems* (pp. 53–69). Prospect Heights, IL: Waveland Press.

Fitzpatrick, P. (1992). *The mythology of modern law*. London: Routledge.

Flanagan, T., & McGarrell, E. (1997). *Sourcebook of criminal justice statistics—1996*. Albany, NY: The Hindelang Criminal Justice Research Center.

Florida Statute Annotated (1992). Sec. 784.048. St. Paul: West.

Florida stalking arrest. (1992, January 13). *USA Today*, p. 9A.

Foreman, J. (1980, March 16). Kidnapped! Parental child-snatching, a world problem. *Boston Globe*, p. B1.

Fox, J., & Levin, J. (1985). *Mass murder: America's growing menace*. New York: Plenum.

Frank, N. (1985). *Crimes against health and safety*. Albany, NY: Harrow and Heston.

Frankel, G. (1997, June 8). Federal agencies duplicate efforts, wage costly turf battles. *The Washington Post*, p. A1.

Franklin, D. (1988). Hooked, not hooked. *Health*, 39–52.

Freeh, L. (1994, April). Responding to violent crime in America. *FBI Law Enforcement Bulletin*. Washington, DC: U.S. Government Printing Office.

Freeman, M. (1994). Networks doubled crime coverage in '93 despite flat violence levels in U.S. society. *Mediaweek*, 4.

Fridell, L., & Pate, A. (1997). Death on patrol. In R. Dunham & G. Alpert (Eds.), *Critical issues in policing* (3rd ed., pp. 580–608). Prospect Heights, IL: Waveland Press.

Friedberg, M. (1992, July 12). Elderly man may be first charged under Florida stalking law. *Houston Chronicle*, p. 16.

Friedman, L. (1993). *Crime and punishment in American history*. New York: Basic Books.

Friedman, P. (1967). Suicide among police. In E. Scheidman (Ed.), *Essays in self-destruction*. New York: Science House.

Furman vs. Georgia, 408 U.S. 238 (1972).

Fyfe, J. (1979). Administrative interventions on police shooting discretion: An empirical examination. *Journal of Criminal Justice, 7*(4), 309–323.

Fyfe, J. (Ed.). (1982). In *Always prepared: Police off duty guns: Readings on police use of deadly force*. Washington, DC: Police Foundation.

Fyfe, J. (1991, March 17). Why won't crime stop? Because we cling to our favorite social myths. *The Washington Post*, p. D1.

Fyfe, J., & Blumberg, M. (1985). Response to Griswold: A more valid test of the justifiability of police actions. *American Journal of Police, 4*(2), 110–132.

Gaines, L., & Van Tubergen, N. (1989). Job stress in police work: An exploratory analysis into structural causes. *American Journal of Criminal Justice, 13*(3), 197–214.

Galiber, J. L. (1990). A bill to repeal criminal drug laws: Replacing prohibition with regulation. *Hofstra Law Review, 18,* 831–849.

Galliher, J., & Walker, A. (1977). The puzzle of the social origins of the Marijuana Tax Act of 1937. *Social Problems, 24,* 371–373.

Gallup News Service. (1998, November 24). As confidence in police rises, American fear of crime diminishes: Public's more positive feelings may reflect real decline in crime as well as own precautionary measures.

Gardiner, J. (1970). *The politics of corruption: Organized crime in an American city*. New York: Russell Sage Foundation.

Gardiner, J., & Lyman, T. (1978). *Decisions for sale: Corruption and reform in land-use and building regulations*. New York: Praeger.

Garner, J., & Clemmer, E. (1986). Danger to police in domestic disturbances—A new look. In R. Dunham and G. Alpert (Eds.), *Critical issues in policing: Contemporary readings* (2nd ed.). Prospect Heights, IL: Waveland Press.

Gavzer, B. (1995, August 13). Life behind bars. *Chicago Tribune*, Parade, pp. 4–7.

General Accounting Office. (1998, May). *Report to the honorable Charles Rangel, House of Representatives. Law enforcement: Information on drug-related police corruption*. Washington, DC: United States Government Printing Office.

General Social Survey, (1994).

Gerbner, G. (1972). Communication and social environment. *Scientific American, 227,* 153–160.

Gerbner, G. (1994, July). Television violence: The art of asking the wrong question. *Currents in Modern Thought*, 385–397.

Gibbs, N. (1994, November 14). Death and deceit. *Time*, 43–48.

Gideon v. Wainwright, 372 U.S. 335 (1963).

Gieringer, D. (1988). Marijuana, driving and accident safety. *Journal of Psychoactive Drugs, 20,* 1.

Glass, A. (1997, September 15). The young and the feckless. *The New Republic*.

Glassner, B. (1999). *The culture of fear: Why Americans are afraid of the wrong things*. New York: Basic Books.

Gleick, E. (1995, June 19). Rich justice, poor justice. *Time*, 41.

Godfrey, M. J. & Schiraldi, V. (1995). *How have homicide rates been affected by California's death penalty?* Report from the Center on Juvenile & Criminal Justice.

Godwin, J. (1978). *Murder USA*. New York: Ballantine.

Goldstein, P., Brownstein, H., Ryan, P., & Bellucci, P. (1997). Crack and homicide in New York City: A case study in the epidemiology of violence. In C. Reinarman &

H. Levine (Eds.), *Crack in America: Demon drugs and social justice* (pp. 113–130). Berkeley: University of California Press.

Goode, E. (1994, July 25). The selling of reality. *U.S. News & World Report.*

Goode, E. (1997) *Between politics and reason: The drug legalization debate.* New York: St. Martin's Press.

Goode, E. (1999). *Drugs in American society* (5th ed.). New York: Alfred A. Knopf.

Goode, E., & Ben-Yehuda, N. (1994). *Moral panics: The social construction of deviance.* Cambridge, MA: Blackwell.

Goodman, E. (1995, July 18). Our problem with strangers. *Chicago Tribune,* p. 11.

Gordon, D. (1990). *The justice juggernaut.* New Brunswick, NJ: Rutgers University Press.

Gordon, J. (1992, September). *America's Most Wanted* takes credit for a killing. *EXTRA!,* pp. 1–2.

Gottfredson, D., Neithercutt, M., Nuffield, J., & O'Leary, V. (1973). Four thousand lifetimes: A study of time served and parole outcomes. *Law and Contemporary Problems, 41.*

Gover, A., Styve, G., & MacKenzie, D. (1999). Evaluating correctional boot camp programs: Issues and concerns. In K. Haas & G. Alpert (Eds.), *The dilemmas of corrections* (4th ed., pp. 384–402). Prospect Heights, IL: Waveland Press.

Graber, D. (1980). *Crime news and the public.* New York: Praeger.

Graves, W. (1956). A doctor looks at capital punishment. *Medical Arts and Sciences, Journal of the Loma Linda University School of Medicine, 10*(4), 137–141.

Graysmith, R. (1987). *Zodiac.* New York: Berkley.

Green, M., Monroe, B., & Wasserstein, B. (1972). *The closed enterprise system: Ralph Nader's study group report on anti-trust enforcement.* New York: Grossman.

Greene, J., & Klockars, C. (1991). What police do. In C. Klockars & S. Mastrofski (Eds.), *Thinking about police: Contemporary readings* (2nd ed.). New York: McGraw-Hill.

Greenfield, L. (1985). Examining recidivism. *Bureau of Justice Statistics Special Report.* Washington, DC: U.S. Government Printing Office.

Greenfield, L. (1996, March 3). Child victimizers: Violent offenders and their victims. Bureau of Justice Statistics.

Gregg v. Georgia, 428 U.S. 158 (1976).

Grinspoon, L., & Bakalar, J. (1994). The war on drugs—A peace proposal. *New England Journal of Medicine, 330,* 357.

Gropper, B. (1985). Probing the links between drugs and crime. National Institute of Justice: *Research in Brief.* Washington, DC: U.S. Government Printing Office.

Gross, S. & Mauro, R. (1989). *Death and discrimination: Racial disparities in capital sentencing.* Boston, MA: Northeastern University Press.

Gusfield, J. (1963). *Symbolic crusade: Status politics and the American temperance movement.* Urbana, IL: University of Illinois Press.

Gusfield, J. (1981). *The culture of public problems.* Chicago: University of Chicago Press.

Guy, R. (1993). The nature and constitutionality of stalking laws. *Vanderbilt Law Review, 46,* 991.

Hagan, F. (1998). *Introduction to criminology* (4th ed.). Chicago: Nelson-Hall.

Hagan, J., Nagel, I., & Albonetti, C. (1980, September). The differential sentencing of white-collar offenders in ten federal district courts. *American Sociological Review, 45,* 802–820.

Haller, M. (1987, November). Business partnerships in the coordination of illegal enterprise. Paper presented at the annual meetings of the American Society of Criminology, Montreal.

Hallin, D. (1990). Whatever happened to the news? *Media & Values, 50*, 2–4.
Hallman, T. (1992, March 9). Stalker robs girl of innocence. *Oregonian*, p. A1.
Halloween Candy Hotline. (1991, September). *Police Chief*, 70.
Heckathorn, D. (1985). Why punishment does not deter. In A. Blumberg & E. Niederhoffer (Eds.), *The ambivalent force: Perspectives on the police* (3rd ed.). New York: Holt, Rinehart and Winston.
Heilbroner, R. (1973). *In the name of profit: Profiles in corporate irresponsibility*. New York: Warner Paperback Library.
Hellman, D. (1980). *The economics of crime*. New York: St. Martin's Press.
Hernandez, J. (1989). *The Custer syndrome*. Salem, WI: Sheffield Publishing.
Hickey, E. (1986, November). The etiology of victimization in serial murder. Paper presented to ASC, Atlanta, GA.
Higham, C. (1982). *Trading with the enemy: An exposé of the Nazi-American money plot, 1933–1949*. New York: Delacourte Press.
Hills, S. (1971). *Crime, power, and morality*. Scranton, PA: Chandler.
Hills, S. (Ed.). (1987). *Corporate violence*. Totowa, NJ: Rowman and Littlefield.
Hindelang, M., Gottfredson, M., Dunn, C., & Parisi, N. (1977). *Sourcebook of criminal justice statistics–1976*. Albany, NY: Criminal Justice Research Center.
Hirschel, J., Dean, C., & Lumb, R. (1994). The relative contribution of domestic violence to assault and injury of police officers. *Justice Quarterly, 11*(1), 99–117.
Hitz, D. (1973). Drunken sailors and others: Drinking problem in specific occupations. *Quarterly Journal of Studies on Alcohol, 34*, 496–505.
Holden, R. (1991, March 6). *Mortal danger in law enforcement: A statistical comparison of police mortality with those of other occupations*. Paper presented at the annual meeeting of the Academy of Criminal Justice Sciences, Nashville, TN.
Holmes, R. (1993). Stalking in America: Types and methods of criminal stalkers. *Journal of Contemporary Criminal Justice, 9*(4), 317–319.
Horowitz, R., & Pottieger, A. (1991). Gender bias in juvenile justice handling of seriously crime-involved youth. *Journal of Research in Crime and Delinquency, 28*, 75–100.
Hoshen, J., Sennett, J., & Winkler, M. (1995). Keeping tabs on criminals. *IEEE Spectrum, 21*(2), 26–32.
Hubbard, R., Marsden, M., Rachal, J., Harwood, H., Cavanaugh, E., & Ginsburg, H. (1989). *Drug abuse treatment, a national survey of effectiveness*. Washington, DC: NIDA.
Hunter, R., & Wood, R. (1994). Impact of felony sanctions: An analysis of weaponless assaults upon police. *American Journal of Police, 13*(1), 65–89.
Hynds, P. (1990). Balance bias with critical questions. *Media & Values, 50*, 5–7.
Ianni, F. (1972). *A family business: Kinship and social control in organized crime*. New York: Russell Sage Foundation.
Ianni, F. (1974). *Black mafia: Ethnic succession in organized crime*. New York: Simon and Schuster.
Inciardi, J. (1992). *The war on drugs II: Heroin, cocaine, crime, and public policy*. Palo Alto, CA: Mayfield.
Injustice will be done: Women drug couriers and the Rockefeller drug laws. (1992, February). New York: Correctional Association of New York.
Innes, C. (1986, December). *Population density in state prisons*. Washington, DC: Bureau of Justice Statistics.
Institute of Medicine (1982). *Marijuana and health*. Washington, DC: National Academy of Sciences.

Irwin, J. (1980). *Prisons in turmoil*. Boston: Little, Brown.

Irwin, J., & Austin, J. (1997). *It's about time: America's imprisonment binge* (2nd ed.). Belmont, CA: Wadsworth.

Isaacson, W., & Gorey, H. (1981, September 21). Let the buyer beware: Consumer advocates retrench for hard times. *Time*, 22–23.

Jackson, P., & Carroll, L. (1981). Race and the war on crime: The sociopolitical determinants of municipal police expenditures in 90 non-southern U.S. cities. *American Sociological Review, 46*, 290–305.

Jehl, D. (1994, February 10). Clinton to use drug plan to fight crime. *The New York Times*, p. D20.

Jenkins, P. (1994). *Using murder: The social construction of serial homicide*. London: Aldine de Gruyter.

Jenkins, P. (1994). *Using murder*. New York: Aldine de Gruyter.

Jenkins, P. (1998). *Moral panic*. New Haven: Yale University Press.

Jenkins, P., & Katkin, D. (1987, November). Benefit of law. Paper presented to ASC, Montreal.

Jenkins, P., & Katkin, D. (1988). Protecting victims of child sexual abuse: A case for caution. *Prison Journal, 58*(2), 25–35.

Jensen, E. L. & Metsger, L. K. (1994). A test of the deterrent effect of legislative waiver on violent juvenile crime. *Crime and Delinquency, 40*(1), 96–104.

Jensen, G., & Karpos, M. (1993). Managing rape: Exploratory research on the behavior of rape statistics. *Criminology, 31*, 363–385.

Johanson, C. E., & Fischman, M. W. (1989). The pharmacology of cocaine related to its abuse. *Pharmacology Reviews, 41*, 3–52.

Johnson, J., & Secret, P. (1990). Race and juvenile court decision making revisited. *Criminal Justice Policy Review, 4*(2), 159–187.

Johnson, L., Bachman, J., & O'Malley, P. (1996). *National survey results from the Monitoring the Future Study, Vol. 1*. Washington, DC: U.S. Government Printing Office.

Johnson, R. (1996). *Hard time: Understanding and reforming the prison* (2nd ed.). Pacific Grove, CA: Brooks/Cole.

Johnson, R., & Toch, H. (1982). *The pains of imprisonment*. Prospect Heights, IL: Waveland Press.

Josephson, R. & Reiser, M. (1990). Officer suicide in the Los Angeles Police Department: A twelve-year follow-up. *Journal of Police Science and Administration, 17*(3), 227–229.

Joyce, F, (1983, November 4). Two suspects' stories of killings culled. *The New York Times*.

Judicial Conference of the United States (1998). *Federal death penalty cases: Recommendations concerning the cost and quality of defense representation*. Washington, DC: U.S. Government Printing Office.

Kagan, D. (1984). Serial murderers. *OMNI*.

Kahler, K. (1986, May 25). The mob is winning: Organized crime in the United States is richer than ever. *Gannett Westchester Newspapers*, pp. B1, B6.

Kantrowitz, B. (1997, Spring/Summer Special Issue). Off to a good start: Why the first three years are so crucial to a child's development. *Newsweek*, 8.

Kantrowitz, B. (1999, August 23). The new age of anxiety. *Newsweek, 134*, 39–40.

Kaplan, J. (1983). *The hardest drug: Heroin and public policy*. Chicago: University of Chicago Press.

Kappeler, V., Sluder, R., & Alpert, G. (1998). *Forces of deviance: Understanding the dark side of policing* (2nd ed.). Prospect Heights, IL: Waveland Press.

Kappeler, V., & Vaughn, J. (1988). The myth and fear of child abduction: Defining the problem and solutions. *The Justice Professional, 3*(1), 56–69.

Karmen, A. (1978). How much heat? How much light: Coverage of New York City's blackout and looting in the print media. In C. Winick (Ed.), *Deviance and mass media*. Beverly Hills: Sage Publications.

Karmen, A. (1995). Women victims of crime: Introduction. In B. Price & N. Sokoloff (Eds.), *The criminal justice system and women: Offenders, victims, and workers* (pp. 181–196). New York: McGraw-Hill.

Keil, T., & Vito, G. (1992). Effects of the *Furman* and *Gregg* decisions on black-white execution ratios in the South. *Journal of Criminal Justice, 20*(3), 217–226.

Kelling, G., Pate, T., Dieckman, D., & Brown, C. (1974). *The Kansas City preventive patrol experiment: A summary report.* Washington, DC: Police Foundation.

Kelly, K. (1992, June 29). How did Sears blow this gasket? Some say the retailer's push for profits spurred its auto-repair woes. *Business Week,* 38.

Keyes, D. (1986). *Unveiling Claudia.* New York: Bantam.

Kidder, T. (1974). *The road to Yuba City.* New York: Doubleday.

Kidnapping and abuse: Rep. Hyde seeks life in prison or mandatory death sentence for crimes against children. (1985, July 1). *Juvenile Justice Digest,* 4.

Kiernan, L. (1999, August 30). Doors shut on one theory as youth prison opens. *Chicago Tribune,* p. 1, 9

Klausner, L. (1981). *Son of Sam.* New York: McGraw-Hill.

Kleber, H. (1994). Our current approach to drug abuse: Progress, problems, proposals. *New England Journal of Medicine, 330,* 361.

Klofas, J. (1992). The effects of incarceration. In S. Stojkovic & R. Lovell (Eds.), *Corrections: An introduction* (pp. 295–327). Cincinnati: Anderson.

Kolarik, G. (1992, November). Stalking laws proliferate. *American Bar Association Journal,* 35–36.

Kolko, G. (1963). *The triumph of conservatism.* New York: Free Press.

Konstantin, D. (1984). Homicides of American law enforcement officers, 1978–1980. *Justice Quarterly, 1*(1), 29–45.

Kramer, M. (1994, March 14). Frying them isn't the answer. *Time,* 32.

Kraska, P. (1990). The unmentionable alternative: The need for, and the argument against, the decriminalization of drug laws. In R. Weisheit (Ed.), *Drugs, crime and the criminal justice system*. Cincinnati, OH: Anderson.

Kraska, P., & Kappeler, V. (1988). A theoretical and descriptive study of police on duty drug use. *American Journal of Police, 8*(1), 1–36.

Kraska, P., & Kappeler, V. (1999). Militarizing American police: The rise and normalization of paramilitary units. In V. Kappeler, (Ed.), *The police and society* (2nd ed., pp. 463–479). Prospect Heights, IL: Waveland Press.

Kroes, W. (1976). *Society's victim, the policeman: An analysis of job stress in policing.* Springfield, IL: Charles C Thomas.

Kuczka, S. (1999, September 23). Abduction tape offers parents tips on reaction. *Chicago Tribune,* Sec. 2, p. 3.

Kuehnle, J., Mendelson, J. H., Davis, K. R., & New, P. F. J. (1977). Computed topographic examination of heavy marijuana smokers. *Journal of the American Medical Association, 237,* 1231–1232.

Labovitz, S., & Hagedorn, R. (1971). An analysis of job suicide rates among occupational categories. *Sociological Inquiry, 41*(1).

Lacayo, R. (1994, February 7). Lock 'em up. *Time,* 51–53.

Ladinsky, J. (1984). The impact of social background of lawyers in legal practice and the law. In Bonsignore et al., (Eds.), *Before the law*. Boston, MA: Houghton-Mifflin.

LaFree, G. (1989). *Rape and criminal justice: The social construction of sexual assault.* Belmont, CA: Wadsworth.

Lang, K., & Lang, G. (1969). *Television and politics.* Chicago: Quadrangle Books.

Langan, P., & Harlow, C. (1994, June). Child rape victims, 1992. Bureau of Justice Statistics.

Leavitt, P. (1993, April 28). Tennis coach was stalking suspect. *USA Today*, p. 3A.

Lehtinen, M. (1977). The voice of life: An argument for the death penalty. *Crime & Delinquency, 23,* 237–252.

Lernoux, P. (1984). *In banks we trust.* New York: Doubleday.

Lester, D. (1983). Stress in police officers: An American perspective. *The Police Journal, 56*(2), 184–193.

Letwin, M. (1994, April 18). Sentencing Angela Thompson. *New York Law Journal,* 2.

Levinson, R. (1982). Try softer. In R. Johnson & H. Toch (Eds.), *The pains of imprisonment* (pp. 241–255). Prospect Heights, IL: Waveland Press.

Leyton, E. (1986). *Compulsive killers.* New York University Press.

Lichtenberger, J. (1968). *Divorce: A study in social causation.* New York: AMS Press.

Lichter, R., & Lichter, L. (1983). *Prime time crime: Criminals and law enforcement in TV entertainment.* Washington, DC: Center for Media and Public Affairs.

Lichter, R., & Lichter, L. (Eds.). (1994). *Media monitor: 1993—the year in review.* VIII, 1. Washington DC: Center for Media and Public Affairs.

Lindeman, L. (1995, January 22). Between bars: Wondering how the war on crime is going? *Chicago Tribune*, pp. 19–22.

Lindsey, R. (1984, January 22). Officials cite a rise in killers who roam US for victims. *The New York Times.*

Liska, A., & Baccaglini, W. (1990). Feeling safe by comparison: Crime in the newspapers. *Social Problems, 37,* 360–374.

Liska, A., & Chamlin, M. (1984). Social structure and crime control among Mmacrosocial units. *American Journal of Sociology, 98,* 383–395.

Livingston, J. (1996). *Crime and criminology*, (2nd ed.). Englewood Cliffs, NJ: Prentice-Hall.

Lock 'em up, throw away the future. (1995, June 21). *Chicago Tribune*, p. 20.

Lockwood, D. (1980). *Prison sexual violence.* New York: Elsevier Books.

Lockwood, D. (1994). Issues in prison sexual violence. In M. Braswell, S. Dillingham, & R. Montgomery, Jr. (Eds.), *Prison violence in America* (2nd ed., pp. 97–102). Cincinnati: Anderson.

Lofquist, L., & Davis, R. (1969). *Adjustment of work.* New York: Appleton-Century-Crofts.

Long v. State, 931 S.W.2d 285 (Tex. 1996).

Lotke, E. (1997). Youth homicide: Keeping perspective on how many children kill. *Valparaiso Law Review, 31,* 2.

Lotke, E. (1998, April). The prison-industrial complex. *Multinational Monitor,* 4.

Lowenstein, J. (1995, March 12). How free is speech in cyberspace? *Chicago Tribune*, p. 1.

Luksetich, W., & White, M. (1982). *Crime and public policy: An economic approach.* Boston: Little, Brown.

Lunde, D. (1976). *Murder and madness.* New York: W.W. Norton.

Lunde, D., & Morgan, J. (1980). *The die song.* New York: W.W. Norton.

Lyman, M., & Potter, G. (1998). *Drugs in society*, (3rd ed.). Cincinnati, OH: Anderson.

Lyman, M., & Potter, G. (2000). *Organized crime* (2nd ed.). Engelwood Cliffs, NJ: Prentice-Hall.

Lynch, J. (1988). A comparison of prison use in England, Canada, West Germany, and the United States: A limited test of the punitive hypothesis. *Journal of Criminal Law and Criminology, 79*, 1.

Mastrofski, S. (1983). *The police and non-crime services.* In G. Whitaker & C. Phillips (Eds.), *Evaluating performance of criminal justice agencies.* Beverly Hills: Sage.

Maguire, K., & Flanagan, T. (1997). *Sourcebook of criminal justice statistics—1996.* Albany, NY: The Hindelang Criminal Justice Research Center.

Maguire, K., & Pastore, A. (Eds.). (1994). *Sourcebook of criminal justice statistics—1993.* Washington, DC: Bureau of Justice Statistics.

Maguire, K., & Pastore, A. (Eds.). (1995). *Sourcebook of criminal justice statistics—1994.* Washington, D.C. Bureau of Justice Statistics.

Males, M. A. (1998, April 20). Five myths and why adults believe they are true. *The New York Times.*

Mallory, T., & Mays, G. (1984). The police stress hypothesis: A critical evaluation. *Criminal Justice and Behavior, 11*(2), 197–224.

Mannheim, K. (1936). *Ideology and utopia.* New York: Harcourt, Brace and World.

Marenin, O. (1991, September/October). Making a tough job tougher: The legacy of conservatism. *ACJS Today, 10*(2), 1, 17, 19.

Marquart, J., & Sorensen, J. (1988). Institutional and postrelease behavior of *Furman*-commuted inmates in Texas. *Criminology, 26*, 677–693.

Marsh, H. (1991). A comparative analysis of crime coverage in newspapers in the United States and other countries from 1960–1989: A review of the literature. *Journal of Criminal Justice, 19*(4), 67–79.

Marshall, J. (1991). CIA assets and the rise of the Guadalajara connection. *Crime, Law and Social Change, 16*(1), 85–96.

Martin, M., Khoury, M., Cordero, J., & Waters, G. (1992). Trends in rates of multiple vascular disruption defects, Atlanta 1968–1989: Is there evidence of a cocaine teratogenic epidemic? *Teratology, 45*, 647–653.

Marx, G. (1995a, April 6). Captive readers. *Chicago Tribune*, Sec. 5, pp. 1–2.

Marx, G. (1995b, May 12). War zone. *Chicago Tribune*, Sec. 5, p. 2.

Mauer, M. (1992). *Americans behind bars: One year later* (February). Washington, DC: The Sentencing Project.

Mauer, M. (1994). *Americans behind bars: The international use of incarceration, 1992–1993.* Washington, DC: The Sentencing Project.

Mauer, M. (1997). *Americans behind bars: U.S. and international use of incarceration.* Washington, DC: The Sentencing Project.

Mauer, M. (1999). "Lock 'em up and throw away the key": African-American males and the criminal justice system. In K. Haas & G. Alpert (Eds.), *The dilemmas of corrections* (4th ed., pp. 30–43). Prospect Heights, IL: Waveland Press.

Mauer, M., & Huling, T. (1995). *Young black Americans and the criminal justice system: Five years later.* Washington, DC: The Sentencing Project.

Maxwell v. City of Indianapolis, 998 F.2d 431 (7th Cir. 1993).

Mayer, A., & Bishop, J. (1976, June 14). Antitrust: Snap, crackle and pop. *Newsweek*, 14.

McCaffrey, B. (1998, July 24). Statement of ONDCP director Barry McCaffrey on Mayor Giuliani's recent comments on methadone therapy. Washington, DC: ONDCP.

McCaghy, C., Capron, T., & Jamieson, J. D. (2000). *Deviant behavior* (5th ed.). Boston: Allyn and Bacon.

McCaghy, C., & Cernkovich, S. (1987). *Crime in American society*. New York: Macmillan.

McCarthy, B. (1991). Social structure, crime, and social control: An examination of factors influencing rates and probabilities of arrest. *Journal of Criminal Justice, 19,* 19–29.

McClelland, D. (1961). *The achieving society*. New York: Free Press.

McCormick, A., Jr. (1977). Rule enforcement and moral indignation: Some observations on the effects of criminal antitrust convictions upon societal reaction process. *Social Problems, 25,* 30–39.

McGlothlin, W., Anglin, M., & Wilson, B. (1978, November). Narcotic addiction and crime. *Criminology, 16,* 293–315.

Mcleary, R., Nienstedt, B., & Erven, J. (1982). Uniform crime reports as organizational outcomes: Three time series quasi-experiments. *Social Problems, 29,* 361–372.

Medalia, N., & Larsen, O. (1958). Diffusion and belief in a collective delusion: The Seattle windshield pitting epidemic. *American Sociological Review, 23,* 180–186.

Meddis, S. (1991, July 30). U.S. role in bank probe criticized. *USA Today*, p. 9A.

Meierhoffer, B. (1992). *The general effect of mandatory minimum prison terms: A longitudinal study of federal sentences imposed*. Washington, DC: Federal Judicial Center.

Merton, R. (1949). *Social theory and social structure*. Glencoe, IL: The Free Press.

Messerschmidt, J. (1986). *Capitalism, patriarchy, and crime: Toward a socialist feminist criminology*. Totowa, NJ: Rowman and Littlefield.

Messner, S., & Rosenfeld, R. (1997). *Crime and the American dream* (2nd ed.). Belmont, CA: Wadsworth.

Miami Herald. July 10, 1988.

Michaud, S. (1986, October 26). The FBI's new psyche squad. *New York Times Magazine*.

Michaud, S., & Aynesworth, H. (1983). *The only living witness*. New York: Simon and Schuster.

Mikuirya, T. H., & Aldrich, M. (1988). Cannabis 1988, old drug, new dangers, the potency question. *Journal of Psychoactive Drugs, 20,* 1.

Mills, C. (1952). A diagnosis of moral uneasiness. In I. Horowitz (Ed.), *Power, politics and people* (pp. 330–339). New York: Ballantine.

Mills, J. (1986). *The underground empire: Where crime and governments embrace*. New York: Doubleday.

Mills, S. (1999, May 2). On the record: Interview with Frank Zimring. *Chicago Tribune,* Sec. 2, p. 3.

Mishan, E. (1990). Narcotics: The problem and the solution. *Political Quarterly, 61,* 441–458.

Missing Children's Assistance Act of 1983, 28 U.S.C. 534.

Missing Children's Assistance Act of 1984, 42 U.S.C. 5772.

Moldea, J. (1986). *Dark victory: Ronald Reagan, MCA, and the mob*. New York: Viking.

Morris, N., & Hawkins, G. (1970). *The honest politician's guide to crime control*. Chicago: University of Chicago Press.

Mugford, S., & Cohen, P. (1989). *Drug use, social relations and commodity consumption: A study of recreational users in Sydney, Canberra and Melbourne*. Canberra, Australia: Research into Drug Abuse Advisory Committee, National Campaign Against Drug Abusers.

Muir, W., Jr. (1977). *Police: Streetcorner politicians*. Chicago: University of Chicago Press.

Munger, M. (1997, Summer). The drug threat: Getting priorities straight. *Parameters*.

Murray, J. (1986). Marijuana's effects on human cognitive functions, psychomotor functions, and personality. *Journal of General Psychology, 113*(1), 23–55.

Musto, D. (1973). *The American disease: Origins of narcotics control.* New Haven, CT: Yale University Press.

Muwakkil, S. (1999, August 30). The problem with anti-drug fairy tales. *Chicago Tribune*, p. 13.

Nacci, P. & Kane, T. (1983, December). The incidence of sex and sexual aggression in federal prisons. *Federal Probation, 47*(4), 31–36.

Nadelmann, E. (1988, October 2). Isn't it time to legalize drugs? *The Boston Sunday Globe*, p. A23.

Nadelmann, E. (1989, September). Drug prohibition in the United States: Costs, consequences, and alternatives. *Science, 245*, 939–947.

Nadelmann, E. (1999, October 10). New approach to drugs that's grounded not in ignorance or fear but common sense. *Chicago Tribune*, p. 23.

Nader, R. (1985, May 19). America's crime without criminals. *The New York Times*, p. F3.

Nader, R., Green, M., & Seligman, J. (1976). *Taming the giant corporation.* New York: Norton.

Nakell, B. (1982). The cost of the death penalty. In H. Bedau (Ed.), *The death penalty in America* (3rd ed.). Oxford: Oxford University Press.

National Center for Institutions and Alternatives. (1998). *A prison term punishes only the prisoner.* Washington, DC: Author.

National Center for Institutions and Alternatives. (1999). *Myths of the month* [On-line]. Available: www.ncianet.org

National Center for Missing and Exploited Children. (1999, September). Kathy Mattea & Michael McDonald duet focuses attention on the search for missing children [On-line]. Available: http://missingkids.com/html/fl_vol36.html

National Center on Addiction and Substance Abuse at Columbia University. (1998, January 8). *Behind bars: Substance abuse and America's prison population.* New York: Author.

National Criminal Justice Association. (1993). *Project to develop a model anti-stalking code for states.* Washington, DC: National Institute of Justice.

National Institute on Drug Abuse. (1987). *Data from the 1985 National Household Survey on drug abuse.* Rockville, MD: Author.

National Institute on Drug Abuse. (1991). *National household survey on drug abuse: Population estimates 1990* (DHHS Publication Number ADM 91-1732). Washington, DC: U.S. Government Printing Office.

National Institute on Drug Abuse. (1992). *Annual medical examiner data 1991, data from the drug abuse warning network.* NIDA Statistical Series, Series I, Number 11-B, 50.

National Institute on Drug Abuse and National Institute on Alcohol Abuse and Alcoholism. (1998). *The economic costs of alcohol and drug abuse in the United States, 1992.* Washington, DC: U.S. Department of Health and Human Services.

National missing children's day raises awareness. (1998). *Juvenile Justice Journal, 5*, 1.

NCAVC. (1986). The National Center for the Analysis of Violent Crime. Behavioral Science Services, FBI Academy, Quantico, VA (revised 4/7/86).

Nehra v. Uhlar, 43 N.Y. 2d 242 (1977).

Nelli, H. (1976). *The business of crime.* New York: Oxford University Press.

Nettier, G. (1982). *Killing one another.* Cincinnati: Anderson.

Neuspiel, D. (1996). Racism and perinatal addiction. *Ethnicity and Disease, 6*, 47–55.

Niederhoffer, A., & Niederhoffer, E. (1978). *The police family: From station house to ranch house*. Lexington, MA: Lexington Books.

Norvell, N., Belles, D., & Hills, H. (1988, March). Perceived stress levels and physical symptoms in supervisor law enforcement personnel. *Journal of Police Science and Administration, 16*, 75–79.

NY Daily News, July 28, 1998.

O'Brien, D. (1985). *Two of a kind*. New York: New American Library.

Office of National Drug Control Policy. (1998). *Drug facts*. Washington, DC: Office of National Drug Control Policy Website.

OJJDP (1997, March 20). Press release. *All 50 states show progress in protecting children from abduction and exploitation*.

Olsen, J. (1974). *The man with the candy*. New York: Simon and Schuster.

Olsen, J. (1983). *Son: A psychopath and his victims*. New York: Dell.

O'Neill, M., & Bloom, C. (1972). The field officer: Is he really fighting crime? *Police Chief, 39*, 30–32.

Orcutt, J., & Turner, J. B. (1993). Shocking numbers and graphic accounts: Quantified images of drug problems in the print media. *Social Problems, 40*(2), 190–205.

Organized Crime Digest. (1987, March 25).

OSAP. (1991). Promoting health development through school-based prevention: New approaches. In United States Department of Health and Human Services, *Preventing adolescent drug use: From theory to practice*, OSAP Prevention Monograph-8, DHHS Pub. No. (ADM) 91–1725.

Ostrowski, J. (1989, May 25). *Thinking about drug legalization*. Cato Institute Policy Analysis No. 121.

Ostrowski, J. (1990). The moral and practical case for drug legalization. *Hofstra Law Review, 18*, 607–650.

Pace, D., & Styles, J. (1975). *Organized crime: Concepts and control*. Englewood Cliffs, NJ: Prentice-Hall.

Page, C. (1995, August 2). The murky line between who gets life or death. *Chicago Tribune*, p. 15.

Page, C. (1999, January 13). Hasta la vista, baby. *Chicago Tribune*, p. 17.

Pagelow, M. (1984). *Family violence*. New York: Praeger.

Passell, P., & Taylor, J. (1976). The deterrent controversy: A reconsideration of the time series evidence. In H. Bedau & C. Pierce (Eds.), *Capital punishment in the United States*. New York: AMS Press.

Paternoster, R. (1991). *Capital punishment in America*. New York: Lexington Books.

Paulette, T. (1994, May 12). Making crime pay: Triangle of interests creates infrastructure to fight lawlessness. *The Wall Street Journal*, p. A1

Pearce, F. (1976). *Crimes of the powerful*. London: Pluto Press.

Pennsylvania Crime Commission. (1986). *Report*. Conshohocken: Commonwealth of Pennsylvania.

Petersilia, J. (1983). *Racial disparities in the criminal justice system*. Santa Monica, CA: The Rand Corporation.

Platt, A., & Pollack, R. (1975). Changing lawyers: The careers of public defenders. *Issues in Criminology, 9*.

Polan, M., Dombrowski, M., Ager, J., & Sokol, R. (1993). Punishing pregnant drug users: Enhancing the flight from care. *Drug and Alcohol Dependence, 31*, 199–203.

Potter, G. (1986). *The porn merchants*. Dubuque, IA: Kendall Hunt.

Potter, G. (1994). *Criminal organizations: Vice, racketeering, and politics in an American city*. Prospect Heights, IL: Waveland Press.

Potter, G., Gaines, L., & Holbrook, B. (1990). Blowing smoke: Marijuana eradication in Kentucky. *American Journal of Police, 9*.

Potter, G., & Jenkins, P. (1985). *The city and the syndicate: Organizing crime in Philadelphia*. Lexington, MA: Ginn Press.

Potter, G. W., & Kappeler, V. E. (1998). *Constructing crime: Perspectives on making news and social problems*. Prospect Heights, IL: Waveland Press.

Potter, K. (1998, October 19). Fletcher ad lacks sensitivity for rape victims. *Lexington Herald-Leader*.

Powell, D. (1990). Study of police discretion in six southern cities. *Journal of Police Science and Administration, 17*(1), 1–7.

President's Commission on Organized Crime. (1984). *The impact: Organized crime today*. Washington, DC: U.S. Government Printing Office.

Puente, D. (1992, January 21). Legislators tackling the terror of stalking. *USA Today*, p. 9A.

Quinn, J. (1999). *Corrections: A concise introduction*. Prospect Heights, IL: Waveland Press.

Quinney, R. (1970). *The social reality of crime*. Boston: Little, Brown.

Radelet, M., & Pierce, G. (1991). Choosing those who will die: Race and the death penalty in Florida. *Florida Law Review, 43*(1), 1034.

Rand Corporation. (1993). *The effect of marijuana decriminalization on hospital emergency room episodes: 1975–1978*. Santa Monica, CA: Author.

The random killers (1984, November 26). *Newsweek*.

Rasmussen, D., & Benson, B. (1994). *The economic anatomy of a drug war*. Lanham, MD: Rowman & Littlefield Publishers, Inc.

Raub, R. (1988). Death of police officers after retirement. *American Journal of Police, 7*(1), 91–102.

Ray, O. (1999). *Drugs, society and human behavior* (8th ed.). New York: McGraw-Hill.

Reddington, F. P., & Sapp, A. D. (1997). Juveniles in adult prisons: Problems and prospects. *Journal of Crime and Justice, 20*(2).

Redfield, R. (1952). The primitive world view. *Proceedings of the American Philosophical Society, 96*, 30–36.

Regnery, A. (1986). A federal perspective on juvenile justice reform. *Crime and Delinquency, 32*, 39–51.

Reiman, J. (1998). *The rich get richer and the poor get prison* (5th ed.). Boston: Allyn and Bacon.

Reinarmann, C. (1996). The social construction of drug scares. In E. Goode (Ed.), *Social deviance*. Boston: Allyn and Bacon.

Reinarmann, C., & Levine, H. (1989). Crack in context: Politics and media in the making of a drug scare. *Contemporary Drug Problems, 16*, 535–577.

Reiss, A., Jr. (1971). *The police and the public*. New Haven: Yale University Press.

Reiss, A., & Roth, J. (Eds.). (1993). *Understanding and preventing violence*. Washington, DC: National Academy Press.

Rentschler, W. (1994, November 29). The death penalty a pivotal issue. *Chicago Tribune*, p. 19.

Ressler, R., & Schachtman, T. (1992). *Whoever fights monsters*. New York: St. Martin's.

Reuter, P. (1983). *Disorganized crime*. Cambridge: MIT Press.

Reuter, P., MacCoun, R., & Murphy, P. (1990). *Money from crime: A study of the economics of drug dealing in Washington, D.C.* Santa Monica, CA: The Rand Corporation.

Reuter, P., Rubinstein, J., & Wynn, S. (1983). *Racketeering in legitimate industries: Two case studies*. Washington, DC: National Institute of Justice.

Rosenbaum, D. (1998). *Assessing the effects of school-based drug education: A six year multilevel analysis of Project DARE*. Chicago: University of Illinois.

Rosenbaum, M., Washburn, A., Knight, K., Kelley, M., & Irwin, J. (1996). Treatment as harm reduction, defunding as harm maximization: The case of methadone maintenance. *Journal of Psychoative Drugs, 28,* 241–249.

Rosenthal, E. (1990, June 20). U.S. is by far the homicide capital of the industrialized nations. *The New York Times*.

Rowan, R. (1986, November 10). The 50 biggest mafia bosses. *Fortune*, 24–38.

Rule, A. (1980). *The stranger beside me*. New York: NAL.

Ryan, W. (1976). *Blaming the victim*. New York: Vintage Books.

Rydell, C., & Everingham, S. (1994). *Controlling cocaine*. Santa Monica, CA: Drug Policy Research Center, RAND.

Salekin, R. T., & Aexander, B. K. (1991). Cocaine and crime. In A. S. Trebach & K. B. Zeese (Eds.), *New frontiers in drug policy* (pp. 105–111). Washington, DC: Drug Policy Foundation.

Salerno, R., & Tompkins, J. (1969). *The crime confederation*. Garden City, NY: Doubleday.

Schiraldi, V., & Keppelhoff, M. (1997, June 5). As juvenile crime drops, experts backpedal and public policy pays the price. *Star Tribune,* p. 24A.

Schiraldi, V., & Soler, M. (1998). The will of the people? The public's opinion of the violent and repeat juvenile offender act of 1997. *Crime and Delinquency, 44*(4), 590–601.

Schmaltz, J. (1988, October 12). Banks indicted by U.S. for money laundering case. *The New York Times*, p. A56.

Schmich, M. (1999, May 2). Littleton lessons reflect a century of good and bad. *Chicago Tribune*, Sec. 4, p. 1.

Schneider, A., & Flaherty, M. (1991, August 11). Presumed guilty: The law's victims in the war on drugs. *The Pittsburgh Press.*

Schodolski, V. (1999, September 7). Sex-offender registries create new challenges. *Chicago Tribune*, p. 10.

Schoenberger, R., & Thomas, W. (1985). Missing children in Michigan: Facts, problems, recommendations. *Juvenile Justice Digest, 31,* 7–8.

Schoenfeld, A., Meier. R., & Griffin, R. (1979). Constructing a social problem: The press and the environment. *Social Problems, 27,* 38–61.

School crime not increasing, according to surveys. (1998). *Justice Bulletin, 18*(4). National Criminal Justice Association.

Schraeger, L., & Short, J., Jr. (1978). Toward a sociology of organizational crime. *Social Problems, 25,* 407–419.

Schwartz, I. M., Steketee, M. W., & Schneider, V. W. (1990). Federal juvenile justice policy and the incarceration of girls. *Crime and Delinquency, 36*(4), 503–520.

Schwartz, T. (1982). *The Hillside Strangler*. New York: Signet.

Seagal, D. (1993, November). Tales from the cutting room floor: The reality of "reality-based" television. *Harper's Magazine, 51*

Seidman, D., & Couzens, M. (1974). Getting the crime rate down: Political pressure and crime reporting. *Law and Society Review, 8,* 457–493.

Selke, W., & Pepinsky, H. (1984). The politics of police reporting in Indianapolis, 1948–1978. In W. Chambliss (Ed.), *Criminal law in action*. New York: John Wiley.

Sellin, T. (1980). *The penalty of death*. Beverly Hills: Sage Publications.

Senate Permanent Subcommittee on Investigations, Committee on Governmental Affairs. (1983). 98th Congress, First Session, August 3.

The Sentencing Project. (1998). *Facts about prisons and prisoners.* Washington, DC: Author.

Shafer, R. (1972). *Marihuana: A signal of misunderstanding.* Washington, DC: National Commission on Marihuana and Drug Abuse.

Shameless: Ten worst corporations. (1995, December). *Multinational Monitor, 16,* 12.

Shannon, L. (1982). Reassessing the relationship of adult criminal careers to juvenile careers: A summary. *Report for the U.S. Department of Justice.* Washington, DC.

Sherman, L. (1982). Learning police ethics. *Criminal Justice Ethics, 1*(1), 10–19.

Sherman, L. (1983). Reducing police gun use: Critical events, administrative policy, and organizational change. In M. Punch (Ed.), *Control in the police organization.* Cambridge: MIT Press.

Sherman, L. (1998, December 3). Needed: Better ways to count crooks. *The Wall Street Journal.*

Sherman, L., & Cohn, E. with Garten, P., Hamilton, E., & Rogan, D. (1986). *Citizens killed by big city police—1970–84.* Washington, DC: Crime Control Institute.

Sherman, L., Gottfredson, D., MacKenzie, D. L., Eck, J., Reuter, P., & Bushway, S. (1997). *Preventing crime: What works, what doesn't, what's promising.* A report to the U.S. Congress prepared for the National Institute of Justice (NCJ-165366).

Sherman, L., & Langworthy, R. (1979). Measuring homicide by police officers. *Journal of Criminal Law and Criminology, 70*(4), 546–560.

Shin, K. (1978). *Death penalty and crime.* Fairfax, VA: Center for Economic Analysis.

Sickmund, M., Snyder, H. N., & Poe-Yamagata, E. (1997). *Juvenile offenders and victims: 1997 update on violence.* Office of Juvenile Justice and Delinquency Prevention. Washington, DC.

Siegel, R. K. (1984). Changing patterns of cocaine use. In J. Grabowski (Ed.), *Cocaine: Pharmacology, effects, and treatment of abuse.* (DHHS Publication Number ADM 84–1326; pp. 92–110). Rockville, MD: U.S. Government Printing Office.

Silverman, B. (1983). The search for a solution to child snatching. *Hofstra Law Review, 11,* 1073–1117.

Simon, D. (1999). *Elite deviance (*6th ed.). Boston: Allyn and Bacon.

Simpson, S., Harris, A., & Mattson, B. (1995). Measuring corporate crime. In M. Blankenship (Ed.), *Understanding corporate criminality* (pp. 115–140). New York: Garland: 115–140

Singer, S., & McDowall, D. (1988). Criminalizing delinquency: The deterrent effects of the New York juvenile offender law. *Law and Society Review, 22,* 521–535.

Sjoerdsma, A. (1994, November 14). Justice: Eighteen months for a wife's life. *Chicago Tribune,* p. 21.

Skolnick, J. (1966). *Justice without trial: Law enforcement in a democratic society.* New York: John Wiley and Sons.

Sluder, R. (1995). Double celling. In M. McShane & F. Williams (Eds.), *Encyclopedia of American prisons.* New York: Garland.

Smith, B. (1998). Children in custody: 20-year trends in juvenile detention, correctional, and shelter facilities. *Crime and Delinquency, 44*(4), 526–543.

Smith, D. (1975). *The mafia mystique.* New York: Basic Books.

Smith, D. (1976). Mafia: The prototypical alien conspiracy. *The Annals of the American Academy of Political and Social Science, 423,* 75–88.

Smith, D. (1978). Organized crime and entrepreneurship. *International Journal of Criminology and Penology, 6,* 161–177.

Smith, M. (1990). Patriarchal ideology and wife beating: A test of a feminist hypothesis. *Violence and Victims, 5,* 257–274.

Smolowe, J. (1994a, February, 28). . . . And throw away the key. *Time.*

Smolowe, J. (1994b, August 1). Race and the O.J. case. *Time,* 25–26.

Smolowe, J. (1994c, November 14). Going soft on crime. *Time,* 63.

Smolowe, J. (1994d, December 19). A high price to pay. *Time,* 59.

Snell, T. L. (1998). *Capital punishment, 1997.* Washington, DC: Bureau of Justice Statistics.

Snider, L. (1982). Traditional and corporate theft: A comparison of sanctions. In P. Wickman & T. Daily (Eds.), *White-collar and economic crime* (pp. 235–258). Lexington, MA: Lexington.

Snortum, J., & Bodal, K. (1992). Conditions of confinement within security prisons: Scandinavia and California. In M. Carlie & K. Minor (Eds.), *Prisons around the world* (pp. 38–60). Dubuque, IA: William C. Brown.

Snyder, H. (1998). *Juvenile arrests 1997.* Office of Juvenile Justice and Delinquency Prevention. Washington, DC.

Sohn, E. (1994). Antistalking statutes: Do they actually protect victims? *Criminal Law Bulletin, 13,* 203–241.

Spangenberg, R., & Walsh, E. (1989). Capital punishment or life imprisonment?: Some cost considerations. *Loyola of Los Angeles Law Review, 23,* 45–58.

Special report: America under the gun. (1999, August 23). *Newsweek, 134,* 20–49.

Spire, R. (1990). Breaking up the old boy network. *Trial, 26*(2), 57–58.

Spohn, C., & Cederblom, J. (1991). Race and disparities in sentencing: A test of the liberation hypothesis. *Justice Quarterly, 8*(3), 305–327.

Stack, A. (1984). *The 15 killer.* New York: Signet.

Stack, S. (1987). Publicized executions and homicide, 1950–1980. *American Sociological Review, 52,* 532–540.

Stack, S., & Kelley, T. (1994). Police suicide: An analysis. *American Journal of Police, 13*(4), 73–90.

Statman, P. (1995). *On the safe side.* New York: HarperCollins.

Steffensmeier, D., & Harer, M. (1991, August). Did crime rise or fall during the Reagan presidency?: The effects of an 'aging' United States population on the nation's crime rate. *Journal of Research in Crime and Delinquency, 28*(3).

Steinberg, J. (1999). Ideas and trends: Storm warning; the coming crime wave is washed up. *The New York Times,* Sec. 4, p. 4.

Stephan, J., & Jankowski, L. (1991, June). *Jail inmates, 1990.* Washington, DC: Bureau of Justice Statistics.

Stickler, G. B., Salter, M., Broughton, D. D., & Alario, A. (1991). Parents' worries about children compared to actual risks. *Clinical Pediatrics, 30*(9), 522–528.

Stone, H. (1915). Legal education and democratic principles. *American Bar Journal,* 639–646.

Straus, M., Gelles, R., & Steinmetz, S. (1980). *Behind closed doors: Violence in the American family.* Garden City, NY: Anchor Books.

Streib, V. (1987). *Death penalty for juveniles.* Bloomington: Indiana University Press.

Streib, V. (1998). *The juvenile death penalty today: Death sentences and executions for juvenile crime, January 1973–October 1998.* Ada, OH: Claude W. Pettit College of Law, Ohio Northern University.

Streisand, B. (1994, October 3). Can he get a fair trial? *U.S. News & World Report,* 61–63.

Substance Abuse and Mental Health Services Administration. (1997). *National household survey on drug abuse: Population estimates 1996.* Rockville, MD: Author.

Sullivan, T., & Maiken, P. (1983). *Killer clown: The John Wayne Gacy murders.* New York: Grosset and Dunlap.

Surette, R. (1998). *Media, crime and criminal justice: Images and realities.* (2nd ed.). Pacific Grove, CA: Wadsworth.

Sutherland, E. (1949). *White collar crime.* New York: Holt, Rinehart and Winston.

Sutherland, E. (1950). The diffusion of sexual psychopath laws. *American Journal of Sociology, 56,* 142–148.

Sutherland, E. H., & Cressey, D. J. (1970). *Criminology.* Philadelphia: Lippincott.

Sykes, G. (1958). *The society of captives: A study of a maximum security prison.* Princeton: Princeton University Press.

Tabak, R., & Lane, J. (1989). The execution of injustice: A cost and lack-of-benefit analysis of the death penalty. *Loyola of Los Angeles Law Review, 23,* 136.

Tappan, P. (1955). Some myths about the sex offender. *Federal Probation, 19,* 1–12.

Task Force on Organized Crime. (1967). *Task force report: Organized crime.* Washington, DC: U.S. Government Printing Office.

The ten worst corporations of 1996. (December). *Multinational Monitor, 17,* 12.

Teresa, V. (1973, February). A mafioso cases the mafia craze. *Saturday Review,* 23–29.

Terry, M. (1987). *The ultimate evil.* Garden City, NY: Dolphin.

Terry, W., III (1981). Police stress: The empirical evidence. *Journal of Police Science and Administration, 9*(1), 61–75.

Terry, W., III (1983). Police stress as an individual and administrative problem: Some conceptual and theoretical difficulties. *Journal of Police Science and Administration, 11*(2), 156–165.

Tewksbury, R. (1989, Spring/Summer). Fear of sexual assault in prison inmates. *The Prison Journal,* 62–71.

Thomas, C. (1995). *Private adult correctional facility census* (8th ed.). Gainsville, FL. Private Corrections Project. University of Florida.

Thomas, K. (1993). How to stop the stalker: State antistalking laws. *Criminal Law Bulletin, 12,* 124–136.

Thomson, E. (1997). Deterrence versus brutalization: The case of Arizona. *Homicide Studies, 1*(2), 110–128.

Thornton, J. (1983, October 24). The tragedy of America's missing children. *U.S. News and World Report,* 63–64.

Tillman, R., & Pontell, H. (1992). Is justice "collar-blind"? Punishing Medicaid provider fraud. *Criminology, 30,* 547–573.

Tjaden, P., & Thoennes, N. (1998a). Stalking in America: Findings from the National Violence Against Women Survey. *Research in Brief.* Washington, DC: National Institute of Justice.

Tjaden, P., & Thoennes, N. (1998b). Prevalence, incidence, and consequences of violence against women: Findings from the National Violence Against Women Survey. *Research in Brief.* Washington, DC: National Institute of Justice.

Toch, H. (1969, revised 1980). *Violent men.* Chicago: Aldine.

Toch, H. (1994). Social climate and prison violence. In M. Braswell, S. Dillingham, & R. Montgomery, Jr. (Eds.), *Prison violence in America* (2nd ed., pp. 345–352). Cincinnati: Anderson.

Torbet, P., Gable, R., Hurst IV, H., Montgomery, I., Szymanski, L., & Thomas, D. (1996). *State responses to serious and violent juvenile crime.* Office of Juvenile Justice and Delinquency Prevention. Washington, DC.

Torbet, P., & Szymanski, L. (1998). *State legislative responses to violent juvenile crime:*

1996–97 update. Office of Juvenile Justice and Delinquency Prevention. Washington, DC.

Trade and Environment Database. (1997). *TED case studies: Colombia coca trade.* Washington, DC: American University.

Treanor, B. (1986, February 1). Picture our missing children: The problem is blown far out of proportion. *The Houston Chronicle.*

Treaster, J. (1994, February 1). Survey finds marijuana use is up in high schools. *The New York Times,* pp. A1, A14.

Trebach, A. (1989, March 13). *Drug policies for the democracies.* Statement before the public hearing on drug control, Interior Committee of the Deutscher Bundestag, The Parliament of the Federal Republic of Germany.

Trebach, A., & Engelsman, E. (1989, Summer). Why not decriminalize? *New Perspectives Quarterly,* 40–45.

Tunnell, K. (1992). Film at eleven: Recent developments in the commodification of crime. *Sociological Spectrum, 12,* 293–313.

U.S. Congress. (1993). United States Departments of Commerce, Justice, and State, and Senate Judiciary, and Related Agencies. *Appropriations Act for Fiscal Year 1993.* Pub. L. 102–395, Section 109(b).

U.S. Department of Commerce, Bureau of Census. (1994). *Current population reports.* Washington, DC: U.S. Government Printing Office.

U.S. Department of Justice. (1983). *Sixth report to Congress on implementation of the Parental Kidnapping Prevention Act of 1980.* Washington, DC: U.S. Department of Justice.

U.S. Sentencing Commission. (1995, February). *Special report to Congress: Cocaine and federal sentencing policy.* Washington, DC: Sentencing Commission.

Uniform Crime Reports. (1997). *Crime in the United States 1996.* Washington, DC: Federal Bureau of Investigation.

Uniform Crime Reports. (1998). *Crime in the United States 1997.* Washington, DC: Federal Bureau of Investigation.

United Kingdom Royal Commission On Capital Punishment (1953). *United Kingdom Royal Commission On Capital Punishment 1949–1953.* London, Her Majesty's Stationery Office.

United States Attorneys Bulletin. (1983, April 29), 31.

Vachss, A. (1993, January 5). Sex predators can't be saved. *The New York Times.*

van den Haag, E. (1978). In defense of the death penalty: A legal-practical-moral analysis. *Criminal Law Bulletin, 14,* 51–68.

Van Wormer, K. (1995). Execution-inspired murder: A form of suicide? *Journal of Offender Rehabilitation, 22*(3/4), 1–10.

Vaughn, J., & Kappeler, V. (1986, March 18). *A descriptive study of law enforcement officers killed, 1974–1984.* Paper presented at the annual meeting of the Academy of Criminal Justice Sciences, Orlando, FL.

Vetter, H., & Rieber, R. (1986, November). Dissociative states and processes. Paper presented to ASC, Atlanta, GA.

Violanti, J., Vena, J., & Marshall, J. (1986). Disease risk and mortality among police officers: New evidence and contributing factors. *Journal of Police Science and Administration, 14*(1), 17–23.

Violent and Repeat Juvenile Offender Act of 1997, S. Rep. No. 105–108, 105th Congress, 1st Session 173 (1997).

Vito, G., Koester, P., & Wilson, D. (1991). Return of the dead: An update on the status of Furman-commuted death row inmates. In R. Bohm (Ed.), *The death penalty in*

America: Current research. Cincinnati, OH: Anderson and Academy of Criminal Justice Sciences.

Vold, G. (1997). *Theoretical criminology* (4th ed.). New York: Oxford University Press.

Wagner, M., & Brzeczek, R. (1983, August). Alcoholism and suicide: A fatal connection. *FBI Law Enforcement Bulletin*, 8–15.

Wainwright v. Witt, 105 S. Ct. 844 (1985).

Waldman, S., Mabry, M., Bingham, C., & Levinson, M. (1991, September 23). The unified scandal theory. *Newsweek*, 22–23.

Walker, S. (1998). *Sense and nonsense about crime and drugs* (4th ed.). Belmont, CA: Wadsworth.

Wal-Mart (1999). How does the program work [On-line]. Available: www.walmart.com/community/missing

Warr, M. (1995). Public perceptions of crime and punishment. In J. Sheley (Ed.), *Criminology: A contemporary handbook* (pp. 15–31). Belmont, CA: Wadsworth.

Watson, N., & Sterling, J. (1969). *Police and their opinions*. Gaithersburg, MD: International Association of Chiefs of Police.

Weinstein, J. (1968). *The corporate ideal in the liberal state: 1900–1918*. Boston: Beacon Press.

Welch, M., Fenwick, M., & Roberts, M. (1998). State managers, intellectuals, and the media: A content analysis of ideology in experts' quotes in feature newspaper articles on crime. In G. W. Potter & V. E. Kappeler (Eds.), *Constructing crime: Perspective on making news and social problems*. Prospect Heights, IL: Waveland Press.

Wellford, H. (1972). *Sowing the wind: A report from Ralph Nader's Center for Study of Responsive Law*. New York: Grossman.

Westley, W. (1956). Secrecy and the police. *Social Forces, 34*(3), 254–257.

White paper of narcotics control. (1998). Washington, DC: Embassy of Colombia.

Whitehouse, J. (1965, May–June). A preliminary inquiry into the occupational disadvantages of Llaw enforcement officers. *Police*.

Wickman, P., & Whitten, P. (1980). *Criminology: Perspectives on crime and criminality*. Lexington, MA: D.C. Heath.

Williams, C. (1991). The federal death penalty for drug-related killings. *Criminal Law Bulletin, 27*(5), 387–415.

Williams, H., & Murphy, P. (1999). The evolving strategy of police: A minority view. In V. Kappeler (Ed.), *The police and society: Touchstone readings* (2nd ed., pp. 27–50). Prospect Heights, IL: Waveland.

Wills, T. (1996, Fall). Maryland's missing children. *Trooper*, 39–42.

Wilson, C. (1972). *Order of assassins*. London: Rubert Hart-Davis.

Wilson, C., & Seaman, D. (1983). *Encyclopaedia of modern murder*. New York: Perigee.

Wilson, J. (1983). *Thinking about crime* (Rev. ed.). New York: Basic Books.

Wilson, J., & Herrnstein, E. (1985). *Crime and human nature*. New York: Simon and Schuster.

Wisotsky, S. (1986). *Breaking the impasse in the war on drugs*. New York: Greenwood Press.

Wolfson, W. (1982). The deterrent effect of the death penalty upon prison murder. In H. Bedau (Ed.), *The death penalty in America* (3rd ed.). Oxford: Oxford University Press.

Woodbury, R. (1993, August 23). A convict's view: People don't want solutions. *Time*, 33.

Woodward, A., Epstein, J., Gfroerer, J., Melnick, D., Thoreson, R., & Wilson, D.

(1997). The drug abuse treatment gap: Recent estimates. *Health Care Financing Review, 18,* 5–17.

Wright, R. (1995, May 15). What do 167 deaths justify? *Time,* 86.

Zawitz, M., Klaus, P., Bachman, R., Bastian, L., DeBerry, M., Jr., Rand, M., & Taylor, B. (1993). *Highlights from 20 years of surveying crime victims: The National Crime Victimization Survey, 1973–92.* Washington, DC: Bureau of Justice Statistics.

Zeisel, H. (1977). The deterrent effect of the death penalty: Facts v. faith. In P. Kurland (Ed.), *The Supreme Court Review 1976.* Chicago: University of Chicago Press.

Zimring, F., & Hawkins, G. (1986). *Capital punishment and the American agenda.* Cambridge: Cambridge University Press.

Zimring, F., & Hawkins, G. (1997). *Crime is not the problem: Lethal violence in America.* New York: Oxford University Press.

Zion, S. (1993, December 15). Battle lines in the war on drugs. Make them legal. *The New York Times,* p. A27.

Zorn, E. (1995a, May 18). Davis' execution may reveal folly of eye for an eye. *Chicago Tribune,* Sec. 2, p. 1.

Zorn, E. (1995b, May 25). Fear of abductions is bad for parents good for business. *Chicago Tribune,* Sec. 2, p. 1.

Zuckerman, M. (1994, July 25). The limits of the TV lens. *U.S. News & World Report,* 64.

Index

340   Index